Tracy Traynor

Teacher's Guide

Renewed Framework Edition

Part of Pearson

Heinemann is an imprint of Pearson Education Limited, a company incorporated in England and Wales, having its registered office at Edinburgh Gate, Harlow, Essex, CM20 2JE. Registered company number: 872828

www.pearsonschoolsandfecolleges.co.uk

Heinemann is a registered trademark of Pearson Education Limited

First published 2010

14 13 12 11 10
10 9 8 7 6 5 4 3 2 1

British Library Cataloguing in Publication Data is available from the British Library on request.

ISBN: 978 0 435088 66 8

Edited by Rosemary Morlin
Designed by Ken Vail Graphic Design, Cambridge
Typeset by TechType
Cover photo/illustration © Getty Images
Printed in the UK by Ashford Colour Press Ltd

Acknowledgements
Every effort has been made to contact copyright holders of material reproduced in this book. Any omissions will be rectified in subsequent printings if notice is given to the publishers.

We would like to thanks Jackie Coe and Charonne Prosser for their conributions to this new edition.

Websites
The websites used in this book were correct and up-to-date at the time of publication. It is essential for tutors to preview each website before using it in class so as to ensure that the URL is still accurate, relevant and appropriate. We suggest that tutors bookmark useful websites and consider enabling students to access them through the school/college intranet.

Important notice
This software is suitable for use on PCs only. It will not run on a Mac.

If the CD is loaded into a CD drive on a PC it should autorun automatically. If it does not, please click on RB32.exe (D:Mira1TGRFSoW/RB32.exe).

Active content
Your browser security may initially try to block elements of this product. If this problem occurs, please refer to the Troubleshooting document which can be found in the root of this CD (D:Mira1TGRFSoW/Troubleshooting.doc).

Installation instructions
This product may be installed to your local hard drive or to the network. Further instructions on how to do this are available from the main menu.

VLE Pack
The root of this CD contains the content from this product as a zipped SCORM 1.2 Content Pack to allow for convenient uploading to your VLE.

Please follow the usual instructions specific to your VLE system to upload this content pack.

Contents

¡Mira! 2 Teacher's Guide Introduction

¡Mira! is a lively and easy-to-use Key Stage 3 Spanish course for the full ability range starting Spanish in Year 7:

¡Mira! 1 for Year 7 pupils
¡Mira! 2 for Year 8 pupils
¡Mira! 3 for Year 9 pupils

There are differentiated books (*Rojo* and *Verde*) for Year 9.

It is written to support Foundation Subjects MFL including the Framework for Teaching MFL.

The *¡Mira! 2 Teacher's Guide Nueva Edición* has been updated in the following ways:

- Updated references to the most recent QCA Programme of Study for MFL (2008)
- New references to the Resource and Assessment Pack and the Teacher Presentations software
- Updated references to the most recent QCA KS3 Framework for Languages

Teaching Foundation Subjects MFL and the MFL Framework using *¡Mira! 2* Framework objectives (2009)

¡Mira! 2 ensures that there is comprehensive coverage of all five strands of the framework:

- **Listening and speaking (L&S)** – teaching pupils to extend their linguistic capability in listening, speaking and spoken interaction.
- **Reading and writing (R&W)** – helping pupils to appreciate and make use of a wide range of texts and to write for a range of purposes and audiences.
- **Intercultural understanding (IU)** – encouraging pupils to recognise different beliefs, attitudes and different ways of seeing the world.
- **Knowledge about language (KAL)** – helping pupils to develop their understanding of how a language works and how to manipulate it.
- **Language learning strategies (LLS)** – showing pupils how to manage their own learning by selecting, using and evaluating different language learning strategies.

Opportunities for delivering all of the strands of the 2009 MFL Framework are offered in *¡Mira! 2*. References can be found in the following places in the Teacher's Guide:

a in the Framework Overview grid on pages 5–6 to help you with your **long-term planning**

b in the overview grids at the beginning of each module (e.g. pages 17–19) to help you with your **medium-term planning**

c in the overview boxes at the start of each teaching unit to help with your **short-term planning** (i.e. **lesson planning**)

In addition, all activities in the Pupil's Book are cross-referenced to the 2009 MFL Framework to allow you to deliver the teaching objectives at different points in the course if you wish. The references are given in the Teacher's Guide at the start of each activity.

The CD-Rom which accompanies this Teacher's Guide provides a customisable scheme of work showing the complete coverage of the framework.

Lesson starters

For every unit in the Pupil's Book the Teacher's Guide contains two lesson starters, the first at the beginning of every unit, the second approximately half-way through, at the point when a second lesson is likely to begin. Most of them are simple ideas that allow you to recap on previous knowledge or prepare the pupils for new language to be learnt in the unit. They are designed to get the lesson off to a brisk start, focusing the pupils' attention and promoting engagement in a challenging way.

Plenaries

Every unit in the Pupil's Book ends with a plenary session. Again these are simple ideas described in the Teacher's Guide. They aim to draw out the key learning points. Pupils are actively involved and are expected to demonstrate and explain what they have learnt in the unit. They identify links with what the pupils have learnt so far and what they will learn later in the course.

Thinking Skills

Throughout the Pupil's Book and Cuadernos there are activities which challenge the pupils to think about the language they are learning and the skills required to do so.

Assessment for learning

Throughout the course pupils are encouraged and given ample opportunity to reflect on their own learning and set themselves targets for further progress:

- Plenary sessions suggested in the teacher's notes for each unit focus on activities to help pupils gain an understanding of what they have learnt and what they still need to work on.
-

- At the end of every third unit in each module there is a *Mini-test*, a checklist of what pupils have learnt so far in the module.
- The *Resumen* at the end of each module provides a longer checklist for pupils to test themselves on the content of the whole module. This checklist also features in the *¡Mira! 2* Resource and Assessment Pack.
- *Pruebas* in the Resource and Assessment Pack allow pupils to test their knowledge in a summative test.
- *I can …* pages in the Resource and Assessment Pack help pupils to understand why they are working at a particular level, and to target specific areas of improvement to help them move on to the next level.
- *¡Progreso!* pages in the Resource and Assessment Pack and Workbooks allow pupils to set targets for improvement. These are accompanied in the workbooks by pupil-friendly National Curriculum level descriptors to help them understand the difference between each level.

All the tests are matched to the National Curriculum Attainment Target levels. By the end of *¡Mira! 2* pupils have the opportunity to reach National Curriculum Level 6. The pattern of assessment is as follows:

Module 1	Levels 1–5
Module 2	Levels 1–5
Module 3	Levels 1–5
Module 4	Levels 1–6
Module 5	Levels 1–6
End-of-year	Levels 1–6

¡Mira! 2 2009 Framework Objectives (Year 8) long-term plan

Teaching Objective	Module and Unit
1.1/Y8 Listening – understanding on first hearing	M1 U1 M2 ¡Extra! 1
1.2/Y8 Listening – new contexts	M3 U2 M5 ¡Extra! 1
1.3/Y8 Listening – (a) understanding language for specific functions	M2 U3 M4 U2
1.3/Y8 Speaking – (b) using language for specific functions	M2 U3 M4 U2
1.4/Y8 Speaking – (a) classroom exchanges (pupil-pupil) (teacher-pupil)	M1 U2 (p-p) M5 ¡Extra! 1 (t-p)
1.4/Y8 Speaking – (b) unscripted conversations	M2 ¡Extra! 1 M4 U4
1.5/Y8 Speaking – (a) unscripted talks	M3 U5 M4 ¡Extra! 1
1.5/Y8 Speaking – (b) using simple idioms	M2 U3 M3 U4
2.1/Y8 Reading – authentic materials	M1 ¡Extra! 2 M3 ¡Extra! 2
2.2/Y8 Reading – (a) longer, more complex texts	M3 ¡Extra! 1 M4 ¡Extra! 2
2.2/Y8 Reading – (b) personal response to text	M2 U5 M4 ¡Extra! 1
2.3/Y8 Reading – text features: emotive	M3 U5 M6 U1
2.4/Y8 Writing – (a) using text as stimulus	M3 U3 M6 U5
2.4/Y8 Writing – (b) sequencing paragraphs	M1 U5 M3 U3
2.5/Y8 Writing – using researched language	M1 U4 M6 U1
3.1/Y8 Culture – changes in everyday life	M5 ¡Extra! 2 (S) M6 ¡Extra! 1 (S)
3.2/Y8 Culture – (a) young people: aspirations	M1 U5 M2 U2
3.2/Y8 Culture – (b) customs, traditions	M4 U3 M5 U2
4.1/Y8 Language – sounds/spelling exceptions	M3 U3 M5 U5
4.2/Y8 Language – increasing vocabulary	M1 U2 M4 U1
4.3/Y8 Language – gender and plurals	M1 U2 M5 U1
4.4/Y8 Language – developing sentences	M2 U2 M3 U4
4.5/Y8 Language – (a) range of verb tenses	M2 U1 M3 U2
4.5/Y8 Language – (b) range of modal verbs	M2 U4 M2 U5
4.6/Y8 Language – (a) range of questions	M1 U1 M5 U4
4.6/Y8 Language – (b) range of negatives	M2 U4 M4 U5

Teaching Objective	Module and Unit
5.1 Strategies – patterns	M1 U1 M4 U4
5.2 Strategies – memorising	M1 U3 M4 U3
5.3 Strategies – English/other languages	M1 U3 M3 U1
5.4 Strategies – working out meaning	M3 U1 M6 U2
5.5 Strategies – reference materials	M4 ¡Extra! 2 M5 U5
5.6 Strategies – reading aloud	M1 ¡Extra! 2 M2 ¡Extra! 2
5.7 Strategies – planning and preparing	M3 U5 M4 ¡Extra! 1
5.8 Strategies – evaluating and improving	M1 U4 M4 U5

Expressions offering praise and suggestions

Here are some words and phrases that you can use to praise pupils' work or to offer advice for improvement.

¡Buen trabajo!
¡Has realizado un buen trabajo!
¡Bien hecho!
¡Excelente!
¡Estupendo!
¡Bien!
¡Qué bien!
¡Muy bien!
¡Lo has hecho muy bien!
¡Has sacado un 10!
¡Genial!
¡Muy gracioso/a!
¡Buena idea!
¡Qué interesante!
¡Está perfecto!
¡Atención!
¡Cuidado con los acentos!
Cuidado con las concordancias (son muy importantes en español)
No os olvidéis de poner los acentos
Puedes hacerlo mejor
Tienes que mejorar
¡Venga, ánimo, tú puedes hacerlo mejor!
Si sigues así, llegarás a ser el/la primero/a de la clase
Presta más atención a tu ortografía / Tienes que mejorar tu ortografía
Hay que repetir / Tienes que repetir
¿Dónde están tus deberes?
Escribe cinco veces: trabajé
No te olvides de poner la fecha / el título
Rellena todos los espacios y no dejes ninguno en blanco
<u>Subraya</u> las palabras/las frases, por favor

Symbols used in the teaching notes

 extension material/suggestion for extending an activity for the more able

 reinforcement material/suggestion for simplifying an activity for the less able

 activity to practise thinking skills

 ICT activity

suggestions on how to use the Zona Cultura material in the Pupil's Book

Differentiation

¡Mira! 2 provides one book for the full ability range. The following aspects of the course help to cater to a range of abilities within the classroom:

- There are differentiated activities at a range of AT levels throughout the Pupil's Book.
- Ideas are given in the Teacher's Guide for simplifying and extending the Pupil's Book activities.
- *¡Extra!* units at the end of every module contain longer reading and listening passages to provide opportunities for extension work.
- The *Te toca a ti* section at the back of the Pupil's Book provides extra reading and writing activities at reinforcement and extension levels.
- The Cuadernos are differentiated at two levels: reinforcement (*Cuaderno A*) and extension (*Cuaderno B*).

¡Mira! 1 takes pupils up to Level 5 of the National Curriculum.
¡Mira! 2 takes pupils up to Level 6 of the National Curriculum.

¡Mira! 3 Verde takes pupils up to Level 5 of the National Curriculum.
¡Mira! 3 Rojo takes pupils up to Levels 6/7 of the National Curriculum.

Grammar

Grammar is fully integrated into the teaching sequence in *¡Mira! 2* to ensure that pupils have the opportunity to learn thoroughly the underlying structures of the Spanish language. Each unit has a grammar objective so that the pupils can see clearly what grammar structures they are learning in each unit. The key grammar points are presented in the *Gramática* boxes on the Pupil's Book pages with short explanations. Fuller explanations and practice activities are provided in the *Gramática* section at the back of the Pupil's Book.

Grammar points explained and practised in *¡Mira! 2*:

1. Nouns

Gender
Singular/Plural
The indefinite article ('a'/'an', 'some')
The definite article ('the')

2. Pronouns

3. Adjectives

Agreement of adjectives
Position of adjectives
Comparatives
Superlatives
Possessive adjectives ('my', etc.)
Demonstrative adjectives ('this', 'these')

4. Verbs

The infinitive
The present tense
The near future tense
The preterite
Recognising different tenses
Making verbs negative
me gusta, etc.
se puede/se pueden
Verbs with the infinitive

5. Prepositions

6. Question words

The components

¡Mira! 2 consists of:

Pupil's Book with audio CDs
Cuadernos
Teacher's Guide and CD-Rom
Resource and Assessment Pack (R & A Pack)
¡Mira! and *¡Mira! Express 2* Teacher Presentations
Flashcards

Pupil's Book

The Pupil's Book consists of six modules sub-divided as follows:

- Five double-page core units. These units contain the core material in all four skills that must be taught to ensure that all the key language and grammar is covered.
- *Resumen* – this is a checklist, allowing the pupils to keep a check on their progress as part of assessment for learning (see 'Teaching Foundation Subjects MFL' above).
- *Prepárate* – optional revision activities that can be used as a 'mock' test.
- *¡Extra! 1* and *2* – two optional units. No new core language is introduced in *¡Extra! 1* and *2* and therefore they can be left out if you are short of time. However, the units contain lots of useful consolidation activities and material covering the cultural knowledge and contact strand of the MFL Framework.
- *Palabras* – two pages of module wordlists for vocabulary learning and revision plus an *Estrategia* tip box to help pupils acquire the skills they need to learn vocabulary more effectively.

At the back of the Pupil's Book there are three further sections:

- *Te toca a ti* – self-access differentiated reading and writing activities. *Te toca a ti A* contains reinforcement activities for lower-ability and *Te toca a ti B* has extension activities for higher-ability pupils. These are ideal for use as homework.
- *Gramática* – the grammar reference and practice section where all the grammar points introduced in the core units are explained fully and accompanied by practice activities.
- *Vocabulario* – a comprehensive Spanish–English word list and a shorter English–Spanish word list.

Cuadernos

There are two parallel workbooks to accompany *¡Mira! 2*, one for reinforcement (*Cuaderno A*) and one for extension (*Cuaderno B*). There is a page of activities for each double-page unit in the Pupil's Book. The workbooks fulfil a number of functions:

- They provide self-access reading and writing activities designed to offer the pupils enjoyable ways of consolidating and practising the language they have learnt in each unit.
- They give extra practice in grammar and thinking skills with integrated activities throughout the Cuadernos.
- Revision pages at the end of each module

(*Prepárate*) help pupils revise what they have learnt during the module.

- *Palabras* pages provide the word lists from the end of each module in the Pupil's Book to help pupils with independent workbook-based work and vocabulary learning.
- *¡Progreso!* pages at the end of each module allow pupils to record their National Curriculum level in each Attainment Target and set themselves improvement targets for the next module.
- National Curriculum level descriptors in pupil-friendly language at the back of the Cuadernos allow pupils to see what they must do to progress up through the NC levels in all four Attainment Targets.

Teacher's Guide

The Teacher's Guide contains:

- a long-term plan grid for the teaching objectives of the MFL Framework
- overview grids for each module to help with medium-term planning
- mapping of activities to the National Curriculum Programmes of Study
- clear teaching notes for short-term planning together with a full audio transcript
- suggestions for ICT activities
- indications of how the course covers aspects of maths, English and citizenship
- ideas for using the flashcards and other games in the classroom

The CD-Rom which accompanies the Teacher's Guide provides a customisable scheme of work showing the complete coverage of the framework.

Resource and Assessment Pack (R & A Pack)

The Resource and Assessment Pack provides the following types of photocopiable materials:

Resource sheets

- *Gramática* worksheets, including thinking skills activities, homework sheets and activities suitable for use as starters and plenaries
- *Palabras* sheets

Assessment for learning materials

- *Resumen* – revision checklists for each module
- *Pruebas* – end-of-module tests at National Curriculum levels 1–5
- *Prueba fin del año* – end-of-year tests at National Curriculum levels 1–5
- *I can …* – pages related to National Curriculum levels identify areas of progress and set concrete targets for future learning

All of the sheets are provided in a customisable format on the CD-Rom which comes with the Pack. In addition there is an audio CD containing material for the listening tests.

Teacher Presentations

The Teacher Presentations are an electronic resource for use with a data projector or interactive whiteboard for front-of-class teaching. They are exactly matched to the Pupil's Book and contain the following resources.

In every module:

- Concept maps (*Sumarios*) give a visual picture of each module and help review learning objectives
- Vocab animations and flashcards present new language
- Interactive listening activities engage and help with language comprehension
- Games reinforce new language
- A video story and worksheet, provide a strong authentic context for learning

Additional support:

- Module overviews giving detailed lists of the screens provided
- Audio and video transcripts (for printing or whiteboard work)
- Texts from the Pupil's Book (for printing or whiteboard work)
- Useful ideas on how to use the screens for starters and plenaries

Flashcards

There are 96 full-colour single-sided flashcards with the name of the object on the reverse. A complete list of flashcards is given on pages 9–10. They can be used for presentation of new language or practice. Here are some imaginative methods of using the flashcards to help pupils learn and memorise new vocabulary more effectively.

Method 1

Show one card, say the word or phrase and pupils repeat in fun and varied ways (loud/soft, high/low etc.).

Do four cards as above. Show one that you've just done and give a choice of two words. Pupils say the correct word. Keep going until they know about eight.

Method 2

Once you've been through about six to nine cards and they've heard the words a few times stick a selection on the board, numbered. Say one in

Spanish and a pupil gives you the number. Do this a few times until most of the class recognise the words. Then say the number, and a pupil gives you the word. This can then be done from pupil to pupil.

Method 3

Put nine cards on the board, in rows of three; divide the class into two teams and play noughts and crosses. Pupils choose a card and say the Spanish. A correct answer wins a nought/cross. The aim is to get three in a row.

Method 4

Stick a series of cards on the board. Two pupils stand by the board. You or another pupil say a word. The two pupils compete to be the first to point to the correct card.

Method 5

See who can win the most cards by naming as many words as possible from the set they have just learnt.

Method 6

Guess the card. You conceal a card behind your back (look at it quickly first). The pupils have to guess which one it is by going through the words in the set.

Method 7

After term 1 use the cards to elicit phrases, negatives, opinions (*me gusta, no me gusta,* etc.). Encourage pupils to use the cards creatively. Aim for longer sentences incorporating the word.

List of flashcards

1	divertido / divertida	amusing
2	hablador / habladora	talkative
3	serio / seria	serious
4	perezoso / perezosa	lazy
5	inteligente	intelligent
6	generoso / generosa	generous
7	guapo / guapa	good-looking
8	alto / alta	tall
9	bajo / baja	short
10	delgado / delgada	thin
11	Me despierto.	I wake up.
12	Me levanto.	I get up.
13	Me ducho.	I have a shower.
14	Me peino.	I comb my hair.
15	Me visto.	I get dressed.
16	Desayuno.	I have breakfast.
17	Voy al instituto.	I go to school.
18	Ceno.	I have dinner.
19	Me lavo los dientes.	I brush my teeth.
20	Me acuesto.	I go to bed.
21	Tengo que hacer mis deberes.	I have to do my homework.
22	Tengo que ordenar mi dormitorio.	I have to tidy up my room.
23	Tengo que pasear al perro.	I have to walk the dog.
24	Tengo que lavarme el pelo.	I have to wash my hair.
25	No quiero.	I don't want to.
26	No tengo dinero.	I don't have any money.
27	No tengo tiempo.	I don't have time.
28	Lo siento, no puedo.	I am sorry, I can't.
29	en tren	by train
30	en avión	by plane
31	en autocar	by coach
32	en coche	by car
33	en monopatín	on skateboard
34	a pie	on foot
35	en barco	by boat
36	en bicicleta	by bike
37	cereales	cereals
38	tostadas	toast
39	magdalenas	fairy cakes
40	carne con verduras	meat and vegetables
41	pizza	pizza
42	patatas fritas	chips
43	galletas	biscuits
44	fruta	fruit
45	un bocadillo	a sandwich
46	pescado con ensalada	fish and salad
47	pasta	pasta
48	pollo	chicken
49	Cola Cao	drinking chocolate
50	té	tea
51	zumo de naranja	orange juice
52	nada	nothing
53	un kilo de peras	1 kg pears
54	medio kilo de tomates	1/2 kg tomatoes
55	dos kilos de manzanas	2 kg apples
56	un kilo de zanahorias	1 kg carrots
57	cien gramos de jamón	100 grams of ham
58	doscientos gramos de queso	200 grams of cheese
59	quinientos gramos de uvas	500 grams of grapes

60	un chorizo	a chorizo (spicy Spanish sausage)
61	una lechuga	a lettuce
62	una barra de pan	a baguette/loaf of bread
63	una botella de agua	a bottle of water
64	un cartón de leche	a carton of milk
65	un jersey	a jumper
66	un vestido	a dress
67	una falda	a skirt
68	una gorra	a cap
69	una camisa	a shirt
70	una camiseta	a t-shirt
71	una sudadera	a sweatshirt
72	unos vaqueros	some jeans
73	unos pantalones	some trousers
74	unos zapatos	some shoes
75	unas botas	some boots
76	unas zapatillas de deporte	some trainers
77	una panadería	a baker's
78	una cafetería	a café
79	una carnicería	a butcher's
80	una pastelería	a cake shop
81	una joyería	a jeweller's
82	una zapatería	a shoe shop
83	una librería	a bookshop
84	una tienda de música	a music shop
85	una tienda de ropa	a clothes shop
86	un supermercado	a supermarket
87	Sigue todo recto.	Continue straight on.
88	Dobla a la derecha.	Turn right.
89	Dobla a la izquierda.	Turn left.
90	Cruza la plaza.	Cross the square.
91	Toma la segunda calle a la derecha.	Take the second street on the right.
92	Toma la segunda calle a la izquierda.	Take the second street on the left.
93	Está al final de la calle.	It's at the end of the street.
94	Está a la derecha.	It's on the right.
95	Está a la izquierda.	It's on the left.
96	Está aquí.	Here it is.

Integrating ICT

Suggestions for ICT activities have been included in the Teacher's Guide. The following grid shows the location in *¡Mira! 2* and nature of these activities.

Unit reference	Activity type
Module 1 Unit 1	Emailing
Module 1 Unit 5	Word-processing
Module 1 ¡Extra! 2	Internet research
Module 2 Unit 2	Exchanging emails
Module 2 Unit 3	Internet research
Module 3 Unit 1	Producing a presentation using a presentation package
Module 3 Unit 3	Word-processing
Module 3 ¡Extra! 2	Internet research
Module 4 Unit 4	Internet research
Module 5 Unit 1	Emailing
Module 5 Unit 2	Producing a survey chart
Module 5 Unit 3	Producing a presentation using a presentation package
Module 5 ¡Extra! 2	Internet research
Module 6 Unit 5	Word-processing
Module 6 ¡Extra! 2	Internet research

Games and other teaching suggestions

Reading aloud

There are many reading activities in the Pupil's Book which give scope for further activities.

1. Use the texts to practise reading aloud. As an incentive, award points to a pupil who can read a text without any errors.
2. Ask a volunteer pupil to predict how many mistakes he/she will make before having a go, then seeing if he/she can do better than predicted.
3. Texts could be read round the class with pupils simply reading up to a full-stop and then passing it on to someone else in the room.

Reading follow-up

Motivation and participation can be enhanced by dividing the class into two teams and awarding points.

1. You read aloud and stop (or insert the word 'beep') for pupils to complete the sentence.
2. You read aloud and make a deliberate mistake. Pupils put up their hands as soon as they spot a mistake.

3. *Hot-potato*: pupils read a bit and pass it on quickly to someone who may not be expecting it.
4. *Random reading*: you read a phrase at random and the pupils have to say the next bit.

Mime activities

Mimes are a motivating way to help pupils to learn words.

1. You say a word which could be a job, sport, hobby or an adjective and the pupils mime it. It can be done silently with the whole class responding.
2. Pupils say a word or phrase and you mime – but only if the pupils say it correctly. This really puts you on the spot and gets the pupils trying very hard.
3. You mime and pupils say the word or phrase.
4. (*Un(a) voluntario/a*) One person goes out of the room. The rest of the class decide on a character-adjective to mime. The volunteer comes back into the room and has to guess the adjective that the class are miming. Again encourage the use of whole sentences.
5. (*Class knock down*) As above but this time everyone in the class can choose different qualities to mime. The volunteer returns to the room with everyone doing his/her own mime. The volunteer points to each pupil and names their character-adjective. If correct, the pupil sits down. This works well as a timed or team activity. The aim is to sit your team down as quickly as possible.
6. A version of charades: a good activity at the end of the lesson. Organise two teams, A and B. Have all the adjectives written on separate cards, masculine forms only. Put the cards in a pile at the front. A volunteer from team A comes to the front, picks up the first card and mimes it. The rest of the team must not see the word on the card. Anyone from Team A can put up his/her hand and is then invited by the volunteer to say the word. If correct, the volunteer picks up the next card and mimes it. The aim is to get through the whole list as quickly as possible. Note down the time for Team A. Team B then tries to beat that time.

Exploiting the songs

1. Pupils sing along. Fade out certain bits while they continue. When most of them know the song quite well, you can pause the audio to let them give you the next line by heart. Then try the whole chorus, followed by a few verses completely from memory.
2. You could try the 'pick up song' game: you fade the song after a few lines, the pupils continue singing and then you fade the song up again towards the end and they see whether they have kept pace with the recording.

Translation follow-up

All of the activities suggested above for Reading follow-up will also work for activities that involve translating from Spanish to English. For the first one, for example, translate the text aloud instead of reading it, stopping to ask pupils to complete the sentences.

Writing follow-up (Text dissection)

Mini-whiteboards are useful for these activities (individual, between two, or one per team).

After reading a text in some detail:

1. Display some anagrams of key words from the text and ask pupils to write them correctly. Prepare these in advance and check carefully. Award points for correct answers on each board.
2. Display some jumbled phrases from the text (words in the wrong order), e.g. *baloncesto el sábado juego al*. Pupils rewrite the phrase correctly. They could work in teams, producing one answer per team on paper.
3. Display an incorrect word or phrase in Spanish. See if they can spot the mistake and correct it. This can also be done as 'spot the missing word' or 'spot the word that is in the wrong place'.
4. Ask pupils to spell certain words from memory. Differentiate by first reading out a few words in Spanish and then giving a few in English for them also to write out in Spanish.

Comprehension follow-up

1. Ask questions in English about the text.
2. Ask questions in Spanish about the text.
3. True or False?
4. Who ... ?

Vocabulary treasure hunt

1. Find the word for ...
2. Find (3) opinions.

Grammar treasure hunt

1. Find (3) adjectives.
2. Find (2) feminine adjectives.
3. Find a verb in the *nosotros* form.
4. Find a plural noun.
5. Find a negative.

A variation on pair work

Musical pass the mobile. One pupil operates the CD player. He/she has to face away from the class. While the music is playing, a toy mobile phone (or a real one if you are prepared to risk it) is passed from pupil to pupil. As soon as the pupil stops the music, he/she (who is ideally also equipped with a phone) says the first statement of a dialogue. The other pupil who has ended up with the phone replies. They can, if they like, disguise their voices. The pupil who operated the CD player tries to guess who is speaking. The game then continues.

Personal Learning and Thinking Skills (PLTS)

In planning for progression, it is important to develop a clear picture of how learners demonstrate PLTS in the context of teaching and learning Spanish, and how those skills can raise achievement in this subject.

PLTS	Examples in ¡Mira! 2
1 Independent enquirers	Student Book activities throughout the course (e.g. exploring different perspectives when they compare alternative cultures with their own in M4 Unit 3 ex. 7 or M5 Unit 2 exs 4 and 6); ICT-based research (see suggestions to go with M3 ¡Extra! 2 exs 5-6 and M4 ¡Extra! 2 ex. 4)
2 Creative thinkers	Regular activities developing skills strategies (how to work out new vocabulary, etc.) (e.g. M2 Unit 1 Starter 1 or M4 Unit 1 Starter 1); Starters requiring students to apply logic and make connections (e.g. M5 Unit 1 Starter 2, M6 Unit 2 Starter 1 and M6 Unit 4 Starter 1); regular activities encouraging pupils to identify patterns and work out rules (e.g. M4 Unit 4 ex. 3)
3 Reflective learners	Ongoing opportunities to assess work and identify areas for improvement (e.g. M2 Unit 3 Plenary and M6 Unit 1 Plenary), including all Mini-tests, Resumen and Plenaries (e.g. M1 Unit 3 Plenary)
4 Team workers	Regular pair work activities (M3 Unit 4 ex. 4 or M6 Unit 1 Starter 1); class survey activities (M5 Unit 2 ex. 6); links with partner schools (e.g. M5 Unit 1 ICT suggestion after ex. 7)
5 Self-managers	Ongoing advice on managing learning (e.g. M1 Unit 2 Plenary on using the Palabras section), including strategies to improve learning (e.g. M2 Unit 1 Starter 1 – strategies for working out the meaning of new words)
6 Effective participators	Opportunities throughout the course for students to contribute (e.g. M3 Unit 1 ex. 2 working through strategies to understand new words), M4 Unit 5 Plenary (getting the most out of the Resumen section) or M6 Unit 5 Plenary (choosing a unit to review)

Covering the Programmes of Study

1 Key concepts

There are a number of key concepts outlined in the QCA Programmes of Study which underpin the study of languages. Pupils need to understand these concepts in order to deepen and broaden their knowledge, skills and understanding. These are addressed in all modules of *¡Mira! 2*, so are not included in the module grids, but are listed here for reference.

Linguistic competence

1.1 **a** developing the skills of listening, speaking, reading and writing in a range of situations and contexts
b applying linguistic knowledge and skills to understand and communicate effectively

1.2 Knowledge about language
a understanding how a language works and how to manipulate it
b recognising that languages differ but may share common grammatical, syntactical or lexical features

1.3 Creativity
a using familiar language for new purposes and in new contexts
b using imagination to express thoughts, ideas, experiences and feelings

1.4 Intercultural understanding
a appreciating the richness and diversity of other cultures
b recognising that there are different ways of seeing the world, and developing an international outlook

The table below indicates where in *¡Mira! 2*, pupils have the opportunity to progress in the **Key processes, Range and content**, and **Curriculum opportunities** prescribed in the QCA Programmes of Study. For each area we have indicated where these appear in the units of the Pupil's Book. There are further opportunities both in the Pupil's Book and the supplementary components. More detail is provided in the grids at the beginning of each module in this Teacher's Guide.

2 Key processes

These are the essential skills and processes in languages that pupils need to learn to make progress.

2.1 Developing language-learning strategies – pupils should be able to:	
a identify patterns in the target language	Module 2 Unit 4, Module 3 Unit 3, Module 4 Unit 2
b develop techniques for memorising words, phrases and spellings	Module 1 Unit 2, Module 4 Unit 3, Module 6 Unit 2
c use their knowledge of English or another language when learning the target language	Module 1 Unit 2, Module 2 Unit 3, Module 6 Unit 2
d use previous knowledge, context and other clues to work out the meaning of what they hear or read	Module 1 Unit 5, Module 3 Unit 1, Module 4 Unit 4
e use reference materials such as dictionaries appropriately and effectively	Module 1 Unit 4, Module 4 Unit 4, Module 5 Unit 1
2.2 Developing language skills – pupils should be able to:	
a listen for gist or detail	Module 3 Unit 1, Module 4 Unit 3, Module 5 Unit 4
b skim and scan written texts for the main points or details	Module 2 Unit 5, Module 4 ¡Extra! 2, Module 6 Unit 5
c respond appropriately to spoken and written language	Module 1 Unit 4, Module 2 Unit 4, Module 6 Unit 3
d use correct pronunciation and intonation	Module 1 Unit 3, Module 2 Unit 2, Module 3 Unit 2
e ask and answer questions	Module 2 Unit 4, Module 4 Unit 2, Module 5 Unit 3
f initiate and sustain conversations	Module 2 Unit 4, Module 4 Unit 3, Module 6 Unit 3
g write clearly and coherently, including an appropriate level of detail	Module 3 Unit 3, Module 4 Unit 4, Module 6 Unit 1
h redraft their writing to improve accuracy and quality	Module 2 Unit 3, Module 3 Unit 3, Module 5 Unit 1
i re-use language that they have heard or read in their own speaking and writing	Module 4 Unit 5, Module 5 Unit 5, Module 6 Unit 5
j adapt language they already know in new contexts for different purposes	Module 3 Unit 3, Module 4 Unit 2, Module 5 Unit 5
k deal with unfamiliar language, unexpected responses and unpredictable situations	Module 2 Unit 2, Module 5 Unit 1, Module 6 Unit 4

3 Range and content

This section outlines the breadth of the subject on which teachers should draw when teaching the key concepts and key processes. The study of languages should include:

a	the spoken and written form of the target language	Module 2 Unit 1, Module 5 ¡Extra! 1, Module 6 Unit 3
b	the interrelationship between sounds and writing in the target language	Module 1 Unit 3, Module 3 Unit 2, Module 4 Unit 2
c	the grammar of the target language and how to apply it	Module 1 Unit 1, Module 2 Unit 4, Module 5 Unit 4
d	a range of vocabulary and structures	Module 2 Unit 3, Module 5 Unit 4, Module 6 Unit 1
e	learning about different countries and cultures	Module 3 ¡Extra! 2, Module 4 Unit 3, Module 6 Unit 4
f	comparing pupils' own experiences and perspectives with those of people in countries and communities where the target language is spoken	Module 2 Unit 2, Module 5 Unit 1, Module 6 Unit 4

4 Curriculum opportunities

During the key stage pupils should be offered the following opportunities that are integral to their learning and enhance their engagement with the concepts, processes and content of the subject. The curriculum should provide opportunities for pupils to:

a	hear, speak, read and write in the target language regularly and frequently within the classroom and beyond	all units
b	communicate in the target language individually, in pairs, in groups and with speakers of the target language, including native speakers, where possible, for a variety of purposes	Module 1 Unit 1, Module 4 Unit 2, Module 5 Unit 4
c	use an increasing range of more complex language	Module 2 Unit 5, Module 5 Unit 4, Module 6 Unit 5
d	make links with English at word, sentence and text level	Module 1 Unit 4, Module 2 Unit 3, Module 3 Unit 2
e	use a range of resources, including ICT, for accessing and communicating information	Module 2 Unit 2, Module 4 Unit 3, Module 6 Unit 1
f	listen to, read or view a range of materials, including authentic materials in the target language, both to support learning and for personal interest and enjoyment	¡Extra! 2 all modules, Module 2 Unit 4, Module 4 Unit 4
g	use the target language in connection with topics and issues that are engaging and may be related to other areas of the curriculum	Module 3 ¡Extra ! 1, Module 4 ¡Extra ! 1, Module 6 ¡Extra ! 1

Gramática

Answers

Exercise 1

1 *más seria que* **2** menos generosa que
3 más alto que **4** más guapo que
5 más perezosa que **6** menos habladora que

Exercise 2

1 *Este vestido es el más caro.*
This dress is the most expensive.
2 Estas botas son las más incómodas.
These boots are the most uncomfortable.
3 Estos vaqueros son los menos caros.
These jeans are the least expensive.
4 Estos zapatos son los más bonitos.
These shoes are the nicest.
5 Esta chaqueta es la menos cómoda.
This jacket is the least comfortable.
6 Estos pantalones son los más feos.
These trousers are the ugliest.
7 Esta corbata es la menos anticuada.
This tie is the least old-fashioned.
8 Este jersey es el más guay.
This jersey is the greatest.

Exercise 3

1 *esta* corbata **2** estos cómics **3** este coche
4 estas camisetas **5** este jersey **6** esta chica
7 estos fotos **8** estas patatas fritas **9** esta tienda
10 estos pantalones

Exercise 4

1 *Queremos* – We want to go to the disco.
2 No quiero – I don't want to tidy my bedroom.
3 Puede – He can do his homework tomorrow.
4 No puedo – I can't take the dog for a walk.
5 Quieren – They want to watch a football match.
6 Podéis – You can watch a film.
7 Quiere – She wants to play football.
8 Quieres – Do you want to go shopping?

Exercise 5

1 Normalmente me despierto muy temprano.
Normally I wake up very early.
2 Mi madre se levanta a las siete.
My mother gets up at 7 o'clock.
3 Desayunamos en la cocina y luego nos lavamos los dientes.
We have breakfast in the kitchen and then we brush our teeth.
4 Mis hermanos se peinan y luego van al instituto.
My brothers comb their hair and then go to school.
5 ¿Te duchas por la mañana?
Do you have a shower in the morning?
6 Por la tarde cenáis y os acostáis muy tarde.
In the evening you have dinner and go to bed very late.

Exercise 6

1 tiene – My friend is 15 years old.
2 son – My sisters are funny.
3 es – Penélope Cruz is very small.
4 Tengo – I'm good-looking. I have blond hair.
5 Tienes – Do you have brothers or sisters, Patricia?
6 soy – I'm 12 years old and I'm talkative.
7 tienen – The boys have brown eyes.
8 somos – My mother and I are a bit lazy.

Exercise 7

1 Tengo que – I have to tidy my bedroom.
2 Tengo – I have a dog and a cat.
3 tengo – I'm sorry, I don't have time.
4 tengo que – I don't have to take the dog for a walk.
5 Tengo – I'm 13 years old.
6 Tengo que – I have to go shopping.

Exercise 8

1 Barcelona ***está*** en la costa.
4 **Están** al final de la calle.
7 **Son** las dos y diez.
9 **Está** aquí.
10 Mi piso **es** moderno.

Exercise 9

1 *Voy a ver una película.*
I'm going to watch a film.
2 Van a ver la televisión.
They're going to watch television.
3 ¿Qué vas a hacer?
What are you going to do?
4 Va a jugar al futbolín.
He's/She's going to play table football.
5 Va a escuchar música.
He's/She's going to listen to music.
6 Voy a ver un partido de fútbol.
I'm going to watch a football match.
7 Van a ir a España.
They're going to go to Spain.
8 Voy a ir a la playa y voy a tomar el sol.
I'm going to go to the beach and I'm going to sunbathe.
9 Voy a salir con mis amigos.
I'm going to go out with my friends.
10 Voy a bailar en una discoteca.
I'm going to dance in a disco.

Exercise 10

1 *Mis hermanos **visitaron** monumentos.*
My brothers visited monuments.
2 Mi amigo y yo **bailamos** en la discoteca.
My friend and I danced at the disco.
3 Carmen **montó** en bicicleta.
Carmen rode a bike.
4 ¿**Escuchaste** música?
Did you listen to music?
5 Fui a la playa y **descansé**.
I went to the beach and I relaxed.
6 Diego y Juan, ¿**tomáis** el sol?
Diego and Juan, did you sunbathe?
7 Los chicos **jugaron** al fútbol.
The boys played football.
8 Fui a la discoteca pero no **bailé**.
I went to the disco but I didn't dance.

Exercise 11

1 bebí – In the evening I went to the café and I drank lemonade.
2 comieron – Carmen and Ana ate ice cream.
3 recibió – Miguel received some presents.
4 saliste – Did you go out with your friend?
5 bebimos – We went (in) to a bar and we drank wine.
6 escribió – Antonio wrote a letter.
7 salí – On Wednesday I didn't go out: I listened to music in my bedroom.
8 recibieron – Diego and Juan received some messages from their friend.

Exercise 12

1 *Did you go to Madrid by plane?*
2 He/She went to Germany with his family.
3 It was very boring.
4 Last year we went to Granada.
5 They went on holiday by boat.
6 My trip to Argentina was terrific.
7 Where did you go?
8 What was it like?
9 Did you (plural) go by car?
10 I went to a restaurant. It was very expensive.

Exercise 13

1 *Mañana **voy a ir** al cine.*
2 Este fin de semana Carmen **va a ir** a la piscina.
3 Esta tarde Juan **va a escuchar** música.
4 Mañana **voy a hacer** mucho deporte.
5 *Los jueves **hago** esquí.*
6 Por la mañana Enrique **habla** por teléfono.
7 Normalmente **bailamos**.
8 Los fines de semana **jugáis** con el ordenador.

Exercise 14

1 *Normalmente **voy** a Madrid.*
2 Los viernes Juan **va** de compras.
3 Generalmente **descansamos** en la playa.
4 Los sábados Diego y María **bailan**.
5 *El fin de semana pasado **escuchó** música.*
6 El verano pasado **tomamos** el sol.
7 El año pasado **fui** a Escocia.
8 El jueves pasado **jugaron** al fútbol.

Exercise 15

1 *Ayer fui de compras.*
2 Normalmente llevamos vaqueros.
3 El año pasado fue a Francia.
4 Mañana voy a tomar el sol.
5 La próxima vez va a ver una película.
6 Los fines de semana juegan al fútbol.
7 El verano pasado compré una camiseta.

Exercise 16

1 me interesa **2** le encantan **3** me gusta
4 te gusta **5** le gusta **6** le interesa **7** te gusta
8 le gustan

Exercise 17

1 *Se puede comprar carne en una carnicería.*
2 Se pueden comprar CDs en una tienda de música.
3 Se puede comprar comida en un supermercado.
4 Se pueden comprar joyas en una joyería.
5 Se pueden comprar libros en una librería.
6 Se puede comprar pan en una panadería.
7 Se pueden comprar pasteles en una pastelería.
8 Se pueden comprar zapatos en una zapatería.

Module 1 La gente (Pupil's Book pages 6–23)

Unit	Framework	Levels and PoS	Key language	Grammar	Skills
1 Presentaciones (pp. 6–7) Talking about activities Expressing opinions using *me gusta…*	**1.1/Y8** Listening – understanding on first hearing **4.6/Y8** Language – (a) range of questions **5.1** Strategies – patterns	**2–4** **2.1a** identify patterns **2.1e** use reference materials **2.2e** ask and answer questions **3c** apply grammar **4b** communicate in pairs etc. **4e** use a range of resources	*¿Qué haces en tu tiempo libre?* *Bailo.* *Chateo por internet.* *Escucho música.* *Hago deporte.* *Juego con el ordenador.* *Mando mensajes.* *Salgo con mis amigos.* *Voy de compras.* *¿Qué te gusta?* *Me gusta/interesa/encanta…* *el fútbol/la música/la natación* *Me gustan/interesan/encantan…* *los cómics/los videojuegos/las hamburguesas* *¿Qué no te gusta?* *No me gusta la música.* *Odio el fútbol.* *No me interesan los cómics.*	Present tense ('I'/'you' singular forms): • *-ar* verbs • irregular verbs *salir, hacer, ir* Verb structures which change with plural nouns: *(no) me gusta(n), me encanta(n), me interesa(n)*	Understanding the concept of person in verbs Using reference resources Applying recognised patterns to new language Communicating with native speakers
2 Mis amigos (pp. 8–9) Describing friends using adjectives Using *y, pero, también, nunca*	**1.4/Y8** Speaking – (a) classroom exchanges (pupil-pupil) **4.2/Y8** Language – increasing vocabulary **4.3/Y8** Language – genders and plurals	**2–4** **2.1b** memorising **2.1c** knowledge of language **2.1d** previous knowledge **2.1e** use reference materials **3c** apply grammar **4b** communicate in pairs etc.	*¿Cómo es (tu mejor amigo/a)?* *Es…* *alto/a* *bajo/a* *delgado/a* *guapo/a* *¿Cómo es de carácter?* *Es…* *No/Nunca es…* *divertido/a* *generoso/a* *hablador(a)* *inteligente* *perezoso/a* *serio/a* *¿Cómo es su pelo?* *Tiene el pelo…* *castaño/negro/pelirrojo/rubio* *corto/largo/ondulado* *¿De qué color son sus ojos?* *Tiene los ojos…* *azules/grises/marrones/verdes*	Adjective agreement (all forms) Present tense of *ser/tener* (full paradigm receptive; 'I'/'you' singular, 'he/she' forms productive)	Using reading strategies to work out new words Developing vocabulary learning skills Extending sentences, using connectives and negatives

continued

Module 1 La gente (Pupil's Book pages 6–23)

Unit	Framework	Levels and PoS	Key language	Grammar	Skills
3 Las estrellas (pp. 10–11) Describing celebrities Comparing things using *más... que* (more... than)	**5.2** Strategies – memorising **5.3** Strategies – English/other languages	2–4 **2.2d** pronunciation and intonation **3b** sounds and writing **3c** apply grammar **4f** language for interest/enjoyment	*¿Quién es más alto/a?* *¿Quién es menos alto/a?* *más (viejo/a) que* *menos (joven) que*	Comparatives: *más... que* *menos... que*	Pronunciation: *j, z* Reviewing progress/checking work using the Mini-test
4 Mi rutina diaria (pp. 12–13) Using reflexive verbs Using sequencing words	**2.5/Y8** Writing – using researched language **5.8** Strategies – evaluating and improving	2–4 **2.1c** knowledge of language **2.1e** use reference materials **2.2c** respond appropriately **2.2e** ask and answer questions **2.2g** write clearly and coherently **3c** apply grammar **4b** communicate in pairs etc. **4d** make links with English	*¿Qué haces por la mañana/tarde?* *Por la mañana/tarde...* *me despierto* *me levanto* *me ducho* *me peino* *me visto* *desayuno* *voy al instituto* *hago mis deberes* *ceno* *veo la televisión* *me lavo los dientes* *me acuesto* *después* *luego* *normalmente* *por la mañana* *por la tarde* *primero*	Reflexive verbs (singular: 'you' singular, 'he/she' forms receptive; 'I' form productive) (including example of stem-changing verb – *despertarse* (*e* → *ie*))	Using reading strategies to work out new words Carrying out a survey in the classroom Structuring a longer text using sequencing words Using reference resources
5 Tu nacionalidad (pp. 14–15) Understanding nationalities Writing an extended text	**2.4/Y8** Writing – (b) sequencing paragraphs **3.2/Y8** Culture – (a) young people: aspirations	2–4 **2.1d** previous knowledge **2.1e** use reference materials **2.2g** write clearly and coherently **2.2h** redraft to improve writing **3c** apply grammar **3b** sounds and writing **4e** use a range of resources	*¿Cuál es tu nacionalidad?* *Soy...* *argentino/a* *chileno/a* *colombiano/a* *escocés/escocesa* *español(a)* *estadounidense* *galés/galesa* *inglés/inglesa* *irlandés/irlandesa* *mexicano/a*	Adjective agreement: nationalities	Using reading strategies to work out new words Developing vocabulary learning skills Writing an extended text in Spanish

continued

Module 1 La gente (Pupil's Book pages 6–23)

Unit	Framework	Levels and PoS	Key language	Grammar	Skills
Resumen/ Prepárate (pp. 16–17) Pupils' checklist and practice test		3			Reviewing progress/ checking work
¡Extra! 1 (pp. 18–19) Using frequency words Practising reflexive verbs		4 **2.2f** initiate/sustain conversations **4b** communicate in pairs etc. **4e** use a range of resources **4f** language for interest/ enjoyment	*siempre* *a menudo* *a veces* *de vez en cuando* *nunca* Revision of language from Module 1	Expressions of frequency	Understanding a longer/authentic text in Spanish (magazine questionnaire)
¡Extra! 2 (pp. 20–21) Reading a story in Spanish Practising verbs in the present tense	**2.1/Y8** Reading – authentic materials **5.6** Strategies – reading aloud	3–4 **2.2d** pronunciation and intonation **2.2g** write clearly and coherently **3e** different countries/ cultures **3f** compare experiences **4e** use a range of resources **4f** language for interest/ enjoyment	*lo siento* *mucho gusto* *conocí a* *hoy* Revision of language from Module 1	Present tense	Understanding a longer text in Spanish (ongoing photo story) Working on sounding authentic by copying Spanish models Writing creatively in Spanish
Te toca a ti (pp. 114–115)	Self-access reading and writing at two levels				

1 Presentaciones (Pupil's Book pages 6–7)

Learning objectives

- Talking about activities
- Expressing opinions using *me gusta...*

Framework objectives

1.1/Y8 Listening – understanding on first hearing
4.6/Y8 Language – (a) range of questions
5.1 Strategies – patterns

Grammar

- Present tense ('I'/'you' singular forms):
  - *-ar* verbs
  - irregular verbs *salir, hacer, ir*
- Verb structures which change with plural nouns: *(no) me gusta(n), me encanta(n), me interesa(n)*

Key language

¿Qué haces en tu tiempo libre?
Bailo.
Chateo por internet.
Escucho música.
Hago deporte.
Juego con el ordenador.
Mando mensajes.
Salgo con mis amigos.
Voy de compras.

¿Qué te gusta?
Me gusta...
Me interesa...
Me encanta...
el fútbol/la música/la natación
Me gustan...
Me interesan...
Me encantan...
los cómics/los videojuegos/las hamburguesas

¿Qué no te gusta?
No me gusta la música.
Odio el fútbol.
No me interesan los cómics.

High-frequency words

el, la, los, las
me, te
con
en
y
pero
no
¿cómo?
¿cuántos?
¿qué?
también
hacer (hago, haces)
escuchar (escucho, escuchas)
jugar (juego)
ir (voy, vas)
tener (tienes)

Cross-curricular

English: Verb forms
ICT: Email contact with a Spanish school

Resources

CD1, tracks 2–4
Cuadernos A & B, p. 2
R & A Pack, Gramática p. 5

Teacher Presentations

Screen 1 – Module 1 overview
Screen 2 – Vocabulary: Flashcards
Screen 3 – p. 6 ex. 1
Screen 4 – p. 7 ex. 4
Screen 5 – p. 7 ex. 5

Suggestion ▸▸1.1/Y8◂◂

When pupils carry out listening exercises (e.g. 4 and 5 in this unit), encourage them to pick up certain key information on the first hearing, and then to listen again for further detail.

Starter 1 ▸▸4.5a/Y8 5.1◂◂

Aim
To revise some high-frequency regular verbs and the concept of verb endings.

Write up the following and ask pupils working in pairs to list and translate into English all the verbs in the text.

El sábado no trabajo. Escucho música en mi dormitorio. Hablo por teléfono con mi amigo. Como una pizza y bebo agua. Leo y escribo un poco.

Check answers.

Suggestion

Ask pupils what all the verb forms in the Starter text have in common. What does this tell them about the 'I' form of the verb? Can they think of any exceptions to this rule? (e.g. *soy*, *voy*)
Say that in this unit you will look at verb endings in more detail.

1 Escucha a Fernanda Famosa y escribe la letra correcta. (1–8) (AT1.2) ▸▸4.5a/Y8◂◂

Listening. Pupils listen to someone talking about what she does in her free time and note the letter of each activity mentioned using the pictures *a–h*.

Audioscript Track 2

1 – *Fernanda Famosa, ¿qué haces en tu tiempo libre?*
– *Escucho música. Me encanta la música.*
2 – *¿Bailas también?*
– *Pues, sí. Bailo.*
3 – *¿Y qué más?*
– *A ver... mando mensajes...*
4 – *... y juego con el ordenador...*
5 – *Chateo por internet.*

6 – *¿Vas de compras también?*
– *Sí. Voy de compras.*
7 – *¿Haces mucho deporte?*
– *A ver... sí, hago deporte. ¡El esquí es mi deporte favorito!*
8 – *¿Y sales con amigos?*
– *Sí, sí, salgo con mis amigos.*

Answers

1 d **2** c **3** b **4** e **5** a **6** f **7** h **8** g

Gramática: verb endings ▸▸5.1◂◂

This gives the 1st and 2nd person of *escuchar* and of the irregular verbs *hacer*, *salir* and *ir* in the present tense.

Remind pupils that Spanish has a greater variety of verb endings than English and that it is important to learn endings as they go along.

Ask them where they would find out about the endings for the different groups of regular verbs and for the forms of irregular verbs, reintroducing them to the Gramática section at the back of the Pupil's Book. Explain that this section gives useful summaries of grammar points, often going into more detail and giving more examples than are contained in the Gramática sections on the page. It also contains exercises on specific grammar points, which you will ask them to do at certain points.

You could set them the task of finding the Spanish for 'he/she speaks' by using the Gramática section.

➕ Ask pupils to list the infinitives of all the verbs in exercise 1 and label them regular or irregular.

2 Con tu compañero/a, empareja las preguntas con las respuestas del ejercicio 1. (AT2.3) ▸▸4.6a/Y8◂◂

Speaking. In pairs pupils match the eight questions listed with the appropriate responses from exercise 1 (*a–h*), taking it in turn to supply the question/give the answer. A sample exchange is given.

Once they feel confident, suggest pupils try this with their books closed.

3 Escribe un texto sobre ti. (AT4.3) ▸▸4.4/Y8◂◂

Writing. Using the key expressions in exercise 1, pupils write a text saying what they do in their own free time. A sample opening is given.

Point out the connectives used in the example – *y* and *también*. Ask why connectives are used and if pupils can think of any others they could use in this context, reminding them of *pero* as necessary. Encourage them to include connectives in their writing here and whenever possible to make their Spanish more interesting and varied.

Starter 2 ▸▸5.1◂◂

Aim

To reintroduce *me gusta* and *me gustan* (etc.) with nouns. To encourage pupils to apply a pattern to new language.

Write up:

Me gusta el fútbol pero no me gustan los videojuegos.
Me gusta la música pero no me gustan los cómics.

Ask pupils working in pairs to use these model sentences to write two further sentences, featuring *me interesa/me interesan* and *me encanta/me encantan* and the following words:

el tenis *los cómics*
la natación *las hamburguesas*

Check answers, asking pupils also to translate their sentences. Ask pupils how they worked out which nouns went with with each phrase and get them to summarise the rule on how *me gusta(n)* (etc.) is used with nouns.

Suggestion

Ask pupils to close their books. Write up *me gusta* and *me gustan*. Then prompt with the nouns in the key language box on p. 7 of the Pupil's Book (e.g. *la música*). Pupils respond using the correct form, *me gusta* or *me gustan*. Do the same activity with *me interesa(n)* and *me encanta(n)*.

4 Escucha y escribe la letra correcta. (1–6) Escucha otra vez. ¿Positivo ☺ o negativo ☹? (AT1.2) ▸▸1.1/Y8 4.2/Y8◂◂

Listening. Pupils listen and note the items in the order they are mentioned, using the pictures *a–f*.

They then listen again, this time noting whether the speaker expresses a positive opinion (by drawing a smiley face) or a negative opinion (by drawing a sad face).

Audioscript Track 3

1 *Me gusta la natación.*
2 *Me encantan los cómics.*
3 *Odio el fútbol. Es muy, muy aburrido.*
4 *Me interesan los videojuegos.*
5 *Me gusta la música, especialmente la música electrónica.*
6 *No me gustan las hamburguesas. Puagh, ¡qué asco!*

Answers

1 *b*☺ **2** f☺ **3** c☹ **4** a☺ **5** e☺ **6** d☹

5 Escucha y lee. Copia y rellena la tabla. (AT1.3) ▸▸1.1/Y8 4.5a/Y8◂◂

Listening. Pupils copy out the grid. They listen to the two speakers, following the text at the same time in the book. They then complete the grid with the speakers' personal information and details of what they like/dislike.

Audioscript Track 4

a *Me llamo Blondi, Jaume Blondi.*
Soy el agente secreto 00Ñ y soy español.
Tengo treinta años.
En mi tiempo libre mando mensajes y hago deporte.
Me gustan los cómics. Odio las hamburguesas.

b *Me llamo Pria Fredericks.*
Soy presentadora de 'Las mañanas con Pria'.
Tengo veinticinco años.
A ver, en mi tiempo libre escucho música, salgo con mis amigos y voy de compras.
Me encantan los videojuegos pero odio el fútbol. ¿Y tú?

Answers

Nombre	*Jaume Blondi*	*Pria Fredericks*
Edad	30 años	25 años
Actividades	mando mensajes, hago deporte	escucho música, salgo con mis amigos, voy de compras
☺	los cómics	los videojuegos
☹	las hamburguesas	el fútbol

6 Con tu compañero/a, pregunta y contesta por Jaume Blondi y Pria Fredericks. (AT2.4) ▸▸1.4a/Y8 4.6a/Y8◂◂

Speaking. In pairs pupils take it in turn to ask questions and to answer as though they were Jaume Blondi or Pria Fredericks. The questions are supplied and a sample exchange shown.

Ask pupils to use the texts in exercise 5 as a model and write an email describing themselves in a similar way. Encourage them to use a dictionary as necessary.

If lower-ability pupils need support, start by identifying with them the phrases that need to be changed in one of the model texts.

Email contact with a Spanish school will give your pupils an enjoyable forum in which to practise the Spanish they are learning. They could use this email as a way of introducing themselves, including the questions listed in exercise 6 for their Spanish contacts to respond to.

Plenary ▸▸5.1◂◂

Ask pupils to summarise how *me gusta* and *me gustan* are used with nouns and to give you two examples of other expressions which work in the same way (*me interesa(n)*, *me encanta(n)*).

Put pupils into small teams. Tell them they have two minutes to come up with examples of *me interesa/me interesan* plus an appropriate noun. A correct answer with *me interesa* will win one point; a correct answer with *me interesan* two points. The team with the highest score is the winner.

The teaching notes throughout *¡Mira! 2* suggest a variety of Starters and Plenaries which involve pupils working in teams. You may want to allocate teams at this stage which students can stay in throughout the year. This will save time whenever a team activity comes up. You could also keep an ongoing tally of points won in these activities and award a prize to the team with the highest score at the end of each term/half-term.

Cuaderno A, page 2

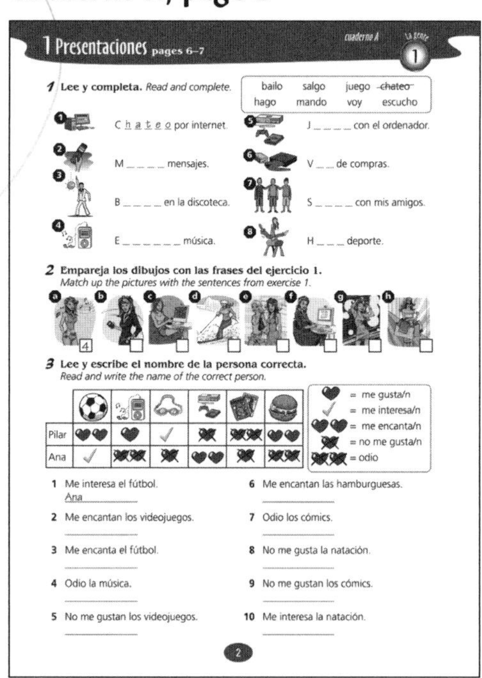
1 Presentaciones pages 6–7

1 Lee y completa. *Read and complete.*

bailo salgo juego ~~chateo~~ hago mando voy escucho

1 Chateo por internet.
2 M____ mensajes.
3 B____ en la discoteca.
4 E______ música.
5 J____ con el ordenador.
6 V__ de compras.
7 S____ con mis amigos.
8 H___ deporte.

2 Empareja los dibujos con las frases del ejercicio 1. *Match up the pictures with the sentences from exercise 1.*

3 Lee y escribe el nombre de la persona correcta. *Read and write the name of the correct person.*

= me gusta/n
= me interesa/n
= me encanta/n
= no me gusta/n
= odio

1 Me interesa el fútbol. Ana
2 Me encantan los videojuegos.
3 Me encanta el fútbol.
4 Odio la música.
5 No me gustan los videojuegos.
6 Me encantan las hamburguesas.
7 Odio los cómics.
8 No me gusta la natación.
9 No me gustan los cómics.
10 Me interesa la natación.

2

1 (AT3.2, AT4.1)

Answers

1 *Chateo* **2** Mando **3** Bailo **4** Escucho **5** Juego **6** Voy **7** Salgo **8** Hago

2 (AT3.2)

a *4* **b** 2 **c** 5 **d** 8 **e** 7 **f** 1 **g** 3 **h** 6

3 (AT3.2)

Answers

1 *Ana* **2** Ana **3** Pilar **4** Ana **5** Pilar **6** Pilar
7 Pilar **8** Ana **9** Ana **10** Pilar

Cuaderno B, page 2

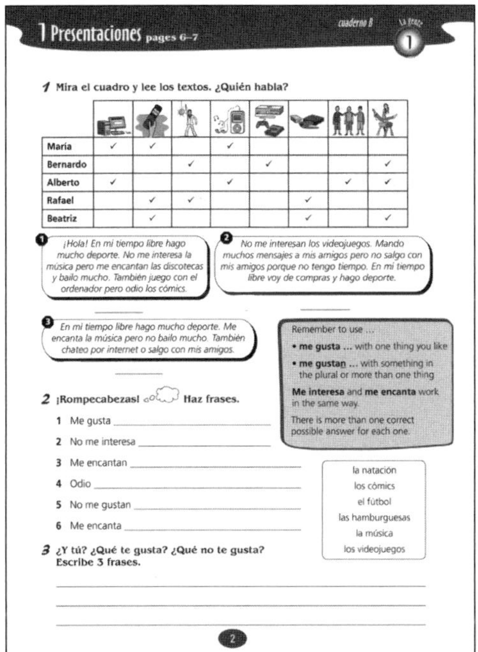

1 Presentaciones pages 6–7 cuaderno B La gente 1

1 **Mira el cuadro y lee los textos. ¿Quién habla?**

María	✓	✓		✓				
Bernardo			✓		✓			✓
Alberto	✓			✓			✓	✓
Rafael		✓	✓			✓		
Beatriz		✓				✓		✓

1 *¡Hola! En mi tiempo libre hago mucho deporte. No me interesa la música pero me encantan las discotecas y bailo mucho. También juego con el ordenador pero odio los cómics.*

2 *No me interesan los videojuegos. Mando muchos mensajes a mis amigos pero no salgo con mis amigos porque no tengo tiempo. En mi tiempo libre voy de compras y hago deporte.*

3 *En mi tiempo libre hago mucho deporte. Me encanta la música pero no bailo mucho. También chateo por internet o salgo con mis amigos.*

Remember to use …
- **me gusta …** with one thing you like
- **me gustan …** with something in the plural or more than one thing

Me interesa and **me encanta** work in the same way.

There is more than one correct possible answer for each one.

2 **¡Rompecabezas! Haz frases.**

1 Me gusta ______
2 No me interesa ______
3 Me encantan ______
4 Odio ______
5 No me gustan ______
6 Me encanta ______

la natación
los cómics
el fútbol
las hamburguesas
la música
los videojuegos

3 **¿Y tú? ¿Qué te gusta? ¿Qué no te gusta? Escribe 3 frases.**

2

1 (AT3.3)

1 Bernardo **2** Beatriz **3** Alberto

2 (AT4.2)

3 (AT4.3)

R & A Pack, Gramática page 5

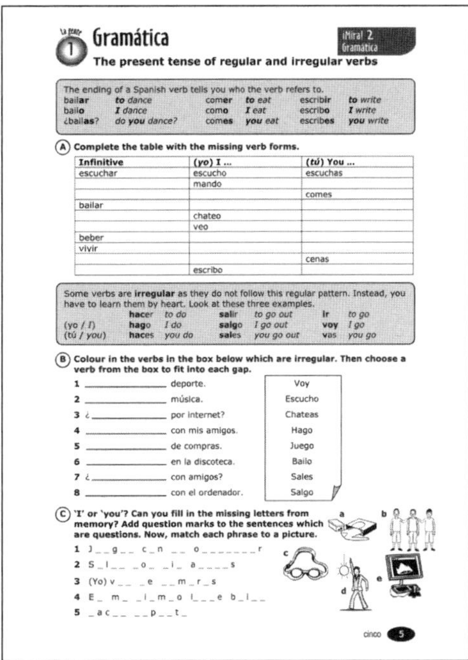

La gente 1 **Gramática** ¡Mira! 2 Gramática

The present tense of regular and irregular verbs

The ending of a Spanish verb tells you who the verb refers to.

bail**ar**	**to** *dance*	com**er**	**to** *eat*	escrib**ir**	**to** *write*
bail**o**	***I*** *dance*	com**o**	***I*** *eat*	escrib**o**	***I*** *write*
¿bail**as**?	*do* ***you*** *dance?*	com**es**	***you*** *eat*	escrib**es**	***you*** *write*

(A) **Complete the table with the missing verb forms.**

Infinitive	**(*yo*) I …**	**(*tú*) You …**
escuchar	escucho	escuchas
	mando	
		comes
bailar		
	chateo	
	veo	
beber		
vivir		
		cenas
	escribo	

Some verbs are **irregular** as they do not follow this regular pattern. Instead, you have to learn them by heart. Look at these three examples.

	hacer	*to do*	**salir**	*to go out*	**ir**	*to go*
(yo / *I*)	**hago**	*I do*	**salgo**	*I go out*	**voy**	*I go*
(tú / *you*)	**haces**	*you do*	**sales**	*you go out*	**vas**	*you go*

(B) **Colour in the verbs in the box below which are irregular. Then choose a verb from the box to fit into each gap.**

1 ______ deporte.
2 ______ música.
3 ¿ ______ por internet?
4 ______ con mis amigos.
5 ______ de compras.
6 ______ en la discoteca.
7 ¿ ______ con amigos?
8 ______ con el ordenador.

Voy
Escucho
Chateas
Hago
Juego
Bailo
Sales
Salgo

(C) **'I' or 'you'? Can you fill in the missing letters from memory? Add question marks to the sentences which are questions. Now, match each phrase to a picture.**

1 J _ _ g _ _ c _ n _ _ o _ _ _ _ _ _ r
2 S _ l _ _ _ o _ _ i _ a _ _ _ s
3 (Yo) v _ _ _ e _ _ m _ r _ s
4 E _ m _ _ i _ m _ o l _ _ _ e b _ i _ _
5 _ a c _ _ _ _ p _ _ t _

a b c d e

cinco 5

(A) mandar, mandas; comer, como; bailo, bailas; chatear, chateas; ver, ves; bebo, bebes; vivo, vives; cenar, ceno; escribir, escribes

(B) irregular verbs – voy, hago, juego, sales, salgo
1 hago **2** escucho **3** chateas **4** salgo **5** voy
6 bailo **7** sales **8** juego

(C) **1** ¿Juegas con el ordenador? e
2 Salgo con mis amigos. b **3** voy de compras. a
4 En mi tiempo libre bailo. d **5** ¿Haces deporte? c

2 Mis amigos (Pupil's Book pages 8–9)

Learning objectives

- Describing friends using adjectives
- Using *y, pero, también, nunca*

Framework objectives

1.4/Y8 Speaking – (a) classroom exchanges (pupil-pupil)
4.2/Y8 Language – increasing vocabulary
4.3/Y8 Language – genders and plurals

Grammar

- Adjective agreement (all forms)
- Present tense of *ser/tener* (full paradigm receptive; 'I'/'you' singular, 'he/she' forms productive)

Key language

¿Cómo es (tu mejor amigo/a)?
Es... alto/a, bajo/a, delgado/a, guapo/a
¿Cómo es de carácter?
Es...
No/Nunca es...
divertido/a, generoso/a, hablador(a), inteligente, perezoso/a, serio/a
¿Cómo es su pelo?
Tiene el pelo...
castaño/negro/pelirrojo/rubio
corto/largo/ondulado
¿De qué color son sus ojos?
Tiene los ojos...
azules/grises/marrones/verdes

High-frequency words

un, una
el, los
mi, tu, su
se
de
y
pero
no, sí
¿cómo?
¿cuántos?
también
ser, tener
nunca

Resources

CD1, tracks 5–9
Cuadernos A & B, p. 3
R & A Pack, Gramática pp. 6–7
Flashcards 1–10

Teacher Presentations

Screen 1 – Module 1 overview
Screen 2 – Vocabulary: Flashcards
Screen 3 – p. 8 ex. 1
Screen 4 – p. 8 ex. 2
Screen 5 – p. 8 ex. 3
Screen 6 – p. 9 ex. 5
Screen 7 – p. 9 ex. 6
Screen 8 – Game

Suggestion ▸▸4.2/Y8◂◂

You may like to discuss which of the new words in this unit express abstract attributes and which express physical attributes.

Starter 1 ▸▸4.2/Y8 5.4◂◂

Aim

To introduce adjectives for describing people. To use strategies to work out new vocabulary.

Write up the following, jumbling the order of the second column (in correct order here for reference only) and give pupils two minutes working in pairs to match the Spanish expressions with the correct English versions.

Mi amigo es...

generoso	generous
muy guapo	very attractive
serio	serious
divertido	amusing
un poco perezoso	a bit lazy
delgado	slim
bastante alto	quite tall
bajo	short
inteligente	intelligent
hablador	talkative

Check the answers and ask pupils what strategies they used to work out the pairings. Remind them as necessary: using what you know (the intensifiers), using cognates in English (*serio*/ serious) and in Spanish (*hablar/hablador*), using a process of elimination.

Suggestion

Write up *¿Cómo es tu mejor amigo? Mi amigo es generoso y divertido.*

Ask the class to translate it. Then ask them how they would ask and answer the question if they were talking about a female friend.

Remind pupils as necessary that adjectives agree with the noun they describe, i.e. they have a particular form depending on whether the noun is masculine or feminine, singular or plural. Adjectives which end in *-o* in the masculine singular change to *-a* in the feminine.

Use Flashcards 1–10 and prompt with the masculine version of the adjective, getting pupils to give you the feminine version. Then, as a class, read through the key language box in exercise 1 before playing the recording. Point out the feminine forms of the adjectives *inteligente* and *hablador* as you do so, and say that adjective endings will be covered in more detail later in the unit.

1 Escucha y escribe la letra correcta. (1–10) (AT1.2) ▸▸4.2/Y8◂◂

Listening. Pupils listen to the descriptions of friends and note the letter of each characteristic mentioned (from *a–j*).

Audioscript Track 5

1 *¿Cómo es tu mejor amigo?*
Mi mejor amigo es generoso.
2 *¿cómo es tu mejor amiga?*
Mi mejor amiga es baja.
3 *¿Cómo es tu mejor amigo?*
Mi mejor amigo es serio.
4 *Mi mejor amiga es alta.*
5 *¿Y cómo es tu mejor amigo?*
Mi mejor amigo es guapo.
6 *¿Y cómo es tu mejor amigo?*
Mi mejor amigo es perezoso.
7 *Mi mejor amigo es delgado.*
8 *Mi mejor amiga es habladora.*
9 *Mi mejor amiga es inteligente.*
10 *Mi mejor amigo es divertido.*

Answers

1 f **2** i **3** c **4** h **5** g **6** d **7** j **8** b **9** e
10 a

R Prompt with *Mi mejor amigo es...* or *Mi mejor amiga es...* for pupils to respond with an adjective in the appropriate form.

You could now cover adjective endings in detail using the Gramática box. Alternatively, you could do this just before pupils tackle exercise 4.

2 Escucha y describe a la persona en inglés. (1–6) (AT1.3) ▸▸1.1/Y8 4.3/Y8◂◂

Listening. Pupils listen to six people describing their best friends and note in English whether the person described in each case is a boy or a girl and what he/she is like.

Audioscript Track 6

1 – *Mi mejor amigo es hablador. También es inteligente. No es serio.*
2 – *¿Cómo es tu mejor amigo?*
– *A ver, mi mejor amigo es perezoso y serio pero es generoso.*
3 – *¿Cómo es tu mejor amiga?*
– *Mi mejor amiga es alta y guapa.*
4 – *¿Y cómo es tu mejor amiga, Carmen?*
– *Es una chica inteligente. Nunca es perezosa.*
5 – *¿Cómo es tu mejor amigo, Pepe?*
– *Mi mejor amigo es bajo y muy guapo. Tiene muchos, muchos años – ¡es mi abuelo!*
6 – *¿Cómo es tu mejor amiga, Ana? ¡Cuéntame!*
– *Es divertida y es muy habladora, pero es perezosa.*

Answers

1 boy – talkative, intelligent, not serious
2 boy – lazy, serious, generous
3 girl – tall, pretty
4 girl – intelligent, never lazy
5 boy – short, very attractive
6 girl – amusing, very talkative, lazy

3 Escucha otra vez. Escribe la palabra o las palabras del cuadro que entiendes. (AT1.3) ▸▸1.3a/Y8◂◂

Listening. Pupils listen to the recording again, this time noting down for each speaker the words *y, pero, no, también* and *nunca* whenever they hear them.

Audioscript Track 7

As for exercise 2.

Answers

1 *también, no* **2** y, pero **3** y **4** y, nunca
5 y, y **6** y, pero

R Pupils write a short description of a friend incorporating *y, pero, no, también* and *nunca.* Check first that pupils know how *nunca* is used, writing up the model *Nunca es seria* for support if necessary.

Gramática: agreement of adjectives

This shows the agreement of adjectives ending in *-o/-a*, *-e*, or a consonant in the singular and plural.

Point out that most adjectives ending in a consonant in the masculine singular don't change in the feminine singular: *habladora* is an exception.

4 Elige cinco personas de tu clase. Tu compañero/a adivina quién es. (AT2.3) ▸▸1.4a/Y8◂◂

Speaking. In pairs: one pupil chooses a person from their class; the other guesses who it is by asking yes/no questions. They should take it in turn to think up/guess five people each. A sample exchange is given.

¡Mira! 2 provides regular opportunities for pupils to practise short unscripted exchanges and also suggests strategies to help them cope in these situations. To give pupils as much practice as possible, encourage them to use Spanish routinely in class when asking for information or help.

Starter 2 ▸▸ 4.5a/Y8 ◂◂

Aim
To review the high-frequency irregular verbs *ser* and *tener*.

Write up the following, replacing the words in brackets with a gap. Give pupils three minutes working in pairs to complete the text with the correct forms of *ser/tener*. You could supply the missing words in random order if pupils need support.

Carmen (es) mi mejor amiga. (Tiene) trece años. (Es) divertida y inteligente. (Tiene) dos hermanos y una hermana. ¡Sus hermanos (son) muy perezosos!

Suggestion

Select a few pupils to come, one by one, to the front of the class. Describe their hair using ... *tiene el pelo (largo/corto/ondulado)*, then ... *tiene el pelo (rubio/negro/pelirrojo/castaño)*. Do the same with eye colour.

When the class has understood the structures ... *tiene el pelo* and ... *tiene los ojos*, read through the first half of the language box on page 9 together. Reinforce the structures by making a few statements about pupils in the class, making deliberate errors in the details (*largo/corto*, etc.).

Go through the same process to describe eyes. Point out the use of verbs in the question forms: *¿Cómo es... ?* for hair, *¿Cómo son... ?* for eyes.

5 Escucha y escribe los datos. (1–6) (AT1.2–3) ▸▸ 1.1/Y8 4.2/Y8 ◂◂

Listening. Pupils listen to six people describing their best friends and note down in Spanish the details of hair/eye colour mentioned. You could warn them that speakers 1–3 each give details of one feature and speakers 4–6 each give details of two.

Audioscript Track 8

1. *Mi mejor amiga, pues... tiene el pelo largo y ondulado.*
2. *Mi mejor amigo tiene los ojos azules. Tiene unos ojos muy bonitos.*
3. *Mi mejor amigo se llama Javier. Tiene el pelo rubio y largo.*
4. *Mi mejor amigo tiene el pelo corto y los ojos grises.*
5. – *¿Cómo se llama tu mejor amiga?*
   – *Mi mejor amiga se llama Juana.*
   – *¿Cómo es su pelo?*
   – *Tiene el pelo pelirrojo.*
   – *¿Y de qué color son sus ojos?*
   – *Tiene los ojos azules.*
6. – *¿Cómo se llama tu mejor amiga?*
   – *Mi mejor amiga se llama Vanesa.*
   – *¿Y cómo es su pelo?*
   – *¿Su pelo? Pues... tiene el pelo negro.*
   – *¿Y de qué color son sus ojos?*
   – *Tiene los ojos marrones.*

Answers

1	*el pelo largo y ondulado*	**2**	los ojos azules (y bonitos)
3	el pelo rubio y largo	**4**	el pelo corto, los ojos grises
5	el pelo pelirrojo, los ojos azules	**6**	el pelo negro, los ojos marrones

Suggestion

After checking answers, ask pupils to tell you what sort of words the following are: *rubio, largo, azules*. What can they tell you about the form *azules?* (plural because it agrees with *ojos*) Using the examples in the language box in exercise 5, can they give a rule on the position of adjectives?

6 Escucha y lee. Cierra el libro y escribe cinco datos. (AT1.4) ▸▸ 5.2 ◂◂

Listening. Pupils listen to someone describing his best friend, Antonio, following the text at the same time in the book. They then close their Pupil's Books and try to note down in Spanish five details that were given about Antonio.

Audioscript Track 9

– *¿Cómo se llama tu mejor amigo?*
– *Mi mejor amigo se llama Antonio.*
– *¿Cuántos años tiene?*
– *Tiene dieciocho años.*
– *¿Cómo es?*
– *Tiene el pelo corto y castaño. Tiene los ojos marrones. También es alto y delgado.*
– *¿Cómo es de carácter?*
– *Es divertido y generoso, pero nunca es serio.*

Answers

Any five of: se llama Antonio, tiene dieciocho años, el pelo corto, el pelo castaño, los ojos marrones, alto, delgado, divertido, generoso, nunca es serio

Gramática: *ser* (to be) and *tener* (to have)

This gives the full present tense paradigms of the irregular verbs *ser* (to be) and *tener* (to have). It also reminds pupils of the use of *tener* when giving your age (*Tengo catorce años*). There is practice on this on page 131 of the Pupil's Book.

R Ask pupils to identify and translate all the examples of *ser* and *tener* in the dialogue in exercise 6.

7 Escribe un diálogo sobre un(a) amigo/a. Utiliza el ejercicio 6 como modelo. (AT4.4) ▸▸2.4a/Y8◂◂

Writing. Using exercise 6 as a model, pupils write their own dialogue describing a friend. Remind them to think about adjective agreement.

Pupils could swap texts and check each other's work.

Plenary ▸▸4.2/Y8◂◂

Ask pupils what they have learned in this unit and ask them to give examples. As a class, can they remember all the phrases introduced so far? Explain that the end of each unit is a good time to look back over all the new material they have covered and to test themselves on it.

Use the language in exercise 1 to remind pupils of the importance of noting down new vocabulary and learning it as they go along. Suggest they use colour to show different genders, endings, etc.: they could, for example, use blue/pink to highlight the endings of masculine/feminine adjectives.

Use this as an opportunity to talk about how to use the Palabras section at the end of each module. This provides a useful list of the key vocabulary that pupils need to learn: the two-column layout (Spanish–English) makes it easy for pupils to test themselves. The Palabras section also has an Estrategia feature: in Module 1 this offers tips on memorising vocabulary.

Cuaderno A, page 3

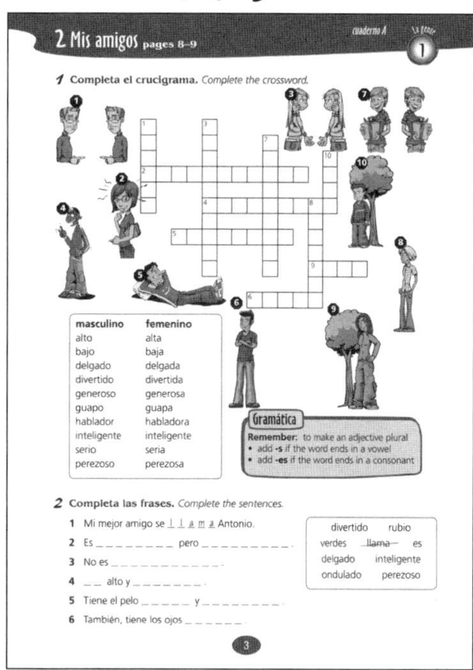
2 Mis amigos pages 8–9 cuaderno A La gente 1

1 Completa el crucigrama. *Complete the crossword.*

masculino	femenino
alto	alta
bajo	baja
delgado	delgada
divertido	divertida
generoso	generosa
guapo	guapa
hablador	habladora
inteligente	inteligente
serio	seria
perezoso	perezosa

Gramática
Remember: to make an adjective plural
- add **-s** if the word ends in a vowel
- add **-es** if the word ends in a consonant

2 Completa las frases. *Complete the sentences.*

1 Mi mejor amigo se l l a m a Antonio.
2 Es _ _ _ _ _ _ _ _ pero _ _ _ _ _ _ _ _ _ _.
3 No es _ _ _ _ _ _ _ _ _ _ _ _.
4 _ _ alto y _ _ _ _ _ _ _.
5 Tiene el pelo _ _ _ _ _ y _ _ _ _ _ _ _ _.
6 También, tiene los ojos _ _ _ _ _ _.

divertido rubio verdes ~~llama~~ es delgado inteligente ondulado perezoso

3

1 (AT4.1)

1 serios **2** inteligente **3** habladoras **4** divertido **5** perezoso **6** guapo **7** generosos **8** delgado **9** alta **10** bajo

2 (AT3.2, AT4.1)

1 llama **2** perezoso, divertido **3** inteligente **4** Es, delgado **5** rubio, ondulado **6** verdes

Cuaderno B, page 3

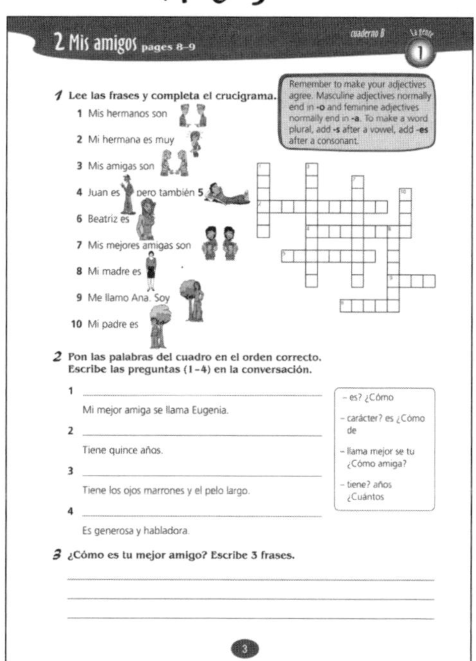
2 Mis amigos pages 8–9 cuaderno B La gente 1

1 Lee las frases y completa el crucigrama.

Remember to make your adjectives agree. Masculine adjectives normally end in **-o** and feminine adjectives normally end in **-a**. To make a word plural, add **-s** after a vowel, add **-es** after a consonant.

1 Mis hermanos son
2 Mi hermana es muy
3 Mis amigas son
4 Juan es pero también 5
6 Beatriz es
7 Mis mejores amigas son
8 Mi madre es
9 Me llamo Ana. Soy
10 Mi padre es

2 Pon las palabras del cuadro en el orden correcto. Escribe las preguntas (1–4) en la conversación.

1 ______________
Mi mejor amiga se llama Eugenia.
2 ______________
Tiene quince años.
3 ______________
Tiene los ojos marrones y el pelo largo.
4 ______________
Es generosa y habladora.

– es? ¿Cómo
– carácter? es ¿Cómo de
– llama mejor se tu ¿Cómo amiga?
– tiene? años ¿Cuántos

3 ¿Cómo es tu mejor amigo? Escribe 3 frases.

3

1 (AT3.2, AT4.1)

1 serios **2** inteligente **3** habladoras **4** divertido **5** perezoso **6** guapa **7** generosas **8** delgada **9** alta **10** bajo

2 (AT3.2, AT4.2)

1 ¿Cómo se llama tu mejor amiga?
2 ¿Cuántos años tiene?
3 ¿Cómo es?
4 ¿Cómo es de carácter?

3 (AT4.3)

R & A Pack, Gramática page 6

La gente 1 **Gramática** ¡Mira! 2 Gramática

The present tense of the irregular verbs *ser* (to be) and *tener* (to have)

(A) Learn the irregular verbs *ser* and *tener* then fill in the parts of each verb from memory.

_ _ _	to be	_ _ _ _ _	to have
_ _ _	I am	_ _ _ _ _	I have
_ _ _ _	you are	_ _ _ _ _ _	you have
_ _	he/she is	_ _ _ _ _	he/she has
_ _ _ _ _	we are	_ _ _ _ _ _ _	we have
_ _ _ _	you (plural) are	_ _ _ _ _ _	you (plural) have
_ _ _	they are	_ _ _ _ _ _	they have

(B) Underline the words in the Spanish text which have the same meaning as the words in bold in the English text.

I am Rosa and **I am** fifteen. **I am** good looking. **I am** also tall but **I am not** thin. **I have** brown eyes. My best friend **is** Juan. **He is** short but **he is** good looking. **He has** grey eyes and **is** intelligent. **Juan and I have** curly, black hair. **We are** talkative but **we are** never lazy.

Soy Rosa y tengo quince años. Soy guapa. También soy alta pero no soy delgada. Tengo los ojos marrones. Mi mejor amigo es Juan. Es bajo pero es guapo. Tiene los ojos grises y es inteligente. Juan y yo tenemos el pelo ondulado y negro. Somos habladores pero nunca somos perezosos.

(C) Fill in the gaps with the correct forms of *ser* or *tener*.

¡Hola! ________ Jorge y ________ trece años. ________ inteligente y hablador pero nunca ________ perezoso. ________ los ojos azules. ________ alto pero no ________ delgado. ________ el pelo corto y rubio. Mi mejor amiga ________ Pili y ________ catorce años. ________ inteligente y seria. También ________ perezosa. Pili no ________ alta. ________ baja, delgada y ________ guapa. ________ el pelo corto y negro y los ojos grises. Y tú, ¿cuántos años ________? ¿________ alto o bajo? ¿De qué color ________ tus ojos?

(D) Use the exercises above and the scaffolding to help you translate these sentences into 100% accurate Spanish.

1 I am not thin but I am short. — baja.
2 Isabel is good looking and she is also generous. — también
3 Rosa and I are lazy and serious. — perezosas
4 My best friend is 15. — amigo
5 I have short blond hair. — el
6 Juan and Paca have blue eyes. — los

6 seis — *¡Mira! 2 © Pearson Education Limited 2008*

R & A Pack, Gramática page 7

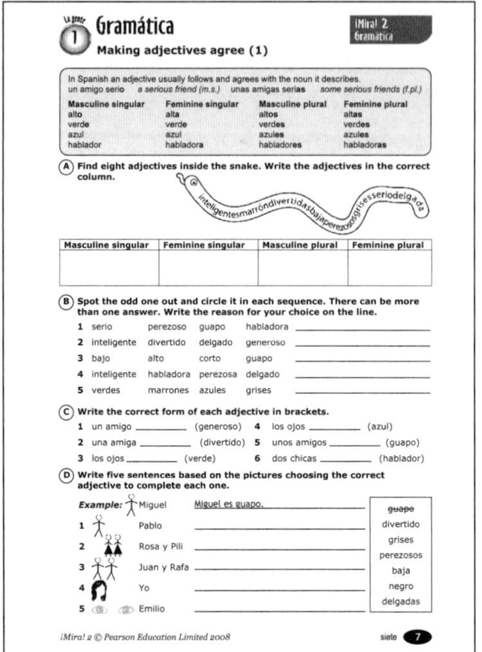
La gente 1 **Gramática** ¡Mira! 2 Gramática

Making adjectives agree (1)

In Spanish an adjective usually follows and agrees with the noun it describes.
un amigo serio *a serious friend (m.s.)* unas amigas serias *some serious friends (f.pl.)*

Masculine singular	Feminine singular	Masculine plural	Feminine plural
alto	alta	altos	altas
verde	verde	verdes	verdes
azul	azul	azules	azules
hablador	habladora	habladores	habladoras

(A) Find eight adjectives inside the snake. Write the adjectives in the correct column.

Masculine singular	Feminine singular	Masculine plural	Feminine plural

(B) Spot the odd one out and circle it in each sequence. There can be more than one answer. Write the reason for your choice on the line.

1 serio perezoso guapo habladora ________
2 inteligente divertido delgado generoso ________
3 bajo alto corto guapo ________
4 inteligente habladora perezosa delgado ________
5 verdes marrones azules grises ________

(C) Write the correct form of each adjective in brackets.

1 un amigo ________ (generoso) 4 los ojos ________ (azul)
2 una amiga ________ (divertido) 5 unos amigos ________ (guapo)
3 los ojos ________ (verde) 6 dos chicas ________ (hablador)

(D) Write five sentences based on the pictures choosing the correct adjective to complete each one.

Example: Miguel — Miguel es guapo.
1 Pablo ________
2 Rosa y Pili ________
3 Juan y Rafa ________
4 Yo ________
5 Emilio ________

~~guapo~~ divertido grises perezosos baja negro delgadas

¡Mira! 2 © Pearson Education Limited 2008 siete 7

(A) ser soy eres es somos sois son
tener tengo tienes tiene tenemos tenéis tienen

(B) soy, tengo, soy, soy, no soy, tengo, es, es, es, tiene, es, Juan y yo tenemos, somos, somos

(C) soy, tengo, soy, soy, tengo, soy, soy, tengo
es, tiene, es, es, es, es, es, tiene
tienes, eres, son

(D) **1** No soy delgada pero soy baja.
2 Isabel es guapa y también es generosa.
3 Rosa y yo somos perezosas y serias.
4 Mi mejor amigo tiene quince años.
5 Tengo el pelo corto y rubio.
6 Juan y Paca tienen los ojos azules.

(A) masculine singular – marrón, serio; feminine singular – baja, delgada, marrón; masculine plural – inteligentes, perezosos, grises; feminine plural – inteligentes, divertidas, grises

(B) *possible answers:* **1** habladora (a feminine singular adjective – the rest are masculine singular) **2** inteligente (the only adjective ending in 'e') **3** corto (the other adjectives describe people) **4** delgado (the other adjectives can be feminine singular) **5** verdes (the other adjectives end in a consonant in their singular form)

(C) **1** generoso **2** divertida **3** verdes **4** azules **5** guapos **6** habladoras

(D) **1** Pablo es divertido.
2 Rosa y Pili son delgadas.
3 Juan y Rafa son perezosos.
4 (Yo) tengo el pelo negro.
5 Emilio tiene los ojos grises.

3 Las estrellas (Pupil's Book pages 10–11)

Learning objectives
- Describing celebrities
- Comparing things using *más... que* (more... than)

Framework objectives
5.2 Strategies – memorising
5.3 Strategies – English/other languages

Grammar
- Comparatives:
  más ... que
  menos ... que

Pronunciation
j, z

Key language
¿Quién es más alto/a?
¿Quién es menos alto/a?
más (viejo/a) que
menos (joven) que

High-frequency words
¿quién?
ser (es)
más
menos

Cross-curricular
English: Comparatives

Resources
CD1, tracks 10–12
Cuadernos A & B, p. 4

Teacher Presentations
Screen 1 – Module 1 overview
Screen 2 – p. 10 ex. 1
Screen 3 – p. 11 ex. 4

Starter 1 4.3/Y8

Aim
To revise adjectives and adjective agreement.

Write up the following:

mi padre	*mi madre*
mis amigos	*mis hermanas*

Give pupils three minutes working in pairs to write four sentences, each featuring one of the phrases you have written up and an adjective from Unit 2.

Check answers, recapping on the rule of adjective agreement.

Suggestion

Ask three male pupils of varying sizes to come to the front of the class. Put them in height order and make statements about them using first *más alto que* and then *menos alto que*. Once pupils have worked out the meaning of the expressions, ask *¿Quién es más/menos alto, X o Y?* Pupils respond with the correct name. Repeat with three female pupils, this time getting the class to make the statements and ask each other questions.

1 Escucha y repite. Escribe las frases en inglés. (1–8) (AT1.2)

5.3 5.4 5.6

Listening. Pupils listen to the eight sentences, each comparing two people, and repeat them. They then write out an English translation of each of the sentences.

Audioscript Track 10

¿Quién es más alto?
¿Quién es menos alto?

1. *Paco es más alto que Alfredo.*
2. *Alfredo es más alto que Sergio.*
3. *Alfredo es menos alto que Paco.*
4. *Sergio es menos alto que Alfredo.*

¿Quién es más vieja?
¿Quién es menos vieja?

5. *Cristina es más vieja que Fabricia.*
6. *Carolina es más vieja que Cristina.*
7. *Cristina es menos vieja que Carolina.*
8. *Fabricia es menos vieja que Cristina.*

Answers

1. Paco is taller than Alfredo.
2. Alfredo is taller than Sergio.
3. Alfredo is less tall than Paco.
4. Sergio is less tall than Alfredo.
5. Cristina is older than Fabricia.
6. Carolina is older than Cristina.
7. Cristina is less old than Carolina.
8. Fabricia is less old than Cristina.

Gramática: comparatives

This gives the comparative forms of the adjective *más* + adjective + *que* (more… than) and *menos* + adjective + *que* (less… than). There is practice on this on page 128 of the Pupil's Book.

Emphasise that when the comparative form is used, the adjective must agree with the noun it describes.

2 Mira las fichas. Escribe frases utilizando 'más ... que' o 'menos ... que'. (AT4.3) ▸▸4.3/Y8◂◂

Writing. Pupils use the forms giving details of Eva Longoria and Jennifer Lopez to write sentences with *más ... que* ('more ... than') and *menos ... que* ('less ... than'). An example is given.

Starter 2 ▸▸4.3/Y8◂◂

Aim

To revise comparatives.

Write up:

inteligente guapa divertido habladora

Give pupils three minutes working in pairs to write four sentences, each comparing two people and using one of the adjectives. The people can be friends or celebrities. Review how the comparative is formed and give a few examples orally, e.g. *Mike Myers es más divertido que Brad Pitt. / Mike Myers es menos divertido que Jack Black.*

Check answers, emphasising as necessary the need for adjectives to agree.

AT2.2, AT1.1

Write up the following words and ask pupils to read them aloud:

videojuegos, mensajes, mejor, bajo
perezoso, azules

Ask pupils to tell you how *j* and *z* are pronounced. Confirm and get a few volunteers to read through the text in the Pronunciation box. Then play the recording for the class to repeat, line by line.

Audioscript Track 11

Alejandro Sanz no es viejo, es joven.
No es perezoso. Juega al ajedrez.

3 Con tu compañero/a, mira las fotos y las fichas. Pregunta y contesta. (AT2.3) ▸▸1.4a/Y8 4.3/Y8◂◂

Speaking. In pairs, using the photos and the forms giving details of celebrities, pupils take it in turn to ask and answer questions comparing two of the celebrities. A sample exchange is given.

Remind pupils to pay attention to adjective agreement, making sure they know where they can check this in their books.

R You could make up a series of true/false statements comparing the height/age of the people whose details are given. The class responds using *verdadero/falso* or by standing up whenever they think a statement is true.

+ In pairs pupils take it in turn to ask and answer questions about people in the class, using the full range of adjectives introduced in Unit 2.

4 Escucha y rellena los espacios en blanco con palabras del cuadro. (AT1.4) ▸▸1.1/Y8 1.3a/Y8◂◂

Listening. Pupils listen to the song and complete the gap-fill version by finding the missing words. The words are supplied in jumbled order for support.

Audioscript Track 12

Mi mejor amigo

Mi mejor amigo
se llama Rodrigo.
*Es **alto** y delgado*
*y más **guapo** que yo.*

*Es **más** atractivo*
que Ronaldo y Luis Figo.
También es divertido,
*nunca es **aburrido**.*

*Es muy, muy **generoso**,*
nunca es perezoso.
Le gustan los animales.
Soy su gato, me llamo González.

¡Rodrigo, yo te quiero!
Eres el señor del universo,
*totalmente **perfecto**,*
¡Mi mejor amigo!

Answers

*See also **bold** in the audioscript.*

1 alto **2** guapo **3** más **4** aburrido **5** generoso **6** perfecto

Plenary ▸▸5.2◂◂

Introduce pupils to the Mini-test feature: this will appear at the end of Unit 3 in every module, summarising what has been introduced in the module up to that point. It gives pupils an ideal opportunity to check on how they are progressing. Read through it as a class, asking for examples in each category. Ask pupils which of these areas they have found most difficult. If their responses vary, suggest they make a point of looking at that area at home. If there is a general consensus, also schedule time to come back to the topic in future lessons.

Cuaderno A, page 4

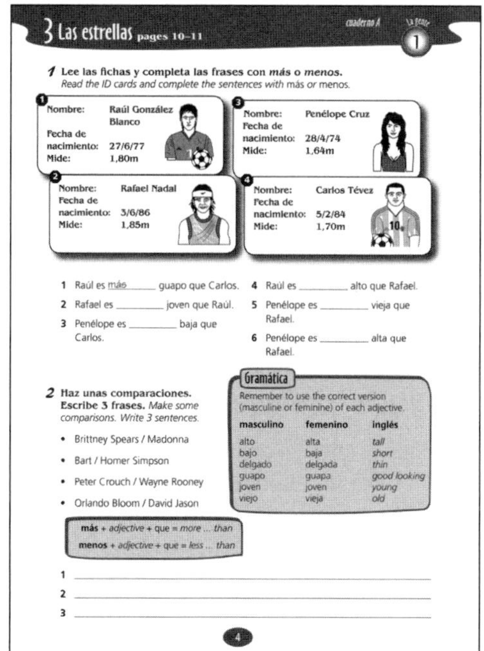

3 Las estrellas pages 10–11 — cuaderno A — La gente 1

1 Lee las fichas y completa las frases con *más* o *menos*. *Read the ID cards and complete the sentences with* más *or* menos.

1. **Nombre:** Raúl González Blanco **Fecha de nacimiento:** 27/6/77 **Mide:** 1,80m
2. **Nombre:** Rafael Nadal **Fecha de nacimiento:** 3/6/86 **Mide:** 1,85m
3. **Nombre:** Penélope Cruz **Fecha de nacimiento:** 28/4/74 **Mide:** 1,64m
4. **Nombre:** Carlos Tévez **Fecha de nacimiento:** 5/2/84 **Mide:** 1,70m

1 Raúl es más ______ guapo que Carlos.
2 Rafael es ______ joven que Raúl.
3 Penélope es ______ baja que Carlos.
4 Raúl es ______ alto que Rafael.
5 Penélope es ______ vieja que Rafael.
6 Penélope es ______ alta que Rafael.

2 Haz unas comparaciones. Escribe 3 frases. *Make some comparisons. Write 3 sentences.*

- Brittney Spears / Madonna
- Bart / Homer Simpson
- Peter Crouch / Wayne Rooney
- Orlando Bloom / David Jason

más + *adjective* + que = *more ... than*
menos + *adjective* + que = *less ... than*

Gramática

Remember to use the correct version (masculine or feminine) of each adjective.

masculino	femenino	inglés
alto	alta	*tall*
bajo	baja	*short*
delgado	delgada	*thin*
guapo	guapa	*good looking*
joven	joven	*young*
viejo	vieja	*old*

1 ______
2 ______
3 ______

4

Cuaderno B, page 4

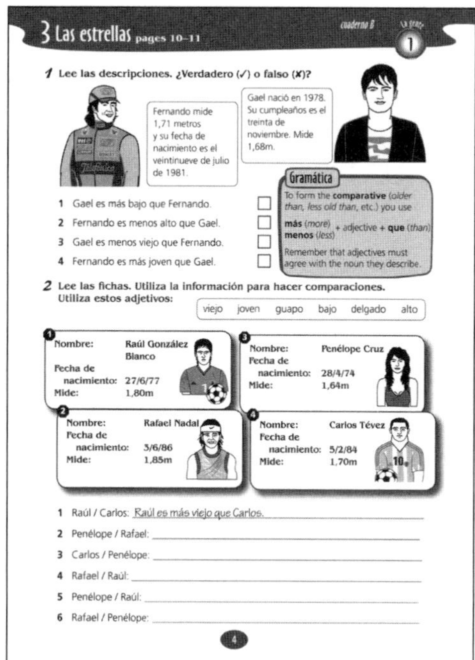

3 Las estrellas pages 10–11 — cuaderno B — La gente 1

1 Lee las descripciones. ¿Verdadero (✓) o falso (✗)?

Fernando mide 1,71 metros y su fecha de nacimiento es el veintinueve de julio de 1981.

Gael nació en 1978. Su cumpleaños es el treinta de noviembre. Mide 1,68m.

1 Gael es más bajo que Fernando. ☐
2 Fernando es menos alto que Gael. ☐
3 Gael es menos viejo que Fernando. ☐
4 Fernando es más joven que Gael. ☐

Gramática

To form the **comparative** (*older than, less old than*, etc.) you use

más (*more*) / **menos** (*less*) + adjective + **que** (*than*)

Remember that adjectives must agree with the noun they describe.

2 Lee las fichas. Utiliza la información para hacer comparaciones. Utiliza estos adjetivos:

viejo joven guapo bajo delgado alto

1. **Nombre:** Raúl González Blanco **Fecha de nacimiento:** 27/6/77 **Mide:** 1,80m
2. **Nombre:** Rafael Nadal **Fecha de nacimiento:** 3/6/86 **Mide:** 1,85m
3. **Nombre:** Penélope Cruz **Fecha de nacimiento:** 28/4/74 **Mide:** 1,64m
4. **Nombre:** Carlos Tévez **Fecha de nacimiento:** 5/2/84 **Mide:** 1,70m

1 Raúl / Carlos: Raúl es más viejo que Carlos.
2 Penélope / Rafael: ______
3 Carlos / Penélope: ______
4 Rafael / Raúl: ______
5 Penélope / Raúl: ______
6 Rafael / Penélope: ______

4

Cuaderno A

1 (AT3.2)

1 más **2** más **3** más **4** menos **5** más **6** menos

2 (AT4.2)

Cuaderno B

1 (AT3.2)

1 ✓ 2 ✗ 3 ✗ 4 ✓

2 (AT4.3)

4 Mi rutina diaria (Pupil's Book pages 12–13)

Learning objectives

- Using reflexive verbs
- Using sequencing words

Framework objectives

2.5/Y8 Writing – using researched language
5.8 Strategies – evaluating and improving

Grammar

- Reflexive verbs

Key language

¿Qué haces por la mañana/tarde?
Por la mañana/tarde...
me despierto
me levanto
me ducho
me peino
me visto
desayuno
voy al instituto
hago mis deberes
ceno
veo la televisión
me lavo los dientes
me acuesto
después, luego
normalmente
por la mañana, por la tarde
primero

High-frequency words

la, los
me, te, se
mis
a (al)
por
y
también
después
¿qué?
hacer (hago, haces)
ir (voy)
ver (veo)

Cross-curricular

English: Using reference materials

Resources

CD1, tracks 13–16
Cuadernos A & B, p. 5
R & A Pack, Gramática p. 8
Flashcards 11–20

Teacher Presentations

Screen 1 – Module 1 overview
Screen 2 – Vocabulary: Flashcards
Screen 3 – Vocabulary: Flashcards
Screen 4 – p. 12 ex. 4
Screen 5 – p. 13 ex. 5
Screen 6 – Game

Starter 1 ▸▸ 4.5a/Y8 ◂◂

Aim

To recap on verb endings for regular *-ar*, *-er* and *-ir* verbs.

Put the class into teams. Explain each team is going to complete a verb grid featuring examples from all three verb groups. Then supply each team with the following grid (or get them to copy it down).

escuchar –	– to eat	
		vivo –
	comes –	
	– he/she eats	
– we listen		*vivimos* –
	coméis –	
		– they live

Explain the scoring: one point for each correct part of the verb, plus one point for each correct translation; two bonus points for being the first team to finish; one point deducted for any error.

You could fill in more of the details in the grid for pupils who need support.

Suggestion

Write up *me ducho* and *me peino*. Ask pupils to find these expressions in exercise 1 and to tell you what they mean. What kind of words are they?

Explain that *me ducho* and *me peino* are examples of a new type of verb, the reflexive verb. Reflexive verbs always include a pronoun: in the 'I' form this pronoun is *me*. Say that you will be covering reflexives in detail in this unit.

Introduce the vocabulary to describe morning/evening routines using Flashcards 11–20. Ask pupils to identify which of the verbs are reflexive verbs. Teachers can use *¡Mira! 1* Flashcards for *Hago mis deberes* and *Veo la televisión*.

1 Escucha y lee el texto. (AT1.2) ▸▸ 4.2/Y8 ◂◂

Listening. Pupils listen to Luis describing his morning routine, looking at the pictures and reading the text at the same time.

Before you start, ask pupils to find in the text the Spanish for 'in the morning' (*por la mañana*).

Audioscript Track 13

– *¿Qué haces por la mañana?*
– *A ver... por la mañana...*
Me despierto...
Me levanto...
Me ducho...
Me peino...
Me visto...
Desayuno...
Voy al instituto...

R Pupils write out all the reflexive verbs in Luis's text in exercise 1 and translate them into English.

Gramática: reflexive verbs

This introduces reflexive verbs in the singular, using *ducharse* and *despertarse*.

Ask pupils to compare *ducharse* and *escuchar*. What is different? What is the same? Encourage them to identify the pronouns *me*, *te*, etc. (in the conjugated forms and in the infinitive) and also to note that *ducharse* has regular *-ar* endings.

The grammar box explains that reflexive verbs describe an action you do to yourself, e.g. to get (yourself) up, to shower (yourself) (though the word 'yourself' or 'myself' is not always translated in English). Explain that this is why the pronouns *me*, *te*, etc., are included – they 'reflect' or refer back to the subject of the verb.

(French is obviously a useful comparison at this point. If your class also studies French, you could ask them if they have encountered reflexive verbs already. If they have, ask them to explain how they work and to give you examples in French. Point out that in this context many of the verbs which are reflexive in French are also reflexive in Spanish.)

Then ask pupils to look at *despertarse*, the second reflexive verb featured. What else can they tell you about this verb (regular *-ar* endings; stem-changing)?

+ Write up *levantarse* and *peinarse*. Ask pupils working in pairs to choose one and write out all forms in the singular, underlining the reflexive pronoun in each form.

2 Haz un sondeo. (AT2.2) ▸▸1.4a/Y8◂◂

Speaking. Pupils carry out a survey about morning routine in small groups and note answers using the picture prompts in exercise 1 for reference. A sample exchange is given.

+ Pupils could write out their dialogues from exercise 2.

3 Escucha y lee. (AT1.2) ▸▸4.2/Y8◂◂

Listening. Pupils listen to Luis describing his evening routine, looking at the pictures and reading the text at the same time.

Before you start, ask pupils to find in the text the Spanish for 'in the evening' (*por la tarde*).

Audioscript Track 14

– *¿Y qué haces por la tarde, Luis?*
– *Por la tarde...*
A ver... hago mis deberes...
Ceno...
Veo la televisión un poco...
Me lavo los dientes...
Me acuesto...

4 Escucha y escribe las letras correctas de los ejercicios 1 y 3. (1–5) (AT1.3) ▸▸1.1/Y8 4.5a/Y8◂◂

Listening. Pupils listen to five people talking about their daily routines and note the letter of the appropriate picture (from *a–l* in exercises 1 and 3).

Audioscript Track 15

1 – *¿Qué haces por la mañana?*
– *Por la mañana me despierto y desayuno.*
– *¿Y qué haces por la tarde?*
– *Por la tarde... a ver... hago mis deberes y veo la televisión un poco...*

2 – *¿Qué haces por la mañana?*
– *Por la mañana me levanto y me peino.*
– *¿Y qué haces por la tarde?*
– *Por la tarde, ceno y me lavo los dientes.*

3 – *¿Qué haces por la mañana?*
– *Por la mañana me ducho y voy al instituto.*
– *¿Y qué haces por la tarde?*
– *Por la tarde ceno y me acuesto.*

4 – *Por la mañana, me visto y voy al instituto.*
– *Por la tarde, me lavo los dientes y me acuesto.*

5 – *¿Qué haces por la mañana?*
– *Por la mañana me despierto y me levanto.*
– *¿Y qué haces por la tarde?*
– *Por la tarde hago mis deberes y ceno.*

Answers

	mañana	tarde
1	a, f	h, j
2	b, d	i, k
3	c, g	i, l
4	e, g	k, l
5	a, b	h, i

Starter 2 ▸▸ 4.5a/Y8 ◂◂

Aim

To consolidate reflexive verbs.

Write up *Por la mañana...* Ask pupils to complete the text by writing out their own morning routine in chronological order, using the verbs that Luis used in exercise 1. Challenge them to do this from memory, but if they need support supply the Spanish verbs in random order.

5 Escucha y lee. Pon los dibujos en el orden del texto. (AT1.4)

▸▸ 4.5a/Y8 ◂◂

Listening. Pupils listen to someone describing what she does each day, following the text at the same time in the book. Pupils then reread the text, putting the pictures in the order that they are mentioned. There is some vocabulary support.

Audioscript Track 16

Normalmente me levanto temprano, me levanto a las nueve de la mañana.
Primero me ducho, me lavo los dientes y me peino. ¡Soy muy guapo!
Por la mañana juego al fútbol con mi equipo y voy a la sauna. Luego voy a la peluquería. Mi peluquero se llama Rupert y es muy hablador. Después juego con mi ordenador y escucho música. Por la tarde voy al casino con mis amigos. Me encanta jugar al Blackjack. También me gusta bailar. Me encantan el hip hop y la música electrónica. Voy a la discoteca, hablo con mucha gente y me acuesto tarde.

Answers

c, f, b, e, a, d

6 Busca las frases en español en el texto del ejercicio 5. Utiliza la sección Vocabulario. (AT3.4) ▸▸ 5.3 ◂◂

Reading. Pupils reread the text in exercise 5 and find the Spanish phrases for the seven English phrases listed.

Answers

1. *normally – normalmente*
2. in the morning – por la mañana
3. then – luego
4. afterwards – después
5. in the evening – por la tarde
6. also – también
7. first – primero

7 Describe tu rutina diaria. (AT4.4)

▸▸ 2.5/Y8 4.4/Y8 5.8 ◂◂

Writing. Using the text in exercise 5 as a model, pupils write a description of their own daily routine. They should include the expressions highlighted in the text, using them to structure their writing. Encourage them to be inventive in the details and to use a dictionary for any activities not yet covered.

Take in pupils' texts and mark them. Use this as an opportunity to introduce the class to the kind of language that they will come across in feedback on their work. If possible, create a list of the expressions you will use and display this in the classroom, making sure that everyone understands all of the comments. Use these consistently so that pupils become familiar with them.

Plenary ▸▸ 5.2 ◂◂

Put the class into teams and tell pupils to close their books. Write up:

Por la mañana... (7)
Por la tarde... (5)

Give them two minutes working in teams to come up with seven morning activities and five evening activities. Give one point for each correct verb/phrase. The team with the most points is the winner.

Ask pupils to give you an example of a reflexive verb. How are these formed? Get them to list all the reflexive verbs that they used in the team activity.

Cuaderno A, page 5

4 Mi rutina diaria pages 12–13 — cuaderno A — La gente 1

1 Descifra el código y escribe las frases. *Break the code and write the phrases.*

1 = a, 2 = b, 3 = c, 4 = ch, 5 = d, 6 = e, 7 = f, 8 = g, 9 = h, 10 = i, 11 = j, 12 = k, 13 = l, 14 = ll, 15 = m, 16 = n, 17 = ñ, 18 = o, 19 = p, 20 = q, 21 = r, 22 = s, 23 = t, 24 = u, 25 = v, 26 = w, 27 = x, 28 = y, 29 = z

1 15 6 / 5 6 22 19 10 6 21 23 18 me despierto
2 15 6 / 13 6 25 1 16 23 18
3 15 6 / 5 24 4 18
4 15 6 / 19 6 10 16 18
5 15 6 / 25 10 22 23 18
6 5 6 22 1 28 24 16 18
7 25 18 28 / 1 13 / 10 16 22 23 10 23 24 23 18
8 9 1 8 18 / 15 10 22 / 5 6 2 6 21 6 22
9 3 6 16 18
10 25 6 18 / 13 1 / 23 6 13 6 25 10 22 10 18 16
11 15 6 / 13 1 25 18 / 13 18 22 / 5 10 6 16 23 6 22
12 15 6 / 1 3 24 6 22 23 18

2 Empareja los dibujos y las palabras. *Match up the pictures and the words.*

a 7 b c d e f g h i j k l

3 Descifra las palabras y copia las frases. *Unscramble the words and copy the sentences.*

también por la mañana por la tarde primero ~~normalmente~~ luego después

1 **ratmmnnolee** me levanto a las ocho. Normalmente me levanto a las 8.
2 Voy de compras y **spduseé** voy a la peluquería.
3 **reompir** me lavo los dientes.
4 **orp al añmnaa** voy al instituto.
5 **pro al aetdr** ceno y **abéimtn** veo la tele.
6 **ugleo** me acuesto a las once.

5

1 (AT4.1)

1 *me despierto* **2** me levanto **3** me ducho
4 me peino **5** me visto **6** desayuno
7 voy al instituto **8** hago mis deberes
9 ceno **10** veo la televisión
11 me lavo los dientes **12** me acuesto

2 (AT3.1)

a 7 **b** 12 **c** 6 **d** 2 **e** 5 **f** 1 **g** 3 **h** 10 **i** 4 **j** 9
k 8 **l** 11

3 (AT4.2)

1 *normalmente* **2** después **3** primero
4 por la mañana **5** por la tarde, también **6** luego

Cuaderno B, page 5

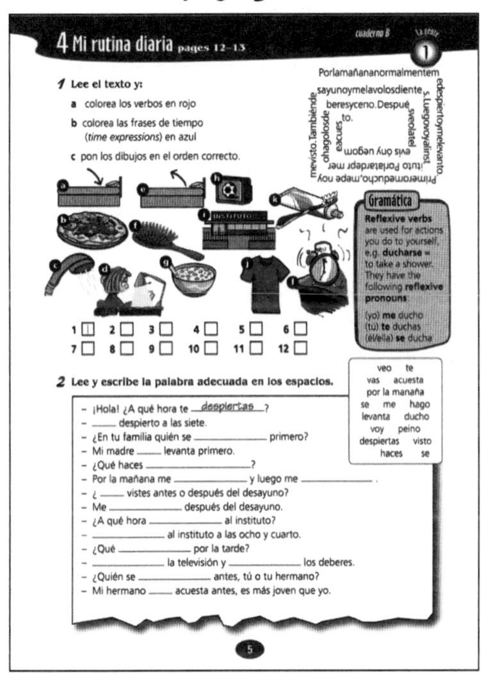

4 Mi rutina diaria pages 12–13

cuaderno B La gente 1

1 **Lee el texto y:**

a colorea los verbos en rojo
b colorea las frases de tiempo (*time expressions*) en azul
c pon los dibujos en el orden correcto.

Porlamañananormalmentem
edespiertoymelevanto.
s.Luegovoyalinst
sayunoymelavolosdiente
ituto Porlatardepr mer
Primeromeducho,mepe noy
mevisto.Tambiénde
beresyceno.Despué
sveolatel
evis óny megow
ohagolosde
eacues
to.

1 [ ] 2 [ ] 3 [ ] 4 [ ] 5 [ ] 6 [ ]
7 [ ] 8 [ ] 9 [ ] 10 [ ] 11 [ ] 12 [ ]

Gramática
Reflexive verbs are used for actions you do to yourself, e.g. **ducharse** = to take a shower. They have the following **reflexive pronouns**:
(yo) **me** ducho
(tú) **te** duchas
(él/ella) **se** ducha

2 **Lee y escribe la palabra adecuada en los espacios.**

veo te vas acuesta por la mañana se me hago levanta ducho voy peino despiertas visto haces se

– ¡Hola! ¿A qué hora te *despiertas*?
– ____ despierto a las siete.
– ¿En tu familia quién se ____ primero?
– Mi madre ____ levanta primero.
– ¿Qué haces ____?
– Por la mañana me ____ y luego me ____.
– ¿ ____ vistes antes o después del desayuno?
– Me ____ después del desayuno.
– ¿A qué hora ____ al instituto?
– ____ al instituto a las ocho y cuarto.
– ¿Qué ____ por la tarde?
– ____ la televisión y ____ los deberes.
– ¿Quién se ____ antes, tú o tu hermano?
– Mi hermano ____ acuesta antes, es más joven que yo.

5

1 (AT3.3)

1 *l* **2** e **3** c **4** f **5** j **6** g **7** k **8** i **9** d
10 b **11** h **12** a

2 (AT4.1)

¡Hola! ¿A qué hora te *despiertas*?
Me despierto a las siete.
¿En tu familia quién se levanta primero?
Mi madre se levanta primero.
¿Qué haces por la mañana?
Por la mañana me ducho y luego me peino.
¿Te vistes antes o después del desayuno?
Me visto después del desayuno.
¿A qué hora vas al instituto?
Voy al instituto a las ocho y cuarto.
¿Qué haces por la tarde?
Veo la televisión y hago los deberes.
¿Quién se acuesta antes, tú o tu hermano?
Mi hermano se acuesta antes, es más joven que yo.

R & A Pack, Gramática page 8

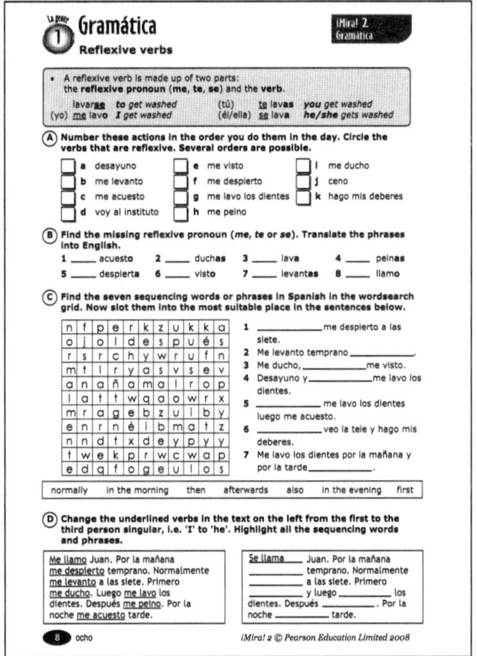

La gente 1 **Gramática** ¡Mira! 2 Gramática

Reflexive verbs

- A reflexive verb is made up of two parts: the **reflexive pronoun** (**me, te, se**) and the **verb**.

lavar**se** *to get washed* (tú) te lav**as** *you get washed*
(yo) me lav**o** *I get washed* (él/ella) se lav**a** *he/she gets washed*

(A) **Number these actions in the order you do them in the day. Circle the verbs that are reflexive. Several orders are possible.**

[ ] **a** desayuno [ ] **e** me visto [ ] **i** me ducho
[ ] **b** me levanto [ ] **f** me despierto [ ] **j** ceno
[ ] **c** me acuesto [ ] **g** me lavo los dientes [ ] **k** hago mis deberes
[ ] **d** voy al instituto [ ] **h** me peino

(B) **Find the missing reflexive pronoun (*me, te* or *se*). Translate the phrases into English.**

1 ____ acuest**o** **2** ____ duch**as** **3** ____ lav**a** **4** ____ pein**as**
5 ____ despiert**a** **6** ____ vist**o** **7** ____ levant**as** **8** ____ llam**o**

(C) **Find the seven sequencing words or phrases in Spanish in the wordsearch grid. Now slot them into the most suitable place in the sentences below.**

n	f	p	e	r	k	z	u	k	k	a
o	j	o	l	d	e	s	p	u	é	s
r	s	r	c	h	y	w	r	u	f	n
m	t	l	r	y	a	s	v	s	e	v
a	n	a	ñ	a	m	a	l	r	o	p
l	a	t	t	w	q	a	o	w	r	x
m	r	a	g	e	b	z	u	i	b	y
e	n	r	n	é	i	b	m	a	t	z
n	n	d	t	x	d	e	y	p	y	y
t	w	e	k	p	r	w	c	w	a	p
e	d	q	f	o	g	e	u	l	o	s

1 ________ me despierto a las siete.
2 Me levanto temprano ________.
3 Me ducho, ________ me visto.
4 Desayuno y ________ me lavo los dientes.
5 ________ me lavo los dientes luego me acuesto.
6 ________ veo la tele y hago mis deberes.
7 Me lavo los dientes por la mañana y por la tarde ________.

normally in the morning then afterwards also in the evening first

(D) **Change the underlined verbs in the text on the left from the first to the third person singular, i.e. 'I' to 'he'. Highlight all the sequencing words and phrases.**

Me llamo Juan. Por la mañana me despierto temprano. Normalmente me levanto a las siete. Primero me ducho. Luego me lavo los dientes. Después me peino. Por la noche me acuesto tarde.

Se llama Juan. Por la mañana ________ temprano. Normalmente ________ a las siete. Primero ________ y luego ________ los dientes. Después ________. Por la noche ________ tarde.

8 ocho

¡Mira! 2 © Pearson Education Limited 2008

(B) **1** me (I go to bed) **2** te (you have a shower) **3** se (he/she gets washed) **4** te (you brush/comb your hair) **5** se (he/she wakes up) **6** me (I get dressed) **7** te (you get up) **8** me (I am called)

(C) **1** normalmente **2** por la mañana **3** luego **4** después **5** primero **6** por la tarde **7** también

N	F	P	E	R	K	Z	U	K	K	A
O	J	O	L	D	E	S	P	U	É	S
R	S	R	C	H	Y	W	R	U	F	N
M	T	L	R	Y	A	S	V	S	E	V
A	N	A	Ñ	A	M	A	L	R	O	P
L	A	T	T	W	Q	A	O	W	R	X
M	R	A	G	E	B	Z	U	I	B	Y
E	N	R	N	É	I	B	M	A	T	Z
N	N	D	T	X	D	E	Y	P	Y	Y
T	W	E	K	P	R	W	C	W	A	P
E	D	Q	F	O	G	E	U	L	O	S

(D) se despierta, se levanta, se ducha, se lava, se peina, se acuesta

5 Tu nacionalidad (Pupil's Book pages 14–15)

Learning objectives

- Understanding nationalities
- Writing an extended text

Framework objectives

2.4/Y8 Writing – (b) sequencing paragraphs
3.2/Y8 Culture – (a) young people: aspirations

Grammar

- Adjective agreement: nationalities

Key language

¿Cuál es tu nacionalidad?
Soy...
argentino/a
chileno/a
colombiano/a
escocés/escocesa
español(a)
estadounidense
galés/galesa
inglés/inglesa
irlandés/irlandesa
mexicano/a

High-frequency words

de
¿cómo?
¿cuál?
¿cuántos?
¿qué?
ser (soy)
y
pero
también

Cross-curricular

English: Evaluating and improving written work; Recognising the features of different text types
ICT: Word-processing

Resources

CD1, tracks 17–18
Cuadernos A & B, p. 6

Teacher Presentations

Screen 1 – Module 1 overview
Screen 2 – Vocabulary: Flashcards
Screen 3 – p. 14 ex. 1
Screen 4 – p. 14 ex. 3
Screen 5 – Game
Screen 6 – Video

Suggestion ▶▶2.4a/Y8◀◀

Draw pupil's attention to paragraph structure in reading (exercise 5) and in writing (exercise 6).

Starter 1 ▶▶5.4◀◀

Aim

 To use reading strategies to work out new vocabulary.

Write up the following, jumbling the order of the nationalities in the second column. Give pupils two minutes working in pairs to match the two columns. If they need support, discuss first what kind of words appear in each column.

Vivo en...	*Soy...*
Londres	*inglés*
Nueva York	*estadounidense*
Edimburgo	*escocés*
Dublín	*irlandés*
Cardiff	*galés*
Buenos Aires	*argentino*
Barcelona	*español*

When checking answers, get pupils to translate the nationalities and ask them how they worked out the new words.

Suggestion

Use the pictures in exercise 1 on page 14 to introduce the vocabulary for nationalities. Go round the class getting the pupils in turn to translate the speech bubbles. Then say *Alba es colombiana – Diego es mexicano*, stressing the agreement in the endings. Explain that nationalities are adjectives and so agree with the person being described. Go through the speech bubbles again as a class, asking pupils to predict what the female form is for all the boys' bubbles and the male form for all the girls'. (Do this orally and don't worry about explaining accents at this stage.)

1 Escucha y escribe el nombre correcto. (1–10) (AT1.2–3) ▶▶5.3◀◀

Listening. Pupils listen to the ten people giving their nationalities and identify each speaker using the pictures in the Pupil's Book.

Audioscript Track 17

1 – *¿Cuál es tu nacionalidad?*
– *Soy galesa.*
2 – *¿Cuál es tu nacionalidad?*
– *Soy argentino.*
3 – *¿Cuál es tu nacionalidad?*
– *Soy mexicano.*
4 – *¿Cuál es tu nacionalidad?*
– *Soy española.*
5 – *¿Cuál es tu nacionalidad?*
– *Soy colombiana.*
6 – *¿Cuál es tu nacionalidad?*
– *Soy inglés. Vivo en Londres.*
7 – *¿Y tú? ¿Cuál es tu nacionalidad?*
– *No soy inglés. Soy escocés.*
8 – *¿Cuál es tu nacionalidad?*
– *Soy chilena.*

9 – *¿Cómo estás?*
– *Bien, gracias.*
– *¿Cuál es tu nacionalidad?*
– *Soy estadounidense. Vivo en Los Ángeles.*

10 – *¡Hola! ¿Qué tal?*
– *Bien gracias, ¿y tú?*
– *Muy bien, gracias. Dime, ¿cuál es tu nacionalidad?*
– *Soy irlandesa. Vivo en Dublín.*

Answers

1 *Meryl* **2** Tico **3** Diego **4** Patricia **5** Alba
6 Dan **7** Lachlan **8** Angélica **9** Chuck
10 Margaret

Gramática: adjective endings

This covers agreement of nationalities. Point out the patterns:

- ending in consonant: add *-a* in the feminine
- ending in *-o*: change to *-a* in the feminine
- ending in *-e*: no change in the feminine

Write up *inglés* and *inglesa* and ask pupils what other change has taken place in the feminine form. Can they work out why the accent has been dropped? Use this as an opportunity to review the rules on stress in Spanish. Ask pupils to then identify and note down the other nationalities that change like this (*escocés*, *irlandés*, *galés*) and to come up with a way of remembering them.

2 Juego de memoria. (AT2.2) ▸▸5.2◂◂

Speaking. Memory game in pairs. Pupils close their books and take it in turn to give a nationality (e.g. *Soy irlandesa*) and to respond with the correct person (e.g. *Eres Margaret*). A sample exchange is given.

3 Escucha. Copia y rellena la ficha. (AT1.4) ▸▸1.1/Y8◂◂

Listening. Pupils copy out the form. They then listen to Fernando talking about himself and complete the form with his details in Spanish.

Before you play the recording, ask pupils to use the form to predict what kind of language will come up in the recording.

Audioscript Track 18

– *¿Cómo te llamas?*
– *Hola, me llamo Fernando.*
– *¿Cuál es tu nacionalidad?*
– *Soy español, de San Sebastián.*
– *¿Cuántos años tienes?*
– *Tengo quince años.*
– *¿Qué te gusta?*
– *Me gustan los cómics y me encantan los videojuegos. Mi videojuego favorito es Tomb Rider.*
– *¿Qué haces en tu tiempo libre?*
– *Juego con el ordenador y mando mensajes a mis amigos.*
– *¿Cómo eres?*
– *Soy inteligente pero perezoso.*
– *¿Cómo es tu pelo?*
– *¿Mi pelo? Pues… tengo el pelo moreno y rizado. ¡Soy bastante guapo!*
– *¿De qué color son tus ojos?*
– *Tengo los ojos marrones.*

Answers

Nombre	*Fernando*
Nacionalidad	español
Edad	quince años
☺	los cómics, los videojuegos
Actividades	juego con el ordenador, mando mensajes
Carácter	inteligente, perezoso
Pelo	moreno, rizado
Ojos	marrones

Starter 2 ▸▸4.3/Y8◂◂

Aim
To revise descriptions of how people look. To revise adjective agreement and position.

Write up:

Javier *María*
pelo – castaño/negro/pelirrojo/rubio y corto/largo/ondulado
ojos – azules/grises/marrones/verdes

Give pupils three minutes working in pairs to come up with two sentences for each person, one describing his/her hair and one describing his/her eyes.

If they need support, remind them of the verb form to use (*tiene*). You could also talk through an example before they start.

4 Con tu compañero/a, lee y completa el diálogo por Lola. (AT2.4) ▸▸1.4a/Y8◂◂

Speaking. In pairs pupils read the form giving Lola's details and use it to complete the gap-fill dialogue.

Answers

- ✦ *¿Cómo te llamas?*
- ■ *Me llamo* ***Lola****.*
- ✦ *¿Cuál es tu nacionalidad?*
- ■ *Soy* ***estadounidense****.*
- ✦ *¿Cuántos años tienes?*
- ■ *Tengo* ***trece años****.*
- ✦ *¿Qué te gusta?*
- ■ *Me gusta* ***el fútbol*** *y* ***la natación****.*
- ✦ *¿Qué haces en tu tiempo libre?*
- ■ *En mi tiempo libre* ***voy de compras*** *y* ***bailo. No juego con el ordenador****.*
- ✦ *¿Cómo eres?*
- ■ *Soy* ***divertida*** *y* ***habladora****.*
- ✦ *¿Cómo es tu pelo?*
- ■ *Tengo el pelo* ***largo*** *y* ***rubio.***
- ✦ ¿De qué color son tus ojos?
- ■ *Tengo* ***los ojos azules****.*

R Pupils complete the dialogue with their own details.

5 Lee el texto y contesta a las preguntas en inglés. (AT3.4) ▸▸2.2a/Y8 3.2a/Y8◂◂

Reading. Pupils read the text about Gerardo and answer the eight questions in English.

Answers

1. He is Colombian. He is 14.
2. It is the capital of Colombia; it is a very important city.
3. He likes video games and football.
4. He plays football in the park with his friends; he also plays in a team at school; tomorrow he is going to play in a match.
5. He plays on his computer or goes out with his friends.
6. He has brown eyes; he has short black hair; he wears glasses; he is taller than his sister Silvia but not as tall as his brother Rodrigo.
7. He says he's intelligent but a bit lazy.
8. **a** In the morning he wakes up, gets up and has a shower; (he doesn't comb his hair); he has breakfast and then goes to school.
   b In the afternoon he does his homework, has dinner, watches a little television and goes to bed at 10.

R Use the text for a reading aloud activity round the class. Give feedback (or ask pupils to give feedback) on accuracy of pronunciation, fluency and expression.

+ Ask pupils to find five reflexive verbs in the text.

6 Escribe una respuesta a Gerardo. (AT4.4–5) ▸▸2.4a/Y8 2.4b/Y8◂◂

Writing. Pupils write a reply to Gerardo. They should make sure they include answers to the questions in exercise 4 and also cover the other points listed.

+ Pupils include some information about the future, using the near future tense. This is not covered in this module, so either review it quickly before pupils start writing or direct them to the Gramática section at the back of the Pupil's Book.

An extended writing activity like this can be done on computer. It makes the process of correcting/redrafting much easier and more encouraging.

You could also use this as an opportunity to introduce pupils to any electronic reference tools your school has, such as a Spanish dictionary or grammar.

Plenary ▸▸4.2/Y8 5.2 5.8◂◂

To introduce/reintroduce the class to the Resumen section, ask pupils to close their books. Use the Resumen section to give a sentence in English (e.g. 'I like music') to prompt a Spanish structure from each unit.

Tell pupils that they have just worked through key language from all five units of the module. Explain that the Resumen section summarises this language and is a very useful tool for self-testing. Encourage pupils to use it to work out what they know and what they need more practice in at the end of a module. They will also find it helpful for ongoing revision.

Cuaderno A, page 6

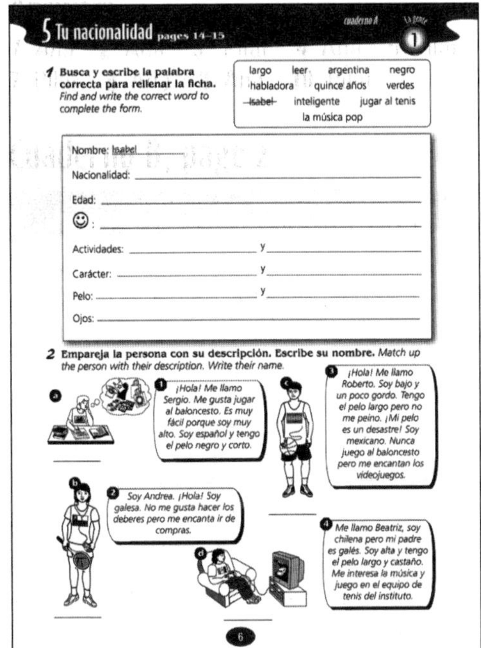
5 Tu nacionalidad pages 14–15

cuaderno A La gente 1

1 **Busca y escribe la palabra correcta para rellenar la ficha.** *Find and write the correct word to complete the form.*

largo leer argentina negro habladora quince años verdes ~~Isabel~~ inteligente jugar al tenis la música pop

Nombre: Isabel
Nacionalidad: ______
Edad: ______
☺: ______
Actividades: ______ y ______
Carácter: ______ y ______
Pelo: ______ y ______
Ojos: ______

2 **Empareja la persona con su descripción. Escribe su nombre.** *Match up the person with their description. Write their name.*

1 ¡Hola! Me llamo Sergio. Me gusta jugar al baloncesto. Es muy fácil porque soy muy alto. Soy español y tengo el pelo negro y corto.

2 Soy Andrea. ¡Hola! Soy galesa. No me gusta hacer los deberes pero me encanta ir de compras.

3 ¡Hola! Me llamo Roberto. Soy bajo y un poco gordo. Tengo el pelo largo pero no me peino. ¡Mi pelo es un desastre! Soy mexicano. Nunca juego al baloncesto pero me encantan los videojuegos.

4 Me llamo Beatriz, soy chilena pero mi padre es galés. Soy alta y tengo el pelo largo y castaño. Me interesa la música y juego en el equipo de tenis del instituto.

6

Cuaderno B, page 6

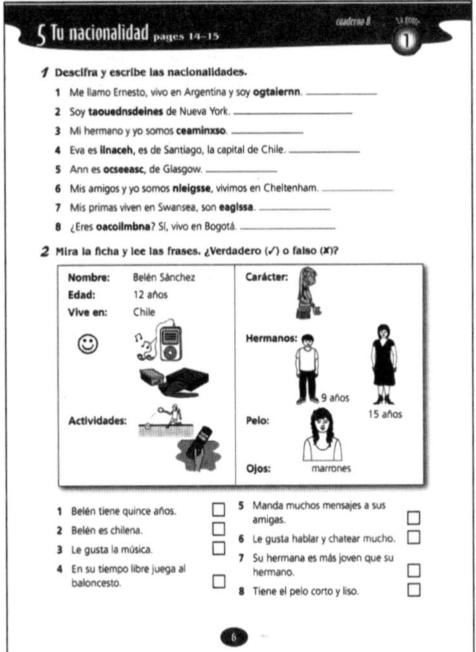
5 Tu nacionalidad pages 14–15

cuaderno B La gente 1

1 **Descifra y escribe las nacionalidades.**

1 Me llamo Ernesto, vivo en Argentina y soy **ogtaiernn**. ______
2 Soy **taouednsdeines** de Nueva York. ______
3 Mi hermano y yo somos **ceaminxso**. ______
4 Eva es **ilnaceh**, es de Santiago, la capital de Chile. ______
5 Ann es **ocseeasc**, de Glasgow. ______
6 Mis amigos y yo somos **nleigsse**, vivimos en Cheltenham. ______
7 Mis primas viven en Swansea, son **eaglssa**. ______
8 ¿Eres **oacoilmbna**? Sí, vivo en Bogotá. ______

2 **Mira la ficha y lee las frases. ¿Verdadero (✓) o falso (✗)?**

Nombre: Belén Sánchez
Edad: 12 años
Vive en: Chile
☺
Actividades:
Carácter:
Hermanos: 9 años 15 años
Pelo:
Ojos: marrones

1 Belén tiene quince años. ☐
2 Belén es chilena. ☐
3 Le gusta la música. ☐
4 En su tiempo libre juega al baloncesto. ☐
5 Manda muchos mensajes a sus amigas. ☐
6 Le gusta hablar y chatear mucho. ☐
7 Su hermana es más joven que su hermano. ☐
8 Tiene el pelo corto y liso. ☐

6

1 (AT3.2, AT4.1)

Nombre: *Isabel*
Nacionalidad: argentina
Edad: quince años
☺: la música pop
Actividades: leer y jugar al tenis
Cárácter: inteligente y habladora
Pelo: largo y negro
Ojos: verdes

2 (AT3.3)

a 2 **b** 4 **c** 1 **d** 3

1 (AT4.1, AT3.2)

1 argentino **2** estadounidense **3** mexicanos **4** chilena **5** escocesa **6** ingleses **7** galesas **8** colombiana

2 (AT3.2)

1 ✗ **2** ✓ **3** ✓ **4** ✗ **5** ✓ **6** ✓ **7** ✗ **8** ✗

Resumen y Prepárate (Pupil's Book pages 16–17)

Resumen

This is a checklist of language covered in Module 1. Pupils can work on this in pairs to check what they have learned and remembered. There is a Resumen page in the Resource and Assessment Pack. Encourage them to look back at the module and to use the grammar section, to revise what they are unclear about. You can also use the Resumen as a useful plenary at the end of each unit.

Prepárate

These revision tests can be used for pupils to practise prior to the assessment tasks in the Resource and Assessment Pack.

Resources

CD1, track 19
R & A Pack, Module 1: Resumen, Prueba, I can ...

1 Escucha. ¿Quién habla? ¿Paco o Pepe? (AT1.3) ▸▸1.1/Y8◂◂

Listening. Pupils listen and, using the pictures given for each person, identify whether the speaker is Paco or Pepe.

Audioscript Track 19

Me gusta el fútbol y me gustan mucho los cómics.
En mi tiempo libre, normalmente juego con el ordenador o mando mensajes a mis amigos.
Me encanta bailar, bailo break dance y hip hop. También me gusta mucho ir al cine.

Answer

Paco

2 Con tu compañero/a, haz diálogos. (AT2.3) ▸▸1.4a/Y8◂◂

Speaking. In pairs: pupils make up dialogues, taking it in turn to ask and answer questions about nationality and personal characteristics. Picture prompts are supplied. A sample exchange is given.

3 Escribe los nombres correctos. (AT3.3) ▸▸5.1◂◂

Reading. Pupils read the short text about the five girls and use it to identify each person pictured.

Answers

a *Andrea* **b** Gloria **c** Raquel **d** Letizia **e** Belén

4 Escribe frases. (AT4.3) ▸▸4.5a/Y8◂◂

Writing. Pupils use the picture prompts to write sentences about their morning and evening routines.

¡Extra! 1 (Pupil's Book pages 18–19)

Learning objectives
- Using frequency words
- Practising reflexive verbs

Grammar
- Expressions of frequency

Key language
siempre
a menudo
a veces
de vez en cuando
nunca

Revision of language from Module 1

High-frequency words
Revision of language from Module 1

Resources
CD1, track 20
Cuadernos A & B, pp. 7–8

Starter ▸▸ 4.5a/Y8 ◂◂

Aim
To revise reflexive verbs.

Give pupils working in pairs three minutes to come up with as many reflexive verbs as they can. Each different form of the verb (e.g. *me acuesto*, *te acuestas*, etc.) counts as a separate verb. The pair with the most correct verbs is the winner.

When checking answers, ask pupils to translate the verbs.

1 Escucha y apunta las respuestas de Alba y Tico. (AT1.4)
▸▸2.1/Y8 2.3/Y8 5.4◂◂

Listening. Pupils listen to Alba and Tico doing a quiz and note the answer each gives for each question.

Before you play the recording, ask pupils where you would find a text like this. Ask them to pick out the features that make this typical of a questionnaire in a magazine (e.g. layout, repetition in answers, points system, etc.).

Tell pupils that although the text on the page is quite dense, the recording is structured to make the information accessible. The labels (*a–e*) and the intonation used for lists will help them.

After checking answers to the listening activity, get pupils to calculate Alba's and Tico's scores and to check out what this means about pupils using the summary at the end of the quiz. Get pupils to translate this into English.

Audioscript Track 20

– *A ver, Alba, número uno: ¿bailas en la discoteca?*
– *Por supuesto, me encanta bailar. Siempre –* ***a****.*
– *Y yo a veces, entonces* ***c****.*
– *Muy bien. Número dos, Tico. Te acuestas muy tarde…*
 a *siempre*
 b *a menudo*
 c *a veces*
 d *de vez en cuando*
 e *nunca*
– *A ver… Me acuesto muy tarde… pues… de vez en cuando –* ***d****.*
– *Y yo, bueno…* ***b*** *a menudo.*
– *Número tres… Haces tus deberes*
– ***a*** *– siempre hago mis deberes. Es muy importante para mí.*
– *Para mí,* ***e****. Nunca hago mis deberes. Soy muy perezoso.*
– *Número cuatro. Tico, te levantas tarde…*
 a *nunca*
 b *de vez en cuando*
 c *a veces*
 d *a menudo*
 e *siempre*
– ***b****, de vez en cuando.*
– *Yo también* ***b****, de vez en cuando.*
– *Y el número cinco. ¿Haces deporte?*
– *Me gusta mucho el deporte.* ***a****, siempre hago deporte.*
– *No me gusta tanto. Para mí* ***c*** *– a veces.*
– *Vale, ahora el número seis. Vas de compras…*
– *A menudo. Me gusta ir de compras a menudo, entonces* ***b****.*
– *Odio ir de compras. Nunca voy de compras.*
– *Entonces* ***e****, Tico.*
– *Número siete. Comes hamburguesas…*
– *Pues de vez en cuando.*
– *Lo mismo: de vez en cuando, entonces para los dos* ***b****.*
– *Número ocho: chateas por internet…*
 a *siempre*
 b *a menudo*
 c *a veces*
 d *de vez en cuando*
 e *nunca*
– *A ver, a veces,* ***c****.*
– *Sí, la opción* ***c*** *para mí también.*
– *Nueve: ¿Lees cómics?*
– *Nunca, no me gustan nada. Para mí:* ***e****.*
– *Me gustan mucho los cómics. Leo a menudo, entonces* ***b****.*
– *Finalmente, el número diez: En una fiesta eres la persona más habladora…*
– *A menudo, sí, para mí* ***b****.*
– *La opción* ***b*** *para mí también.*

Answers

1	*Alba a – Tico c*	**6**	Alba b – Tico e
2	Alba b – Tico d	**7**	Alba b – Tico b
3	Alba a – Tico e	**8**	Alba c – Tico c
4	Alba b – Tico b	**9**	Alba b – Tico e
5	Alba c – Tico a	**10**	Alba b – Tico b

2 Con tu compañero/a, pregunta y contesta: haz el test del ejercicio 1. (AT2.4) ▸▸2.2b/Y8◂◂

Speaking. In pairs pupils do the magazine quiz in exercise 1, taking it in turn to ask and answer the questions. They should work out their scoring and read the text that applies to them.

Encourage them to copy the intonation they heard on the recording in exercise 1 when reading out the options, taking care to pace them appropriately.

3 Escribe un texto: describe tus pasatiempos, utilizando el test como modelo. (AT4.4) ▸▸2.4a/Y8◂◂

Writing. Pupils write a text describing what they do in their free time. They should include details on all the points covered in the quiz in exercise 1. A sample opening is given.

4 Lee el texto y escribe la letra o las letras correctas. (AT3.4) ▸▸2.2a/Y8◂◂

Reading. Pupils read the text and identify the correct picture(s) (from *a–j*) for each section 1–7. Some vocabulary support is given.

Answers

1 *a* **2** g **3** c, d **4** b **5** h, i **6** j, e **7** f

5 Lee el texto otra vez. Contesta a las preguntas en español. (AT3.4) ▸▸4.5a/Y8◂◂

Reading. Pupils read the text again and answer the five questions in Spanish. Warn pupils that this involves changing the 1st person verb forms in the text to the 3rd person. Remind them to use the wording of the questions to help them in putting together the answers.

Answers

1. Es inteligente pero un poco perezosa.
2. En su tiempo libre escucha música y va de compras también.
3. Le gusta la música.
4. Su pelo es rizado.
5. Sus ojos son marrones.

Plenary ▸▸5.2◂◂

To revise the frequency expressions, give a range of prompts (e.g. *hago mis deberes*). Pupils respond with a sentence incorporating an appropriate frequency expression (e.g. *Hago mis deberes de vez en cuando*). Another pupil translates the sentence. Then ask pupils to do the prompts too.

Cuaderno A, page 7

¡Extra! 1 page 18 — cuaderno A — La gente 1

1 **Lee el día de Andrea Activa. Luego mira los dibujos. ¿Qué hora es?** *Read Andrea Active's diary page. Then look at the pictures. What time is it?*

09:00	mando mensajes
10:00	voy de compras
12:00	chateo por internet
~~13:30~~	escucho música, me gusta la música pop.
15:00	hago deporte, no me interesan los videojuegos.
19:30	salgo con mis amigos
23:00	bailo en la discoteca

1 13:30
2 ______
3 ______
4 ______
5 ______
6 ______
7 ______

2 **Lee y corrige las frases.** *Read and correct the sentences.*

1. Voy **mensajes**. *Voy de compras*
2. Hago **los videojuegos**. ______
3. Chateo **de compras**. ______
4. Mando **deporte**. ______
5. No me interesan **por internet**. ______

7

1 (AT3.2)

1 *13:30* **2** 19:30 **3** 10:00 **4** 15:00 **5** 23:00 **6** 12:00 **7** 09:00

2 (AT4.2)

1 *Voy de compras.*
2 Hago deporte.
3 Chateo por internet.
4 Mando mensajes.
5 No me interesan los videojuegos.

Cuaderno A, page 8

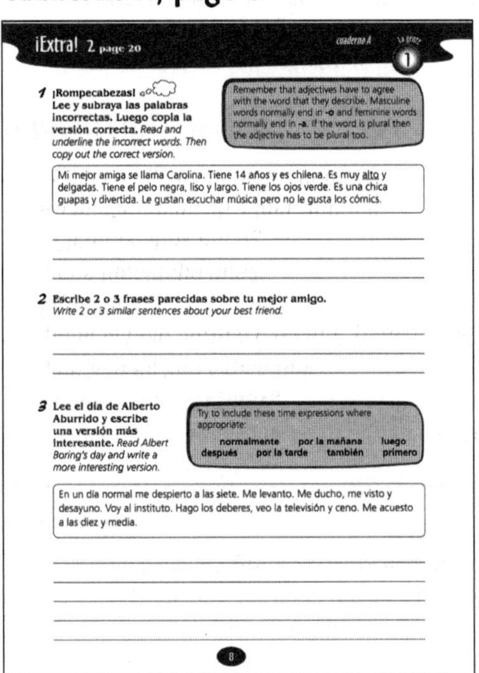

¡Extra! 2 page 20 — cuaderno A — La gente 1

1 **¡Rompecabezas! Lee y subraya las palabras incorrectas. Luego copia la versión correcta.** *Read and underline the incorrect words. Then copy out the correct version.*

Remember that adjectives have to agree with the word that they describe. Masculine words normally end in **-o** and feminine words normally end in **-a**. If the word is plural then the adjective has to be plural too.

Mi mejor amiga se llama Carolina. Tiene 14 años y es chilena. Es muy alto y delgadas. Tiene el pelo negra, liso y largo. Tiene los ojos verde. Es una chica guapas y divertida. Le gustan escuchar música pero no le gusta los cómics.

2 **Escribe 2 o 3 frases parecidas sobre tu mejor amigo.** *Write 2 or 3 similar sentences about your best friend.*

3 **Lee el día de Alberto Aburrido y escribe una versión más interesante.** *Read Albert Boring's day and write a more interesting version.*

Try to include these time expressions where appropriate:
normalmente por la mañana luego después por la tarde también primero

En un día normal me despierto a las siete. Me levanto. Me ducho, me visto y desayuno. Voy al instituto. Hago los deberes, veo la televisión y ceno. Me acuesto a las diez y media.

8

1 (AT3.3)

Mi mejor amiga se llama Carolina. Tiene 14 años y es chilena. Es muy alta y delgada. Tiene el pelo negro, liso y largo. Tiene los ojos verdes. Es una chica guapa y divertida. Le gusta escuchar música pero no le gustan los cómics.

2 (AT4.3)

Pupils' personal responses

3 (AT4.3)

Pupils' personal responses

Cuaderno B, page 7

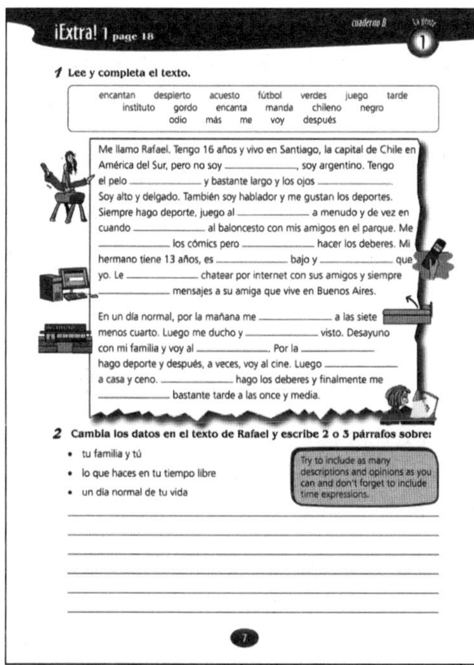
¡Extra! 1 page 18

cuaderno B La gente 1

1 **Lee y completa el texto.**

encantan despierto acuesto fútbol verdes juego tarde instituto gordo encanta manda chileno negro odio más me voy después

Me llamo Rafael. Tengo 16 años y vivo en Santiago, la capital de Chile en América del Sur, pero no soy ________, soy argentino. Tengo el pelo ________ y bastante largo y los ojos ________. Soy alto y delgado. También soy hablador y me gustan los deportes. Siempre hago deporte, juego al ________ a menudo y de vez en cuando ________ al baloncesto con mis amigos en el parque. Me ________ los cómics pero ________ hacer los deberes. Mi hermano tiene 13 años, es ________ bajo y ________ que yo. Le ________ chatear por internet con sus amigos y siempre ________ mensajes a su amiga que vive en Buenos Aires.

En un día normal, por la mañana me ________ a las siete menos cuarto. Luego me ducho y ________ visto. Desayuno con mi familia y voy al ________. Por la ________ hago deporte y después, a veces, voy al cine. Luego ________ a casa y ceno. ________ hago los deberes y finalmente me ________ bastante tarde a las once y media.

2 **Cambia los datos en el texto de Rafael y escribe 2 o 3 párrafos sobre:**

- tu familia y tú
- lo que haces en tu tiempo libre
- un día normal de tu vida

Try to include as many descriptions and opinions as you can and don't forget to include time expressions.

7

1 (AT3.4)

Me llamo Rafael. Tengo 16 años y vivo en Santiago, la capital de Chile en América del Sur, pero no soy chileno, soy argentino. Tengo el pelo negro y bastante largo y los ojos verdes. Soy alto y delgado. También soy hablador y me gustan los deportes. Siempre hago deporte, juego al fútbol a menudo y de vez en cuando juego al baloncesto con mis amigos en el parque. Me encantan los cómics pero odio hacer los deberes. Mi hermano tiene 13 años, es más bajo y gordo que yo. Le encanta chatear por internet con sus amigos y siempre manda mensajes a su amiga que vive en Buenos Aires.

En un día normal, por la mañana me despierto a las siete menos cuarto. Luego me ducho y me visto. Desayuno con mi familia y voy al instituto. Por la tarde hago deporte y después, a veces, voy al cine. Luego voy a casa y ceno. Después hago los deberes y finalmente me acuesto bastante tarde a las once y media.

2 (AT4.4)

Cuaderno B, page 8

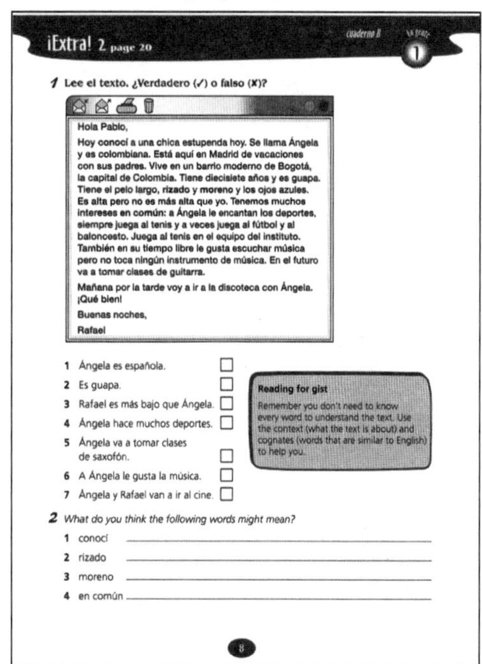
¡Extra! 2 page 20

cuaderno B La gente 1

1 **Lee el texto. ¿Verdadero (✓) o falso (✗)?**

Hola Pablo,

Hoy conocí a una chica estupenda hoy. Se llama Ángela y es colombiana. Está aquí en Madrid de vacaciones con sus padres. Vive en un barrio moderno de Bogotá, la capital de Colombia. Tiene diecisiete años y es guapa. Tiene el pelo largo, rizado y moreno y los ojos azules. Es alta pero no es más alta que yo. Tenemos muchos intereses en común: a Ángela le encantan los deportes, siempre juega al tenis y a veces juega al fútbol y al baloncesto. Juega al tenis en el equipo del instituto. También en su tiempo libre le gusta escuchar música pero no toca ningún instrumento de música. En el futuro va a tomar clases de guitarra.

Mañana por la tarde voy a ir a la discoteca con Ángela. ¡Qué bien!

Buenas noches,

Rafael

1 Ángela es española. ☐
2 Es guapa. ☐
3 Rafael es más bajo que Ángela. ☐
4 Ángela hace muchos deportes. ☐
5 Ángela va a tomar clases de saxofón. ☐
6 A Ángela le gusta la música. ☐
7 Ángela y Rafael van a ir al cine. ☐

Reading for gist

Remember you don't need to know every word to understand the text. Use the context (what the text is about) and cognates (words that are similar to English) to help you.

2 *What do you think the following words might mean?*

1 conocí ________
2 rizado ________
3 moreno ________
4 en común ________

8

1 (AT3.4)

1 ✗ **2** ✓ **3** ✗ **4** ✓ **5** ✗ **6** ✓ **7** ✗

2 (AT3.4)

1 I met **2** curly **3** dark **4** in common

¡Extra! 2 (Pupil's Book pages 20–21)

Learning objectives

- Reading a story in Spanish
- Practising verbs in the present tense

Framework objectives

2.1/Y8 Reading – authentic materials
5.6 Strategies – reading aloud

Grammar

- Present tense

Key language

lo siento
mucho gusto
conocí a
hoy

Revision of language from Module 1

High-frequency words

Revision of language from Module 1

Cross-curricular

Citizenship: Cultural knowledge
ICT: Internet research

Resources

CD1, tracks 21–22

Starter ▸▸4.5a/Y8◂◂

Aim
To practise using present tense verbs.

Write up (answers in brackets for reference only):

1 _____ *español.* (*soy/es*)
2 _____ *el pelo corto.* (*tengo/tiene*)
3 _____ *veinte años.* (*tengo/tiene*)
4 _____ *música.* (*escucho/escucha*)
5 _____ *por internet.* (*chateo* or *navego/chatea* or *navega*)
6 _____ *con el ordenador.* (*juego/juega*)
7 _____ *en Barcelona.* (*vivo/vive*)
8 _____ *mensajes.* (*mando/manda*)

Give pupils three minutes working in pairs to come up with an appropriate verb ('I' form) to fill in each gap.

When checking answers, ask pupils to give the corresponding 3rd person singular form of each verb.

1 Escucha y lee. (AT1.4) ▸▸2.1/Y8 5.4◂◂

Listening. Pupils listen to the recording of the story and read the text at the same time. Ask them to try to work out how Diego and Patricia feel about each other, by listening out for how they talk as well as what they say. Some vocabulary support is given.

Audioscript Track 21

1 – *Lo siento.*
– *Lo siento.*
– *¡Hola! Me llamo Diego. Soy español. Mucho gusto, mucho gusto…*
2 – *¿Cómo te llamas? ¿Cuál es tu nacionalidad?*
– *Me llamo Patricia. Soy mexicana pero vivo en Barcelona.*
3 – *Yo también vivo en Barcelona. ¿Y… te gusta Barcelona, Patricia?*
– *¡Ah sí, me encanta, me encanta! Es una ciudad muy interesante y muy importante también, porque es la capital de la región de Cataluña. Me gustan los monumentos y las galerías de arte.*
4 – *¿Qué haces en tu tiempo libre, Patricia?*
– *Me encanta la música. Escucho de todo. Me gusta bailar.*
5 – *¿Y tú? ¿Qué haces en tu tiempo libre?*
– *Chateo por internet. Me gustan los videojuegos. Juego con el ordenador y mando mensajes. Me gusta mucho la informática. Aquí tienes mi correo electrónico.*
6 – *¡Hola, Ana! ¿Qué tal? Conocí a un chico hoy. Es alto y delgado. Tiene el pelo castaño y los ojos azules…*

2 Con tu compañero/a, lee en voz alta la historia de Diego y Patricia. (AT2.4) ▸▸5.6◂◂

Speaking. In pairs: pupils read the story aloud, each taking the role of Diego or Patricia. Encourage them to focus on pronunciation and stress and to try and sound as fluent as possible, following the model of the recording.

3 Escribe los infinitivos de los verbos (en naranja) de la historia. Luego escríbelos en inglés. (AT4.4) ▸▸4.5a/Y8 5.2◂◂

Reading. Pupils copy out all the verbs shown in orange in the story text: they write out the infinitive form of each and translate both verb forms into English. They should then use the Gramática section at the back of the book to check their answers.

Answers

Present tense	Infinitive
soy = I am	*ser = to be*
vivo = I live	vivir = to live
haces = you do	hacer = to do
escucho = I listen	escuchar = to listen
haces = you do	hacer = to do
chateo = I chat	chatear = to chat
juego = I play	jugar = to play
mando = I send	mandar = to send
tiene = he has	tener = to have

4 Lee la historia otra vez y escribe Diego (D), Patricia (P) o Diego y Patricia (DP). (AT3.4) ▸▸2.2a/Y8◂◂

Reading. Pupils reread the story on page 20 and answer the six questions on it, by identifying who is being described in each – Diego (by writing D), Patricia (P) or both (DP).

Answers

1 D **2** P **3** DP **4** D **5** D **6** P

5 Imagina otra historia de dos personas que se encuentran en Barcelona. Incluye estas expresiones. (AT4.4) ▸▸2.4a/Y8 5.7◂◂

Writing. Pupils make up another story about two people who meet in Barcelona, using Diego and Patricia's exchange as a model and including the expressions supplied.

Encourage pupils to identify the structures they need to include and to use the language they know to vary the content.

6 Escucha el texto de Zona Cultura. (AT1.4) ▸▸2.1/Y8◂◂

ZONA CULTURA This section gives cultural information on Barcelona. The text is also given on the recording.

Pupils listen to the recording and read through the text at the same time. Then translate the text round the class, with each pupil doing a sentence.

You could use the text as a starting point for a general discussion about the city: ask if anyone has visited it and what they did there. What else does the class know about Barcelona?

Pupils could go on to research Barcelona on Spanish websites. You could either give them a particular topic to work on in pairs or you could ask each pair to come up with three differences in Spanish between living in Barcelona and living where they do.

Audioscript Track 22

Zona Cultura – Barcelona

Barcelona está en el noreste de España. Es una ciudad muy importante.

Hay monumentos interesantes, galerías de arte y muchos restaurantes y cafeterías. Barcelona es la capital de la región de Cataluña. En Cataluña se habla catalán.

Plenary ▸▸5.6◂◂

Ask a pair to read out one of the stories they wrote for exercise 5 and ask the rest of the class comprehension questions on it.

Te toca a ti (Pupil's Book pages 114–115)

- Self-access reading and writing at two levels

A Reinforcement

1 *Look at the information. Write six sentences.* (AT4.3) ▸▸2.4a/Y8◂◂

Writing. Using the notes supplied, pupils write six sentences, each comparing two of the celebrities featured. A sample is given.

2 *Copy out the form and fill it in for yourself.* (AT4.2–3) ▸▸2.4a/Y8◂◂

Writing. Pupils copy out the form, omitting the details supplied in the example for Paco Torres. They then complete the form with their own details, using Paco's as a model.

3 *Write four dialogues.* (AT4.3) ▸▸4.5a/Y8◂◂

Writing. Using the picture prompts supplied, pupils write out four dialogues about morning routines. The relevant verbs are supplied for support. A sample dialogue is given.

Answers

✦ *¿Qué haces por la mañana, Isabel?*
■ *Me peino, desayuno y voy al instituto.*
✦ ¿Qué haces por la mañana, Roberto?
■ Me despierto, me levanto y desayuno.
✦ ¿Qué haces por la mañana, Natalia?
■ Me ducho, me visto y voy al instituto.
✦ ¿Qué haces por la mañana, Omar?
■ Me levanto, me ducho y me visto.

B Extension

1 *Choose the correct word.* (AT3.2) ▸▸4.3/Y8 4.5a/Y8◂◂

Reading. Pupils read the sentences about Antonio and complete them by selecting the correct word from the two options given in each case.

Answers

El mejor ***amigo*** de Pepe se llama Antonio. **Tiene** dieciocho años. Es **alto**. Tiene **el pelo** corto y castaño. **Tiene** los ojos marrones. Es divertido **y** generoso. **Le gusta** leer y hacer deporte.

2 *Who is it? Write the correct name. (There is one picture too many.)* (AT3.3) ▸▸2.2a/Y8◂◂

Reading. Pupils read the three descriptions of best friends and use the labelled pictures to identify who is being described in each case.

Answers

1 Tico **2** Silvia **3** Carlos

3 *Write the website text describing these people.* (AT4.3–4) ▸▸2.4a/Y8◂◂

Writing. Using the texts in exercise 2 as models, pupils write a website text describing the two people pictured.

Pupils should use the Palabras and Gramática sections to check their work.

Module 2 ¿Vamos a salir? (Pupil's Book pages 24–41)

Unit	Framework	Levels and PoS	Key language	Grammar	Skills
1 ¿Adónde vas? (pp. 24–25) Talking about places in town Using the near future tense	**4.5/Y8** Language – (a) range of verb tenses (near future)	**2–5** **2.1d** previous knowledge **2.1e** use reference materials **2.2d** pronunciation and intonation **3a** spoken and written language **3c** apply grammar	*¿Adónde vas?* *Voy...* *al centro comercial/cine/estadio/parque/salón recreativo* *a la bolera/discoteca/playa* *¿Qué vas a hacer?* *Voy a...* *bailar* *ir de compras* *jugar al fútbol* *jugar al futbolín* *jugar a los bolos* *tomar el sol* *ver un partido de fútbol* *ver una película* *el lunes/el martes/el miércoles/el jueves/ el viernes/el sábado/el domingo*	*a + el = al* The near future tense	Using reading strategies to work out new words Understanding different tense usage Using reference resources Working on sounding authentic by copying Spanish models
2 Vamos a salir... (pp. 26–27) Practising the present and near future tenses Using sequencing words	**3.2/Y8** Culture – (a) young people: aspirations **4.4/Y8** Language – developing sentences	**4–5** **2.1e** use reference materials **2.2d** pronunciation and intonation **2.2k** deal with unfamiliar language **3f** compare experiences **4b** communicate in pairs etc. **4e** use a range of resources	*¿Qué vas a hacer hoy?* *esta mañana* *esta tarde* *esta noche* *más tarde* *primero* *luego* *después* *este fin de semana* *Voy a... / Vamos a...* *ver la televisión* *escuchar música* *salir* *ir al balneario* *ir a la peluquería* *ir a la bolera*	The near future tense Time phrases associated with the near future tense (*más tarde*, etc.) Distinguishing the present and near future tenses	Using different tenses appropriately Using reference resources Pronunciation: *ue* Structuring a longer text using sequencing words

continued

Module 2 ¿Vamos a salir? (Pupil's Book pages 24–41)

Unit	Framework	Levels and PoS	Key language	Grammar	Skills
3 ¿Te gustaría ir a la bolera? (pp. 28–29) Inviting someone to go out Adding expression to your spoken Spanish	**1.3/Y8** Listening – (a) understanding language for specific functions **1.3/Y8** Speaking – (b) using language for specific functions **1.5/Y8** Speaking – (b) using simple idioms	**4–5** **2.1a** identify patterns **2.1c** knowledge of language **2.1d** previous knowledge **2.2h** redraft to improve writing **2.2j** adapt previously learned language **3a** spoken and written language **3d** use a range of vocab/ structures **3e** different countries/ cultures **4d** make links with English **4e** use a range of resources	*¿Te gustaría... ?* *... ir al parque* *... ir a la bolera* *... ir de compras* *¿A qué hora?* *a la una* *a las tres* *a las cinco y cuarto* *a las seis y media* *a las siete menos cuarto* *a las ocho* *a las nueve* *¿Dónde quedamos?* *delante de la discoteca* *detrás del centro comercial* *en el parque* *en la bolera* *en la calle* *en tu casa* *De acuerdo.* *Vale.* *Muy bien.* *No tengo ganas.* *¡Ni hablar!* *¡Ni en sueños!* *Bueno...* *Pues...* *A ver...* *Hasta luego.* *Adiós.* *Hasta pronto.*	Using prepositions (including *a* + *el* = *al*, *de* + *el* = *del*) *¿Te gustaría... ?* + the infinitive	Using reading strategies to work out new words Participating in an unscripted dialogue Working on sounding authentic by copying Spanish models Reviewing progress/ checking work using the Mini-test

continued

Module 2 ¿Vamos a salir? (Pupil's Book pages 24–41)

Unit	Framework	Levels and PoS	Key language	Grammar	Skills
4 No puedo... (pp. 30–31) Making excuses Using *querer* and *poder*	**4.5/Y8** Language – (b) range of modal verbs **4.6/Y8** Language – (b) range of negatives	**2–4** **2.1a** identify patterns **2.1d** previous knowledge **2.1e** use reference materials **2.2c** respond appropriately **2.2e** ask and answer questions **2.2f** initiate/sustain conversations **3c** apply grammar **4f** language for interest/ enjoyment	*¿Quieres...?* *chatear por internet* *ir a la discoteca* *ir de compras* *jugar a los bolos* *jugar al fútbol* *salir* *ver un partido de fútbol* *ver una película* *Lo siento, no puedo.* *No puedo salir.* *¿Por qué?* *Porque...* *no quiero* *no tengo dinero* *no tengo tiempo* *Tengo que...* *hacer mis deberes* *lavarme el pelo* *ordenar mi dormitorio* *pasear al perro*	*tener/tengo que* *poder* *querer*	Using reading strategies to work out new words Applying recognised patterns to new language Using reference resources Extending sentences using connectives and negatives and sequencing words
5 Tengo un problema (pp. 32–33) Saying what someone else likes or dislikes Using phrases with infinitives	**2.2/Y8** Reading – (b) personal response to text **4.5/Y8** Language – (b) range of modal verbs	**4–5** **2.1e** use reference materials **2.2b** skim and scan **3c** apply grammar **4b** communicate in pairs etc. **4c** use more complex language	*Tengo un problema.* *¿Qué voy a hacer?* *Mi madre es muy severa.* *Me gusta así.* *Mi padre dice que...* *Soy demasiado joven.* *¿Qué le puedo decir a mi madre?* *Tienes que hablar con tus padres.* *Es tu responsabilidad.* *Estoy de acuerdo con tu padre.* *Eres demasiado joven para ir a la discoteca.* *Tienes que pensar en tu hermano.* *Tienes que presentar el amigo a tu madre.* *Tienes que salir más.*	Expressions + infinitive (*me gustaría*, etc.) *A (Sergio) (no) le gusta...* Possessive adjectives (*mi(s)/tu(s)/su(s)*)	Identifying key information by skim-reading a text Applying known patterns to new language Using reference resources Writing an extended text in Spanish
Resumen/ Prepárate (pp. 34–35) Pupils' checklist and practice test		**3–5**			Reviewing progress/ checking work

continued

Module 2 ¿Vamos a salir? (Pupil's Book pages 24–41)

Unit	Framework	Levels and PoS	Key language	Grammar	Skills
¡Extra! 1 (pp. 36–37) Talking about a visit to an adventure park Taking part in an unscripted dialogue	**1.1/Y8** Listening – understanding on first hearing **1.4/Y8** Speaking – (b) unscripted conversation	**4–5** **2.1d** previous knowledge **2.1e** use reference materials **2.2a** listen for gist **2.2g** write clearly and coherently **4c** use more complex language **4f** language for interest/ enjoyment	Revision of language from Module 2	Verb + infinitive expressions	Using reading strategies to work out new words Using reference resources Developing listening skills Participating in an unscripted dialogue Extending sentences, using connectives and negatives
¡Extra! 2 (pp. 38–39) Reading a story in Spanish Practising stem-changing verbs		**2–4** **2.1e** use reference materials **2.2d** pronunciation and intonation **4e** use a range of resources **4f** language for interest/ enjoyment	Revision of language from Module 2	*poder* and *querer* (stem-changing verbs)	Understanding a longer text in Spanish (ongoing photo story) Working on sounding authentic by copying Spanish models Using reference resources
Te toca a ti (pp. 116–117)	Self-access reading and writing at two levels				

continued

1 ¿Adónde vas? (Pupil's Book pages 24–25)

Learning objectives

- Talking about places in town
- Using the near future tense

Framework objectives

4.5/Y8 Language – (a) range of verb tenses (near future)

Grammar

- *a + el = al*
- The near future tense

Key language

¿Adónde vas?
Voy...
al centro comercial/cine/estadio/parque/salón recreativo
a la bolera/discoteca/playa

¿Qué vas a hacer?
Voy a...
bailar
ir de compras
jugar al fútbol
jugar al futbolín
jugar a los bolos
tomar el sol
ver un partido de fútbol
ver una película

el lunes, el martes, el miércoles, el jueves, el viernes, el sábado, el domingo

High-frequency words

el, la, los
un, una
a (a, al)
de
¿qué?
hacer
ver
ir (voy, vas)
jugar
tomar

Cross-curricular

English: Verb tenses; Using reference materials

Resources

CD1, tracks 23–24
Cuadernos A&B, p. 12
R & A Pack, Gramática p. 9

Teacher Presentations

Screen 1 – Module 2 overview
Screen 2 – Vocabulary: Flashcards
Screen 3 – p. 24 ex.1
Screen 4 – p. 25 ex. 4

Starter 1 4.2/Y8

Aim

To revise vocabulary for places in town.
To use reading strategies to work out new vocabulary.

Write up the text below, jumbling the order of the second column. Give pupils two minutes to match each Spanish term with the correct English translation.

centro comercial	shopping centre
cine	cinema
estadio	stadium
parque	park
salón recreativo	amusement arcade
bolera	bowling alley
discoteca	disco
playa	beach

Check answers, asking pupils how they worked out the ones they didn't know.

Suggestion

Write up *Voy al parque* and *Voy a jugar al fútbol*. Ask pupils to translate the sentences, and then to identify the verbs in each sentence. Which tenses are used here? Remind pupils as necessary of when the present and near future tenses are used and of how the near future tense is formed in the 1st person: *voy* + *a* + infinitive. Say that the near future tense will be covered in detail in this unit.

1 Escucha y escribe la letra correcta. (1–8) (AT1.2) 4.5a/Y8

Listening. Pupils listen to eight conversations and identify the picture with the label for each.

Audioscript Track 23

1 – *¿Adónde vas, Julio?*
– *Voy a la playa.*
– *¿Qué vas a hacer?*
– *Voy a tomar el sol.*

2 – *¿Adónde vas, Elena?*
– *Voy al cine. Voy a ver una película.*

3 – *¿Adónde vas, Javier?*
– *Voy al salón recreativo. Voy a jugar al futbolín.*

4 – *¿Adónde vas, Paco?*
– *Voy al parque.*
– *¿Qué vas a hacer?*
– *Voy a jugar al fútbol.*

5 – *¿Adónde vas, Marta?*
– *Voy a la discoteca. Voy a bailar.*

6 – *¡Hola, Silvia! ¿Adónde vas?*
– *Ehmm, voy al centro comercial.*
– *¿Qué vas a hacer en el centro comercial?*
– *Voy a ir de compras.*

7 – *¿Qué tal, Alfredo?*
– *Muy, muy bien, gracias.*
– *¿Adónde vas?*
– *Voy al estadio. Voy a ver un partido de fútbol.*

8 – *¡Hola, Carolina! ¿Qué tal?*
– *Bien, bien. ¿Adónde vas?*
– *Voy a la bolera. Voy a jugar a los bolos.*

Answers

1 f **2** a **3** e **4** b **5** h **6** c **7** d **8** g

Gramática: *a* + *el* = *al*

This shows how *a* when followed by *el* changes to *al*.

R In pairs: pupils take it in turn to prompt with a place, using the correct form of *a* (e.g. *al parque*) and to respond with an appropriate activity (e.g. *jugar al fútbol*). Once they feel confident, pupils could try this with their books closed.

2 Escribe una lista de los infinitivos del ejercicio 1. Luego escríbelos en inglés. (AT4.1, AT3.3) ▸▸5.4◂◂

Writing. Pupils write out a list of all the infinitives used in exercise 1 and translate them into English.

Pupils then check their translations using the Vocabulario section at the back of the Pupil's Book.

Answers

hacer = to do
ver = to see
jugar = to play
ir = to go
(ir de compras = to go shopping)
jugar = to play
tomar = to take
(tomar el sol = to sunbathe)
jugar = to play
bailar = to dance
ver = to watch

Starter 2 ▸▸4.5a/Y8 5.3◂◂

Aim
To revise the present tense of *ir*.

Write up:

ir	to go
	I go
	you go (singular)
	he/she/it goes
	we go
	you go (plural)
	they go

Give pupils two minutes working in pairs to complete the table with the full present tense paradigm of *ir*.

You could supply all the verb forms in jumbled order if pupils need support.

To check answers, complete the table as a class. Then ask pupils to check these are correct using the verb tables in the Gramática section at the back of the Pupil's Book.

3 Elige un sitio. Tu compañero/a dice la actividad. (AT2.3) ▸▸1.4a/Y8 4.5a/Y8◂◂

Speaking. In pairs pupils take it in turn to prompt with a place from exercise 1 and to respond with the appropriate activity. The text to be changed is underlined.

Gramática: the near future tense

This shows how the near future tense is formed. There is practice on this on page 131 of the Pupil's Book.

R Ask pupils to come up with other examples of the near future tense in the 1st or 3rd person using different infinitives.

+ Ask pupils to rewrite the sentences which use the near future tense in exercise 1 using a different part of the verb *ir* (e.g. *Vamos a ver una película*) and translating each sentence into English (e.g. 'We are going to see a film').

4 Escucha a Milena. Copia y rellena la tabla. (1–6) (AT1.4) ▸▸1.1/Y8◂◂

Listening. Pupils copy out the table. They listen to Milena and complete the table with the details of what she does each day.

Audioscript Track 24

1 *A ver, mi semana va a ser muy interesante. El lunes, hmm, voy a jugar al fútbol en el parque.*
2 *El martes voy al cine. Voy a ver una película. Me encanta ir al cine.*
3 *El miércoles voy al salón recreativo. Voy a jugar al futbolín.*
4 *Y el jueves… voy a la playa. Voy a tomar el sol – perfecto.*
5 *El viernes… a ver, el viernes voy a la discoteca con mis amigos. ¡Estupendo! Voy a bailar. Vamos a bailar toda la noche.*
6 *El sábado, el sábado… ¿Adónde voy el sábado? ¿Qué voy a hacer? A ver… Voy al centro comercial y voy a ir de compras. Después voy a jugar a los bolos. Voy a la bolera con mis amigos. Me gusta jugar a los bolos: es muy divertido.*

Answers

Día	Sitio(s)	Actividad(es)
lunes	*parque*	*fútbol*
martes	cine	película
miércoles	salón recreativo	futbolín
jueves	playa	tomar el sol
viernes	discoteca	bailar
sábado	centro comercial, bolera	ir de compras, bolos

Explain to pupils that the recording contains lots of examples of techniques they can copy to make what they say more interesting and to sound more authentic in Spanish: expressions to gain thinking time (*a ver*, *hmm*, repetition – *el sábado, el sábado*), exclamations giving opinion (*perfecto*, *¡Estupendo!*), rhetorical questions (*¿Adónde voy el sábado?*, *¿Qué voy a hacer?*), using stress to convey opinion (*mi semana va a ser muy interesante, es muy divertido*).

Play the recording again, asking pupils to listen out for these features. Encourage them to use them in their own speech.

5 Lee el texto y mira los dibujos. ¿Verdadero o falso? Escribe V o F. (AT3.5) ▶▶2.2a/Y8◀◀

Reading. Pupils read the text describing Sergio's week and decide whether each of the pictures is a true (V) or false (F) depiction of what he is going to do.

Answers

1 F **2** F **3** F **4** V **5** V **6** F

R Working in pairs, pupils take it in turn to give an activity from Sergio's diary and to respond with the appropriate day of the week.

+ Use Sergio's text for a translation activity: go round the class with each pupil translating a sentence.

6 Describe tu semana ideal. Da opiniones. (AT4.4–5) ▶▶2.2b/Y8 4.5a/Y8◀◀

Writing. Using Sergio's text as a model, pupils describe their own ideal week. They should include opinions on what they are going to do. A sample opening is given.

Plenary ▶▶4.5a/Y8◀◀

Ask pupils to say how the near future tense is formed and to give examples using different verbs from the unit. Prompt (as appropriate to the level of the class) so that they produce the tense in different persons.

Play a chain game round the class to practise forming the near future tense. Explain the aim: to make the longest possible sentence describing the things you are all going to do at the weekend, using the near future tense for each. Each person adds a word in turn, so (e.g.) P1 *Voy* + P2 *a* + P3 *ver* + P4 *una* + P5 *película*, etc.

Once pupils are feeling confident, encourage them to go as quickly as possible. You could also suggest they vary the person of the verbs.

Cuaderno A, page 12

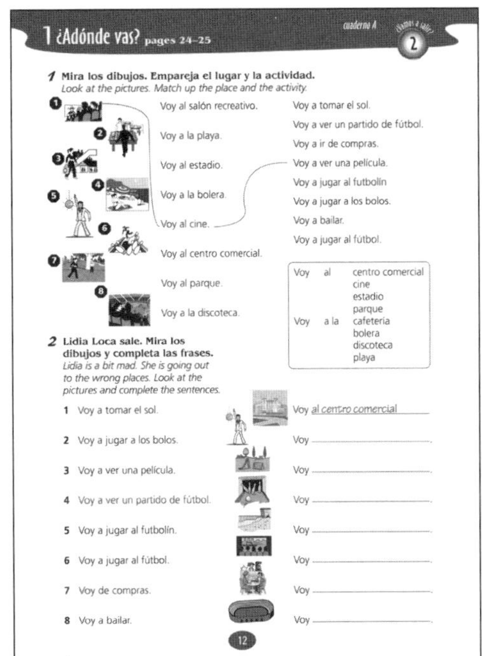

1 (AT3.2)

1 *Voy al cine. Voy a ver una película.*
2 Voy al salón recreativo. Voy a jugar al futbolín.
3 Voy al centro comercial. Voy a ir de compras.
4 Voy a la playa. Voy a tomar el sol.
5 Voy a la discoteca. Voy a bailar.
6 Voy a la bolera. Voy a jugar a los bolos.
7 Voy al parque. Voy a jugar al fútbol.
8 Voy al estadio. Voy a ver un partido de fútbol.

2 (AT4.2)

1 *Voy al centro comercial.* **2** Voy a la discoteca.
3 Voy al parque. **4** Voy a la bolera.
5 Voy a la playa. **6** Voy al cine.
7 Voy a la cafetería. **8** Voy al estadio.

Cuaderno B, page 12

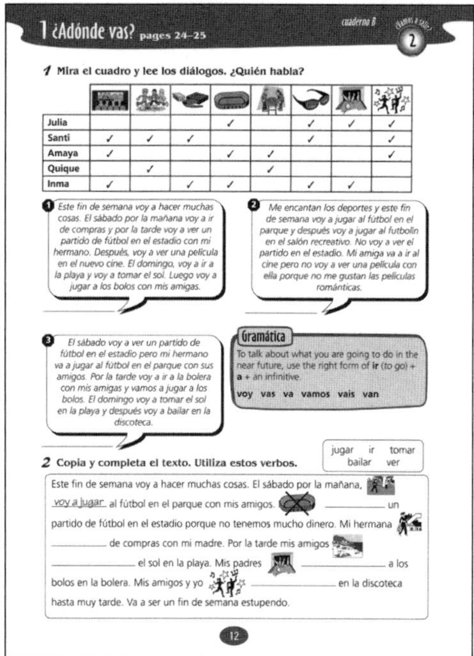

1 ¿Adónde vas? pages 24–25

cuaderno B ¿Vamos a salir? 2

1 **Mira el cuadro y lee los diálogos. ¿Quién habla?**

Julia				✓		✓	✓	✓
Santi	✓	✓	✓			✓		✓
Amaya	✓			✓	✓			✓
Quique		✓			✓			
Inma	✓		✓	✓		✓	✓	

1 *Este fin de semana voy a hacer muchas cosas. El sábado por la mañana voy a ir de compras y por la tarde voy a ver un partido de fútbol en el estadio con mi hermano. Después, voy a ver una película en el nuevo cine. El domingo, voy a ir a la playa y voy a tomar el sol. Luego voy a jugar a los bolos con mis amigas.*

2 *Me encantan los deportes y este fin de semana voy a jugar al fútbol en el parque y después voy a jugar al futbolín en el salón recreativo. No voy a ver el partido en el estadio. Mi amiga va a ir al cine pero no voy a ver una película con ella porque no me gustan las películas románticas.*

3 *El sábado voy a ver un partido de fútbol en el estadio pero mi hermano va a jugar al fútbol en el parque con sus amigos. Por la tarde voy a ir a la bolera con mis amigas y vamos a jugar a los bolos. El domingo voy a tomar el sol en la playa y después voy a bailar en la discoteca.*

Gramática

To talk about what you are going to do in the near future, use the right form of **ir** (*to go*) + **a** + an infinitive.

voy vas va vamos vais van

2 **Copia y completa el texto. Utiliza estos verbos.**

jugar ir tomar bailar ver

Este fin de semana voy a hacer muchas cosas. El sábado por la mañana, voy a jugar al fútbol en el parque con mis amigos. ________ un partido de fútbol en el estadio porque no tenemos mucho dinero. Mi hermana ________ de compras con mi madre. Por la tarde mis amigos ________ el sol en la playa. Mis padres ________ a los bolos en la bolera. Mis amigos y yo ________ en la discoteca hasta muy tarde. Va a ser un fin de semana estupendo.

12

1 (AT3.3)

1 Inma **2** Quique **3** Julia

2 (AT3.3, AT4.3)

Este fin de semana voy a hacer muchas cosas. El sábado por la mañana, *voy a jugar* al fútbol en el parque con mis amigos. No vamos a ver un partido de fútbol en el estadio porque no tenemos mucho dinero. Mi hermana va a ir de compras con mi madre. Por la tarde mis amigos y yo vamos a tomar el sol en la playa. Mis padres van a jugar a los bolos en la bolera. Mis amigos y yo vamos a bailar en la discoteca hasta muy tarde. Va a ser un fin de semana estupendo.

R & A Pack, Gramática page 9

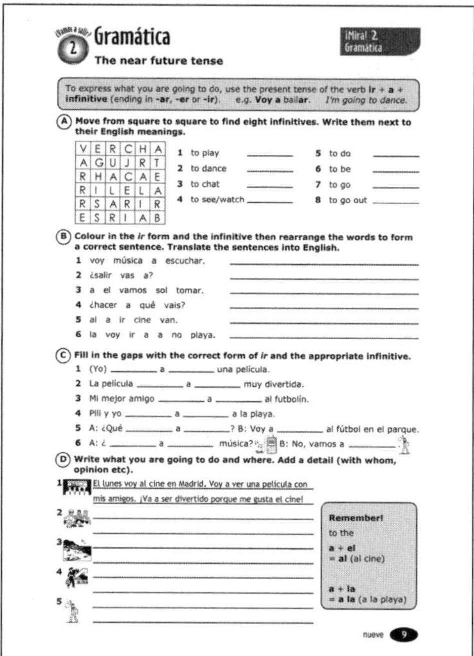

¿Vamos a salir? 2 **Gramática** ¡Mira! 2 Gramática

The near future tense

To express what you are going to do, use the present tense of the verb **ir** + **a** + **infinitive** (ending in **-ar**, **-er** or **-ir**). e.g. **Voy a** bail**ar**. *I'm going to dance.*

Ⓐ **Move from square to square to find eight infinitives. Write them next to their English meanings.**

V	E	R	C	H	A
A	G	U	J	R	T
R	H	A	C	A	E
R	I	L	E	L	A
R	S	A	R	I	R
E	S	R	I	A	B

1 to play ________ 5 to do ________
2 to dance ________ 6 to be ________
3 to chat ________ 7 to go ________
4 to see/watch ________ 8 to go out ________

Ⓑ **Colour in the *ir* form and the infinitive then rearrange the words to form a correct sentence. Translate the sentences into English.**

1 voy música a escuchar. ________
2 ¿salir vas a? ________
3 a el vamos sol tomar. ________
4 ¿hacer a qué vais? ________
5 al a ir cine van. ________
6 la voy ir a a no playa. ________

Ⓒ **Fill in the gaps with the correct form of *ir* and the appropriate infinitive.**

1 (Yo) ________ a ________ una película.
2 La película ________ a ________ muy divertida.
3 Mi mejor amigo ________ a ________ al futbolín.
4 Pili y yo ________ a ________ a la playa.
5 A: ¿Qué ________ a ________? B: Voy a ________ al fútbol en el parque.
6 A: ¿ ________ a ________ música? B: No, vamos a ________.

Ⓓ **Write what you are going to do and where. Add a detail (with whom, opinion etc).**

1 El lunes voy al cine en Madrid. Voy a ver una película con mis amigos. ¡Va a ser divertido porque me gusta el cine!
2 ________
3 ________
4 ________
5 ________

Remember!
to the
a + el = **al** (al cine)
a + la = **a la** (a la playa)

nueve 9

Ⓐ **1** jugar **2** bailar **3** chatear **4** ver **5** hacer **6** ser **7** ir **8** salir

Ⓑ **1 Voy** a **escuchar** música. I'm going to listen to music.
2 ¿**Vas** a **salir**? Are you going to go out?
3 Vamos a **tomar** el sol. We are going to sunbathe.
4 ¿Qué **vais** a **hacer**? What are you going to do?
5 Van a **ir** al cine. They are going to go to the cinema.
6 No **voy** a **ir** a la playa. I'm not going to go to the beach.

Ⓒ **1** voy, ver **2** va, ser **3** va, jugar **4** vamos, ir **5** A: vas, hacer B: jugar **6** A: vais, escuchar B: bailar

Ⓓ **1** Voy al parque. Voy a jugar al fútbol. **2** Voy a la playa. Voy a tomar el sol. **3** Voy al centro comercial. Voy a ir de compras. **4** Voy a la discoteca. Voy a bailar.

2 Vamos a salir... (Pupil's Book pages 26–27)

Learning objectives

- Practising the present and near future tenses
- Using sequencing words

Framework objectives

3.2/Y8 Culture – (a) young people: aspirations

4.4/Y8 Language – developing sentences

Grammar

- The near future tense
- Time phrases associated with the near future tense (*más tarde*, etc.)
- Distinguishing the present and near future tenses

Key language

¿Qué vas a hacer hoy?
esta mañana
esta tarde
esta noche
más tarde
primero
luego
después
este fin de semana
Voy a... / Vamos a...
ver la televisión
escuchar música
salir
ir al balneario
ir a la peluquería
ir a la bolera

High-frequency words

la, los
a (a, al)
de
hoy
después
luego
y
¿qué?
escuchar
hacer
ir (voy, vas, vamos)
ver
más
esta

Cross-curricular

Citizenship: Cultural knowledge
English: Using reference materials
ICT: Email contact with a Spanish school

Resources

CD1, tracks 25–27
Cuadernos A & B, p. 13
R & A Pack, Gramática p. 10

Teacher Presentations

Screen 1 – Module 2 overview
Screen 2 – p. 26 ex. 1
Screen 3 – p. 27 ex. 4
Screen 4 – Game

Starter 1 ▸▸ 4.5a/Y8 ◂◂

Aim
To practise forming the near future tense.

Write up: *juego, tomo, chateo*
voy, salgo, veo
escucha, baila, es

Give pupils three minutes working in pairs to write out the near future tense forms of the nine verbs given in the present tense.

Suggestion

Ask pupils to describe in English what they are going to do this evening, incorporating the following words: 'first', 'then', 'afterwards'. Take one of the sentences as an example and write it up in Spanish. Ask pupils to identify the tense of the verb used (near future) and to translate the time expression (*primero*, *luego* or *después*, as appropriate). Write up the time expressions not used, say what they mean and explain that these are time expressions: recognising words like this can help pupils identify which tense is being used in a text and which tense they need to use in their own speech or writing. Say that this unit focuses on time expressions that can be used with the near future tense.

1 Escucha y lee. (AT1.5) ▸▸ 4.4/Y8 4.5a/Y8 ◂◂

Listening. Pupils listen to Estela Estrella describing what she is going to do today, following the text at the same time in the book. Some vocabulary support is given.

Audioscript Track 25

1 – *¡Hola! Me llamo Estela Estrella. Soy una gran estrella. Normalmente no me levanto de la cama por menos de 40 millones de dólares.*
Hoy es un día normal para mí.
– *¿Qué vas a hacer hoy?*
2 – *Esta mañana no voy a salir.*
3 – *Primero voy a ver la televisión...*
4 – *... y luego voy a escuchar música.*
5 – *Esta tarde voy a salir a las dos.*
6 – *Después voy a ir al balneario por la tarde...*
7 – *... y más tarde voy a ir a la peluquería.*
8 – *Esta noche voy a ir al casino...*
9 – *... y por último a la discoteca. Voy a bailar toda la noche. ¡Va a ser muy divertido!*

2 Busca el equivalente en español en los textos. (AT3.4)

4.4/Y8 5.4

Reading. Pupils reread the text in exercise 1 and find the Spanish phrases for the eight English phrases listed.

Get pupils to check their answers in the Vocabulario section at the back of the Pupil's Book.

Answers

1 *después* **2** primero **3** esta mañana
4 esta tarde **5** luego **6** más tarde
7 esta noche **8** por último

R Prompt using the sentences in exercise 1, but omitting the time expression (e.g. *voy a escuchar música*). Pupils respond with the appropriate time expression (e.g. *luego*).

3 Con tu compañero/a, haz dos diálogos utilizando estos dibujos. (AT2.5)

1.4/Y8 4.4/Y8

Speaking. In pairs using the picture prompts supplied, pupils make up two dialogues. A sample exchange is given.

AT2.2, AT1.1

Write up the following words and ask pupils to read them aloud:

jueves, después, juego, luego, acuesto

Ask pupils to tell you how *ue* is pronounced. Confirm and get a few volunteers to read through the text in the Pronunciation box. Then play the recording for the class to repeat, line by line.

Audioscript Track 26

Los jueves escucho música.
Después juego al futbolín
y luego me acuesto...

+ Write up:

dueño, fuego, cuenta, pueden, cuero

Can pupils apply the pronunciation rule to these words?

Starter 2 4.5a/Y8

Aim

To practise the near future tense.

Write up the following in two columns, jumbling the order of the second column (given in the correct order here for reference) and ask pupils to match the sentence halves.

1	*Esta mañana*	*no voy a salir.*
2	*Después voy a*	*ir a la peluquería.*
3	*Esta noche voy*	*a ir al casino.*
4	*Voy a ver*	*la televisión.*
5	*Voy a salir a*	*las dos.*
6	*¿Qué vas*	*a hacer hoy?*

Pupils could work in pairs for support.

4 Escucha y lee. Luego corrige las frases en inglés. (AT1.5)

3.2a/Y8 4.5a/Y8

Listening. Pupils listen to Ramón and Mireya talking about what they usually do in their free time and what they are going to do. They then read the eight sentences in English, identify the errors in them and rewrite them correctly.

Audioscript Track 27

Ramón *Generalmente chateo por internet y no salgo mucho, pero hoy voy a ver un partido de fútbol muy especial, un partido internacional: España e Italia. Va a ser muy, muy divertido y el equipo español va a ganar (¡espero!). Después, voy a ir al salón recreativo con mis amigos y vamos a jugar al futbolín un rato. Más tarde vamos a ir a la discoteca y vamos a bailar.*

Mireya *Generalmente los fines de semana juego con el ordenador o escucho música pero este fin de semana voy a hacer otra cosa. Es un fin de semana especial porque es el cumpleaños de mi mejor amiga, Susa.*
Primero vamos a ir de compras, luego vamos a ir al balneario juntas y después a la peluquería. Más tarde vamos a ir a la bolera y vamos a jugar a los bolos.

Answers

1. *Normally Ramón* ***chats on the internet*** *and doesn't go out much.*
2. He is going to see an international **football** game.
3. It is going to be very **entertaining**.
4. Afterwards he is going to play **table football**.
5. Mireya is going to go shopping with her **best friend**.
6. Then they are going to go to the **spa**.
7. Afterwards they are going to go to the **hairdresser's**.
8. Later on they are going to **go bowling**.

+ Pupils close their books and in pairs try to remember three things that Ramón is going to do and three things that Mireya is going to do. They write a sentence for each thing, e.g. *Ramón va a ver un partido de fútbol.*

Gramática: verb tenses

This prompts pupils to check which tense is being used. They should put the verbs in exercise 4 into two lists, present tense and near future tense. There is practice on this on page 133 of the Pupil's Book.

Answers

Presente	Futuro
chateo	*voy a ver*
salgo	va a ser
juego	va a ganar
escucho	voy a ir
es	vamos a jugar
es	vamos a ir
	vamos a bailar
	voy a hacer
	vamos a ir
	vamos a ir

5 Describe un fin de semana para Cenicienta. (AT4.5) ▸▸2.4a/Y8 4.5a/Y8◂◂

Writing. Using the texts in exercise 4 as a model, pupils write a description of what Cinderella usually does at the weekend and what she is going to do this weekend. Picture prompts are supplied to give ideas, but offer pupils the alternative of using their own ideas. A framework is supplied for support: if necessary, talk it through, highlighting the sequencing words used to structure it.

You could use the word 'ball' to highlight potential pitfalls in using a dictionary: how will pupils know whether to use *balón* or *baile*? Stress that using resources such as dictionaries effectively is an important skill to acquire in order to work more independently.

▸▸3.2a/Y8◂◂

If you have contact with a school in Spain, pupils could exchange emails on what they usually do at the weekend and what they are going to do this weekend. Ask your pupils to pool their information in groups and to list the similarities/differences between what they do and what their Spanish counterparts do.

Plenary ▸▸4.5a/Y8◂◂

To practise distinguishing the present and near future tenses, read out a series of sentences at random from Units 1 and 2 of Module 2. Pupils put their hands on their heads if they recognise a present tense and stand up if they recognise a near future tense. Vary the verb persons to suit the level of the class.

Cuaderno A, page 13

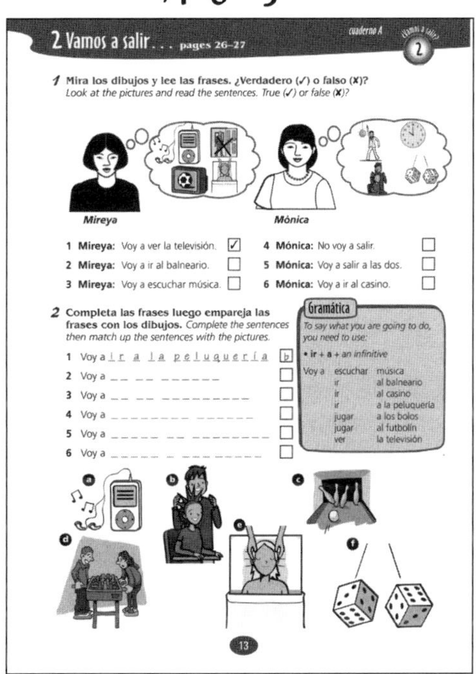
2 Vamos a salir... pages 26–27 cuaderno A ¿Vamos a salir? 2

1 **Mira los dibujos y lee las frases. ¿Verdadero (✓) o falso (✗)?** *Look at the pictures and read the sentences. True (✓) or false (✗)?*

Mireya Mónica

1 **Mireya:** Voy a ver la televisión. ✓
2 **Mireya:** Voy a ir al balneario. ☐
3 **Mireya:** Voy a escuchar música. ☐
4 **Mónica:** No voy a salir. ☐
5 **Mónica:** Voy a salir a las dos. ☐
6 **Mónica:** Voy a ir al casino. ☐

2 **Completa las frases luego empareja las frases con los dibujos.** *Complete the sentences then match up the sentences with the pictures.*

1 Voy a ir a la peluquería b
2 Voy a __ __ ______ ☐
3 Voy a __ __ _________ ☐
4 Voy a _______ ______ ☐
5 Voy a _____ __ ________ ☐
6 Voy a _____ _ ___ _____ ☐

Gramática
To say what you are going to do, you need to use:
• **ir + a** + *an infinitive*

Voy a	escuchar	música
	ir	al balneario
	ir	al casino
	ir	a la peluquería
	jugar	a los bolos
	jugar	al futbolín
	ver	la televisión

13

1 (AT3.2)

1 ✓ 2 ✓ 3 ✓ 4 ✗ 5 ✗ 6 ✓

2 (AT4.2)

1	*Voy a ir a la peluquería.*	*b*
2	Voy a ir al casino.	f
3	Voy a ir al balneario.	e
4	Voy a escuchar música.	a
5	Voy a jugar al futbolín.	d
6	Voy a jugar a los bolos.	c

Cuaderno B, page 13

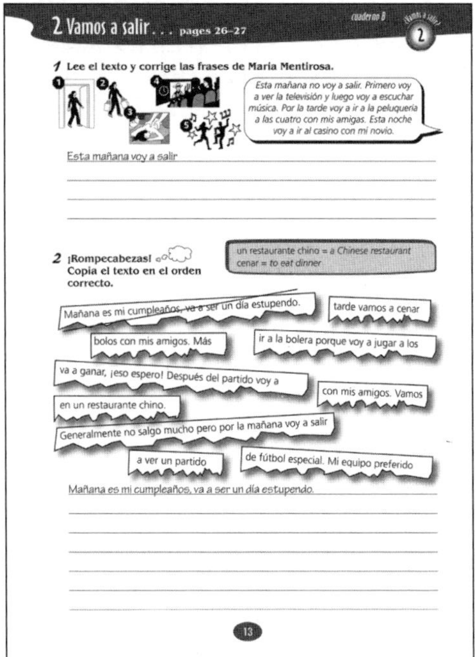

2 Vamos a salir . . . pages 26–27

cuaderno B

¿Vamos a salir? 2

1 **Lee el texto y corrige las frases de María Mentirosa.**

1
2
3
4
5
Esta mañana no voy a salir. Primero voy a ver la televisión y luego voy a escuchar música. Por la tarde voy a ir a la peluquería a las cuatro con mis amigas. Esta noche voy a ir al casino con mi novio.

Esta mañana voy a salir

2 **¡Rompecabezas! Copia el texto en el orden correcto.**

un restaurante chino = *a Chinese restaurant*
cenar = *to eat dinner*

Mañana es mi cumpleaños, va a ser un día estupendo.
tarde vamos a cenar
bolos con mis amigos. Más
ir a la bolera porque voy a jugar a los
va a ganar, ¡eso espero! Después del partido voy a
con mis amigos. Vamos
en un restaurante chino.
Generalmente no salgo mucho pero por la mañana voy a salir
a ver un partido
de fútbol especial. Mi equipo preferido

Mañana es mi cumpleaños, va a ser un día estupendo.

13

1 (AT4.4)

Esta mañana *voy a salir*. Primero voy a ir de compras y luego voy a ir al balneario. Por la tarde voy a ir al cine a las cuatro con mis amigas. Esta noche voy a bailar en la discoteca con mi novio.

2 (AT3.5)

Mañana es mi cumpleaños, va a ser un día estupendo. Generalmente no salgo mucho pero por la mañana voy a salir con mis amigos. Vamos a ver un partido de fútbol especial. Mi equipo preferido va a ganar, ¡eso espero! Después del partido voy a ir a la bolera porque voy a jugar a los bolos con mis amigos. Más tarde vamos a cenar en un restaurante chino.

R & A Pack, Gramática page 10

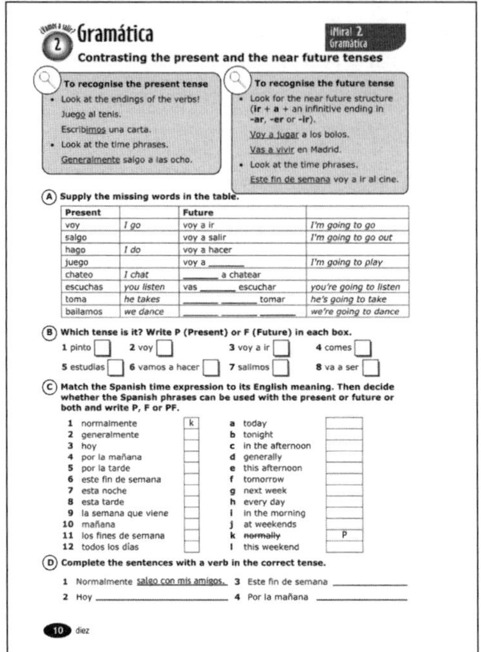

¿Vamos a salir? 2 Gramática

¡Mira! 2 Gramática

Contrasting the present and the near future tenses

To recognise the present tense
- Look at the endings of the verbs!
  Juego al tenis.
  Escribimos una carta.
- Look at the time phrases.
  Generalmente salgo a las ocho.

To recognise the future tense
- Look for the near future structure (**ir** + **a** + an infinitive ending in **-ar**, **-er** or **-ir**).
  Voy a jugar a los bolos.
  Vas a vivir en Madrid.
- Look at the time phrases.
  Este fin de semana voy a ir al cine.

(A) **Supply the missing words in the table.**

Present		Future	
voy	*I go*	voy a ir	*I'm going to go*
salgo		voy a salir	*I'm going to go out*
hago	*I do*	voy a hacer	
juego		voy a ______	*I'm going to play*
chateo	*I chat*	______ a chatear	
escuchas	*you listen*	vas ______ escuchar	*you're going to listen*
toma	*he takes*	______ ______ tomar	*he's going to take*
bailamos	*we dance*	______ ______ ______	*we're going to dance*

(B) **Which tense is it? Write P (Present) or F (Future) in each box.**

1 pinto ☐ **2** voy ☐ **3** voy a ir ☐ **4** comes ☐
5 estudias ☐ **6** vamos a hacer ☐ **7** salimos ☐ **8** va a ser ☐

(C) **Match the Spanish time expression to its English meaning. Then decide whether the Spanish phrases can be used with the present or future or both and write P, F or PF.**

1	normalmente	k	**a**	today	
2	generalmente		**b**	tonight	
3	hoy		**c**	in the afternoon	
4	por la mañana		**d**	generally	
5	por la tarde		**e**	this afternoon	
6	este fin de semana		**f**	tomorrow	
7	esta noche		**g**	next week	
8	esta tarde		**h**	every day	
9	la semana que viene		**i**	in the morning	
10	mañana		**j**	at weekends	
11	los fines de semana		**k**	~~normally~~	P
12	todos los días		**l**	this weekend	

(D) **Complete the sentences with a verb in the correct tense.**

1 Normalmente salgo con mis amigos. **3** Este fin de semana ______
2 Hoy ______ **4** Por la mañana ______

10 diez

(A) I go out; I'm going to do; I play, jugar; voy, I'm going to chat; a; va a; vamos a bailar

(B) **1** P **2** P **3** F **4** P **5** P **6** F **7** P **8** F

(C) **1** k P; **2** d P; **3** a PF; **4** i PF; **5** c PF; **6** l F; **7** b F; **8** e F; **9** g F; **10** f F; **11** j P; **12** h P

3 ¿Te gustaría ir a la bolera? (Pupil's Book pages 28–29)

Learning objectives

- Inviting someone to go out
- Adding expression to your spoken Spanish

Framework objectives

1.3/Y8 Listening – (a) understanding language for specific functions
1.3/Y8 Speaking – (b) using language for specific functions
1.5/Y8 Speaking – (b) using simple idioms

Grammar

- Using prepositions (including *a* + *el* = *al*, *de* + *el* = *del*)
- *¿Te gustaría... ?* + the infinitive

Key language

¿Te gustaría... ?
... ir al parque
... ir a la bolera
... ir de compras
¿A qué hora?
a la una
a las tres
a las cinco y cuarto
a las seis y media
a las siete menos cuarto
a las ocho
a las nueve
¿Dónde quedamos?
delante de la discoteca
detrás del centro comercial
en el parque
en la bolera
en la calle
en tu casa
De acuerdo.
Vale.
Muy bien.
No tengo ganas.
¡Ni hablar!
¡Ni en sueños!
Bueno.../Pues.../A ver...
Hasta luego.
Adiós.
Hasta pronto.

High-frequency words

el, la, las
a (al)
de (del)
en
te
tu
y
muy
no
bueno
¿dónde?
¿qué?
ir
menos

Cross-curricular

English: Prepositions; Recognising the features of different text types
ICT: Internet research

Resources

CD1, tracks 28–30
Cuadernos A & B, p. 14

Teacher Presentations

Screen 1 – Module 2 overview
Screen 2 – p. 28 ex. 1
Screen 3 – p. 28 ex. 2
Screen 4 – p. 29 ex. 3
Screen 5 – Game

Starter 1 ▸▸ 5.4 ◂◂

Aim

To use reading strategies to work out new vocabulary.

Ask pupils to read the text in exercise 1. What is happening? What clues did they use (dialogue format, picture, known vocabulary)?

Then write up the following three questions from the dialogue and give pupils working in pairs two minutes to work out what they mean. *¿Te gustaría... ?, ¿A qué hora?, ¿Dónde quedamos?*

Check answers, asking pupils how they worked out this new vocabulary.

Suggestion

Use a soft toy or item of similar size and put it in various positions in the classroom to illustrate: 'in', 'in front of', 'behind'. Ask pupils to say in English where the toy is. What kind of words are 'in', 'in front of', 'behind'? Ask what prepositions do in a sentence. (show position or relationship) Can pupils think of any others in English?

Ask the Spanish for 'in', 'in front of', 'behind' and write it up: *en, delante de, detrás de*. Add *a* and get pupils to translate this preposition too.

1 Escucha y lee el diálogo. (AT1.4) ▸▸ 1.3a/Y8 ◂◂

Listening. Pupils listen to the dialogue, following the text at the same time in the book.

Audioscript Track 28

– *Hola, Rico, ¿qué tal?*
– *Muy bien, ¿y tú?*
– *Muy bien. Oye, ¿te gustaría ir al estadio el jueves?*
– *Muy bien. ¿A qué hora?*
– *Bueno... a las tres.*
– *¿Dónde quedamos?*

- *Delante del estadio.*
- *Hasta luego.*
- *Hasta luego.*

Ask pupils what they notice about the expression *¿Te gustaría... ?* (followed by an infinitive) (You could point out the link to *me gusta/¿te gusta?*)

Summarise the point using the tip box on page 28.

Pupils come up with examples of invitations using *¿Te gustaría... ?* and as many different verbs as they can.

Suggestion

Read through the key language box as a class. To consolidate the expressions, use the language in the left-hand column (e.g. *¿Te gustaría ir... ?* or *¿A qué hora?*) for pupils to respond with an example from the right-hand column (e.g. *a la bolera* or *a las ocho*). A good class could aim to come up with responses not included in the key language box.

2 Escucha y rellena la tabla en inglés. (1–6) (AT1.4) ▸▸1.3a/Y8 1.5b/Y8◂◂

Listening. Pupils copy the table. They listen to the recording and complete the table in English.

Audioscript Track 29

1 – *¿Te gustaría ir a la bolera el martes?*
– ***Vale.*** *¿A qué hora?*
– *A las siete menos cuarto.*
– *¿Dónde quedamos?*
– *En la bolera.*
– ***Hasta luego.***
– ***Hasta luego.***

2 – *¿Te gustaría ir de compras el viernes?*
– ***De acuerdo.*** *¿A qué hora?*
– *A las ocho.*
– *¿Dónde quedamos?*
– *Detrás del centro comercial.*
– ***Adiós.***
– ***Adiós.***

3 – *¿Te gustaría ir al parque el sábado?*
– *¿A qué hora?*
– ***Pues...*** *a las tres.*
– *¿Dónde quedamos?*
– *En la calle.*
– ***Hasta pronto.***
– ***Hasta pronto.***

4 – *¿Te gustaría ir a la bolera el lunes?*
– ***¡Ni hablar!***
– *Pues... ¿te gustaría ir al salón recreativo?*
– ***Bueno.*** *¿A qué hora?*
– *A las seis y cuarto.*
– *¿Dónde quedamos?*
– *En tu casa.*
– ***Hasta luego.***
– ***Hasta luego.***

5 – *¡Hola, Roberto! ¿Qué tal?*
– *Muy bien, gracias.*
– *¿Te gustaría ir a la discoteca el jueves?*
– ***De acuerdo.*** *¿A qué hora?*
– ***A ver...*** *a las nueve.*
– *¿Dónde quedamos?*
– *Delante de la discoteca.*
– ***Hasta luego.***
– ***Hasta luego.***

6 – *¡Hola, Alfredo! ¿Qué tal?*
– *Bien, gracias.*
– ***Oye...*** *¿te gustaría ir de compras el miércoles?*
– ***¡Ni en sueños!*** *Odio ir de compras.*
– *¿Y al cine?*
– *No,* ***no tengo ganas.***
– ***¿Pues...*** *te gustaría ir al estadio?*
– ***Vale,*** *¿quedamos el miércoles a las siete?*
– *Sí, ¿dónde quedamos?*
– *En tu casa.*

Answers

	Place to go/activity	Day	Time to meet	Place to meet
1	*bowling alley*	*Tuesday*	*6:45*	*in bowling alley*
2	go shopping	Friday	8:00	behind the shopping centre
3	park	Saturday	3:00	in the street
4	amusement arcade	Monday	6:15	in your house
5	disco	Thursday	9:00	in front of the disco
6	estadio	Wednesday	7.00	in your house

Gramática: prepositions

This lists useful prepositions and reminds pupils that *a + el = al* and *de + el = del*.

 Get pupils to research on the internet new vocabulary for things to do in the city, by keying in *¿Qué hacer?* plus the name of a Spanish city. Set them the goal of finding five activities, including three new expressions in Spanish which they can use with *¿Te gustaría... ?*

Starter 2 ▸▸5.2◂◂

Aim

To revise the vocabulary for the days of the week.

Write up all the days of the week as anagrams, e.g. *rensive* (= *viernes*). Give pupils three minutes working in pairs to solve the anagrams and put the words in order. You can decide whether or not to tell them that they are all days of the week: a good class should be able to work it out.

Suggestion

As a class read through the speech bubbles in exercise 3 on page 29. Ask pupils when they would use each set of words (respectively: to accept an invitation, to refuse an invitation, to gain thinking time, to say goodbye).

Can they translate all of the phrases? Encourage them to use reading strategies as usual. You could also read the phrases aloud using expression to help convey the meanings.

3 Escucha otra vez. Escribe las frases que entiendes. (AT1.4)

▸▸ **1.5b/Y8 4.2/Y8** ◂◂

Listening. Pupils listen to the recording from exercise 2 again, this time writing down the phrases they hear.

Point out that using colloquial expressions of the sort introduced in this activity is a good way of sounding authentic in Spanish.

Audioscript Track 30

As for exercise 2.

Answers

*See **bold** in audioscript for exercise 2.*

4 Con tu compañero/a, haz cuatro diálogos. Utiliza las frases de los ejercicios 2 y 3. (AT2.4)

▸▸ **1.3b/Y8 1.4a/Y8 1.5a&b/Y8** ◂◂

Speaking. In pairs: pupils make up four dialogues using the picture prompts supplied and the phrases in exercises 2 and 3.

Remind them to include colloquial expressions and thinking time expressions when taking part in these unscripted dialogues.

If pupils do need support, they should use the dialogue in exercise 1 on page 28 as a model.

5 Lee el texto y dibuja ☺ o ☹ para cada actividad. (AT3.5)

▸▸ **1.5b/Y8 2.3/Y8** ◂◂

Reading. Pupils read the text of an online chat and draw the appropriate symbol (a smiley face or a sad face) to show the opinion expressed of each of the four activities depicted.

Before pupils do the activity, ask them what kind of language they would expect to be used in a chatroom (colloquialisms, nicknames, use of odd spellings for effect), prompting them with options as necessary. After they have done the activity, ask them to identify these features in the text.

You could also use the text to remind pupils of the negative structure *no me gusta nada.*

Answers

1 ☺ 2 ☹ 3 ☹ 4 ☹

6 Escribe un diálogo entre dos personas chateando. Utiliza el ejercicio 5 como modelo. (AT4.4–5)

▸▸ **1.5b/Y8 2.4a/Y8 4.6b/Y8** ◂◂

Writing. Using the text in exercise 5 as a model, pupils write a dialogue between two people chatting online.

Encourage them to include colloquialisms and the negative expression *no... nada.*

Plenary ▸▸ 5.2 5.8 ◂◂

Remind pupils that the Mini-test is an ideal opportunity to check on how they are progressing in each module.

In pairs: give pupils time to read through the bullet points and write a sentence for each, illustrating that they can do all the things listed. They should then swap texts with another pair and check the other pair's work. Ask for examples of mistakes made and take feedback from the class on where pupils should look for help in these areas (where summaries of adjective endings, verb endings, etc., are to be found).

Cuaderno A, page 14

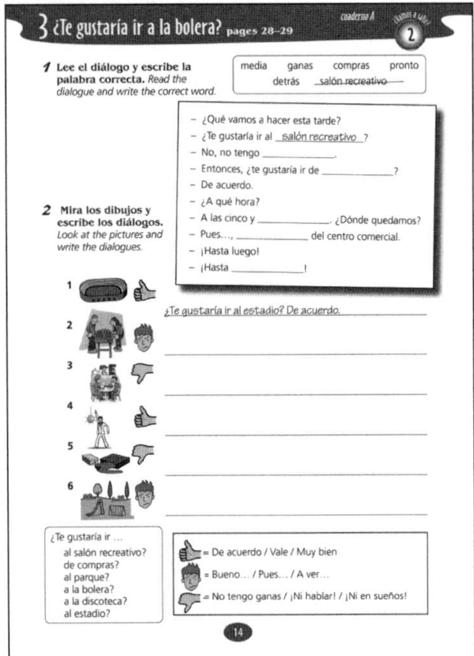

3 ¿Te gustaría ir a la bolera? pages 28–29

1 **Lee el diálogo y escribe la palabra correcta.** *Read the dialogue and write the correct word.*

media ganas compras pronto detrás ~~salón recreativo~~

– ¿Qué vamos a hacer esta tarde?
– ¿Te gustaría ir al *salón recreativo*?
– No, no tengo ______.
– Entonces, ¿te gustaría ir de ______?
– De acuerdo.
– ¿A qué hora?
– A las cinco y ______. ¿Dónde quedamos?
– Pues..., ______ del centro comercial.
– ¡Hasta luego!
– ¡Hasta ______!

2 **Mira los dibujos y escribe los diálogos.** *Look at the pictures and write the dialogues.*

1 *¿Te gustaría ir al estadio? De acuerdo.*
2
3
4
5
6

¿Te gustaría ir ...
al salón recreativo?
de compras?
al parque?
a la bolera?
a la discoteca?
al estadio?

= De acuerdo / Vale / Muy bien
= Bueno... / Pues... / A ver...
= No tengo ganas / ¡Ni hablar! / ¡Ni en sueños!

14

1 (AT3.3, AT4.1)

¿Qué vamos a hacer esta tarde?
¿Te gustaría ir al *salón recreativo*?
No, no tengo ganas.
Entonces, ¿te gustaría ir de compras?
De acuerdo.
¿A qué hora?
A las cinco y media. ¿Dónde quedamos?
Pues..., detrás del centro comercial.
¡Hasta luego!
¡Hasta pronto!

2 (AT4.2)

1. *¿Te gustaría ir al estadio? De acuerdo.*
2. ¿Te gustaría ir al salón recreativo? Bueno... / Pues... / A ver...
3. ¿Te gustaría ir a la cafetería? No tengo ganas / ¡Ni hablar!/¡Ni en sueños!
4. ¿Te gustaría ir a la discoteca? De acuerdo / Vale / Muy bien.
5. ¿Te gustaría ir de compras? No tengo ganas /¡Ni hablar! /¡Ni en sueños!
6. ¿Te gustaría ir al parque? Bueno... / Pues... / A ver...

Cuaderno B, page 14

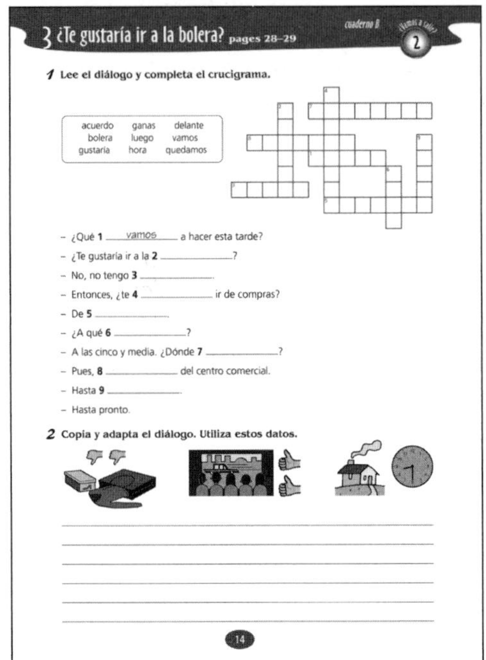

3 ¿Te gustaría ir a la bolera? pages 28–29

1 **Lee el diálogo y completa el crucigrama.**

acuerdo ganas delante
bolera luego vamos
gustaría hora quedamos

– ¿Qué 1 *vamos* a hacer esta tarde?
– ¿Te gustaría ir a la 2 ______?
– No, no tengo 3 ______.
– Entonces, ¿te 4 ______ ir de compras?
– De 5 ______.
– ¿A qué 6 ______?
– A las cinco y media. ¿Dónde 7 ______?
– Pues, 8 ______ del centro comercial.
– Hasta 9 ______.
– Hasta pronto.

2 **Copia y adapta el diálogo. Utiliza estos datos.**

14

1 (AT3.3, AT4.1)

1 *vamos* **2** bolera **3** ganas **4** gustaría **5** acuerdo **6** hora **7** quedamos **8** delante **9** luego

2 (AT4.3)

4 No puedo . . . (Pupil's Book pages 30–31)

Learning objectives

- Making excuses
- Using *querer* and *poder*

Framework objectives

4.5/Y8 Language – (b) range of modal verbs

4.6/Y8 Language – (b) range of negatives

Grammar

- *tener/tengo que*
- *poder*
- *querer*

Key language

¿Quieres...?
chatear por internet
ir a la discoteca
ir de compras
jugar a los bolos
jugar al fútbol
salir
ver un partido de fútbol
ver una película
Lo siento, no puedo.
No puedo salir.
¿Por qué?
Porque...
no quiero
no tengo dinero
no tengo tiempo
Tengo que...
hacer mis deberes
lavarme el pelo
ordenar mi dormitorio
pasear al perro

High-frequency words

el, la, los
un, una
mi, mis
a (al)
de
por
porque
luego
después
no
¿por qué?
hacer
ir
jugar
poder
querer
tener (tengo)
ver
más

Cross-curricular

English: Using reference materials

Resources

CD1, tracks 31–33
Cuadernos A & B, p. 15
R & A Pack, Gramática p. 11
Flashcards 21–28

Teacher Presentations

Screen 1 – Module 2 overview
Screen 2 – Vocabulary: Flashcards
Screen 3 – p. 30 ex. 1
Screen 4 – p. 30 ex. 2
Screen 5 – p. 31 exs 4 & 5

Starter 1 5.4

Aim

To introduce the concept of non-literal meanings. To use reading strategies to work out new language.

Write up the following and give pupils two minutes working in pairs to translate it into English.

– *¿Quieres salir el viernes?*
– *No puedo salir. No tengo tiempo. Tengo que hacer mis deberes.*

Check answers, asking pupils how they worked out that *tengo que* was not translated *I have that*. How did they work out what it meant?

Suggestion

Use Flashcards 21–28 to introduce excuses for turning down an invitation. Start with 25–28, then move on to the cards featuring *tengo que.*

Write up *Tengo un perro* and *Tengo que pasear al perro* and ask pupils to translate these. Explain that, as pupils saw in Starter 1, in certain contexts some words don't have the literal meaning they would expect. This can be confusing: suggest they note down examples of these as they come across them and make a point of learning them as separate vocabulary items.

1 Escucha. ¿Quién habla? Escribe el nombre. (1–8) (AT1.2) 4.5b/Y8 4.6a/Y8

Listening. Pupils listen and use the pictures with speech bubbles to identify the person turning down the invitation in each conversation.

Audioscript Track 31

1 – *¿Quieres salir?*
– *No. Tengo que pasear al perro.*
2 – *¿Quieres salir?*
– *No. Tengo que hacer mis deberes.*
3 – *¿Quieres salir?*
– *Hmm... No. Tengo que ordenar mi dormitorio.*
4 – *¿Quieres salir?*
– *Pues no... tengo que lavarme el pelo.*
5 – *¿Quieres salir?*
– *No, no tengo tiempo.*
6 – *¿Quieres salir mañana?*
– *No, no quiero.*
7 – *¿Quieres salir este fin de semana?*
– *No, lo siento, no puedo.*
8 – *¿Quieres salir esta tarde?*
– *Lo siento mucho, pero no tengo dinero.*

Answers

1 Antonio **2** Carolina **3** Sergio **4** Rosa **5** María **6** Sergio **7** Alejandro **8** Eduardo

R Pupils work in pairs: one prompts with a name (e.g. *Sergio*), the other responds with the appropriate excuse (e.g. *No quiero*). More able pupils could play this as a memory game, with their books closed.

Gramática: *tener / tener que* + infinitive

This contrasts the verb *tener* ('to have') and the phrase *tener que* + infinitive ('to have to'). There is practice on this on page 130 of the Pupil's Book.

+ Pupils in pairs see how many other excuses they can come up with using *tener que*.

2 Escucha y rellena la tabla en inglés. (1–6) (AT1.3) ▸▸4.5b/Y8 4.6a/Y8◂◂

Listening. Pupils copy out the grid. They listen to the six conversations and fill in the details in the grid in English. In 5 and 6 two excuses are given.

Audioscript Track 32

1
- *¿Quieres jugar al fútbol, Pepe?*
- *Lo siento, no puedo jugar al fútbol.*
- *¿Por qué?*
- *Porque tengo que pasear al perro.*

2
- *¿Quieres ver una película, Lola?*
- *No, lo siento mucho, no puedo. Tengo que ordenar mi dormitorio.*
- *Chica, ¡ven! ¡Qué aburrida eres!*

3
- *¿Quieres chatear por internet más tarde?*
- *Lo siento, no puedo chatear por internet. No tengo tiempo.*
- *Qué pena.*

4
- *¿Quieres jugar a los bolos con nosotros?*
- *Lo siento. No puedo jugar a los bolos. Tengo que lavarme el pelo. Y además no me gusta jugar a los bolos.*

5
- *¿Quieres ver un partido de fútbol en el estadio, Julio?*
- *Lo siento. No puedo, no tengo tiempo y no tengo dinero.*

6
- *¿Quieres ir a la discoteca este fin de semana?*
- *No. No puedo ir a la discoteca.*
- *¿Por qué?*
- *Porque tengo que hacer mis deberes y tengo que ordenar mi dormitorio. Lo siento.*

Answers

	Activity	Excuse
1	*football*	*has to walk dog*
2	film	has to tidy bedroom
3	chat online	doesn't have time
4	bowling	has to wash hair
5	football match	has no time, has no money
6	disco	has to do homework, has to tidy bedroom

R Pupils working in pairs use their completed grids as a prompt to produce the appropriate questions and answers in Spanish. e.g. *football/has to walk dog.*

P1 *¿Quieres jugar al fútbol?*
P2 *No puedo jugar al fútbol. Tengo que pasear al perro.*

With a less able class, pupils could respond just with *No puedo…* , leaving out the details of the excuse.

3 Con tu compañero/a, haz diálogos. (AT2.3) ▸▸1.4b/Y8 4.5b/Y8 4.6a/Y8◂◂

Speaking. In pairs: pupils make up dialogues, taking it in turn to give an invitation and to refuse it, giving a reason. Draw their attention to the box on *¿por qué?/porque* before they start.

Starter 2 ▸▸5.1◂◂

Aim
To reintroduce the concept of stem-changing verbs.

Write up the following and give pupils working in pairs two minutes to choose the correct verb form for each person and to translate the verbs into English. Make sure they know the infinitive form of the verb and what it means before they start.

juego / jugo
juegas / jugas
juega / juga
juegamos / jugamos
juegáis / jugáis
juegan / jugan

Check answers, asking pupils to summarise which persons of a stem-changing verb change in the present tense.

Suggestion

Explain that while the same persons of a stem-changing verb always change, the actual letters used vary. The letters used depend on the vowel in the infinitive: so, for example, *jugar* → *ue*, *despertarse* → *ie*. Explain that this lesson is going to focus on two more very important stem-changing verbs, *querer* ('to want') and *poder* ('to be able'), and then cover these using the Gramática box on page 31. Ask pupils to summarise the letter change in each.

Gramática: *poder/querer*

This gives the full paradigms of the stem-changing verbs *poder* ('to be able') and *querer* ('to want') and shows how they are usually followed by an infinitive. There is practice on this on page 129 of the Pupil's Book.

4 Escucha y canta. (AT1.4)

▸▸ 2.2a/Y8 4.5b/Y8 4.6a/Y8 ◂◂

Listening. Pupils listen to the song, following the words at the same time in their books. Play the recording again, this time getting pupils to sing along.

Ask pupils how they worked out what *una peli* means.

Audioscript Track 33

¿Por qué?

¿Por qué siempre me dices 'no'?
'No, no puedo',
'No, no quiero',
'No tengo dinero'.

¿Te gustaría ir a la playa
el lunes por la noche?
'Creo que no, lo siento,
porque hoy hace mucho viento.'

¿Por qué siempre me dices 'no'?
'No, no puedo',
'No, no quiero',
'No tengo dinero'.

¿Quieres ver una peli
el martes a las cuatro?
'Lo siento, odio el cine.
Sólo me gusta el teatro.'

¿Por qué siempre me dices 'no'?
'No, no puedo',
'No, no quiero',
'No tengo dinero'.

¿Este fin de semana
quieres ir al balneario?
'No, quiero ver la televisión
y tengo que ordenar el salón.'

¿Por qué siempre me dices 'no'?
'No, no puedo',
'No, no quiero',
'No tengo dinero'.

¿Te gustaría ir de compras
el miércoles a las tres?
'No tengo dinero, pero vale,
si me compras un pastel.'

¿Por qué siempre me dices 'no'?
'No, no puedo',
'No, no quiero',
'No tengo dinero'.

5 Busca estas frases en español en la canción. (AT3.4) ▸▸ 5.4 ◂◂

Reading. Pupils reread the text of the song and find the Spanish for the six English expressions listed.

Answers

1	*No, no puedo.*	**4**	Lo siento.
2	Odio el cine.	**5**	No tengo dinero.
3	No, no quiero.	**6**	Tengo que ordenar el salón.

6 No quieres salir. Inventa la excusa más larga. (AT4.4) ▸▸ 2.5/Y8 4.5b/Y8 4.6a/Y8 ◂◂

Writing. Pupils imagine they are refusing an invitation. To make it clear that they really don't want to go out, they need to write out the longest excuse they can, listing all the possible things that prevent them accepting. Encourage them to use a dictionary to look up other excuses.

Plenary ▸▸ 5.1 ◂◂

Ask the class to tell you what stem-changing verbs are and to give the two examples introduced in the unit. You could go on to test a more able class on the different persons of *querer* and *poder*.

To review the language for excuses put the class into teams. Teams take it in turn to play against the clock. Each team appoints a prompter, who shows his/her team Flashcards 21–28 one at a time. The other members of the team take it in turn to give the correct Spanish expression. Pupils have the option of saying 'pass' and getting the next flashcard as a prompt. Time the team: how long does it take them to identify all the flashcards? Then it is the next team's turn. Can they beat the time?

Cuaderno A, page 15

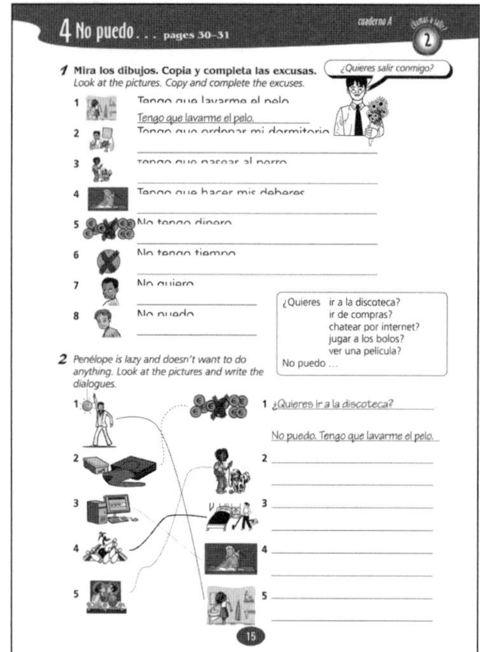
4 No puedo... pages 30–31
cuaderno A
¿Vamos a salir? 2

1 **Mira los dibujos. Copia y completa las excusas.**
Look at the pictures. Copy and complete the excuses.

¿Quieres salir conmigo?

1 Tengo que lavarme el pelo
Tengo que lavarme el pelo.
2 Tengo que ordenar mi dormitorio
3 Tengo que pasear al perro
4 Tengo que hacer mis deberes
5 No tengo dinero
6 No tengo tiempo
7 No quiero
8 No puedo

¿Quieres ir a la discoteca?
ir de compras?
chatear por internet?
jugar a los bolos?
ver una película?
No puedo ...

2 *Penélope is lazy and doesn't want to do anything. Look at the pictures and write the dialogues.*

1 *¿Quieres ir a la discoteca?*
No puedo. Tengo que lavarme el pelo.
2
3
4
5

15

1 (AT4.2)

1. *Tengo que lavarme el pelo.*
2. Tengo que ordenar mi dormitorio.
3. Tengo que pasear al perro.
4. Tengo que hacer mis deberes.
5. No tengo dinero.
6. No tengo tiempo.
7. No quiero.
8. No puedo.

2 (AT4.3)

1. *¿Quieres ir a la discoteca? No puedo. Tengo que lavarme el pelo.*
2. ¿Quieres ir de compras? No puedo. No tengo dinero.
3. ¿Quieres chatear por internet? No puedo. Tengo que hacer mis deberes.
4. ¿Quieres jugar a los bolos? No puedo. Tengo que ordenar mi dormitorio.
5. ¿Quieres ver una película? No puedo. Tengo que pasear al perro.

Cuaderno B, page 15

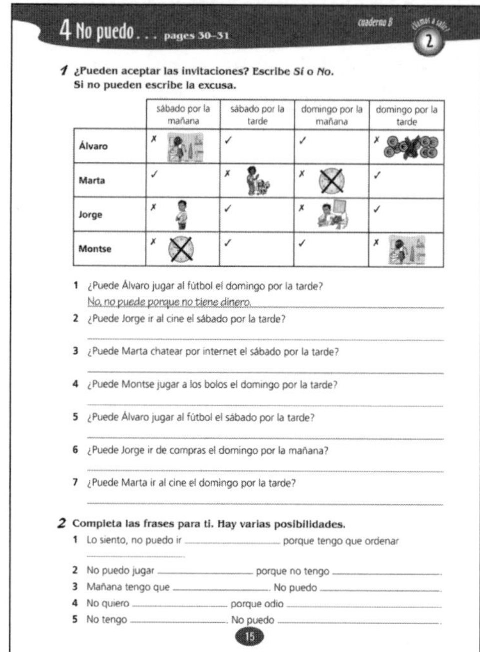
4 No puedo... pages 30–31
cuaderno B
¿Vamos a salir? 2

1 **¿Pueden aceptar las invitaciones? Escribe *Sí* o *No*. Si no pueden escribe la excusa.**

	sábado por la mañana	sábado por la tarde	domingo por la mañana	domingo por la tarde
Álvaro	✗	✓	✓	✗
Marta	✓	✗	✗	✓
Jorge	✗	✓	✗	✓
Montse	✗	✓	✓	✗

1 ¿Puede Álvaro jugar al fútbol el domingo por la tarde?
No, no puede porque no tiene dinero.
2 ¿Puede Jorge ir al cine el sábado por la tarde?
3 ¿Puede Marta chatear por internet el sábado por la tarde?
4 ¿Puede Montse jugar a los bolos el domingo por la tarde?
5 ¿Puede Álvaro jugar al fútbol el sábado por la tarde?
6 ¿Puede Jorge ir de compras el domingo por la mañana?
7 ¿Puede Marta ir al cine el domingo por la tarde?

2 **Completa las frases para ti. Hay varias posibilidades.**
1 Lo siento, no puedo ir ______ porque tengo que ordenar ______.
2 No puedo jugar ______ porque no tengo ______.
3 Mañana tengo que ______. No puedo ______.
4 No quiero ______ porque odio ______.
5 No tengo ______. No puedo ______.

15

1 (AT3.3, AT4.3)

1. *No, no puede porque no tiene dinero.*
2. Sí.
3. No, no puede porque tiene que pasear al perro.
4. No, no puede porque tiene que lavarse el pelo.
5. Sí.
6. No, no puede porque tiene que ordenar su dormitorio.
7. Sí.

2 (AT4.3)

R & A Pack, Gramática page 11

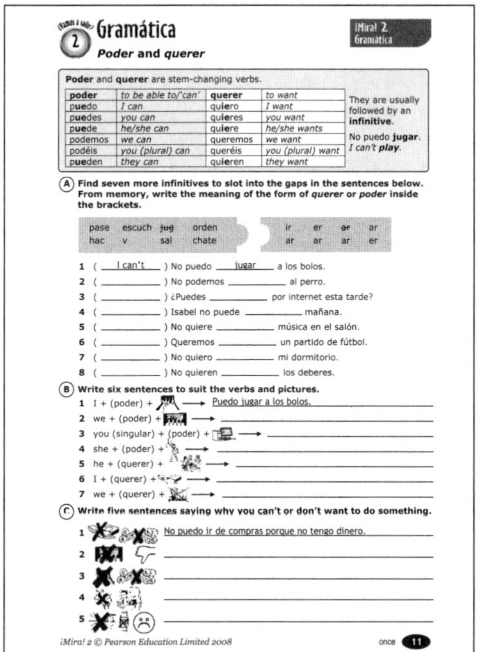

¿Vamos a salir? 2 Gramática

¡Mira! 2 Gramática

Poder* and *querer

Poder and **querer** are stem-changing verbs.

poder	*to be able to/'can'*	**querer**	*to want*
puedo	*I can*	quiero	*I want*
puedes	*you can*	quieres	*you want*
puede	*he/she can*	quiere	*he/she wants*
podemos	*we can*	queremos	*we want*
podéis	*you (plural) can*	queréis	*you (plural) want*
pueden	*they can*	quieren	*they want*

They are usually followed by an **infinitive**.

No puedo **jugar**. *I can't **play**.*

(A) Find seven more infinitives to slot into the gaps in the sentences below. From memory, write the meaning of the form of *querer* or *poder* inside the brackets.

pase escuch ~~jug~~ orden hac v sal chate | ir er ~~ar~~ ar ar ar ar er

1 (I can't) No puedo jugar a los bolos.
2 (______) No podemos ______ al perro.
3 (______) ¿Puedes ______ por internet esta tarde?
4 (______) Isabel no puede ______ mañana.
5 (______) No quiere ______ música en el salón.
6 (______) Queremos ______ un partido de fútbol.
7 (______) No quiero ______ mi dormitorio.
8 (______) No quieren ______ los deberes.

(B) Write six sentences to suit the verbs and pictures.

1 I + (poder) + → Puedo jugar a los bolos.
2 we + (poder) + → ______
3 you (singular) + (poder) + → ______
4 she + (poder) + → ______
5 he + (querer) + → ______
6 I + (querer) + → ______
7 we + (querer) + → ______

(C) Write five sentences saying why you can't or don't want to do something.

1 No puedo ir de compras porque no tengo dinero.
2 ______
3 ______
4 ______
5 ______

¡Mira! 2 © Pearson Education Limited 2008 once 11

(A) **2** pasear **3** chatear **4** salir **5** escuchar **6** ver **7** ordenar **8** hacer
2 We can't **3** Can you? **4** can't **5** He/she doesn't want **6** We want **7** I don't want **8** They don't want

(B) **2** Podemos ir al cine. **3** Puedes chatear por internet. **4** Puede ir a la discoteca. **5** Quiere jugar al fútbol. **6** Quiero ir de compras. **7** No queremos hacer los deberes.

(C) **2** No quiero ir al cine porque no me gusta.
3 No puedo jugar a los bolos porque no tengo dinero.
4 No puedo pasear al perro porque tengo que ordenar mi dormitorio.
5 No quiero ir a la playa porque no tengo tiempo y no me gusta tomar el sol.

5 Tengo un problema (Pupil's Book pages 32–33)

Learning objectives

- Saying what someone else likes or dislikes
- Using phrases with infinitives

Framework objectives

2.2/Y8 Reading – (b) personal response to text
4.5/Y8 Language – (b) range of modal verbs

Grammar

- Expressions + infinitive (*me gustaría*, etc.)
- *A (Sergio) (no) le gusta...*
- Possessive adjectives (*mi(s)/tu(s)/su(s)*)

Key language

Tengo un problema.
¿Qué voy a hacer?
Mi madre es muy severa.
Me gusta así.
Mi padre dice que ...
Soy demasiado joven.
¿Qué le puedo decir a mi madre?
Tienes que hablar con tus padres.
Es tu responsabilidad.
Estoy de acuerdo con tu padre.
Eres demasiado joven para ir a la discoteca.
Tienes que pensar en tu hermano.
Tienes que presentar el amigo a tu madre.
Tienes que salir más.

High-frequency words

el, la
me
mi, mis, tu, tus
a
de
en
muy
que
con
para
¿qué?
hablar
hacer
estar (estoy)
ir (voy)
ser (soy, eres, es)
tener (tengo, tienes)
más

Cross-curricular

English: Possessive adjectives; Using reference materials; Recognising the features of different text types

Resources

CD1, track 34
Cuadernos A & B, p. 16
R & A Pack, Gramática p. 12

Teacher Presentations

Screen 1 – Module 2 overview
Screen 2 – p. 32 ex. 1
Screen 3 – Game
Screen 4 – Video

Suggestion ▸▸2.2b/Y8◂◂

Give pupils an opportunity to show their personal responses to the texts. Ask them which characters they sympathise with and why.

Starter 1 ▸▸4.5b/Y8◂◂

Aim

To revise expressions followed by the infinitive.

Write up: *me gusta, tengo que, puedo, quiero, voy a*

Ask pupils what all these verbs have in common (all followed by the infinitive). Give pupils three minutes working in pairs to come up with a sentence using each verb plus an infinitive. (You could add a range of infinitives to choose from if pupils need support.)

Suggestion

Give pupils one minute to skim-read the text in exercise 1. Ask them to summarise what it is about, prompting them as necessary to come up with the key features: what do all the negative words show? – disagreement; What does Sergio want to do? (*concierto de Shakira*) What does his mother want him to do? (*Vamos a la ópera*) What do the near future tense verbs show? – what Sergio promises to do if allowed to go out.

Point out that it is not necessary to understand all the detail to work out what is going on and that it is a useful skill to be able to pick out key words.

1 Escucha y lee. (AT1.5) ▸▸2.2b/Y8 4.5b/Y8 5.4◂◂

Listening. Pupils listen to the conversation between Sergio and his mother, reading the text at the same time. Some vocabulary support is given.

Audioscript Track 34

– *Mamá, me gustaría ir al concierto de Shakira y luego a la discoteca. ¿Tienes 20 euros?*
– *Pero Sergio, hoy vamos a la ópera. Tu hermana es la cantante principal.*
– *Mamá, ¡ni en sueños! No me gusta nada la ópera. Es muy aburrida. No puedo ir. Sólo me gusta la música moderna. Quiero salir con mis amigos y bailar. Me gusta mucho bailar.*
– *Lo siento, Sergio, pero tienes que ir a la ópera.*
– *Mamá, por favor, odio hacer muchas cosas en casa pero esta semana voy a ordenar el dormitorio y también voy a hacer mis deberes.*
– *Eso es fantástico, en tal caso puedes...*
– *¡Qué guay! ¡Gracias, mamá!*
– *... hacer los deberes ahora, pero tienes que ir a la ópera luego.*
– *Pero, mamá, por favor...*

R Read through the tip box on expressions followed by the infinitive as a class. Ask pupils to read through the text in exercise 1 again and identify all instances of these expressions + infinitive (e.g. *me gustaría ir*).

2 Con tu compañero/a, lee el diálogo. (AT2.5) ⏩5.6⏪

Speaking. In pairs pupils read through the dialogue in exercise 1, playing the part of Sergio or Mamá.

Gramática: *le gusta*

This introduces using *le gusta* with an infinitive or a singular noun to say what someone likes/dislikes. It also shows how to make it clear who you are talking about by using *a* + a name. There is practice on this on page 134 of the Pupil's Book.

Introduce *le gustan* with plural nouns by asking pupils to translate into Spanish 'Ana doesn't like films'.

3 Con tu compañero/a, pregunta y contesta. (AT2.4)
⏩1.4a/Y8 4.6a&b/Y8⏪

Speaking. In pairs: pupils work through the five questions about the conversation in exercise 1, taking it in turn to ask and answer them. Read through the example together and point out that they must answer in full sentences.

Starter 2 ⏩4.5b/Y8⏪

Aim
To practise using *le gusta* + infinitive and *le gusta(n)* + noun.

Write up the following sentences in jumbled order (correct version given in brackets for reference) and give pupils working in pairs three minutes to write them in the correct order.

1 *los le perros a Sergio gustan*
(A Sergio le gustan los perros.)
2 *no mensajes a le Paz gusta mandar*
(A Paz no le gusta mandar mensajes.)
3 *Shakira gusta no le la de música*
(No le gusta la música de Shakira.)
4 *el gusta a ordenador mucho jugar con Diego le*
(A Diego le gusta mucho jugar con el ordenador.)

Check answers, getting pupils to translate the sentences. Ask them to summarise how *le gusta* is used with verbs and with nouns.

4 Empareja los problemas con los consejos de Tatiana. (AT3.5)
⏩2.2a/Y8 5.4⏪

Reading. Pupils read the problem page texts and match each of the three letters with the most appropriate piece of advice. There is one piece of advice too many. Some vocabulary support is given.

Answers
1 b **2** d **3** c

5 Lee los textos otra vez. Busca estas frases en español. (AT3.5)
⏩4.2/Y8 5.3⏪

Reading. Pupils read the problem page texts again and find the Spanish for the eight English sentences listed.

After pupils have done the activity, point out how useful texts like these are as a source of vocabulary. All the key vocabulary in each module is listed in the Palabras section at the end of the module, but it is also important for pupils to add to this core language other phrases which will make their speaking and writing more fluent. Suggest they note down a phrase from each text (e.g. *no salgo mucho, soy demasiado joven*, etc.) to learn. Remind them when noting down new vocabulary that it is useful to cross-check it in a dictionary, to make sure they note correctly the type of word it is (noun, verb, etc.), the gender of the word (if it is a noun), the masculine form (if it is an adjective), etc. Review as necessary the standard abbreviations used for this information in a dictionary (*n, m, f, vt, vi, adj, conj, prep*, etc.). The Estrategia feature in the Palabras section (page 41) contains a useful summary of this advice.

Answers
1 ¿Qué voy a hacer?
2 Mis padres dicen que tengo que salir más.
3 Tu vida es un poco triste.
4 ¿Qué le puedo decir a mi madre?
5 ¡No es justo!
6 Tengo un problema.

R Use the texts for translation practice: go round the class, with each person translating a sentence.

Gramática: Possessive adjectives

This covers the words for 'my', 'your' (singular) and 'his/her'. Point out these adjectives have just one form in the singular and one in the plural.

6 Describe un problema. Utiliza los textos como modelos. (AT4.4–5)

▶▶2.2b/Y8 2.4a/Y8◀◀

Writing. Using the letters in exercise 4 as models, pupils write a letter describing a problem. Encourage them to include possessive adjectives in their texts, checking the forms as necessary in the Gramática box.

➕ Pupils swap letters with a partner and write a response, giving advice on the problem. In this they should aim to include different forms of the possessive adjective.

Plenary ▶▶4.5b/Y8◀◀

Ask pupils to explain how to say 'he/she likes' in Spanish, followed by a verb and by a noun.

Give pupils working in pairs one minute for each to come up with a statement about what his/her partner likes (e.g. *A Hannah le gusta bailar* or *A Hannah le gustan los gatos*). Go round the class with each person giving their statement.

Cuaderno A, page 16

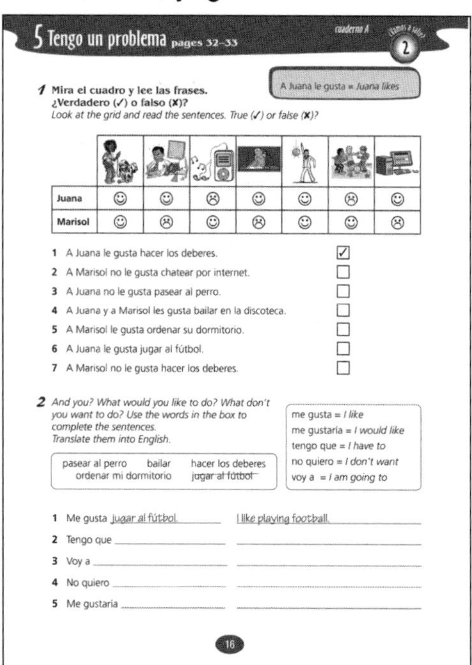

5 Tengo un problema pages 32–33 cuaderno A ¿Vamos a salir? 2

1 Mira el cuadro y lee las frases. ¿Verdadero (✓) o falso (✗)?
Look at the grid and read the sentences. True (✓) or false (✗)?

A Juana le gusta = *Juana likes*

Juana	☺	☺	☹	☺	☺	☹	☺
Marisol	☺	☹	☺	☹	☺	☺	☹

1 A Juana le gusta hacer los deberes. ☑
2 A Marisol no le gusta chatear por internet. ☐
3 A Juana no le gusta pasear al perro. ☐
4 A Juana y a Marisol les gusta bailar en la discoteca. ☐
5 A Marisol le gusta ordenar su dormitorio. ☐
6 A Juana le gusta jugar al fútbol. ☐
7 A Marisol no le gusta hacer los deberes. ☐

2 *And you? What would you like to do? What don't you want to do? Use the words in the box to complete the sentences.*
Translate them into English.

pasear al perro bailar hacer los deberes ordenar mi dormitorio ~~jugar al fútbol~~

me gusta = *I like*
me gustaría = *I would like*
tengo que = *I have to*
no quiero = *I don't want*
voy a = *I am going to*

1 Me gusta jugar al fútbol. I like playing football.
2 Tengo que ______ ______
3 Voy a ______ ______
4 No quiero ______ ______
5 Me gustaría ______ ______

16

1 (AT3.2)

1 ✓ 2 ✓ 3 ✗ 4 ✓ 5 ✗ 6 ✗ 7 ✓

2 (AT4.3)

Cuaderno B, page 16

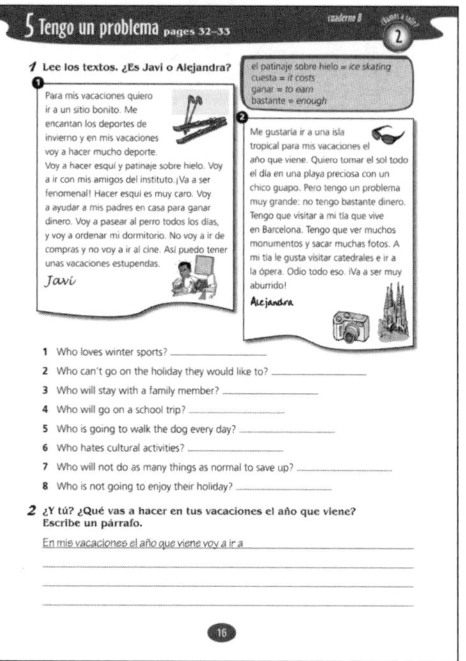

5 Tengo un problema pages 32–33 cuaderno B ¿Vamos a salir? 2

1 Lee los textos. ¿Es Javi o Alejandra?

el patinaje sobre hielo = *ice skating*
cuesta = *it costs*
ganar = *to earn*
bastante = *enough*

❶ Para mis vacaciones quiero ir a un sitio bonito. Me encantan los deportes de invierno y en mis vacaciones voy a hacer mucho deporte. Voy a hacer esquí y patinaje sobre hielo. Voy a ir con mis amigos del instituto. ¡Va a ser fenomenal! Hacer esquí es muy caro. Voy a ayudar a mis padres en casa para ganar dinero. Voy a pasear al perro todos los días, y voy a ordenar mi dormitorio. No voy a ir de compras y no voy a ir al cine. Así puedo tener unas vacaciones estupendas.
Javi

❷ Me gustaría ir a una isla tropical para mis vacaciones el año que viene. Quiero tomar el sol todo el día en una playa preciosa con un chico guapo. Pero tengo un problema muy grande: no tengo bastante dinero. Tengo que visitar a mi tía que vive en Barcelona. Tengo que ver muchos monumentos y sacar muchas fotos. A mi tía le gusta visitar catedrales e ir a la ópera. Odio todo eso. ¡Va a ser muy aburrido!
Alejandra

1 Who loves winter sports? ______
2 Who can't go on the holiday they would like to? ______
3 Who will stay with a family member? ______
4 Who will go on a school trip? ______
5 Who is going to walk the dog every day? ______
6 Who hates cultural activities? ______
7 Who will not do as many things as normal to save up? ______
8 Who is not going to enjoy their holiday? ______

2 ¿Y tú? ¿Qué vas a hacer en tus vacaciones el año que viene? Escribe un párrafo.

En mis vacaciones el año que viene voy a ir a ______

16

1 (AT3.5)

1 Javi **2** Alejandra **3** Alejandra **4** Javi **5** Javi **6** Alejandra **7** Javi **8** Alejandra

2 (AT4.5)

R & A Pack, Gramática page 12

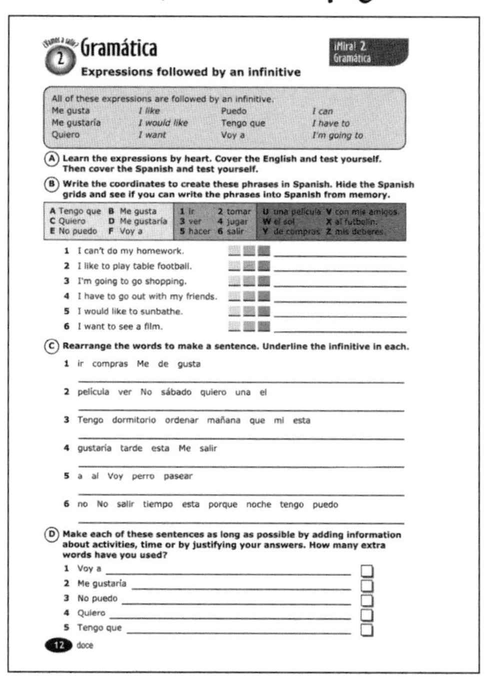

¿Vamos a salir? 2 **Gramática** ¡Mira! 2 Gramática

Expressions followed by an infinitive

All of these expressions are followed by an infinitive.

Me gusta	*I like*	Puedo	*I can*
Me gustaría	*I would like*	Tengo que	*I have to*
Quiero	*I want*	Voy a	*I'm going to*

Ⓐ Learn the expressions by heart. Cover the English and test yourself. Then cover the Spanish and test yourself.

Ⓑ Write the coordinates to create these phrases in Spanish. Hide the Spanish grids and see if you can write the phrases into Spanish from memory.

A Tengo que	**B** Me gusta	**1** ir	**2** tomar	**U** una película	**V** con mis amigos.
C Quiero	**D** Me gustaría	**3** ver	**4** jugar	**W** el sol	**X** al futbolín.
E No puedo	**F** Voy a	**5** hacer	**6** salir	**Y** de compras	**Z** mis deberes.

1 I can't do my homework. ______
2 I like to play table football. ______
3 I'm going to go shopping. ______
4 I have to go out with my friends. ______
5 I would like to sunbathe. ______
6 I want to see a film. ______

Ⓒ Rearrange the words to make a sentence. Underline the infinitive in each.

1 ir compras Me de gusta
2 película ver No sábado quiero una el
3 Tengo dormitorio ordenar mañana que mi esta
4 gustaría tarde esta Me salir
5 a al Voy perro pasear
6 no No salir tiempo esta porque noche tengo puedo

Ⓓ Make each of these sentences as long as possible by adding information about activities, time or by justifying your answers. How many extra words have you used?

1 Voy a ______ ☐
2 Me gustaría ______ ☐
3 No puedo ______ ☐
4 Quiero ______ ☐
5 Tengo que ______ ☐

12 doce

Ⓑ **1** E5Z **2** B4X **3** F1Y **4** A6V **5** D2W **6** C3U

Ⓒ **1** Me gusta <u>ir</u> de compras.
2 No quiero <u>ver</u> una película el sábado.
Tengo que <u>ordenar</u> mi dormitorio esta mañana.
4 Me gustaría <u>salir</u> esta tarde.
5 Voy a <u>pasear</u> al perro.
6 No puedo <u>salir</u> esta noche porque no tengo tiempo.

Resumen y Prepárate (Pupil's Book pages 34–35)

Resumen

This is a checklist of language covered in Module 2. Pupils can work on this in pairs to check what they have learned and remembered. There is a Resumen page in the Resource and Assessment Pack. Encourage them to look back at the module and to use the grammar section, to revise what they are unclear about. You can also use the Resumen as a useful plenary at the end of each unit.

Prepárate

These revision tests can be used for pupils to practise prior to the assessment tasks in the Resource and Assessment Pack.

Resources

CD1, track 35
R & A Pack, Module 2: Resumen, Prueba, I can...

1 Escucha. Copia y rellena la tabla. (1–5) (AT1.4) ▸▸1.1/Y8◂◂

Listening. Pupils copy out the table. They listen to the five conversations and complete the table in English with the details of the arrangements agreed in each (activity, time and place).

Audioscript Track 35

1 – *¿Te gustaría ver un partido de fútbol el jueves?*
– *Vale. ¿Dónde quedamos?*
– *Delante del estadio, ¿no?*
– *Muy bien. Nos vemos.*

2 – *¿Quieres ir al salón recreativo mañana?*
– *Sí, ¿cómo no? A ver... ¿dónde quedamos?*
– *En la calle. A las ocho.*
– *De acuerdo.*

3 – *¿Te gustaría jugar al fútbol esta tarde?*
– *Sí, me gustaría mucho. ¿Dónde quedamos entonces?*
– *En el parque.*
– *Muy bien. Hasta luego.*

4 – *¿Te gustaría ir a la bolera el viernes?*
– *Vale. ¿Dónde quedamos?*
– *En la bolera.*
– *Vale. En la bolera.*

5 – *¿Quieres ir a la discoteca este fin de semana?*
– *Muy bien. ¿Dónde quedamos? ¿Delante de la discoteca?*
– *Sí, delante de la discoteca.*

Answers

	What?	When?	Where?
1	*football match*	*Thursday*	*in front of stadium*
2	amusement arcade	tomorrow/at 8 o'clock	in the street
3	play football	this evening	in the park
4	bowling	Friday	in the bowling alley
5	disco	this weekend	in front of the disco

2 Con tu compañero/a, haz diálogos. (AT2.3) ▸▸1.4b/Y8◂◂

Speaking. In pairs: using the picture prompts supplied, pupils make up dialogues. A sample exchange is given.

3 Pon los dibujos en el orden correcto del texto. (AT3.5) ▸▸2.2a/Y8◂◂

Reading. Pupils read the text, then put the pictures in the order they are mentioned.

Answers

d, f, b, e, c, a

4 Copia y rellena la tabla con los verbos en presente o futuro del ejercicio 3. (AT3.5) ▸▸2.2a/Y8◂◂

Reading. Pupils copy out the table and use it to list all the present tense and near future tense verbs in the text in exercise 3.

Answers

Presente	Futuro
juego	*no voy a jugar*
no hago	voy a ir
tengo	voy a ver
me gusta	no voy a salir
me gusta	voy a estudiar
	voy a chatear
	voy a escuchar
	voy a jugar

5 Describe tu semana. Utiliza las palabras del cuadro (*sequencing words*). (AT4.4) ▸▸4.4/Y8◂◂

Writing. Pupils write a description of their week, incorporating the sequencing words supplied. A sample opening is given.

¡Extra! 1 (Pupil's Book pages 36–37)

Learning objectives

- Talking about a visit to an adventure park
- Taking part in an unscripted dialogue

Framework objectives

1.1/Y8 Listening – understanding on first hearing

1.4/Y8 Speaking – (b) unscripted conversation

Grammar

- Verb + infinitive expressions

Key language

Revision of language from Module 2

High-frequency words

Revision of language from Module 2

Cross-curricular

English: Using reference materials

Resources

CD1, tracks 36–39

Starter ▸▸4.5b/Y8◂◂

Aim

 To revise expressions followed by the infinitive. To revise modal verbs.

Write up:

Followed by infinitive	Not followed by infinitive

odio *me gustaría* *puede* *juega* *queremos* *no puedo* *¿vas a?* *tengo que* *me interesa* *van*

Give pupils two minutes working in pairs to put the words into the appropriate column. How did they work out where *me interesa* went?

1 Escucha y lee. (AT1.4) ▸▸4.5b/Y8 5.3◂◂

Listening. Pupils listen to the radio advert for the Calella adventure park, reading along with the text at the same time. They then make a list of all the cognates in the text.

Check answers, asking pupils to translate all the questions in the text. Point out that looking for cognates is a key reading strategy when tackling harder texts, but that it needs to be used in conjunction with other strategies (e.g. using other clues such as pictures): recognising the cognates *montaña* and *rusa* wouldn't help in translating *montaña rusa*.

Audioscript Track 36

El parque de atracciones de Calella

¿Quieres explorar el mundo perdido del Jurásico?
¿Te gustaría tomar el tren minero?
¿Quieres montar en la montaña rusa?
¿Te interesa practicar las artes circenses?
¿Vas a navegar por los rápidos del Río Rojo?

Answers

el parque = park
atracciones = attractions
explorar = explore
Jurásico = Jurassic
el tren = train
minero = mining
la montaña = mountain
rusa = Russian
interesa = interest
practicar = practise
las artes = arts
circenses = circus
navegar = navigate
los rápidos = rapids

2 Busca los infinitivos en el texto del ejercicio 1. Escríbelos en inglés. (AT3.4) ▸▸4.5b/Y8 5.4◂◂

Reading. Pupils read the advert again. This time they list all the infinitives used in the text and translate them into English. When they have finished, tell them to check their answers using the Vocabulario section at the back of the Pupil's Book.

Answers

explorar = to explore
tomar = to take
montar = to get on
practicar = to practise
navegar = to navigate

3 Escucha el diálogo y pon los dibujos en el orden correcto. (AT1.4) ▸▸1.1/Y8◂◂

Listening. Pupils listen to the dialogue and put the pictures in the order they are mentioned. Warn them that they will hear the recording only once for this activity: what can they do to prepare for this? Give them a minute to look at the pictures shown so they can predict the language that they need to listen out for.

Audioscript Track 37

- *Primero me gustaría mucho practicar las artes circenses Creo que es interesante, ¿y tú?*
- *De acuerdo. Y luego quizás vamos a navegar por los rápidos del Río Rojo.*
- *Ah sí, ¡qué divertido!*
- *¿Y después, quieres montar en la montaña rusa?*
- *No, no, no. ¡Ni en sueños! No me gusta nada eso. No quiero.*
- *Mm, bueno… ¿Quieres explorar el mundo perdido del Jurásico entonces?*
- *Sí, muy bien. Prefiero explorar el mundo perdido porque me encantan los dinosaurios.*
- *¿Más tarde podemos tomar el tren minero?*
- *Por supuesto. También me encantan los trenes.*

Answers

d, e, c, a, b

4 Escucha otra vez. Haz una lista de las opiniones que entiendes. (AT1.4) ▸▸1.2/Y8◂◂

Listening. Pupils listen to the recording for exercise 3 again and note down in Spanish all the phrases the speakers use to say that they like/don't like something.

Audioscript Track 38

As for exercise 3.

Answers

me gustaría mucho	No quiero
es interesante	me encantan
¡qué divertido!	me encantan
no me gusta nada	

5 Con tu compañero/a, planea un día en el parque de atracciones. (AT2.4) ▸▸1.4b/Y8 1.5a/Y8◂◂

Speaking. In pairs: pupils make up a dialogue planning a day at an adventure park. A framework is supplied for support; encourage pupils to familiarise themselves with this and then to close their books and do the dialogue unscripted.

6 Escucha y lee los textos. ¿Verdadero o falso? Escribe V o F. (AT1.5) ▸▸4.5a/Y8◂◂

Listening. Pupils listen to the two descriptions of a day which the speakers are planning to have at an adventure park and follow the text at the same time. They then read the six Spanish sentences on the text and decide whether each is true (V) or false (F).

Audioscript Track 39

- *Primero voy a tomar el tren minero. Luego voy a navegar por los rápidos del Río Rojo. Después voy a explorar el mundo perdido del Jurásico y más tarde me voy a montar en la montaña rusa.*
  Me chiflan los parques de atracciones. Va a ser muy divertido pero no voy a practicar las artes circenses porque ¡no me gusta nada eso!
- *Primero vamos a practicar las artes circenses, ¡qué interesante! Luego vamos a navegar por los rápidos del Río Rojo. Y después vamos a explorar el mundo perdido del Jurásico.*
- *Pero no nos vamos a montar en la montaña rusa. No queremos. Tenemos miedo. Vamos a ir a la cafetería y vamos a comer algo.*

Answers

1 *V* **2** V **3** F **4** F **5** V **6** V

✚ Ask pupils to read the texts in exercise 6 again and to identify the following features:

- negatives (*no, no… nada*)
- connectives (*y, pero, porque*)
- time phrases used for sequencing (*primero, luego, después, más tarde*)
- opinions (*me chiflan, va a ser muy divertido, no me gusta nada, ¡qué interesante!, no queremos*)

7 ¿Qué vas a hacer en el parque de atracciones? Escribe un texto. (AT4.4) ▸▸2.4a/Y8 4.4/Y8◂◂

Writing. Using the texts in exercise 6 as a model, pupils write their own description of what they are going to do at the adventure park. An opening is supplied.

Encourage pupils to write complex sentences using the features they identified as part of exercise 6 (e.g. including reasons with *porque*).

Plenary ▸▸4.5b/Y8◂◂

Ask pupils to recall all the verb + infinitive expressions which were used in the unit (*quieres, ¿te gustaría?*, etc.). Then go round the class prompting with one of the rides at the adventure park. Each pupil has to respond with a sentence or question using one of the verb + infinitive expressions and the ride (e.g. *el tren minero – ¿Quieres tomar el tren minero?*). Encourage more able pupils to use different persons of the verbs.

¡Extra! 2 (Pupil's Book pages 38–39)

Learning objectives
- Reading a story in Spanish
- Practising stem-changing verbs

Key language
Revision of language from Module 2

Cross-curricular
English: Using reference materials

Grammar
- *poder* and *querer* (stem-changing verbs)

High-frequency words
Revision of language from Module 2

Resources
CD1, tracks 40–41
Cuadernos A & B, pp. 17–18

Starter

Aim

To review vocabulary from the module. To recap on grammatical terms.

Draw a grid with the following headings: Verb, Preposition, Possessive Adjective, Connective, Time expression. Ask the class to give you a simple definition of each and a few examples in English and Spanish.

Then put the class into teams. You give a word from the module (e.g. *queremos, delante de, después*) for a pupil to write in the correct column. Each team confers, then sends a member to the front in turn to write the word in the correct column.

Suggestion

To lead into the second episode of the story, ask pupils to recap in English on what they remember of episode 1. Then ask questions in Spanish for pupils to answer as though they were Patricia or Diego, e.g. *Soy mexicana, Soy español,* etc.

1 Escucha y lee. (AT1.4) ▸▸2.1/Y8 5.4◂◂

Listening. Pupils listen to the recording of the story (which in this episode is in the form of an online chat between Patricia and Diego) and read along with the text. Some vocabulary support is given.

Audioscript Track 40

1 – *¡Hola, Patricia! ¿Qué tal?*
– *Bien, gracias, Diego. ¿Y tú? ¿Cómo estás?*

2 – *Muy bien, gracias. Dime, Patricia, ¿te gustaría salir conmigo?*
– *¿Adónde?*

3 – *Pues, no sé, podemos ir a la bolera o quizás a la playa. Tú decides.*

4 – *Me gustaría mucho ir a la playa. Tomo el sol todos los fines de semana.*

5 – *¿Cuándo nos vemos entonces?*
– *¿El viernes por la tarde?*
– *No, Diego. Lo siento, el viernes por la tarde no puedo. Tengo que jugar al fútbol.*

6 – *¿El sábado por la tarde entonces? ¿Está bien?*
– *De acuerdo. Quedamos delante de la estación.*
– *Muy bien. ¡Hasta luego!*

2 Con tu compañero/a, lee en voz alta la historia de Diego y Patricia. (AT2.4) ▸▸5.6◂◂

Speaking. In pairs: pupils read the story aloud, each taking the role of Diego or Patricia. Encourage them to focus on pronunciation and stress and to try and sound as fluent as possible, following the model of the recording.

3 Contesta a las preguntas en español. ¡Cuidado con los verbos! (AT3.4) ▸▸4.5a&b/Y8◂◂

Reading. Pupils answer in Spanish the four comprehension questions on the story. Remind them to use the language of the questions in putting together their answers: they need to think carefully about word order and about verb forms.

Answers

1 *Diego quiere ir a la bolera o a la playa.*
2 Patricia quiere ir a la playa.
3 El viernes por la tarde juega al fútbol.
4 Diego y Patricia van a quedar delante de la estación.

4 Escucha y escribe el verbo correcto. (AT1.2) ▸▸4.5b/Y8 4.6b/Y8◂◂

Listening. Pupils listen to six sentences and select the correct verb from the two options given for each.

Audioscript Track 41

1 *¿**Quieres** salir este fin de semana?*
2 ***No quiero** porque tengo que hacer mis deberes.*
3 *Manuel **quiere** ver una película.*
4 ***Podemos** ir al cine entonces.*
5 *¿**Puedes** mandar un mensaje a Carolina?*
6 *Ay, **no puedo,** mi móvil no funciona.*

Answers

*Also in **bold** in the audioscript.*
1 quieres **2** no quiero **3** quiere **4** podemos
5 puedes **6** no puedo

5 Anita, Miriam, Juan y José quieren salir juntos. ¿Adónde van a ir? Escribe la letra correcta. (AT3.4) ▸▸ 4.5b/Y8 ◂◂

Reading. Pupils read the four texts and identify where the four friends will end up going, using the pictures *a–d*.

Answer

b (la playa)

6 Escribe estas frases en español. (AT4.4) ▸▸ 4.5b/Y8 4.6b/Y8 ◂◂

Writing. Pupils translate the six English sentences into Spanish.

Tell pupils to use the necessary resources to check their answers: a dictionary/the Vocabulario and the Gramática section at the back of the Pupil's Book. Test them to check that they understand the abbreviations used in a dictionary (*n, m, f, vt, vi, adj, conj, prep*, etc.).

Answers

1. *Quiero ir de compras este fin de semana.*
2. Tengo que ir a la playa.
3. Vanesa quiere ir al cine más tarde.
4. Lola no quiere ir a ver el partido de fútbol.
5. Pepe no puede jugar al fútbol el viernes.
6. Norberto puede hacer sus deberes mañana.

Plenary ▸▸ 4.5b/Y8 ◂◂

Put the class into teams for a quiz on the present tense forms of *poder* and *querer*. Team by team, give each pupil a prompt in English (e.g. 'you can') for pupils to give the Spanish translation (e.g. *puedes*). A correct answer wins two points. Pupils can ask you to write up the verb for support, but will then only win one point for a correct answer. The team with the most points wins.

Cuaderno A, page 17

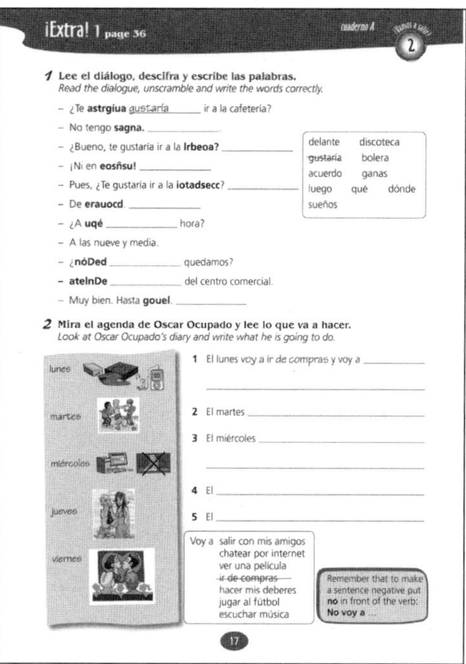

¡Extra! 1 page 36 cuaderno A ¿Vamos a salir? 2

1 Lee el diálogo, descifra y escribe las palabras.
Read the dialogue, unscramble and write the words correctly.

– ¿Te **astrgíua** gustaría ______ ir a la cafetería?
– No tengo **sagna**. ______
– ¿Bueno, te gustaría ir a la **lrbeoa?** ______
– ¡Ni en **eosñsu!** ______
– Pues, ¿Te gustaría ir a la **iotadsecc**? ______
– De **erauocd**. ______
– ¿A **uqé** ______ hora?
– A las nueve y media.
– ¿**nóDed** ______ quedamos?
– **atelnDe** ______ del centro comercial.
– Muy bien. Hasta **gouel**. ______

delante discoteca ~~gustaría~~ bolera acuerdo ganas luego qué dónde sueños

2 Mira el agenda de Oscar Ocupado y lee lo que va a hacer.
Look at Oscar Ocupado's diary and write what he is going to do.

lunes
martes
miércoles
jueves
viernes

1 El lunes *voy a ir de compras* y voy a ______
2 El martes ______
3 El miércoles ______
4 El ______
5 El ______

Voy a salir con mis amigos
chatear por internet
ver una película
~~ir de compras~~
hacer mis deberes
jugar al fútbol
escuchar música

Remember that to make a sentence negative put **no** in front of the verb: **No voy a** ...

17

1 (AT3.3, AT4.1)

1 *gustaría* **2** ganas **3** bolera **4** sueños **5** discoteca **6** acuerdo **7** qué **8** Dónde **9** Delante **10** luego

2 (AT4.2)

1. *El lunes voy a ir de compras y voy a* escuchar música.
2. El martes voy a jugar al fútbol.
3. El miércoles voy a chatear por internet y no voy a hacer los deberes.
4. El jueves voy a salir con mis amigos.
5. El viernes voy a ver una película.

Cuaderno A, page 18

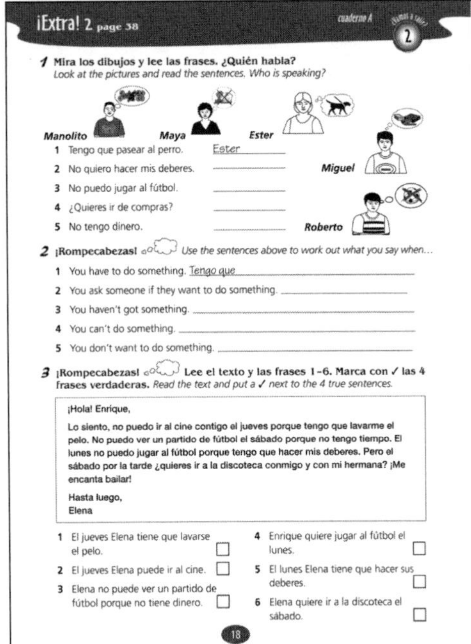

¡Extra! 2 page 38 — cuaderno A — ¿Vamos a salir? 2

1 **Mira los dibujos y lee las frases. ¿Quién habla?**
Look at the pictures and read the sentences. Who is speaking?

Manolito, Maya, Ester, Miguel, Roberto

1 Tengo que pasear al perro. Ester
2 No quiero hacer mis deberes. ______
3 No puedo jugar al fútbol. ______
4 ¿Quieres ir de compras? ______
5 No tengo dinero. ______

2 **¡Rompecabezas!** *Use the sentences above to work out what you say when…*

1 You have to do something. Tengo que ______
2 You ask someone if they want to do something. ______
3 You haven't got something. ______
4 You can't do something. ______
5 You don't want to do something. ______

3 **¡Rompecabezas! Lee el texto y las frases 1–6. Marca con ✓ las 4 frases verdaderas.** *Read the text and put a ✓ next to the 4 true sentences.*

¡Hola! Enrique,

Lo siento, no puedo ir al cine contigo el jueves porque tengo que lavarme el pelo. No puedo ver un partido de fútbol el sábado porque no tengo tiempo. El lunes no puedo jugar al fútbol porque tengo que hacer mis deberes. Pero el sábado por la tarde ¿quieres ir a la discoteca conmigo y con mi hermana? ¡Me encanta bailar!

Hasta luego,
Elena

1 El jueves Elena tiene que lavarse el pelo. ☐
2 El jueves Elena puede ir al cine. ☐
3 Elena no puede ver un partido de fútbol porque no tiene dinero. ☐
4 Enrique quiere jugar al fútbol el lunes. ☐
5 El lunes Elena tiene que hacer sus deberes. ☐
6 Elena quiere ir a la discoteca el sábado. ☐

18

1 (AT3.2)

1 *Ester* **2** Maya **3** Roberto **4** Miguel **5** Manolito

2 (AT4.2)

1 *Tengo que …* **2** ¿Quieres … ? **3** No tengo …
4 No puedo … **5** No quiero …

3 (AT3.3)

1 ✓ **2** ✗ **3** ✗ **4** ✓ **5** ✓ **6** ✓

Cuaderno B, page 17

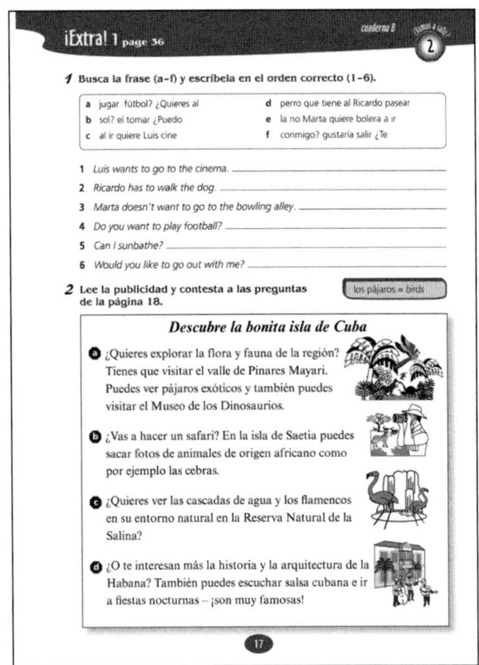

¡Extra! 1 page 36 — cuaderno B — ¿Vamos a salir? 2

1 **Busca la frase (a–f) y escríbela en el orden correcto (1–6).**

a jugar fútbol? ¿Quieres al
b sol? el tomar ¿Puedo
c al ir quiere Luis cine
d perro que tiene al Ricardo pasear
e la no Marta quiere bolera a ir
f conmigo? gustaría salir ¿Te

1 *Luis wants to go to the cinema.* ______
2 *Ricardo has to walk the dog.* ______
3 *Marta doesn't want to go to the bowling alley.* ______
4 *Do you want to play football?* ______
5 *Can I sunbathe?* ______
6 *Would you like to go out with me?* ______

2 **Lee la publicidad y contesta a las preguntas de la página 18.** los pájaros = *birds*

Descubre la bonita isla de Cuba

a ¿Quieres explorar la flora y fauna de la región? Tienes que visitar el valle de Pinares Mayari. Puedes ver pájaros exóticos y también puedes visitar el Museo de los Dinosaurios.

b ¿Vas a hacer un safari? En la isla de Saetia puedes sacar fotos de animales de origen africano como por ejemplo las cebras.

c ¿Quieres ver las cascadas de agua y los flamencos en su entorno natural en la Reserva Natural de la Salina?

d ¿O te interesan más la historia y la arquitectura de la Habana? También puedes escuchar salsa cubana e ir a fiestas nocturnas – ¡son muy famosas!

17

1 (AT4.3)

1 Luis quiere ir al cine.
2 Ricardo tiene que pasear al perro.
3 Marta no quiere ir a la bolera.
4 ¿Quieres jugar al fútbol?
5 ¿Puedo tomar el sol?
6 ¿Te gustaría salir conmigo?

2 (AT3.5)

Cuaderno B, page 18

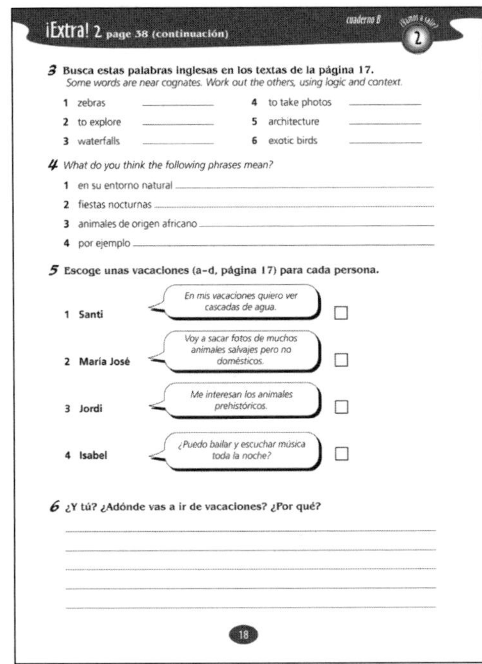

¡Extra! 2 page 38 (continuación) — cuaderno B — ¿Vamos a salir? 2

3 **Busca estas palabras inglesas en los textas de la página 17.**
Some words are near cognates. Work out the others, using logic and context.

1 zebras ______
2 to explore ______
3 waterfalls ______
4 to take photos ______
5 architecture ______
6 exotic birds ______

4 *What do you think the following phrases mean?*

1 en su entorno natural ______
2 fiestas nocturnas ______
3 animales de origen africano ______
4 por ejemplo ______

5 **Escoge unas vacaciones (a–d, página 17) para cada persona.**

1 **Santi** — *En mis vacaciones quiero ver cascadas de agua.* ☐
2 **María José** — *Voy a sacar fotos de muchos animales salvajes pero no domésticos.* ☐
3 **Jordi** — *Me interesan los animales prehistóricos.* ☐
4 **Isabel** — *¿Puedo bailar y escuchar música toda la noche?* ☐

6 **¿Y tú? ¿Adónde vas a ir de vacaciones? ¿Por qué?**

18

3 (AT3.5)

1 cebras **2** explorar **3** cascadas
4 sacar fotos **5** arquitectura **6** pájaros exóticos

4 (AT3.5)

1 in their natural environment
2 night-time parties
3 animals of African origin
4 for example

5 (AT3.5)

1 c **2** b **3** a **4** d

6 (AT3.5)

Te toca a ti (Pupil's Book pages 116–117)

Self-access reading and writing at two levels

A Reinforcement

1 *Write the questions out correctly and underline the infinitives. Then translate them into English.* (AT4.3, AT3.3) ▸▸4.5b/Y8 4.6a/Y8◂◂

Writing. Pupils write out the eight jumbled questions in the correct order and underline the infinitive in each one. They then translate them into English.

Answers

1 *¿Quieres ir al estadio? – Do you want to go to the stadium?*
2 ¿Quieres ir a la discoteca? – Do you want to go to the disco?
3 ¿Quieres ir a la bolera? – Do you want to to go to the bowling alley?
4 ¿Quieres ver una película? – Do you want to watch a film?
5 ¿Quieres salir? – Do you want to go out?
6 ¿Quieres jugar al fútbol? – Do you want to play football?
7 ¿Quieres chatear por internet? – Do you want to chat online?
8 ¿Quieres ir de compras? – Do you want to go shopping?

2 *Where are they going to meet? Match up the two halves of the notes and then translate them into English.* (AT3.2) ▸▸4.5a/Y8 5.4◂◂

Reading. Pupils match the sentence beginnings and endings and translate the completed sentences into English.

Answers

1 *d Quedamos en la bolera. – Let's meet in the bowling alley.*
2 f Quedamos en tu casa. – Let's meet at your house.
3 a Quedamos detrás del centro comercial. – Let's meet behind the shopping centre.
4 e Quedamos delante del estadio. – Let's meet in front of the stadium.
5 b Quedamos en el salón recreativo. – Let's meet in the amusement arcade.
6 c Quedamos delante de la discoteca. – Let's meet in front of the disco.

3 *Write out the words in the wordsnakes with the correct punctuation. Then match the excuses to the pictures.* (AT3.2) ▸▸4.5b/Y8◂◂

Reading. Pupils write out the wordsnakes in sentences, inserting punctuation, and then match each excuse to the appropriate picture.

Answers

1 *Lo siento, no puedo. Tengo que leer mi perro. – b*
2 Lo siento, no puedo. Tengo que comer mi diccionario. – e
3 Lo siento, no puedo. Tengo que pasear a mi hermana. – a
4 Lo siento, no puedo. Tengo que lavarme los pies. – c
5 Lo siento, no puedo. Tengo que escuchar el sol. – d

B Extension

1 *Choose the correct infinitive. Write out the sentence and then translate it into English.* (AT3.2) ▸▸4.5a/Y8 5.4◂◂

Reading. Pupils choose the correct infinitive to complete each sentence, then write out the sentence in Spanish and translate it into English.

Answers

1 *Juanita va a **ver** la nueva película de James Bond.*
Juanita is going to see the new James Bond film.
2 Sergio va a **mandar** mensajes a sus amigos.
Sergio is going to send messages to his friends.
3 Natalia va a **leer** un libro interesante.
Natalia is going to read an interesting book.
4 Jorge va a **escuchar** música.
Jorge is going to listen to music.
5 Carmen va a **hacer** deporte.
Carmen is going to do sport.

2 *Write five sentences about yourself, using the infinitives you didn't use in exercise 1 and the phrases below.* (AT4.4) ▸▸4.5a/Y8◂◂

Writing. Pupils write five sentences, using the discarded infinitives from exercise 1 and the phrases supplied.

Possible answers

Voy a comer mil hamburguesas.
Voy a jugar al voleibol con mi gato.
Va a escuchar tres sinfonías y dos óperas.
Van a beber dos litros de limonada.
Vamos a pintar las estrellas.

3 *Read Jaume's text and complete the sentences in English.* (AT3.5) ▸▸5.4◂◂

Reading. Pupils read the text and complete the six sentences summarising it in English.

Answers

1 *Normally Jaume sends text messages and listens to music.*
2 He also does sport.
3 Jaume likes to waterski and play volleyball.
4 This weekend he wants to have a break.
5 He is going to go to the spa and the hairdresser.
6 In the evening he is going to go out with some friends and go to the disco and the casino.

4 *Write as if you were Pria Fredericks, using the exercise 3 text as a model.* (AT4.5) ▸▸2.4a/Y8◂◂

Writing. Using the text in exercise 3 as a model, pupils write a paragraph as though they were Pria Fredericks, saying what they normally do and what they are going to do this weekend. Prompts are supplied. Pupils can then write a similar paragraph about their own activities.

Module 3 Mis vacaciones (Pupil's Book pages 42–59)

Unit	Framework	Levels and PoS	Key language	Grammar	Skills
1 ¿Adónde fuiste? (pp. 42–43) Saying where you went on holiday Saying what it was like	**5.3** Strategies – English/other languages **5.4** Strategies – working out meaning	**2–5** **2.1d** previous knowledge **2.1e** use reference materials **2.2a** listen for gist **2.2d** pronunciation and intonation **2.2e** ask and answer questions **3b** sounds and writing **3c** apply grammar **4e** use a range of resources	*¿Adónde fuiste de vacaciones?* *el año pasado* *Fui a... de vacaciones.* *Alemania* *Argentina* *Cuba* *Escocia* *España* *Francia* *Gales* *Grecia* *Inglaterra* *Irlanda* *Italia* *México* *Portugal* *la República Dominicana* *¿Cómo fue?* *Fue...* *estupendo* *genial* *guay* *aburrido* *horrible* *un desastre* *¿Con quién fuiste?* *Fui...* *con mi familia* *con mis padres* *con mis amigos*	The preterite tense (*fui, fue*)	Understanding different tense usage Using reading strategies to work out new words Using reference resources Pronunciation: *x* *g + e/i* *c + e/i* Using different tenses appropriately Writing creatively in Spanish

continued

Module 3 Mis vacaciones (Pupil's Book pages 42–59)

Unit	Framework	Levels and PoS	Key language	Grammar	Skills
2 ¡Buen viaje! (pp. 44–45) Saying how you travelled Using the preterite of *ser* and *ir*	**1.2/Y8** Listening – new contexts **4.5/Y8** Language – (a) range of verb tenses (preterite)	**2–5** **2.1a** identify patterns **2.1b** memorising **2.1d** previous knowledge **2.2a** listen for gist **2.2d** pronunciation and intonation **3b** sounds and writing **3c** apply grammar **4d** make links with English **4f** language for interest/ enjoyment	*¿Adónde fuiste de vacaciones?* *Fui a Madrid.* *¿Cómo fuiste?* *Fui…* *en autocar* *en avión* *en barco* *en bicicleta* *en coche* *en monopatín* *en tren* *a pie* *El invierno pasado…* *El verano pasado…*	The preterite tense (*ser, ir*)	Applying recognised patterns to new language Using reading strategies to work out meaning Developing vocabulary learning skills Understanding a longer/authentic text in Spanish (website and newspaper article)
3 ¿Qué hiciste? (pp. 46–47) Saying what you did on holiday Using the preterite of *-ar* verbs	**2.4/Y8** Writing – (a) using text as stimulus **2.4/Y8** Writing – (b) sequencing paragraphs **4.1/Y8** Language – sounds/ spelling exceptions	**3–5** **2.1a** identify patterns **2.2g** write clearly and coherently **2.2h** redraft to improve writing **2.2j** adapt previously learned language **3b** sounds and writing **3c** apply grammar **4e** use a range of resources	*Bailé.* *Descansé.* *Escuché música.* *Fui de excursión.* *Jugué al voleibol en la playa.* *Mandé mensajes.* *Monté en bicicleta.* *Saqué fotos.* *Tomé el sol.* *Visité monumentos.*	The preterite tense (*-ar* verbs)	Applying recognised patterns to new language Using reference resources Structuring a longer text using sequencing words Writing an extended text in Spanish Reviewing progress/ checking work using the Mini-test

continued

Module 3 Mis vacaciones (Pupil's Book pages 42–59)

Unit	Framework	Levels and PoS	Key language	Grammar	Skills
4 ¿Qué tal lo pasaste? (pp. 48–49) Giving more details of your holidays Expressing opinions about past events	**1.5/Y8** Speaking – (b) using simple idioms **4.4/Y8** Language – developing sentences	**2–5** **2.1d** previous knowledge **2.2a** listen for gist **4f** language for interest/ enjoyment	*¿Qué tal lo pasaste?* *¡Lo pasé bomba!* *¡Lo pasé fenomenal!* *¡Lo pasé guay!* *¡Lo pasé bien!* *¡Lo pasé mal!* *¿Cuánto tiempo pasaste allí?* *Pasé…* *diez días* *una semana* *dos semanas* *un mes*	The preterite tense (opinions about the past)	Using reading strategies to work out new words Developing vocabulary learning skills Participating in an unscripted dialogue
5 Un viaje estupendo (pp. 50–51) Giving a presentation about holidays Using the present and the preterite together	**1.5/Y8** Speaking – (a) unscripted talks **2.3/Y8** Reading – text features: emotive **5.7** Strategies – planning & preparing	**5** **2.2a** listen for gist **3c** apply grammar **4c** use more complex language	*Generalmente/Normalmente …* *me quedo en casa* *voy a España* *salgo con mis amigos por la noche* *vamos a la cafetería* *Pero el año pasado…* *fui a Cuba* *fuimos en avión* *fuimos a la playa* *fuimos a un restaurante italiano* *pinté* *hice excursiones muy interesantes*	Distinguishing tenses and using them appropriately (present and preterite)	Understanding different tense usage Using different tenses appropriately Understanding a longer/authentic text in Spanish (website) Developing independence as a learner Delivering a presentation
Resumen/ Prepárate (pp. 52–53) Pupils' checklist and practice test		**2–5**			Reviewing progress/ checking work

continued

Module 3 Mis vacaciones (Pupil's Book pages 42–59)

Unit	Framework	Levels and PoS	Key language	Grammar	Skills
¡Extra! 1 (pp. 54–55) Understanding longer texts Using dictionaries and word lists	**2.2/Y8** Reading – (a) longer, more complex texts	**3–5** **2.1d** previous knowledge **2.1e** use reference materials **4e** use a range of resources **4g** language for a range of purposes	Revision of language from Module 3	The preterite tense (revision)	Understanding a longer/authentic text in Spanish (website) Using reference resources Developing vocabulary learning skills Developing independence as a learner
¡Extra! 2 (pp. 56–57) Reading Spanish out loud Learning about a Spanish painter	**2.1/Y8** Reading – authentic materials	**3–5** **2.2d** pronunciation and intonation **3e** different countries/ cultures **4e** use a range of resources **4f** language for interest/ enjoyment	Revision of language from Module 3	The preterite tense (revision)	Understanding a longer text in Spanish (ongoing photo story) Writing an extended text in Spanish Writing creatively in Spanish
Te toca a ti (pp. 118–119)	Self-access reading and writing at two levels				

1 ¿Adónde fuiste? (Pupil's Book pages 42–43)

Learning objectives

- Saying where you went on holiday
- Saying what it was like

Framework objectives

5.3 Strategies – English/other languages
5.4 Strategies – working out meaning

Grammar

- The preterite tense (*fui, fue*)

Key language

¿Adónde fuiste de vacaciones?
el año pasado
Fui a... de vacaciones.
Alemania/Argentina/Cuba/Escocia/España/Francia/Gales/Grecia/Inglaterra/Irlanda/Italia/México/Portugal/República Dominicana

¿Cómo fue?
Fue...
estupendo
genial
guay
aburrido
horrible
un desastre

¿Con quién fuiste?
Fui...
con mi familia
con mis padres
con mis amigos

Pronunciation

x
g + e/i
c + e/i

High-frequency words

el, la
un
mi, mis
a
de
con
¿cómo?
¿quién?
ir (fui, fuiste)
ser (fue)

Cross-curricular

English: Verb tenses
ICT: Presentation using a presentation package

Resources

CD2, tracks 2–5
Cuadernos A & B, p. 22

Teacher Presentations

Screen 1 – Module 3 overview
Screen 2 – p. 42 ex. 1
Screen 3 – p. 42 ex. 3
Screen 4 – p. 43 exs 4 & 5

Starter 1 ▸▸5.3◂◂

Aim
To reintroduce country names.

Write up the following, explaining that it is a list of countries with the vowels missing:

1	*G_l_s*	8	*_sc_c_ _*
2	*_sp_ñ_*	9	*Gr_c_ _*
3	*P_rt_g_l*	10	*_rg_nt_n_*
4	*Fr_nc_ _*	11	*M_x_c_*
5	*_l_m_n_ _*	12	*C_b_*
6	*_ngl_t_rr_*	13	*R_p_bl_c_ D_m_n_c_n_*
7	*_t_l_ _*		

Give pupils three minutes working in pairs to complete the country names.

Check answers, asking pupils about the location of each country and why they think the last four have been included in the list. (All are Spanish-speaking countries.)

Suggestion

Write up two headings, 'July [current or previous year; must be in the past]' and a similar date that falls next summer. Circle the second (future) date and say *Voy a ir a México.* Then underline the first date and say *Fui a España.* Write up both examples. Ask pupils to translate both sentences, making sure they are clear on the different tenses used. Explain that this tense used to describe an event in the past is called the preterite tense and that they will learn a few preterite forms in this unit. Go round the class getting pupils to give an example of *Fui a* + a country name.

1 Escucha y lee. (1–16) (AT1.2) ▸▸5.3 5.4◂◂

Listening. Pupils listen to 16 people saying where they went on holiday, following the text at the same time. *Fui* ('I went') is glossed.

Audioscript Track 2

1 – *¿Adónde fuiste?*
– *Fui a Irlanda.*
2 *Fui a Gales.*
3 *Fui a Escocia.*
4 *Fui a Inglaterra.*
5 *Fui a Francia.*
6 *Fui a Alemania.*
7 *Fui a Italia.*
8 *Fui a Grecia.*
9 *Fui a Pakistán.*
10 *Fui a India.*
11 *Fui a Argentina.*
12 *Fui a México.*
13 *Fui a Cuba.*
14 *Fui a República Dominicana.*
15 *Fui a Portugal.*
16 *Fui a España.*

R Pupils working in pairs take it in turn to prompt with the name of a city (e.g. *Madrid*) and to respond with a sentence using *Fui* and the appropriate country (e.g. *Fui a España*).

2 Con tu compañero/a, lee estas frases. ¿Qué significan? (AT2.2) ▸▸4.2/Y8 5.3◂◂

Speaking. In pairs pupils read the Spanish sentences and, using the symbols, work out what they mean in English. *Fue* ('it was') is glossed.

Tell them to read through the tip box on reading strategies before they do the activity.

Answers

Pupils may use other words for the positive expressions below: the important thing is that they see the relative strength of the terms in Spanish and respond with an English term that is appropriate.

estupendo – *brilliant*
genial – *fantastic*
guay – *great*
aburrido – *boring*
horrible – *horrible, dreadful*
un desastre – *a disaster*

3 Escucha y escribe el país y la opinión. (1–5) (AT1.3) ▸▸1.1/Y8◂◂

Listening. Pupils listen to the five conversations and note in Spanish the country and opinion mentioned in each.

Audioscript Track 3

1 – *¿Adónde fuiste de vacaciones?*
– *Fui a México.*
– *¿Cómo fue?*
– *Fue genial.*
2 – *¿Adónde fuiste de vacaciones?*
– *Fui a Argentina.*
– *¿A Argentina? ¿Y cómo fue?*
– *Fue aburrido.*
3 – *¿Adónde fuiste de vacaciones?*
– *Fui a Cuba. Es un país muy bonito.*
– *¿Cómo fue?*
– *Fue guay.*
4 – *¿Adónde fuiste de vacaciones?*
– *Fui a Gales.*
– *¡Sí! ¡A Gales! ¿Cómo fue?*
– *Fue horrible, ¡qué frío!*
5 – *¿Adónde fuiste de vacaciones?*
– *Fui a Irlanda a aprender inglés.*
– *¿Cómo fue?*
– *Fue estupendo.*

Answers

1 *México – genial*
2 Argentina – aburrido
3 Cuba – guay
4 Gales – horrible
5 Irlanda – estupendo

❝❞ AT1.1, AT2.2

Write up the following words and ask pupils to read them aloud:

México
Argentina, genial
Francia, Grecia, Escocia

Ask pupils to tell you how *x*, *g* + *e* or *i* and *c* + *e* or *i* are pronounced. Confirm, then get a few volunteers to read through the text in the speech bubbles in the Pronunciation box. Then play the recording for the class to repeat, line by line.

Audioscript Track 4

*Mé**x**ico es e**x**ótico.*
*Ar**g**entina es **g**enial.*
*Esco**ci**a es pre**ci**osa.*

Ask pupils how *c* and *g* are pronounced when followed by other letters, such as *a/o/u* or a consonant.

+ Write up: *colegio, generación, cuatrocientos, carnicería, centígrado.* Can pupils apply the pronunciation rules to these words?

Starter 2 ▸▸4.5a/Y8◂◂

Aim
To revise giving opinions in the past.

Make a set of simple cards showing the six opinion symbols from page 42 of the Pupil's Book (five thumbs up, four thumbs up, three thumbs up, one thumb down + yawning mouth, two thumbs down, three thumbs down). Show each one in turn, asking pupils to give you an appropriate opinion with *fue*. (So, e.g., two thumbs down = *Fue horrible.*) Then show the cards at random for the class or individual pupils in turn to respond.

Suggestion

Make sure that pupils are familiar with the questions already introduced in the unit (*¿Adónde fuiste?* and *¿Cómo fue?*) by modelling a question and answer for each and then asking pupils the questions for them to respond, using *fui/fue*.

Then introduce *¿Con quién?* with a range of answers (*con mi familia/mis padres/mis amigos*, etc.). Once the class have grasped the meaning of the new question, use it to prompt answers from pupils.

4 Escucha y lee. (AT1.5) ▸▸2.1/Y8◂◂

Listening. Pupils listen to three people talking about their holidays and read along with the text at the same time.

Before they do the activity, ask pupils to look at the text briefly. Without reading it, can they tell you where they would see this kind of material? (on a travel website) What are the writers likely to be talking about? (past holiday experiences) What kind of language would pupils expect to find in the texts? (preterite tense, opinons)

Audioscript Track 45

Javier *El año pasado fui a Francia de vacaciones. Fui con mis padres. A mi madre le encanta ir de compras y visitar monumentos pero a mí no me gusta nada. Fue aburrido. Lo siento, pero no me gusta Francia.*

Antonio *El año pasado fui a Cuba de vacaciones. Fui con mis padres y fue guay. Me gusta mucho bailar y me encanta el 'son', la música cubana. También me gusta tomar el sol y en Cuba hace buen tiempo.*

Jessica *El año pasado fui a República Dominicana de vacaciones con mis amigos. Fui a la playa todos los días y luego por la tarde fui a la discoteca. Jugué al beisbol, un deporte muy popular allí. Fue genial.*

R Ask pupils to choose one of the texts and to identify all the verbs in the preterite tense.

5 Lee los textos otra vez. Copia y rellena la tabla en inglés. (AT3.5) ▸▸2.3/Y8◂◂

Reading. Pupils copy out the table. They read the texts in exercise 4 again and complete the table with the details in English.

Answers

Name	Destination	Opinion	Extra details
Javier	France	boring	parents
Antonio	Cuba	great	parents
Jessica	República Dominicana	fantastic	friends

+ Ask pupils to note the activities each person did/likes to do on holiday.

6 Con tu compañero/a, haz diálogos con las personas del ejercicio 4. (AT2.3) ▸▸1.4a/Y8◂◂

Speaking. In pairs pupils make up dialogues with the people in exercise 4. The first one (with Javier) is given as an example. The text they need to change is underlined.

7 Escribe un texto para la página web. (AT4.4–5) ▸▸2.4a/Y8◂◂

Writing. Using the texts in exercise 4 as a model, pupils write their own website text about where they went on holiday.

Get pupils to do this activity on computer. Working in pairs or small groups, they could use a presentation package like PowerPoint and cover a range of destinations, etc., adding in their own photos or pictures from the internet.

Plenary ▸▸4.5a/Y8◂◂

Ask pupils what tenses were used in this unit (present and preterite) and get them to give you some examples of expressions using *fui* and *fue*.

Look at the dialogue in exercise 6 together: explain that each person is going to do a line of dialogue in turn, either asking a question or giving an appropriate answer to the question they have just heard. When answering, pupils should try to include different details each time (country/people/opinion). Get pupils to close their books and stand up. Play this as a game round the class. If a pupil makes an error, he/she sits down. The last pupil standing is the

Cuaderno A, page 22

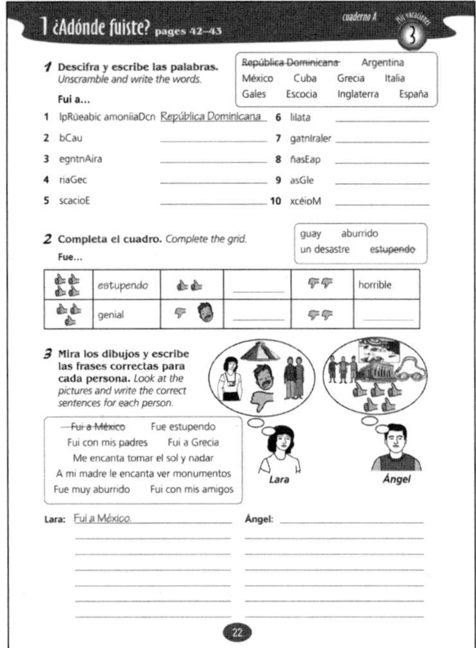
1 ¿Adónde fuiste? pages 42–43

1 **Descifra y escribe las palabras.** *Unscramble and write the words.*

República Dominicana Argentina México Cuba Grecia Italia Gales Escocia Inglaterra España

Fui a...

1 lpRüeabic amoniiaDcn República Dominicana 6 lilata
2 bCau 7 gatnlraler
3 egntnAira 8 ñasEap
4 riaGec 9 asGle
5 scacioE 10 xcéioM

2 **Completa el cuadro.** *Complete the grid.*

guay aburrido un desastre estupendo

Fue...

	estupendo				horrible
	genial				

3 **Mira los dibujos y escribe las frases correctas para cada persona.** *Look at the pictures and write the correct sentences for each person.*

Fui a México Fue estupendo
Fui con mis padres Fui a Grecia
Me encanta tomar el sol y nadar
A mi madre le encanta ver monumentos
Fue muy aburrido Fui con mis amigos

Lara Ángel

Lara: Fui a México **Ángel:**

22

1 (AT4.1)

1 *República Dominicana* **2** Cuba **3** Argentina **4** Grecia **5** Escocia **6** Italia **7** Inglaterra **8** España **9** Gales **10** México

2 (AT3.1, AT4.1)

estupendo, genial, guay, aburrido, *horrible,* un desastre

3 (AT4.2)

Lara: *Fui a México.*
Fui con mis padres.
A mi madre le encanta ver monumentos.
Fue muy aburrido.

Ángel: Fui a Grecia.
Fui con mis amigos.
Me encanta tomar el sol y nadar.
Fue estupendo.

Cuaderno B, page 22

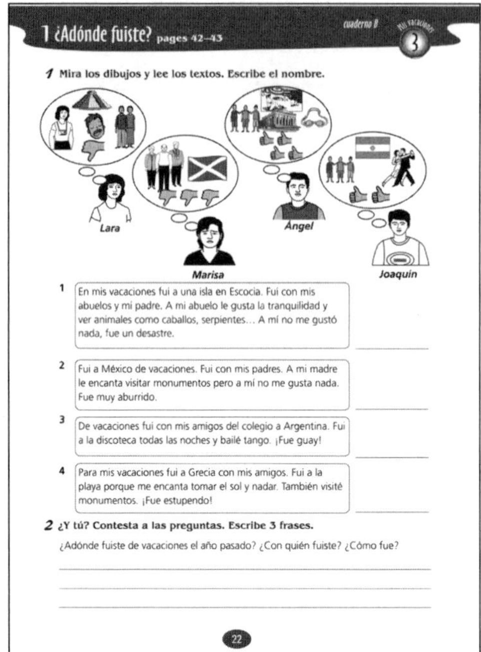
1 ¿Adónde fuiste? pages 42–43

1 **Mira los dibujos y lee los textos. Escribe el nombre.**

Lara Ángel Marisa Joaquín

1 En mis vacaciones fui a una isla en Escocia. Fui con mis abuelos y mi padre. A mi abuelo le gusta la tranquilidad y ver animales como caballos, serpientes… A mí no me gustó nada, fue un desastre.

2 Fui a México de vacaciones. Fui con mis padres. A mi madre le encanta visitar monumentos pero a mí no me gusta nada. Fue muy aburrido.

3 De vacaciones fui con mis amigos del colegio a Argentina. Fui a la discoteca todas las noches y bailé tango. ¡Fue guay!

4 Para mis vacaciones fui a Grecia con mis amigos. Fui a la playa porque me encanta tomar el sol y nadar. También visité monumentos. ¡Fue estupendo!

2 **¿Y tú? Contesta a las preguntas. Escribe 3 frases.**

¿Adónde fuiste de vacaciones el año pasado? ¿Con quién fuiste? ¿Cómo fue?

22

1 (AT3.3)

1 Marisa **2** Lara **3** Joaquín **4** Ángel

2 (AT4.3)

2 ¡Buen viaje! (Pupil's Book pages 44–45)

Learning objectives

- Saying how you travelled
- Using the preterite of *ser* and *ir*

Framework objectives

1.2/Y8 Listening – new contexts
4.5/Y8 Language – (a) range of verb tenses (preterite)

Grammar

- The preterite tense (*ser, ir*)

Key language

¿Adónde fuiste de vacaciones?
Fui a Madrid.
¿Cómo fuiste?
Fui...
en autocar/avión/barco/bicicleta/coche/monopatín/tren
a pie
El invierno/ verano pasado...

High-frequency words

el
a, en
¿cómo?
ir (fui, fuiste)

Cross-curricular

English: Prepositions

Resources

CD2, tracks 6–7
Cuadernos A & B, p. 23
R & A Pack, Gramática p. 13
Flashcards 29–36

Teacher Presentations

Screen 1 – Module 3 overview
Screen 2 – Vocabulary: Flashcards
Screen 3 – p. 44 ex. 1
Screen 4 – p. 45 ex. 4
Screen 5 – Game

Starter 1 ▶▶ 4.5a/Y8 ◀◀

Aim
To revise vocabulary for countries and opinions.
To revise the preterite forms *fui* and *fue*.

Write up:

¿Adónde fuiste de vacaciones? and *¿Cómo fue?*

Ask the class how many responses to these questions they think they could collectively come up with in three minutes: each response must be a correct sentence, with an appropriate verb in the preterite tense (*fui* or *fue*). Write up the numbers they say. If they can beat this target, they win; if they can't, you win. Start the clock.

If pupils need support, give or elicit a model answer for each question and write the verb forms *fui* and *fue* up for reference.

Ask the class to tell you the infinitive of verb forms used in the questions (*fuiste – ir, fue – ser*).

Suggestion

Write up *¿Cómo fuiste?* and *Fui en bicicleta*. Ask pupils to work out what this question means, using the context of the response.

Use Flashcards 29–36 to introduce means of transport. Ask them what prepositions are used in these expressions. (All but one uses *en* [*en barco* – 'by boat', etc.]: the exception is *a pie*.)

1 Escucha y escribe la ciudad y el medio de transporte. (1–8) (AT1.2)

▶▶ 4.2/Y8 ◀◀

Listening. Pupils listen to the eight conversations and note in English the city and the means of transport mentioned in each.

Audioscript Track 6

1 – *¿Adónde fuiste de vacaciones?*
– *Fui a Madrid.*
– *¿Cómo fuiste?*
– *Fui en autocar.*
2 – *¿Cómo fuiste a Pamplona?*
– *Fui en coche.*
3 – *¿Cómo fuiste a Córdoba?*
– *Fui en tren.*
4 – *¿También fuiste a Valencia, no? ¿Cómo fuiste?*
– *Fui a Valencia en avión.*
5 – *¿Cómo fuiste a Lanjarón?*
– *Fui a Lanjarón a pie.*
6 – *¿Cómo fuiste a Santiago de Compostela?*
– *Fui a Santiago de Compostela en bicicleta.*
7 – *¿Fuiste a Palma de Mallorca?*
– *Sí, fui en barco.*
8 – *¿Cómo fuiste a Granada?*
– *Fui en monopatín.*
– *¿Qué? ¿En monopatín?*
– *Pues sí, ¿qué pasa?*

Answers

1 *Madrid – coach*
2 Pamplona – car
3 Córdoba – train
4 Valencia – plane
5 Lanjarón – on foot
6 Santiago de Compostela – bicycle
7 Palma de Mallorca – boat
8 Granada – skateboard

✚ Use the place names in exercise 1 to review the rules for stress in Spanish and the effect an accent has on stress.

2 Con tu compañero/a, haz diálogos utilizando los dibujos del ejercicio 1. (AT2.3) ▸▸1.4a/Y8◂◂

Speaking. In pairs: using the pictures in exercise 1, pupils make up dialogues about where they went on holiday and how they travelled there. A sample exchange is given. The text to be changed is underlined.

Remind pupils that *en* is used for all means of transport except *a pie*. Ask pupils how they could remember this (English too uses a different preposition here – 'on foot').

3 Describe el viaje de Víctor Viaje (ejercicio 1). (AT4.2–3) ▸▸4.4/Y8◂◂

Writing. Pupils write a description of the journey of Víctor Viaje, the traveller shown in exercise 1, detailing where he went and how he travelled for each stage. An opening is supplied.

Answers

Fui a Madrid en autocar, fui a Pamplona en coche, fui a Córdoba en tren, fui a Barcelona en avión, fui a Lanjarón a pie, fui a Santiago de Compostela en bicicleta, fui a Palma de Mallorca en barco, fui a Granada en monopatín.

Starter 2

Aim

To practise using the preterite forms *fui* and *fue*.

Write up the following dialogue, omitting the words in brackets:

- ■ *¿Adónde (fuiste) de vacaciones?*
- ● *(Fui) a España. (Fui) a Sevilla.*
- ■ *¿Cómo (fuiste)?*
- ● *(Fui) en avión.*
- ■ *¿Cómo (fue)?*
- ● *¡(Fue) estupendo!*

Give pupils 3 minutes working in pairs to complete the dialogue with the correct verb form in the preterite tense.

If pupils need support, you could give them the missing words in jumbled order or give two options for each gap for them to choose from.

Suggestion

Write up last year as a number (e.g. *2006*) and *El año pasado fui a Madrid.* Ask the class to translate the sentence.

Then ask them to use this to work out the meaning of *el invierno pasado* and *el verano pasado*, giving them clues as necessary (e.g. for *invierno – Fui a Francia. Me gusta hacer esquí*; for *verano – Fui a España. Me gusta la playa*).

4 Escucha. Copia y rellena la tabla. (1–4) (AT1.4) ▸▸1.2/Y8 4.6a/Y8◂◂

Listening. Pupils copy out the table. They listen to the four speakers and complete the table with the details for each one.

Audioscript Track 7

1 *El verano pasado fui a Madrid de vacaciones. Fui en tren con mis amigos. Fue guay.*

2 *El invierno pasado fui a Lanjarón de vacaciones. Está en el sur de España, en la montaña. Fui en avión con mi madre. Fue estupendo.*

3 *– ¿Adónde fuiste de vacaciones el año pasado?*
– Fui a Pamplona.
– ¿A Pamplona? ¿Con quién fuiste?
– Pues… fui con mis amigos. Fui en tren.
– ¿Cómo fue?
– Fue genial.

4 *– ¿Adónde fuiste de vacaciones el año pasado?*
– Pues… fui a Valencia.
– ¿Y cómo fuiste?
– Fui en coche.
– ¿Con quién fuiste?
– Hmm… con mi familia.
– ¿Cómo fue?
– ¡Fue muy aburrido!
– ¿Por qué?
– Mis padres son muy aburridos.

Answers

	¿Cuándo?	¿Dónde?	¿Cómo?	¿Con quién?	¿Cómo fue?
1	*el verano pasado*	*Madrid*	*tren*	*amigos*	*guay*
2	el invierno pasado	Lanjarón	avión	madre	estupendo
3	al año pasado	Pamplona	tren	amigos	genial
4	el año pasado	Valencia	coche	familia	(muy) aburrido

5 Lee los textos. Escribe los medios de transporte. (AT3.5) ▸▸2.3/Y8 4.5a/Y8◂◂

Reading. Pupils read the two texts and note in English the means of transport that Isabel and Jessica mention. Some vocabulary support is given.

Answers

Jessica – *plane,* on foot, skateboard
Isabel – *boat,* coach, bicycle, horse, train, on foot

Gramática: the preterite (simple past tense)

Use this to introduce the full paradigms of the preterite of *ir* ('to go') and *ser* ('to be'). Point out that these verbs have exactly the same form in the preterite. Ask pupils how they will be able to know which verb is intended. (from the context)

Get them to read through the texts in exercise 5 again, noting each instance of the preterite of *ir* or *ser* and translating the preterite expressions into English.

There is practice on this on page 132 of the Pupil's Book.

Pupils working in pairs take it in turn to prompt with an English verb form (e.g. 'he went' or 'they were') and to respond with the correct Spanish version of *ir* or *ser* in the preterite.

6 Lee los textos otra vez. Corrige cada frase. (AT3.5 AT4.2) ▸▸4.5a/Y8◂◂

Writing. Pupils read the texts again. They then correct the error in each of the eight statements about them.

Answers

1. *Jessica fue a Mallorca con su* ***amiga****.*
2. Su mejor amiga se llama **Alicia**.
3. Por la noche fueron **a la discoteca**.
4. Palma está en la **costa**.
5. Isabel fue a Lima en **barco**.
6. Tacna está en el **sur** de Perú.
7. Cuzco es la capital **del Imperio Inca/de los Incas**.
8. Machu Picchu es **tranquilo** y **precioso**.

Plenary ▸▸4.5a/Y8◂◂

Ask pupils what expressions featuring the preterite were in this unit. What did they find out about the verbs *ir* and *ser*?

Play a game to practise distinguishing *ir* and *ser* in the preterite. Read out a series of statements from Units 1 and 2 featuring these verbs. Pupils stand up if you are using *ir* and put their hands on their heads if you are using *ser*.

Cuaderno A, page 23

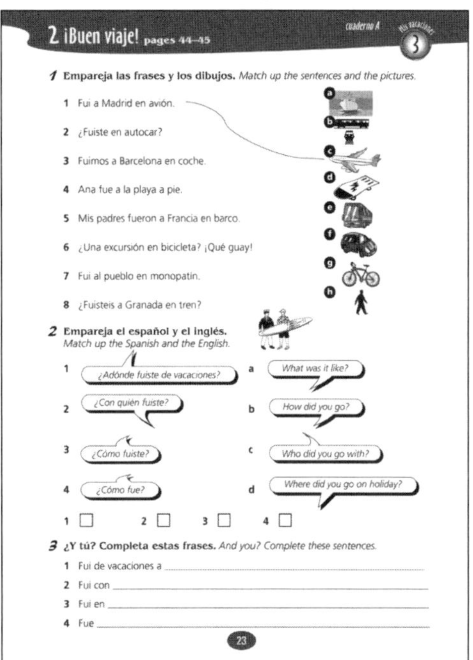

2 ¡Buen viaje! pages 44–45 — cuaderno A — Mis vacaciones 3

1 Empareja las frases y los dibujos. *Match up the sentences and the pictures.*

1. Fui a Madrid en avión.
2. ¿Fuiste en autocar?
3. Fuimos a Barcelona en coche.
4. Ana fue a la playa a pie.
5. Mis padres fueron a Francia en barco.
6. ¿Una excursión en bicicleta? ¡Qué guay!
7. Fui al pueblo en monopatín.
8. ¿Fuisteis a Granada en tren?

a b c d e f g h

2 Empareja el español y el inglés. *Match up the Spanish and the English.*

1. ¿Adónde fuiste de vacaciones?
2. ¿Con quién fuiste?
3. ¿Cómo fuiste?
4. ¿Cómo fue?

a. What was it like?
b. How did you go?
c. Who did you go with?
d. Where did you go on holiday?

1 ☐ 2 ☐ 3 ☐ 4 ☐

3 ¿Y tú? Completa estas frases. *And you? Complete these sentences.*

1. Fui de vacaciones a ______
2. Fui con ______
3. Fui en ______
4. Fue ______

23

1 (AT3.2)

1 c **2** e **3** f **4** h **5** a **6** g **7** d **8** b

2 (AT3.2)

1 d **2** c **3** b **4** a

3 (AT4.2)

Cuaderno B, page 23

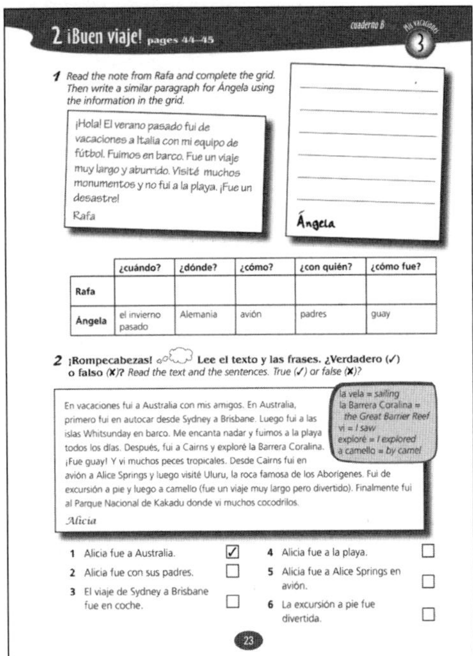

2 ¡Buen viaje! pages 44–45

1 *Read the note from Rafa and complete the grid. Then write a similar paragraph for Ángela using the information in the grid.*

¡Hola! El verano pasado fui de vacaciones a Italia con mi equipo de fútbol. Fuimos en barco. Fue un viaje muy largo y aburrido. Visité muchos monumentos y no fui a la playa. ¡Fue un desastre!
Rafa

Ángela

	¿cuándo?	¿dónde?	¿cómo?	¿con quién?	¿cómo fue?
Rafa					
Ángela	el invierno pasado	Alemania	avión	padres	guay

2 ¡Rompecabezas! Lee el texto y las frases. ¿Verdadero (✓) o falso (✗)? *Read the text and the sentences. True (✓) or false (✗)?*

En vacaciones fui a Australia con mis amigos. En Australia, primero fui en autocar desde Sydney a Brisbane. Luego fui a las islas Whitsunday en barco. Me encanta nadar y fuimos a la playa todos los días. Después, fui a Cairns y exploré la Barrera Coralina. ¡Fue guay! Y vi muchos peces tropicales. Desde Cairns fui en avión a Alice Springs y luego visité Uluru, la roca famosa de los Aborígenes. Fui de excursión a pie y luego a camello (fue un viaje muy largo pero divertido). Finalmente fui al Parque Nacional de Kakadu donde vi muchos cocodrilos.
Alicia

la vela = *sailing*
la Barrera Coralina = *the Great Barrier Reef*
vi = *I saw*
exploré = *I explored*
a camello = *by camel*

1 Alicia fue a Australia. ☑
2 Alicia fue con sus padres. ☐
3 El viaje de Sydney a Brisbane fue en coche. ☐
4 Alicia fue a la playa. ☐
5 Alicia fue a Alice Springs en avión. ☐
6 La excursión a pie fue divertida. ☐

23

R & A Pack, Gramática page 13

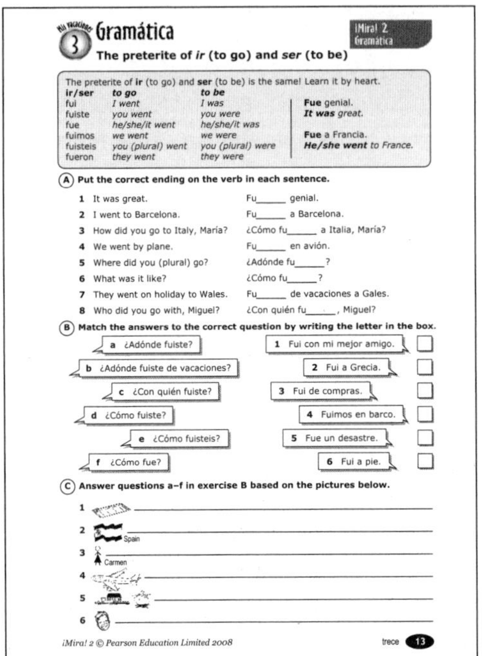

Gramática ¡Mira! 2 Gramática

The preterite of *ir* (to go) and *ser* (to be)

The preterite of **ir** (to go) and **ser** (to be) is the same! Learn it by heart.

ir/ser	to go	to be
fui	I went	I was
fuiste	you went	you were
fue	he/she/it went	he/she/it was
fuimos	we went	we were
fuisteis	you (plural) went	you (plural) were
fueron	they went	they were

Fue genial. *It was great.*
Fue a Francia. *He/she went to France.*

(A) **Put the correct ending on the verb in each sentence.**

1 It was great. Fu____ genial.
2 I went to Barcelona. Fu____ a Barcelona.
3 How did you go to Italy, María? ¿Cómo fu____ a Italia, María?
4 We went by plane. Fu____ en avión.
5 Where did you (plural) go? ¿Adónde fu____?
6 What was it like? ¿Cómo fu____?
7 They went on holiday to Wales. Fu____ de vacaciones a Gales.
8 Who did you go with, Miguel? ¿Con quién fu____, Miguel?

(B) **Match the answers to the correct question by writing the letter in the box.**

a ¿Adónde fuiste? — 1 Fui con mi mejor amigo. ☐
b ¿Adónde fuiste de vacaciones? — 2 Fui a Grecia. ☐
c ¿Con quién fuiste? — 3 Fui de compras. ☐
d ¿Cómo fuiste? — 4 Fuimos en barco. ☐
e ¿Cómo fuisteis? — 5 Fue un desastre. ☐
f ¿Cómo fue? — 6 Fui a pie. ☐

(C) **Answer questions a–f in exercise B based on the pictures below.**

1 ____
2 Spain ____
3 Carmen ____
4 ____
5 ____
6 ____

¡Mira! 2 © Pearson Education Limited 2008 trece 13

1 (AT3.3, AT4.3)

	¿cuándo?	¿dónde?	¿cómo?	¿con quién?	¿cómo fue?
Ángela	*el invierno pasado*	*Alemania*	*avión*	*padres*	*guay*
Rafa	el verano pasado	Italia	barco	equipo de fútbol	un desastre

¡Hola! El invierno pasado fui de vacaciones a Alemania con mis padres. Fuimos en avión. ¡Fue guay!

2 (AT3.4)

1 ✓ **2** ✗ **3** ✗ **4** ✓ **5** ✓ **6** ✓

(A) **1** fue **2** fui **3** fuiste **4** fuimos **5** fuisteis **6** fue **7** fueron **8** fuiste

(B) **a** 3 **b** 2 **c** 1 **d** 6 **e** 4 **f** 5

(C) **1** Fui a la piscina.
2 Fui a España.
3 Fui con mi amiga, Carmen.
4 Fui en avión.
5 Fuimos en tren y en barco.
6 Fue aburrido.

3 ¿Qué hiciste? (Pupil's Book pages 46–47)

Learning objectives

- Saying what you did on holiday
- Using the preterite of *-ar* verbs

Framework objectives

2.4/Y8 Writing – (a) using text as stimulus
2.4/Y8 Writing – (b) sequencing paragraphs
4.1/Y8 Language – sounds/ spelling exceptions

Grammar

- The preterite tense (*-ar* verbs)

Key language

Bailé.
Descansé.
Escuché música.
Fui de excursión.
Jugué al voleibol en la playa.
Mandé mensajes.
Monté en bicicleta.
Saqué fotos.
Tomé el sol.
Visité monumentos.

High-frequency words

la
a (al)
de
en
escuchar (escuché)
ir (fui)
jugar (jugué)
tomar (tomé)

Cross-curricular

English: Evaluating and improving written work
ICT: Word-processing

Resources

CD2, tracks 8–11
Cuadernos A & B, p. 24
R & A Pack, Gramática p. 14

Teacher Presentations

Screen 1 – Module 3 overview
Screen 2 – Vocabulary: Flashcards
Screen 3 – p. 46 ex. 1
Screen 4 – p. 47 ex. 3
Screen 5 – p. 47 ex. 4
Screen 6 – p. 47 ex. 5
Screen 7 – Game

Suggestion ▸▸4.1/Y8◂◂

Make pupils aware of the pronunciation box on page 47 (use of silent u) as you start the first exercise.

Starter 1 ▸▸4.5a/Y8◂◂

Aim

To revise the vocabulary for holiday activities. To apply recognised patterns.

Write up: *visitar* – to visit
Visito monumentos. – I visit monuments.
Visité monumentos. – I visited monuments.

1 *Tomé el sol.*
2 *Bailé.*
3 *Mandé mensajes.*
4 *Escuché música.*
5 *Jugué al voleibol.*

Give pupils three minutes working in pairs to translate the five sentences, using the model provided, and to write out the infinitive of the five verbs used in them.

Check answers, asking pupils what tense all the verbs here are in. What rule can they give about the 'I' form of *-ar* verbs in the preterite tense?

Suggestion

Write up *¿Qué hiciste?* and responses from the unit to make its meaning clear. Ask pupils what verb *hiciste* comes from (*hacer*). Then introduce the key language not covered in the Starter. Write up: *Monté en bicicleta, Saqué fotos, Descansé, Fui de excursión.*

Support with a few mimes as necessary.

Ask why *fui* doesn't follow the pattern of the other verbs. (irregular, not an *-ar* verb)

1 Escucha y escribe la letra correcta. (1–10) (AT1.3) ▸▸4.1/Y8 4.5a/Y8◂◂

Listening. Pupils listen to 10 conversations about what people did on holiday and note the correct picture for each (from *a–j*).

Audioscript Track 8

1 – *¿Qué hiciste?*
– *Fui de excursión.*
2 – *¿Qué hiciste?*
– *Monté en bicicleta.*
3 – *¿Qué hiciste?*
– *Mandé mensajes.*
4 – *¿Qué hiciste?*
– *Descansé.*
5 – *¿Qué hiciste?*
– *Bailé.*
6 – *¿Qué hiciste?*
– *Saqué fotos.*
7 – *¿Qué hiciste?*
– *Tomé el sol.*
8 – *¿Qué hiciste?*
– *Visité monumentos.*
9 – *¿Qué hiciste?*
– *Jugué al voleibol en la playa.*
10 – *¿Qué hiciste durante tus vacaciones?*
– *A ver… escuché música.*

Answers

1 j **2** c **3** e **4** d **5** b **6** h **7** g **8** a **9** i **10** f

Gramática: the preterite of *-ar* verbs

This gives the full paradigm of the preterite of *-ar* verbs, using *visitar*. It also lists the other 1st person preterite verbs used in the unit. Get pupils to read these out aloud, to practise putting the stress on the final syllable. There is practice on this on page 132 of the Pupil's Book.

2 Con tu compañero/a, haz diálogos. (AT2.3) ▶▶1.4b/Y8 4.5a/Y8◀◀

Speaking. In pairs: using the prompts, pupils make up dialogues talking about activities with the preterite tense. A sample exchange is given.

Starter 2 ▶▶4.5a/Y8◀◀

Aim
To practise the preterite tense of *-ar* verbs (1st person) and *fui*. To apply recognised patterns to new language.

Write up:

visitar	to visit	*visité*	I visited
	to listen		
	to dance		
	to play		
	to be		
	to go		
montar	to ride		
llevar	to wear		

Give pupils three minutes to copy and complete the grid.You could give more support to a less able class by supplying all the Spanish infinitives.

Suggestion

Remind pupils of the useful words *primero, luego* and *después*. Can they remember where they used these before? (with the near future tense) Point out that these words can be used with any tense, to sequence information.

3 Escucha a Raúl y haz una lista en inglés de las actividades (8 actividades). (AT1.4) ▶▶1.2/Y8 4.5a/Y8◀◀

Listening. Pupils listen to Raúl's description of his holidays in Alicante and list in English the activities that he did.

Audioscript Track 9

Fui a Alicante de vacaciones. Primero descansé y tomé el sol, mandé mensajes y después jugué al voleibol en la playa. Un día fui de excursión y visité monumentos. Saqué fotos muy bonitas. Me gusta mucho sacar fotos. Luego monté en bicicleta con unos amigos. Fue guay.

Answers
relaxed, sunbathed, sent messages, played volleyball, went on a trip, visited monuments, took photos, went for a bike ride

4 Pon el texto en un orden lógico. Escucha y comprueba tus respuestas. (AT1.5) ▶▶2.4b/Y8 5.4◀◀

Listening. Pupils reorder the seven pieces of text logically. They then listen to check their answers.

Audioscript Track 10

Me llamo Chema. Soy español y tengo catorce años.
Vivo en Granada, en el sur de España.
El año pasado fui de vacaciones a Italia con mi familia. Fui a Trieste.
Está en el norte de Italia, en la costa.
Fuimos en avión. Fue guay.
Tomé el sol en la playa y jugué al voleibol también.
Descansé, escuché música y mandé mensajes a mis amigos.
Fue estupendo. Por la noche bailé en la discoteca con mi hermana y fue genial.
Un día fuimos de excursión en Trieste. Primero visité monumentos y saqué fotos. Luego fuimos a un restaurante italiano. Fue genial.

Answers
7, 3, 5, 4, 6, 1, 2

5 Escucha otra vez. ¿Qué actividades menciona Chema? Escribe las letras del ejercicio 1 (9 actividades). (AT1.5) ▶▶4.5a/Y8◀◀

Listening. Pupils listen again and note the nine activities Chema mentions, using the pictures in exercise 1 (*a–j*).

Audioscript Track 11

As for exercise 4.

Answers
g, i, d, f, e, b, j, a, h

Suggestion

Write up the verb *jugué* and ask pupils what they notice about it. (Remind them as necessary of *jugar* and other 1st person preterite forms, such as *escuché*.) Can they work out why the *u* has been added before the *é* ending?

Confirm that this spelling change is made to keep the pronunciation of the *g* hard, as in the rest of the preterite forms of *jugar*. Explain that a similar thing happens in verbs with a stem (the infinitive minus the ending) that ends in *c*.

Read through the tip box on key spelling changes in the preterite : *g* + *e* or *i* → *gu* and *c* + *e* or *i* → *qu*.

6 Empareja las preguntas con el texto del ejercicio 4. (AT3.5)

4.6a/Y8

Reading. Pupils match each of the seven questions with the corresponding piece of text in exercise 4.

Answers

a 3 **b** 5 **c** 4 **d** 6 **e** 1 **f** 2 **g** 7

7 Describe tus vacaciones. (AT4.4–5)

2.4a&b/Y8

Writing. Using the details of Chema's description in exercise 4 and the questions in exercise 6, pupils write a text introducing themselves and describing a holiday they have had. Encourage them to be as inventive as possible in the details and to check carefully any preterite verb forms used, using either the Gramática box on page 46 or the Gramática section at the back of the Pupil's Book.

Pupils could do this extended writing activity on computer, making the process of correcting/redrafting much easier and more encouraging.

Plenary 5.1

Write up *escuchar* and ask pupils how to say 'I listened' in Spanish. Can they tell you how the 'I' form of the preterite is formed (stem/infinitive minus *-ar* + ending *é*)?

Put the class into teams and tell pupils to close their books. See which team can be the first to remember and write down all 10 key expressions for holiday activities in this unit. All must be given as sentences.

Tell teams to swap papers and check each other's work as you confirm the answers. A correct answer wins two points; an answer with an error in any word except the verb wins one point. The first team to finish gets two bonus points. The team with the most points is the winner.

Cuaderno A, page 24

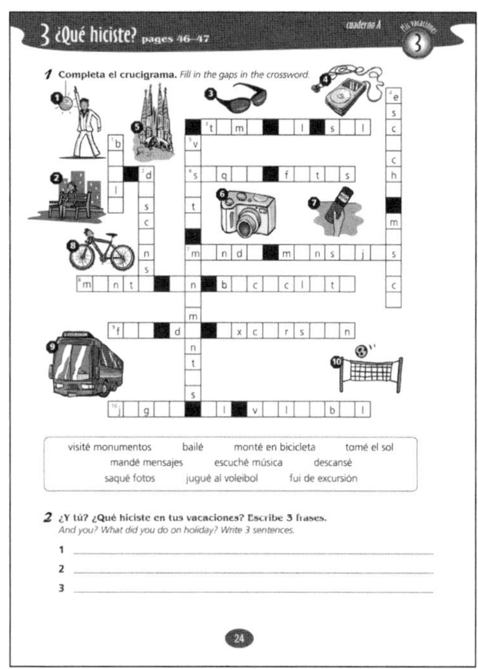

3 ¿Qué hiciste? pages 46–47

1 **Completa el crucigrama.** *Fill in the gaps in the crossword.*

visité monumentos bailé monté en bicicleta tomé el sol mandé mensajes escuché música descansé saqué fotos jugué al voleibol fui de excursión

2 **¿Y tú? ¿Qué hiciste en tus vacaciones? Escribe 3 frases.** *And you? What did you do on holiday? Write 3 sentences.*

1

2

3

24

1 (AT4.1)

1 bailé **2** descansé **3** tomé el sol **4** escuché música **5** visité monumentos **6** saqué fotos **7** mandé mensajes **8** monté en bicicleta **9** fui de excursión **10** jugué al voleibol

2 (AT4.3)

Cuaderno B, page 24

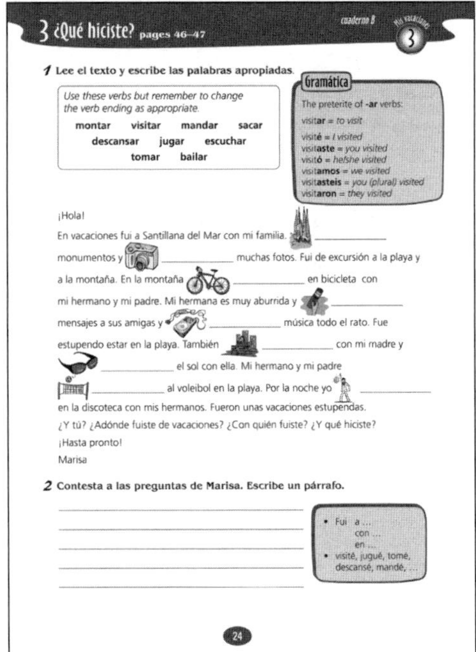

3 ¿Qué hiciste? pages 46–47

cuaderno B — Mis vacaciones 3

1 Lee el texto y escribe las palabras apropiadas.

Use these verbs but remember to change the verb ending as appropriate.

montar visitar mandar sacar descansar jugar escuchar tomar bailar

Gramática

The preterite of **-ar** verbs:

visit**ar** = *to visit*

visit**é** = *I visited*
visit**aste** = *you visited*
visit**ó** = *he/she visited*
visit**amos** = *we visited*
visit**asteis** = *you (plural) visited*
visit**aron** = *they visited*

¡Hola!

En vacaciones fui a Santillana del Mar con mi familia. ______ monumentos y ______ muchas fotos. Fui de excursión a la playa y a la montaña. En la montaña ______ en bicicleta con mi hermano y mi padre. Mi hermana es muy aburrida y ______ mensajes a sus amigas y ______ música todo el rato. Fue estupendo estar en la playa. También ______ con mi madre y ______ el sol con ella. Mi hermano y mi padre ______ al voleibol en la playa. Por la noche yo ______ en la discoteca con mis hermanos. Fueron unas vacaciones estupendas.

¿Y tú? ¿Adónde fuiste de vacaciones? ¿Con quién fuiste? ¿Y qué hiciste?

¡Hasta pronto!

Marisa

2 Contesta a las preguntas de Marisa. Escribe un párrafo.

- Fui a … con … en …
- visité, jugué, tomé, descansé, mandé, …

24

R & A Pack, Gramática page 14

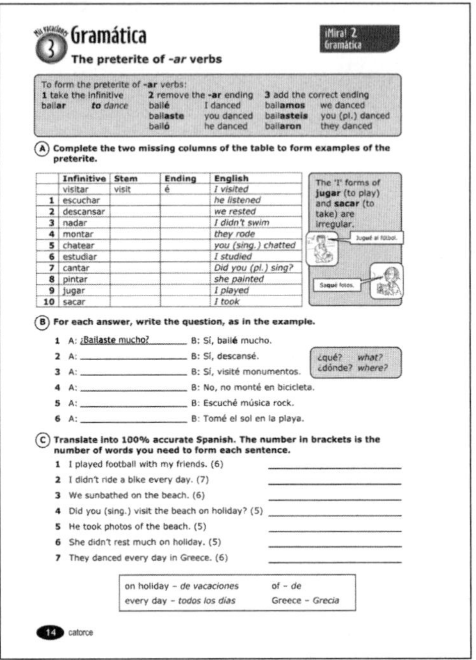

Mis vacaciones 3 **Gramática** — ¡Mira! 2 Gramática

The preterite of *-ar* verbs

To form the preterite of **-ar** verbs:

1 take the infinitive: bail**ar** *to dance*

2 remove the **-ar** ending / **3** add the correct ending:

bail**é** I danced — bail**amos** we danced
bail**aste** you danced — bail**asteis** you (pl.) danced
bail**ó** he danced — bail**aron** they danced

(A) Complete the two missing columns of the table to form examples of the preterite.

	Infinitive	Stem	Ending	English
	visitar	visit	é	*I visited*
1	escuchar			*he listened*
2	descansar			*we rested*
3	nadar			*I didn't swim*
4	montar			*they rode*
5	chatear			*you (sing.) chatted*
6	estudiar			*I studied*
7	cantar			*Did you (pl.) sing?*
8	pintar			*she painted*
9	jugar			*I played*
10	sacar			*I took*

The 'I' forms of **jugar** (to play) and **sacar** (to take) are irregular.

(B) For each answer, write the question, as in the example.

1 A: ¿Bailaste mucho? B: Sí, bailé mucho.
2 A: ______ B: Sí, descansé.
3 A: ______ B: Sí, visité monumentos.
4 A: ______ B: No, no monté en bicicleta.
5 A: ______ B: Escuché música rock.
6 A: ______ B: Tomé el sol en la playa.

¿qué? *what?*
¿dónde? *where?*

(C) Translate into 100% accurate Spanish. The number in brackets is the number of words you need to form each sentence.

1 I played football with my friends. (6)
2 I didn't ride a bike every day. (7)
3 We sunbathed on the beach. (6)
4 Did you (sing.) visit the beach on holiday? (5)
5 He took photos of the beach. (5)
6 She didn't rest much on holiday. (5)
7 They danced every day in Greece. (6)

on holiday – *de vacaciones* — of – *de*
every day – *todos los días* — Greece – *Grecia*

14 catorce

1 (AT3.5, AT4.2)

¡Hola!

Para mis vacaciones fui a Santillana del Mar con mi familia. Visité monumentos y saqué muchas fotos. Fui de excursión a la playa y a la montaña. En la montaña monté en bicicleta con mi hermano y mi padre. Mi hermana es muy aburrida y mandó mensajes a sus amigas y escuchó música todo el rato. Fue estupendo estar en la playa. También descansé con mi madre y tomé el sol con ella. Mi hermano y mi padre jugaron al voleibol en la playa. Por la noche yo bailé en la discoteca con mis hermanos. Fueron unas vacaciones estupendas.

¿Y tú? ¿Adónde fuiste de vacaciones? ¿Con quién fuiste? ¿Y qué hiciste?

¡Hasta pronto!

Marisa

2 (AT4.5)

(A) **1** escuch ó **2** descans amos **3** no nad é
4 mont aron **5** chate aste **6** estudi é
7 ¿cant asteis? **8** pint ó **9** jugu é **10** saqu é

(B) **2** ¿Descansaste? **3** ¿Visitaste monumentos?
4 ¿Montaste en bicicleta? **5** ¿Qué escuchaste?
6 ¿Qué hiciste?

(C) **1** Jugué al fútbol con mis amigos.
2 No monté en bicicleta todos los días.
3 Tomamos el sol en la playa.
4 ¿Visitaste la playa de vacaciones?
5 Sacó fotos de la playa.
6 No descansó mucho de vacaciones.
7 Bailaron todos los días en Grecia.

4 ¿Qué tal lo pasaste? (Pupil's Book pages 48–49)

Learning objectives
- Giving more details of your holidays
- Expressing opinions about past events

Framework objectives
1.5/Y8 Speaking – (b) using simple idioms
4.4/Y8 Language – developing sentences

Grammar
- The preterite tense (opinions about the past)

Key language
¿Qué tal lo pasaste?
¡Lo pasé bomba!
¡Lo pasé fenomenal!
¡Lo pasé guay!
¡Lo pasé bien!
¡Lo pasé mal!
¿Cuánto tiempo pasaste allí?
Pasé…
diez días
una semana, dos semanas
un mes

High-frequency words
un, una
allí
¿cuánto?
¿qué?

Resources
CD2, tracks 12–14
Cuadernos A & B, p. 25

Teacher Presentations
Screen 1 – Module 3 overview
Screen 2 – Vocabulary: Flashcards
Screen 3 – p. 48 ex. 2
Screen 4 – p. 49 ex. 6

Starter 1 ▸▸ 5.4 ◂◂

Aim

To revise time expressions. To revise confusable numbers.

Write up the following, jumbling the order of the phrases (in correct order here for reference):

días x 7 → semana x 4 → mes x 12 → año

dos días	*doce días*	*un año*
una semana	*un mes*	*dieciocho meses*
diez días	*seis semanas*	

Give pupils working in pairs three minutes to put the time expressions in order (from the shortest period of time to the longest) and to translate them into English.

Suggestion

Ask the class to look at the expressions in exercise 1. Do they see any clues in the verb ending that might tell them what tense is being used in the question form (*¿Qué tal lo pasaste?*) and in the responses (*¡Lo pasé bomba!*)? (preterite) Encourage them to use the pictures to work out when you would use these expressions and what they mean.

1 Escucha y repite. (AT1.2) ▸▸ 1.5b/Y8 4.2/Y8 ◂◂

Listening. Pupils listen to the recording, which covers opinions about past events. Pause the recording at the end of each line to give the class time to repeat the question and the five statements.

Audioscript Track 12

¿Qué tal lo pasaste?
¡Lo pasé bomba!
Lo pasé guay.
Lo pasé bien.
Lo pasé fenomenal.
Lo pasé mal.

Read through the tip box, on how these expressions can't be translated word for word: they need to be learned as vocabulary items in their own right. Suggest pupils note expressions like this as a group in a separate section in their vocabulary listings.

They could also use some kind of pictorial way to remember the expressions, e.g. smiley/sad face symbols.

The Estrategia feature in the Palabras section of the Pupil's Book (page 59) contains further ideas for memorising vocabulary.

2 Escucha y contesta a las preguntas para cada persona. (1–5) (AT1.4) ▸▸ 4.5a/Y8 4.6a/Y8 ◂◂

Listening. Pupils listen to five people being interviewed about a holiday in the past. For each of them, they answer the four questions in English. Before you play the recording, read through the key language box as a class.

Audioscript Track 13

1 – *¿Adónde fuiste de vacaciones?*
– *Fui a Grecia.*
– *¿Cuándo?*
– *El invierno pasado.*
– *¿Cuánto tiempo pasaste allí?*
– *Dos semanas.*
– *¿Qué tal lo pasaste?*
– *Lo pasé fenomenal.*

2 – *¿Adónde fuiste de vacaciones?*
– *Fui a Cuba el año pasado.*
– *¿Cuánto tiempo pasaste allí?*
– *Mucho tiempo. Un mes.*
– *¿Qué tal lo pasaste?*
– *Lo pasé bomba.*

3 – *¿Adónde fuiste de vacaciones?*
– *El verano pasado fui a México.*
– *¿Cuánto tiempo pasaste allí?*

- *Hmm… no sé. Tres semanas.*
- *¿Qué tal lo pasaste?*
- *Lo pasé guay. Descansé, tomé el sol y saqué fotos.*

4
- *¿Adónde fuiste de vacaciones?*
- *El invierno pasado fui a Argentina.*
- *¿Cuánto tiempo pasaste allí?*
- *Una semana. No mucho tiempo.*
- *¿Qué tal lo pasaste?*
- *Lo pasé bien. Fui de excursión y visité monumentos. Fue muy interesante.*

5
- *¿Adónde fuiste de vacaciones?*
- *El verano pasado fui a Inglaterra de vacaciones con mi familia.*
- *¿Cuánto tiempo pasaste allí?*
- *Diez días.*
- *¿Y qué tal lo pasaste?*
- *Lo pasé mal. Fue aburrido. No hicimos nada. Mandé mensajes a mis amigos – es todo.*

Answers

1. Greece, last winter, two weeks, wonderful
2. Cuba, last year, a month, fantastic
3. Mexico, last summer, three weeks, great
4. Argentina, last winter, a week, good
5. England, last summer, 10 days, bad/boring

3 Separa las palabras y escribe las preguntas y respuestas. (AT4.2) ▸▸4.5a/Y8 4.6a/Y8◂◂

Writing. Pupils separate out the words in the wordsnake, writing them out as questions and answers. Remind pupils that they will need to add capitals and punctuation as necessary.

Answers

¿Adónde fuiste?	Fui a Cuba.
¿Cuándo?	El año pasado.
¿Cuánto tiempo?	Dos semanas.
¿Qué tal lo pasaste?	¡Lo pasé fenomenal!

Starter 2 ▸▸4.6a/Y8◂◂

Aim

To revise questions using the preterite.

Write up the following, jumbling the order of the second column of words:

1	*¿Adónde*	*fuiste?*
2	*¿Cuánto*	*tiempo pasaste allí?*
3	*¿Con*	*quién fuiste?*
4	*¿Qué*	*hiciste?*
5	*¿Qué tal*	*lo pasaste?*

Give pupils three minutes working in pairs to match the question halves and to translate the questions.

4 Con tu compañero/a, haz diálogos. (AT2.5) ▸▸1.4a/Y8 4.5a/Y8 4.6a/Y8◂◂

Speaking. In pairs pupils make up dialogues using the prompts and the model provided. The text that they need to change in the model is underlined.

+ Pupils in pairs put together a dialogue using their own details, first using the model in the Pupil's Book for support and then attempting the dialogue without a script.

5 Escribe un diálogo del ejercicio 4. (AT4.4) ▸▸4.4/Y8◂◂

Writing. Pupils write out one of the dialogues they made up for exercise 4.

6 Escucha y canta. (AT1.4) ▸▸4.6a/Y8◂◂

Listening. Pupils listen to the song, following the words in their books. Play the recording again, this time getting pupils to sing along.

Audioscript Track 14

Mis vacaciones

Fui de vacaciones
¡la playa es genial!
Fui de vacaciones
¡la playa es genial!
¿Qué tal lo pasaste?
¡Lo pasé fenomenal!

¿Adónde fuiste?
Fui a la playa de Gijón.
¿Cómo fuiste?
Fui en barco y en avión.

¿Con quién fuiste?
Con mi hermana Marisol.
Dime, ¿qué hiciste?
Jugué al fútbol y al voleibol.

Fui de vacaciones
¡la playa es genial!
Fui de vacaciones
¡la playa es genial!
¿Qué tal lo pasaste?
¡Lo pasé fenomenal!

R Pupils working in pairs take it in turn to ask questions on the text of the song (e.g. *¿Con quién fuiste?*), and to answer as though they were the singer (e.g. *Con mi hermana Marisol*).

7 Busca estas frases en español en la canción. (AT3.4) ▸▸5.4◂◂

Reading. Pupils find the Spanish versions of the eight English expressions listed.

Answers

1 *¿Adónde fuiste?* **2** ¿Cómo fuiste?
3 ¿Qué hiciste? **4** ¿Qué tal lo pasaste? **5** dime
6 con **7** fui **8** jugué

Plenary ▸▸4.6a/Y8◂◂

Put the class into teams and allocate each team a question from the dialogue in exercise 4. Give the teams one minute to revise possible answers to their question, looking back at earlier units as necessary. Then all pupils close their books. Ask the teams in turn their allocated question: each team member has to respond with a different answer. Each correct answer wins a point. If someone doesn't have an answer ready, or makes a mistake, the next team can steal the point by coming up with the correct version or an appropriate alternative answer. The team with the most points at the end is the winner.

Cuaderno A, page 25

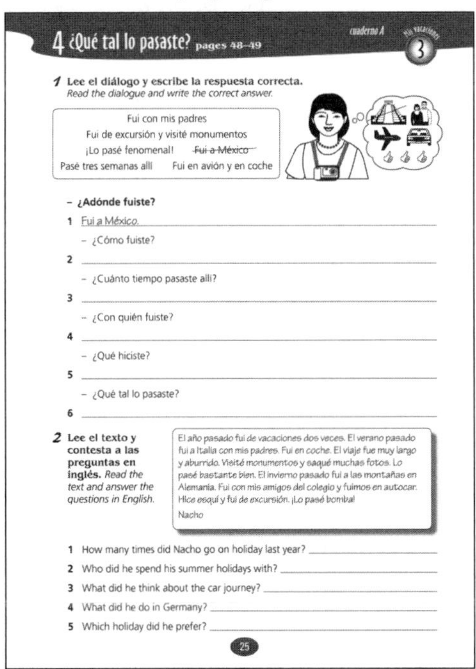

4 ¿Qué tal lo pasaste? pages 48–49
cuaderno A
Mis vacaciones 3

1 **Lee el diálogo y escribe la respuesta correcta.** *Read the dialogue and write the correct answer.*

Fui con mis padres
Fui de excursión y visité monumentos
¡Lo pasé fenomenal! ~~Fui a México~~
Pasé tres semanas allí Fui en avión y en coche

– **¿Adónde fuiste?**
1 Fui a México.
– ¿Cómo fuiste?
2 ______
– ¿Cuánto tiempo pasaste allí?
3 ______
– ¿Con quién fuiste?
4 ______
– ¿Qué hiciste?
5 ______
– ¿Qué tal lo pasaste?
6 ______

2 **Lee el texto y contesta a las preguntas en inglés.** *Read the text and answer the questions in English.*

El año pasado fui de vacaciones dos veces. El verano pasado fui a Italia con mis padres. Fui en coche. El viaje fue muy largo y aburrido. Visité monumentos y saqué muchas fotos. Lo pasé bastante bien. El invierno pasado fui a las montañas en Alemania. Fui con mis amigos del colegio y fuimos en autocar. Hice esquí y fui de excursión. ¡Lo pasé bomba!
Nacho

1 How many times did Nacho go on holiday last year? ______
2 Who did he spend his summer holidays with? ______
3 What did he think about the car journey? ______
4 What did he do in Germany? ______
5 Which holiday did he prefer? ______

25

1 (AT3.3, AT4.2)

1 *Fui a México.* **2** Fui en avión y en coche.
3 Pasé tres semanas allí. **4** Fui con mis padres.
5 Fui de excursión y visité monumentos.
6 ¡Lo pasé fenomenal!

2 (AT3.3)

1 twice (Italy and Germany)
2 his parents
3 It was long and boring.
4 He went skiing and went on a trip.
5 Germany

Cuaderno B, page 25

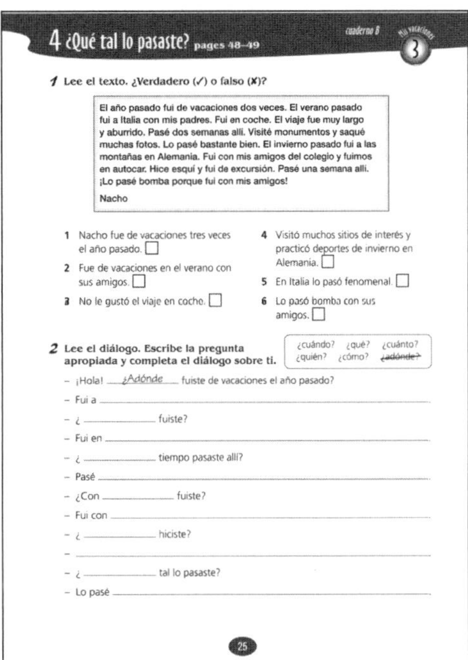

4 ¿Qué tal lo pasaste? pages 48–49
cuaderno B
Mis vacaciones 3

1 **Lee el texto. ¿Verdadero (✓) o falso (✗)?**

El año pasado fui de vacaciones dos veces. El verano pasado fui a Italia con mis padres. Fui en coche. El viaje fue muy largo y aburrido. Pasé dos semanas allí. Visité monumentos y saqué muchas fotos. Lo pasé bastante bien. El invierno pasado fui a las montañas en Alemania. Fui con mis amigos del colegio y fuimos en autocar. Hice esquí y fui de excursión. Pasé una semana allí. ¡Lo pasé bomba porque fui con mis amigos!
Nacho

1 Nacho fue de vacaciones tres veces el año pasado. ☐
2 Fue de vacaciones en el verano con sus amigos. ☐
3 No le gustó el viaje en coche. ☐
4 Visitó muchos sitios de interés y practicó deportes de invierno en Alemania. ☐
5 En Italia lo pasó fenomenal. ☐
6 Lo pasó bomba con sus amigos. ☐

2 **Lee el diálogo. Escribe la pregunta apropiada y completa el diálogo sobre ti.**

¿cuándo? ¿qué? ¿cuánto? ¿quién? ¿cómo? ~~¿adónde?~~

– ¡Hola! ¿Adónde fuiste de vacaciones el año pasado?
– Fui a ______
– ¿ ______ fuiste?
– Fui en ______
– ¿ ______ tiempo pasaste allí?
– Pasé ______
– ¿Con ______ fuiste?
– Fui con ______
– ¿ ______ hiciste?
– ______
– ¿ ______ tal lo pasaste?
– Lo pasé ______

25

1 (AT3.5)

1 ✗ **2** ✗ **3** ✓ **4** ✓ **5** ✗ **6** ✓

2 (AT3.4, AT4.3)

¿*Adónde* fuiste?
¿Cómo fuiste?
¿Cuánto tiempo pasaste allí?
¿Con quién fuiste?
¿Qué hiciste?
¿Qué tal lo pasaste?
and pupils' personal responses

5 Un viaje estupendo (Pupil's Book pages 50–51)

Learning objectives

- Giving a presentation about holidays
- Using the present and the preterite together

Framework objectives

1.5/Y8 Speaking – (a) unscripted talks
2.3/Y8 Reading – text features: emotive
5.7 Strategies – planning & preparing

Grammar

- Distinguishing tenses and using them appropriately (present and preterite)

Key language

Generalmente/Normalmente ...
me quedo en casa
voy a España
salgo con mis amigos por la noche
vamos a la cafetería

Pero el año pasado...
fui a Cuba
fuimos en avión
fuimos a la playa
fuimos a un restaurante italiano
pinté
hice excursiones muy interesantes

High-frequency words

el, la
un
a
me
mis
con
en
por
pero
muy
hacer (hice)
quedar (quedo)
ir (voy, vamos, fui, fuimos)

Cross-curricular

English: Verb tenses

Resources

CD2, tracks 15–17
Cuadernos A & B, p. 26
R & A Pack, Gramática p. 15 & Writing Skills p. 16

Teacher Presentations

Screen 1 – Module 3 overview
Screen 2 – p. 50 ex. 1
Screen 3 – p. 51 exs 5 & 6
Screen 4 – Game
Screen 5 – Video

Starter 1 ▸▸4.5a/Y8◂◂

Aim
To distinguish between present and preterite tense verbs. To identify time expressions that are used with the present and the preterite.

Give pupils two minutes working in pairs to read through the first text on the website featured in exercise 1 and write down the following (answers in brackets for reference):

- the tense of the verbs shown in green (preterite)
- the tense of the verbs shown in orange (present)
- a time expression used with the present tense (*generalmente*)
- a time expression used with the preterite tense (*el verano pasado*)

Suggestion

Tell pupils that this unit focuses on using two tenses together – the present tense, to talk about what you usually do, and the preterite tense, to talk about what you did in the past. Explain that as well as recognising the verb forms for each of the tenses, pupils should look out for particular time expressions as a clue to the tense being used.

1 Escucha y lee. Luego empareja los textos con las fotos correctas. (1–3) (AT1.5) ▸▸2.3/Y8 4.5a/Y8◂◂

Listening. Pupils listen to three people describing their usual holidays and what they did last year, following the text at the same time. They then match each text to the correct photo.

Audioscript Track 15

1 ***Paco***
Generalmente voy de vacaciones a República Dominicana con mis amigos en avión. Por la tarde juego al fútbol en la playa. Salgo con mis amigos por la noche, vamos a la cafetería, a la discoteca y al salón recreativo también.
El verano pasado fui a Portugal con mis amigos. Fui en tren y en autocar, fue guay. Pinté mucho, ¡me encanta pintar! y escuché música. Descansé y lo pasé bien.

2 ***Natalia***
Normalmente voy a Milán con mi familia en coche. Voy de compras, voy a la peluquería y a la sauna. Mando mensajes a mis amigos todos los días.
El año pasado fui a Cuba con mi hermano. Fuimos en avión. Monté en bicicleta y bailé salsa. Hice excursiones muy interesantes. Jugué al fútbol en la playa. Lo pasé fenomenal.

3 ***James***
Normalmente no voy de vacaciones, me quedo en casa. Juego con el ordenador, chateo por internet o a veces mando mensajes. Hago mis deberes y estudio mucho también.
Pero el año pasado fui a la playa en España y lo pasé bomba. ¡Fue genial! Descansé, hice yoga y tomé el sol. Fui con mi amigo Rod. Fuimos en avión.

Answers
1 James **2** Paco **3** Natalia

R Pupils working in pairs take it in turn to read out a word/phrase from the Gramática box on page 51 and to identify it as relating to the present or the past.

2 Escribe los datos sobre Paco, Natalia y James en inglés. (AT3.5) ▸▸2.3/Y8 4.5a/Y8◂◂

Reading. Pupils copy the grid. They read the text in exercise 1 again and complete the grid with the details for each of the three people in English.

Answers

1 Paco normally goes to Dominican Republic. Last year he went to Portugal. **2** Natalia normally goes to Milan. Last year she went to Cuba. **3** James normally stays at home. Last year he went to Spain.

+ Ask pupils to give as many further details as possible about the holidays of Paco, Natalia and James.

Starter 2 ▸▸4.5a/Y8◂◂

Aim

To use the present and preterite tenses appropriately.

Write up: *Normalmente…*
El verano pasado…
Generalmente…
El invierno pasado…

Give pupils three minutes working in pairs to come up with a different ending to each of these sentences, using the appropriate tense in each case. If pupils need support, write up a range of verbs in both tenses that they could use.

Check answers, getting pupils to translate their sentences into English.

Gramática

This gives a checklist for distinguishing the present and preterite tenses, focusing on time expressions associated with each tense and the different verb forms in statements and questions. There is practice on this on page 133 of the Pupil's Book.

Point out that in this unit these tenses are colour-coded for support: present tense verbs appear in orange; preterite tense verbs appear in green.

3 Lee los textos otra vez. ¿Quién es? (AT3.5) ▸▸2.3/Y8 4.5a/Y8 5.4◂◂

Reading. Pupils answer the nine questions on the text in exercise 1 by identifying the person being described in each of them.

Answers

1 Paco **2** Natalia **3** Paco **4** Paco **5** James
6 James **7** Natalia **8** James **9** Paco

R Pupils make up true or false sentences for each other on the texts in exercise 1.

4 Con tu compañero/a, pregunta y contesta por Paco, Natalia y James. (AT2.5) ▸▸1.4a/Y8 4.6a/Y8◂◂

Speaking. In pairs pupils take it in turn to ask and answer the eight questions as though they were Paco, Natalia or James.

5 Escucha y escribe los datos de las vacaciones en inglés. (1–3) (AT1.5) ▸▸4.5a/Y8◂◂

Listening. Pupils copy out the grid. They listen to three people talking about where they usually go on holiday and where they went last year and complete the grid in English with the details for each person. Prompt them to note down all the relevant details they hear, including opinions.

Audioscript Track 16

1 – *¿Adónde vas de vacaciones generalmente?*
– *A ver… normalmente voy a Inglaterra de vacaciones.*
– *¿Y qué haces normalmente?*
– *Voy de excursión y visito monumentos. También descanso.*
– *¿Adónde fuiste de vacaciones el año pasado?*
– *El año pasado fui a Grecia, a la costa.*
– *¿Con quién fuiste?*
– *Fui con mi familia.*
– *¿Cómo fuiste?*
– *Fui en avión.*
– *¿Qué hiciste?*
– *Descansé, tomé el sol y jugué al voleibol en la playa.*
– *¿Cómo fue?*
– *Lo pasé bien.*

2 – *¿Adónde vas de vacaciones generalmente?*
– *Normalmente voy a Francia de vacaciones con mi madre. Voy en tren.*
– *¿Qué haces normalmente?*
– *Voy de compras o al salón recreativo. También tomo el sol en la playa.*
– *¿Y adónde fuiste de vacaciones el año pasado?*
– *Pues, el año pasado fui a Italia.*
– *¿Con quién fuiste?*
– *Con mi padre.*
– *¿Cómo fuiste?*
– *Fui en autocar. Fue horrible.*
– *¿Qué hiciste?*
– *Monté en bicicleta y visité monumentos.*
– *¿Cómo fue?*
– *Fue aburrido. Lo pasé mal, muy mal.*

3 – *¿Adónde vas de vacaciones generalmente?*
– *Voy a Irlanda con mi familia.*
– *¿Qué haces normalmente?*
– *Hum… Juego al fútbol y monto en bicicleta con mi hermano…*
– *¿Y adónde fuiste de vacaciones el año pasado?*
– *Fui a España.*
– *¿Cómo fuiste?*
– *Fui en tren.*

- *¿Con quién fuiste?*
- *Fui con mis amigos.*
- *¿Qué hiciste?*
- *Visité monumentos y tomé el sol.*
- *¿Cómo fue?*
- *¡Fue estupendo! Lo pasé genial.*

Answers

	Normally…	Last year…
1	*England, excursions*, visits monuments, rests	Greece (on the coast), with family, by plane, rested, sunbathed, beach volleyball, had a good time
2	France, with mother, by train, shopping, amusement arcade, sunbathes	Italy, with father, by bus (horrible), rode bike, visited monuments (boring, bad time)
3	Ireland, with family, plays football, rides bike	Spain, by train, with friends, visited monuments, sunbathed (brilliant, fantastic)

6 Escucha otra vez y escribe los verbos que entiendes. (1–3) (AT1.5)

▸▸ 4.5a/Y8 ◂◂

Listening. Pupils copy out the grid. They listen to the recording again and note the verbs they hear, identifying them as present or preterite.

Audioscript Track 17

As for exercise 5.

Answers

	Present	Preterite
1	*vas*, voy, haces, voy, visito, descanso	*fuiste*, fui, fuiste, fui, fuiste, fui, hiciste, descansé, tomé, jugué, fue, pasé
2	vas, voy, voy, haces, voy, tomo	fuiste, fui, fuiste, fuiste, fui, fue, hiciste, monté, visité, fue, fue, pasé
3	vas, voy, haces, juego, monto	fuiste, fui, fuiste, fuiste, fui, hiciste, visité, tomé, fue, fue, pasé

7 Haz una presentación sobre tus vacaciones ideales. Utiliza las preguntas del ejercicio 4. (AT 2.5)

▸▸ 1.5a/Y8 5.7 ◂◂

Speaking. Pupils use the questions in exercise 4 to structure a presentation on their ideal holiday. Encourage them to write out the text of what they want to say, but then to create a short list of notes to use as prompts when actually speaking.

Give students the chance to practise their presentations in pairs.

Plenary ▸▸ 5.2 ◂◂

Put the class into teams and tell pupils that you are going to use the Resumen section to test them. Each team chooses a unit: give them two minutes to review that unit and its summary in the Resumen section. They then close their books.

Ask the teams in turn to give a Spanish example for each point listed in the Resumen section. A correct answer wins a point. The team with the most points wins.

Cuaderno A, page 26

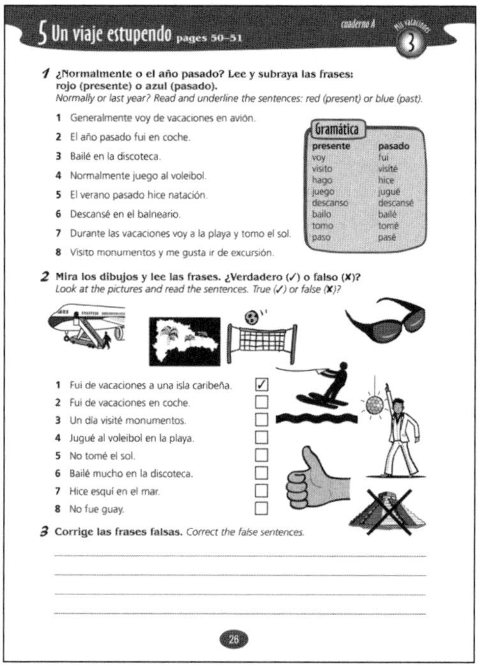

5 Un viaje estupendo pages 50–51 — cuaderno A — Mis vacaciones 3

1 ¿Normalmente o el año pasado? Lee y subraya las frases: rojo (presente) o azul (pasado).
Normally or last year? Read and underline the sentences: red (present) or blue (past).

1 Generalmente voy de vacaciones en avión.
2 El año pasado fui en coche.
3 Bailé en la discoteca.
4 Normalmente juego al voleibol.
5 El verano pasado hice natación.
6 Descansé en el balneario.
7 Durante las vacaciones voy a la playa y tomo el sol.
8 Visito monumentos y me gusta ir de excursión.

Gramática

presente	pasado
voy	fui
visito	visité
hago	hice
juego	jugué
descanso	descansé
bailo	bailé
tomo	tomé
paso	pasé

2 Mira los dibujos y lee las frases. ¿Verdadero (✓) o falso (✗)?
Look at the pictures and read the sentences. True (✓) or false (✗)?

1 Fui de vacaciones a una isla caribeña. ☑
2 Fui de vacaciones en coche. ☐
3 Un día visité monumentos. ☐
4 Jugué al voleibol en la playa. ☐
5 No tomé el sol. ☐
6 Bailé mucho en la discoteca. ☐
7 Hice esquí en el mar. ☐
8 No fue guay. ☐

3 Corrige las frases falsas. *Correct the false sentences.*

26

1 (AT3.5)

1 red **2** blue **3** blue **4** red **5** blue **6** blue **7** red **8** red

2 (AT3.2)

1 ✓ **2** ✗ **3** ✗ **4** ✓ **5** ✗ **6** ✓ **7** ✓ **8** ✗

3 (AT4.2)

2 Fui de vacaciones en avión. **3** No visité monumentos. **5** Tomé el sol. **8** Fue guay.

Cuaderno B, page 26

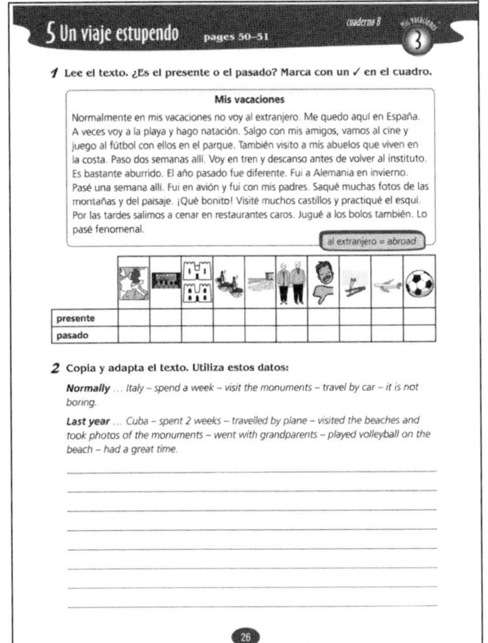

5 Un viaje estupendo pages 50–51 cuaderno B Mis vacaciones 3

1 **Lee el texto. ¿Es el presente o el pasado? Marca con un ✓ en el cuadro.**

Mis vacaciones

Normalmente en mis vacaciones no voy al extranjero. Me quedo aquí en España. A veces voy a la playa y hago natación. Salgo con mis amigos, vamos al cine y juego al fútbol con ellos en el parque. También visito a mis abuelos que viven en la costa. Paso dos semanas allí. Voy en tren y descanso antes de volver al instituto. Es bastante aburrido. El año pasado fue diferente. Fui a Alemania en invierno. Pasé una semana allí. Fui en avión y fui con mis padres. Saqué muchas fotos de las montañas y del paisaje. ¡Qué bonito! Visité muchos castillos y practiqué el esquí. Por las tardes salimos a cenar en restaurantes caros. Jugué a los bolos también. Lo pasé fenomenal.

al extranjero = *abroad*

presente										
pasado										

2 **Copia y adapta el texto. Utiliza estos datos:**

Normally *… Italy – spend a week – visit the monuments – travel by car – it is not boring.*

Last year *… Cuba – spent 2 weeks – travelled by plane – visited the beaches and took photos of the monuments – went with grandparents – played volleyball on the beach – had a great time.*

26

1 (AT3.5)

	a	b	c	d	e	f	g	h	i	j
presente		✓			✓	✓	✓			✓
pasado	✓		✓	✓				✓	✓	

2 (AT4.5)

R & A Pack, Gramática page 15

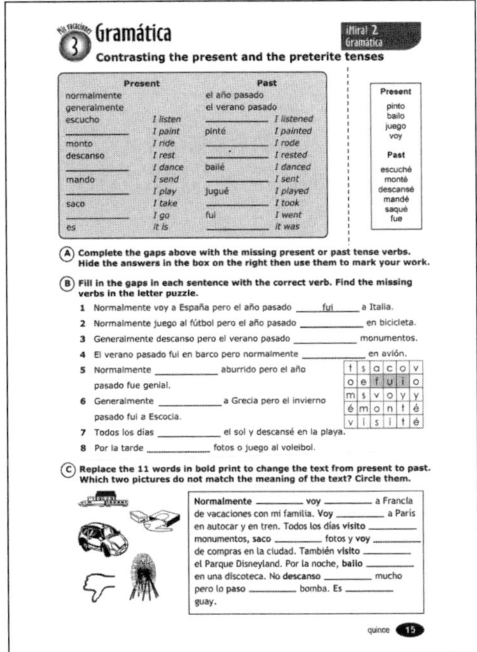

Mis vacaciones 3 Gramática — ¡Mira! 2 Gramática

Contrasting the present and the preterite tenses

Present		Past	
normalmente		el año pasado	
generalmente		el verano pasado	
escucho	*I listen*	________	*I listened*
________	*I paint*	pinté	*I painted*
monto	*I ride*	________	*I rode*
descanso	*I rest*	________	*I rested*
________	*I dance*	bailé	*I danced*
mando	*I send*	________	*I sent*
________	*I play*	jugué	*I played*
saco	*I take*	________	*I took*
________	*I go*	fui	*I went*
es	*it is*	________	*it was*

Present
pinto
bailo
juego
voy

Past
escuché
monté
descansé
mandé
saqué
fue

Ⓐ **Complete the gaps above with the missing present or past tense verbs. Hide the answers in the box on the right then use them to mark your work.**

Ⓑ **Fill in the gaps in each sentence with the correct verb. Find the missing verbs in the letter puzzle.**

1 Normalmente voy a España pero el año pasado ___fui___ a Italia.
2 Normalmente juego al fútbol pero el año pasado ________ en bicicleta.
3 Generalmente descanso pero el verano pasado ________ monumentos.
4 El verano pasado fui en barco pero normalmente ________ en avión.
5 Normalmente ________ aburrido pero el año pasado fue genial.
6 Generalmente ________ a Grecia pero el invierno pasado fui a Escocia.
7 Todos los días ________ el sol y descansé en la playa.
8 Por la tarde ________ fotos o juego al voleibol.

t	s	a	c	o	v
o	e	f	u	i	o
m	s	v	o	y	y
é	m	o	n	t	é
v	i	s	i	t	é

Ⓒ **Replace the 11 words in bold print to change the text from present to past. Which two pictures do not match the meaning of the text? Circle them.**

Normalmente ________ **voy** ________ a Francia de vacaciones con mi familia. **Voy** ________ a París en autocar y en tren. Todos los días **visito** ________ monumentos, **saco** ________ fotos y **voy** ________ de compras en la ciudad. También **visito** ________ el Parque Disneyland. Por la noche, **bailo** ________ en una discoteca. No **descanso** ________ mucho pero lo **paso** ________ bomba. **Es** ________ guay.

quince 15

Ⓐ escuché; pinto; monté; descansé; bailo; mandé; juego; saqué; voy; fue

Ⓑ **2** monté **3** visité **4** voy **5** es **6** voy **7** tomé **8** saco

Ⓒ el año/verano pasado; fui; fui; visité; saqué; fui; visité; bailé; descansé; pasé; fue
Pictures which do not match text – car, thumbs down

R & A Pack, Gramática page 16

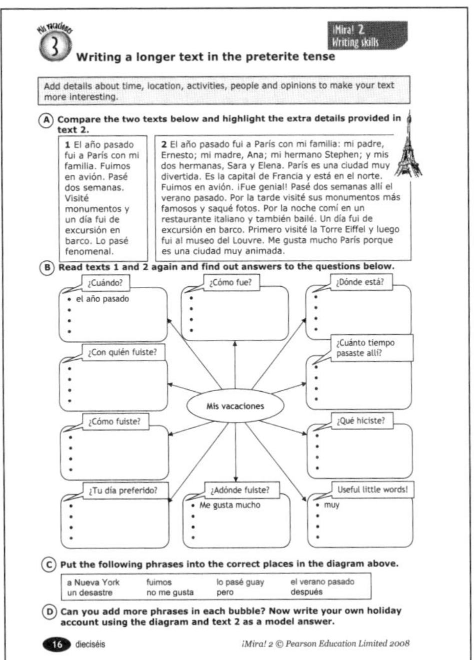

Mis vacaciones 3 — ¡Mira! 2 Writing skills

Writing a longer text in the preterite tense

Add details about time, location, activities, people and opinions to make your text more interesting.

Ⓐ **Compare the two texts below and highlight the extra details provided in text 2.**

1 El año pasado fui a París con mi familia. Fuimos en avión. Pasé dos semanas. Visité monumentos y un día fui de excursión en barco. Lo pasé fenomenal.

2 El año pasado fui a París con mi familia: mi padre, Ernesto; mi madre, Ana; mi hermano Stephen; y mis dos hermanas, Sara y Elena. París es una ciudad muy divertida. Es la capital de Francia y está en el norte. Fuimos en avión. ¡Fue genial! Pasé dos semanas allí el verano pasado. Por la tarde visité sus monumentos más famosos y saqué fotos. Por la noche comí en un restaurante italiano y también bailé. Un día fui de excursión en barco. Primero visité la Torre Eiffel y luego fui al museo del Louvre. Me gusta mucho París porque es una ciudad muy animada.

Ⓑ **Read texts 1 and 2 again and find out answers to the questions below.**

Mis vacaciones
¿Cuándo? • el año pasado
¿Cómo fue?
¿Dónde está?
¿Con quién fuiste?
¿Cuánto tiempo pasaste allí?
¿Cómo fuiste?
¿Qué hiciste?
¿Tu día preferido?
¿Adónde fuiste? • Me gusta mucho
Useful little words! • muy

Ⓒ **Put the following phrases into the correct places in the diagram above.**

a Nueva York	fuimos	lo pasé guay	el verano pasado
un desastre	no me gusta	pero	después

Ⓓ **Can you add more phrases in each bubble? Now write your own holiday account using the diagram and text 2 as a model answer.**

16 dieciséis *¡Mira! 2 © Pearson Education Limited 2008*

Ⓐ mi padre, Ernesto; mi madre, Ana; mi hermano Stephen; y mis dos hermanas, Sara y Elena. París es una ciudad muy divertida. Es la capital de Francia y está en el norte. ¡Fue genial! … allí el verano pasado. Por la tarde… y saqué fotos. Por la noche comí en un restaurante italiano y también bailé. Primero visité la Torre Eiffel y luego fui al museo del Louvre. Me gusta mucho París porque es una ciudad muy animada.

Ⓑ **¿Cuándo?** *el año pasado*, el verano pasado, por la tarde, por la noche; **¿Cómo fue?** genial; **¿Dónde está?** Francia, norte; **¿Con quién fuiste?** familia, padre, Ernesto; madre, Ana; hermano Stephen; dos hermanas Sara y Elena; **¿Cuánto tiempo pasaste allí?** dos semanas; **¿Cómo fuiste?** París/avión, excursión/barco; **¿Qué hiciste?** visité monumentos, saqué fotos, comí, bailé, fui de excursión; **¿Tu día preferido?** un día fui de excursión en barco; **¿Adónde fuiste?** París; **Useful little words!** *muy*, y, también, luego, porque

Ⓒ a Nueva York, ¿Adónde fuiste?; fuimos, ¿Cómo fuiste?; lo pasé guay, ¿Tu día preferido?; el verano pasado, ¿Cuándo?; un desastre, ¿Cómo fue?; no me gusta, pero, después, Useful little words!

Resumen y Prepárate (Pupil's Book pages 52–53)

Resumen

This is a checklist of language covered in Module 3. Pupils can work on this in pairs to check what they have learned and remembered. There is a Resumen page in the Resource and Assessment Pack. Encourage them to look back at the module and to use the grammar section, to revise what they are unclear about. You can also use the Resumen as a useful plenary at the end of each unit.

Prepárate

These revision tests can be used for pupils to practise prior to the assessment tasks in the Resource and Assessment Pack.

Resources

CD2, track 18
R & A Pack, Module 3: Resumen, Prueba, I can...

1 Escucha. Copia y rellena la tabla. (1–5) (AT1.3–4) ▸▸1.1/Y8◂◂

Listening. Pupils copy out the table. They listen to five conversations about holidays and complete the table with the details.

Audioscript Track 18

1 – *¿Adónde fuiste de vacaciones el año pasado?*
– *El año pasado fui a Francia.*
– *¿Cómo fuiste?*
– *Fui en coche.*
– *¿Cómo fue?*
– *Fue horrible.*

2 – *¿Adónde fuiste de vacaciones el año pasado?*
– *El verano pasado fui a Alemania.*
– *¿Cómo fuiste?*
– *Fuimos en tren.*
– *¿Cómo fue?*
– *Fue guay.*

3 – *¿Adónde fuiste de vacaciones el año pasado?*
– *A ver, el año pasado fui a México de vacaciones.*
– *¿Cómo fuiste?*
– *Fui en avión.*
– *¿Cómo fue?*
– *Fue genial.*

4 – *¿Adónde fuiste de vacaciones el año pasado?*
– *El año pasado fui a Grecia.*
– *¡A Grecia! ¡Qué guay! ¿Cómo fuiste?*
– *Fui en barco.*
– *¿Y cómo fue?*
– *Fue estupendo. Me gusta mucho Grecia.*

5 – *¿Adónde fuiste de vacaciones el verano pasado?*
– *A ver... el verano pasado fui a Escocia.*
– *¿Cómo fuiste?*
– *Buagh, fui en autocar.*
– *Pues, ¿cómo fue?*
– *Fue aburrido.*

Answers

País – Transporte – Opinión
1 *Francia – coche – horrible*
2 Alemania – tren – guay
3 México – avión – genial
4 Grecia – barco – estupendo
5 Escocia – autocar – aburrido

2 Con tu compañero/a, pregunta y contesta. (AT2.2) ▸▸1.4a/Y8◂◂

Speaking. In pairs pupils take it in turn to ask and answer questions about what they did on holiday using the prompts in the picture grid. A sample exchange is given.

3 Lee el texto. Contesta a las preguntas en inglés. (AT3.5) ▸▸2.3/Y8◂◂

Reading. Pupils read the text on Jorge's holidays and answer the six questions on it in English.

Answers

1 He normally spends his holidays in France.
2 He went to Italy last summer.
3 He travelled by train.
4 Naples is in the south of Italy, on the coast.
5 He visited monuments, went on trips, danced and listened to music.
6 His holiday was great.

4 Separa estas preguntas. Luego escribe las respuestas utilizando los dibujos. (AT4.4, AT3.2) ▸▸4.6a/Y8◂◂

Writing. Pupils write out the questions concealed in the wordsnake. They then use the picture prompts to write responses to the questions.

Answers

¿Adónde fuiste? – Fui a México.
¿Cómo fuiste? – Fui en avión.
¿Con quién fuiste? – Fui con mi familia.
¿Qué hiciste? – Bailé, visité monumentos, tomé el sol y jugué al fútbol.
¿Qué tal lo pasaste? – ¡Lo pasé bomba!

¡Extra! 1 (Pupil's Book pages 54–55)

Learning objectives
- Understanding longer texts
- Using dictionaries and word lists

Framework objectives
2.2/Y8 Reading – (a) longer, more complex texts

Grammar
- The preterite tense (revision)

Key language
Revision of language from Module 3

High-frequency words
Revision of language from Module 3

Resources
CD2, track 19

Starter

Aim

To introduce the historical figure Christopher Columbus.

Ask pupils working in pairs to come up with as many facts in English as they can about Columbus. Pool answers.

1 Lee los textos. Escucha y pon las frases en el orden correcto. (AT3.5)

▸▸2.2a/Y8 5.4◂◂

Listening. Pupils listen to the recording once. They then listen again and put the five captions to the pictures in the order they hear them.

After playing the recording, ask pupils where they think you might hear a recording like this. (as part of a radio or television documentary)

Audioscript Track 19

Cristóbal Colón fue explorador.
Encontró para España una ruta desde Europa hasta América – un nuevo continente.
En 1492 hizo su primer viaje. Primero fue a San Salvador y luego a Cuba.
Después fue a La Española, otra isla en el mar Caribe.
Regresó del Nuevo Mundo otra el cacao, la patata y el maíz.

Answers

c, d, a, e, b

2 Busca estas frases en español en el texto. (AT3.4) ▸▸5.3 5.4▸▸

Reading. Pupils find the Spanish versions of the five English sentences listed.

Answers

1. *Primero fue a San Salvador.*
2. Regresó del Nuevo Mundo.
3. Cristóbal Colón fue explorador.
4. Después fue a La Española.
5. Encontró para España una ruta desde Europa hasta América.

3 Lee las frases. Tu compañero/a dice 'sí' o 'no'. (AT2.3, AT3.4)

▸▸4.6b/Y8◂◂

Speaking. In pairs pupils take it in turn to read the five statements about the text in exercise 1 and to respond by agreeing or disagreeing.

Answers

1. ***No**, no es una isla en el mar Mediterráneo. Es una isla en el mar Caribe.*
2. **Sí**, Cristóbal Colón regresó del Nuevo Mundo con el cacao, la patata y el maíz.
3. **Sí**, el primer viaje de Cristóbal Colón fue a San Salvador y luego a Cuba.
4. **No**, Cristóbal Colón no fue profesor. Fue explorador.
5. **No**, Cristóbal Colón no encontró para Inglaterra una ruta desde Europa hasta América. Encontró para España una ruta desde Europa hasta América.

4 Copia y completa el texto con las palabras del cuadro. (AT4.4, AT3.5)

▸▸4.5a/Y8◂◂

Writing. Pupils copy out the gap-fill text, using the words supplied to fill in the gaps.

Answers

Me llamo Roberto Buitrago y (1) ***fui*** de viaje con el famoso Cristóbal Colón en 1492. Primero (2) **fuimos** a San Salvador. Probé el cacao. (3) **Fue** delicioso. Muy, muy bueno. Luego (4) **fuimos** en nuestro barco a Cuba. (5) **Fue** genial. Después, fuimos a La Española, otra isla pequeña en el mar Caribe. (6) **Fue** estupendo. No quiero regresar. ¡Me quedo aquí!

5 Contesta a las preguntas en inglés. (AT3.5) ▶▶2.2a/Y8◀◀

Reading. Pupils reread the completed text from exercise 4 and answer the five comprehension questions on it in English.

Answers

1 He travelled with Christopher Columbus.
2 On San Salvador he tried cocoa. He thought it was delicious.
3 The journey to Cuba was great.
4 After Cuba they went to a small island in the Caribbean/La Española.
5 He thought they were brilliant.

6 Lee el texto. Busca las palabras que no entiendes en el Vocabulario. (AT3.4) ▶▶5.3 5.4 5.5◀◀

Reading. Pupils read the website for the Tortuguero National Park, looking up any words they don't know in the Vocabulario section at the back of the Pupil's Book. As a first step they should aim to use reading strategies to work out as much as they can: they should discuss this in pairs. Run through strategies as necessary: looking for cognates in English and Spanish, using context, using other clues such as pictures.

Ask pupils to identify four useful items of vocabulary in the text (single words or phrases) and to note these down and learn them. Remind them to use a dictionary to get any information they need on new words: gender, singular form, infinitive form of verbs, etc. Explain that approaching texts like this is a useful way of developing more independence in learning.

R Ask comprehension questions on the text.

+ Pupils imagine they went to the Tortuguero National Park last year and write a postcard to a friend describing their trip. They could include details as follows:

- where they normally go on holiday
- who they went with
- how they travelled
- what the Park was like
- their opinion of the Park (including reasons)

Plenary

Put the class into teams. Each team chooses a topic – Christopher Columbus, Roberto Buitrago or the Tortuguero National Park. Give them one minute to look again at the details for their chosen topic in the Pupil's Book, then get them to close their books. Each team has to come up with four facts on their topic: a correct fact wins two points, one with a single error wins one point. The team with the most points is the winner.

¡Extra! 2 (Pupil's Book pages 56–57)

Learning objectives
- Reading Spanish out loud
- Learning about a Spanish painter

Framework objectives
2.1/Y8 Reading – authentic materials

Grammar
- The preterite tense (revision)

Key language
Revision of language from Module 3

High-frequency words
Revision of language from Module 3

Cross-curricular
ICT: Internet research

Resources
CD2, tracks 20–21
Cuadernos A & B, pp. 27–28

Starter

Aim
To lead into episode 3 of the photo story by recapping on the first two episodes.

Write up: *¿Quién habla? ¿Patricia? ¿Diego? ¿Los dos?*

Check that pupils know what *¿Los dos?* means.

Then give the class these statements: they need to note down the speaker(s) for each of them.

1 *Conocí a un chico hoy.* (P)
2 *Me gusta bailar.* (P)
3 *Vivo en Barcelona.* (los dos)
4 *Me gustan los videojuegos.* (D)
5 *Es alto y delgado.* (P)
6 *¿Te gustaría salir conmigo?* (D)
7 *Tomo el sol todos los fines de semana.* (P)

1 Escucha y lee. (AT1.5) ⏩2.1/Y8 4.5a/Y8⏪

Listening. Pupils listen to the recording of the story and read along with the text.

Audioscript Track 20

1 – *Diego, ¿adónde fuiste de vacaciones el año pasado?*
– *Pues, no fui de vacaciones, me quedé en Barcelona, pero hice excursiones.*
2 – *¿Ah, sí? ¿Adónde fuiste?*
– *Fui a Cadaqués en barco con un amigo.*
3 – *¿Dónde está?*
– *¿¡Dónde está Cadaqués!? Ah sí, eres mexicana… A ver, Cadaqués está al norte de Barcelona.*
4 – *Es un pueblo muy famoso de pescadores y artistas.*
– *¿Y qué hiciste en Cadaqués?*
5 – *Tomé el sol, jugué al fútbol en la playa y visité la casa de Salvador Dalí. Es un pintor surrealista muy famoso.*
– *¿Dalí? Ah sí, me gustan mucho sus pinturas. Es mi pintor favorito.*
6 – *¿Te gusta el dibujo, Diego?*
– *Sí, me encanta el dibujo.*
– *A mí también me encanta el dibujo…*

2 Con tu compañero/a, lee en voz alta la historia de Diego y Patricia. (AT2.5) ⏩5.6⏪

Speaking. In pairs pupils read the story aloud, each taking the role of Diego or Patricia. Encourage them to focus on pronunciation and stress and to try and sound as fluent as possible, following the model of the recording.

3 Con tu compañero/a, pregunta y contesta. (AT2.5) ⏩1.4a/Y8 4.6a/Y8 5.1⏪

Speaking. In pairs pupils take it in turn to ask and answer the six questions on the story.

You may want to warn pupils that this involves changing the 1st person verb forms in the text to the 3rd person.

Answers
1 El año pasado durante las vacaciones se quedó en Barcelona y hizo excursiones.
2 Fue en barco.
3 Fue con un amigo.
4 Cadaqués está al norte de Barcelona.
5 Tomó el sol, jugó al fútbol en la playa y visitó la casa de Salvador Dalí.
6 A Diego le gusta el dibujo.

4 Copia y completa el texto. (AT4.3, AT3.4) ⏩5.4⏪

Writing. Pupils copy out and complete the gap-fill text, replacing the picture prompts with words.

Answers
El año pasado Diego fue a Cadaqués en (**1**) ***barco*** con un amigo. Cadaqués está al (**2**) **norte** de Barcelona. Es un (**3**) **pueblo** muy famoso de pescadores y artistas. Diego tomó el (**4**) **sol**, jugó al (**5**) **fútbol** en la **playa** y visitó la casa de Salvador Dalí.

5 Escucha y lee el texto sobre Dalí. Luego copia y rellena la tabla. (AT3.4) ▸▸2.1/Y8 5.4◂◂

Reading. Pupils read the Zona cultura feature on Salvador Dalí. Some vocabulary support is given.

They then copy out the table and complete it with information on all six verbs: the infinitive with translation into English and the preterite form of the verb used in the text, also with a translation into English.

ZONA CULTURA This section gives cultural information on Salvador Dalí. The text is also given on the recording.

Pupils listen to the recording and read through the text at the same time. Then translate the text round the class, with each pupil doing a sentence.

You could use the text as a starting point for a general discussion about Dalí. Have pupils heard of him? Have they seen his paintings? What are they like?

You could access some Dalí paintings on the internet or bring in a book on his work to show pupils.

Audioscript Track 21

Zona Cultura – Dalí

Salvador Dalí (1904–89) fue pintor. Estudió en Madrid. Utilizó imágenes surrealistas en sus dibujos. En 1940 fue a los Estados Unidos. Luego en 1948 regresó a España. Trabajó en Cadaqués hasta su muerte.

Answers

Infinitive	English	Preterite	English
ser	*to be*	*fue*	*he was*
estudiar	to study	estudió	he studied
ir	to go	fue	he went
utilizar	to use	utilizó	he used
trabajar	to work	trabajó	he worked
regresar	to return	regresó	he returned

6 Elige a una persona histórica famosa y describe su vida. Utiliza el texto sobre Dalí como modelo. (AT4.4) ▸▸2.1/Y8 2.4a/Y8◂◂

Writing. Using the text on Dalí in exercise 5 as a model, pupils choose a famous historical person and describe his/her life.

Pupils could do research on their chosen person on the internet, using a Spanish website, or accessing both English and Spanish versions of a website like Wikipedia.

Warn pupils that when doing research on Spanish websites, they will encounter a lot of language they don't know. The important thing is to use what they do know and focus on identifying cognates in Spanish and English, using layout/structure/photos, etc., to help them glean the information they need. They should be encouraged by how many of the key points they are able to understand.

Plenary ▸▸5.8◂◂

Choose a few examples of texts pupils have written for exercise 6 and read them out. Ask pupils comprehension questions on them in English.

Cuaderno A, page 27

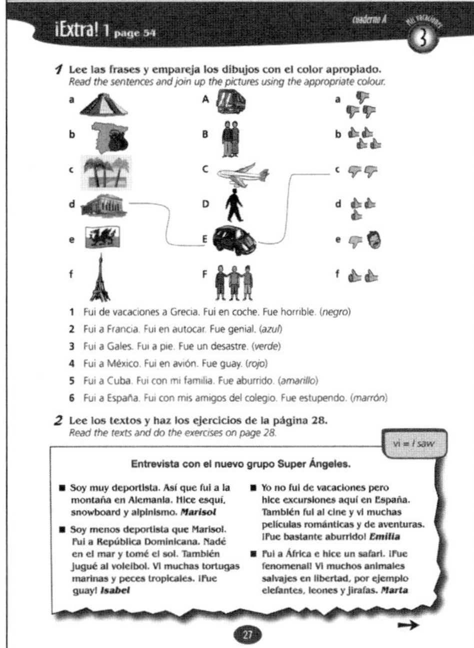

¡Extra! 1 page 54 cuaderno A 3 Mis vacaciones

1 **Lee las frases y empareja los dibujos con el color apropiado.**
Read the sentences and join up the pictures using the appropriate colour.

a A a
b B b
c C c
d D d
e E e
f F f

1 Fui de vacaciones a Grecia. Fui en coche. Fue horrible. (*negro*)
2 Fui a Francia. Fui en autocar. Fue genial. (*azul*)
3 Fui a Gales. Fui a pie. Fue un desastre. (*verde*)
4 Fui a México. Fui en avión. Fue guay. (*rojo*)
5 Fui a Cuba. Fui con mi familia. Fue aburrido. (*amarillo*)
6 Fui a España. Fui con mis amigos del colegio. Fue estupendo. (*marrón*)

2 **Lee los textos y haz los ejercicios de la página 28.**
Read the texts and do the exercises on page 28.

vi = *I saw*

Entrevista con el nuevo grupo Super Ángeles.

- **Soy muy deportista. Así que fui a la montaña en Alemania. Hice esquí, snowboard y alpinismo. *Marisol***
- **Soy menos deportista que Marisol. Fui a República Dominicana. Nadé en el mar y tomé el sol. También jugué al voleibol. Vi muchas tortugas marinas y peces tropicales. ¡Fue guay! *Isabel***
- **Yo no fui de vacaciones pero hice excursiones aquí en España. También fui al cine y vi muchas películas románticas y de aventuras. ¡Fue bastante aburrido! *Emilia***
- **Fui a África e hice un safari. ¡Fue fenomenal! Vi muchos animales salvajes en libertad, por ejemplo elefantes, leones y jirafas. *Marta***

27

1 (AT3.2)

1 d E c (black) **2** f A d (blue) **3** e D a (green)
4 a C f (red) **5** c B e (yellow) **6** b F b (brown)

2 (AT3.3)

Cuaderno A, page 28

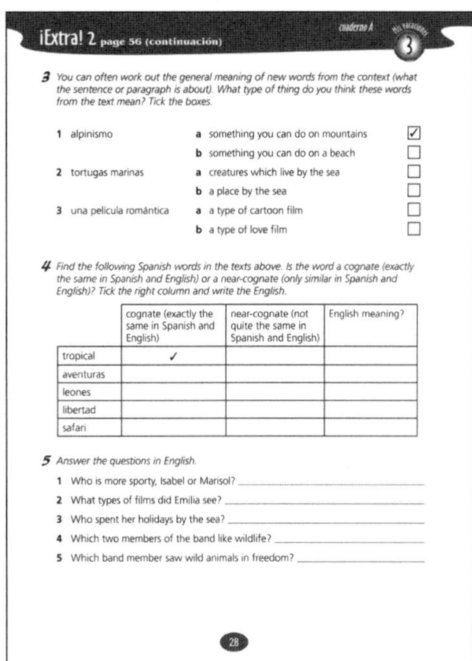

¡Extra! 2 page 56 (continuación) cuaderno A 3 Mis vacaciones

3 *You can often work out the general meaning of new words from the context (what the sentence or paragraph is about). What type of thing do you think these words from the text mean? Tick the boxes.*

1 alpinismo — a something you can do on mountains ☑ — b something you can do on a beach ☐
2 tortugas marinas — a creatures which live by the sea ☐ — b a place by the sea ☐
3 una película romántica — a a type of cartoon film ☐ — b a type of love film ☐

4 *Find the following Spanish words in the texts above. Is the word a cognate (exactly the same in Spanish and English) or a near-cognate (only similar in Spanish and English)? Tick the right column and write the English.*

	cognate (exactly the same in Spanish and English)	near-cognate (not quite the same in Spanish and English)	English meaning?
tropical	✓		
aventuras			
leones			
libertad			
safari			

5 *Answer the questions in English.*

1 Who is more sporty, Isabel or Marisol? ____
2 What types of films did Emilia see? ____
3 Who spent her holidays by the sea? ____
4 Which two members of the band like wildlife? ____
5 Which band member saw wild animals in freedom? ____

28

3 (AT3.3)

1 a **2** a **3** b

4 (AT3.3)

tropical – cognate – tropical
aventuras – near-cognate – adventures
leones – near-cognate – lions
libertad – near-cognate – liberty
safari – cognate – safari

5 (AT3.3)

1 Marisol **2** romantic and adventure films
3 Isabel **4** Marta and Isabel **5** Marta

Cuaderno B, page 27

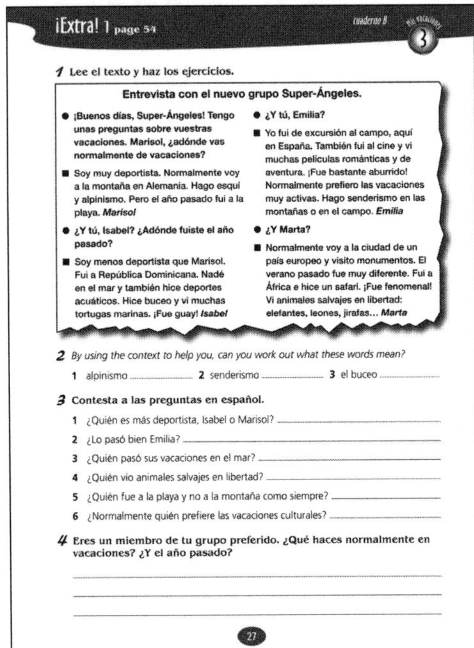

¡Extra! 1 page 54 — cuaderno B — Mis vacaciones 3

1 **Lee el texto y haz los ejercicios.**

Entrevista con el nuevo grupo Super-Ángeles.

- **¡Buenos días, Super-Ángeles! Tengo unas preguntas sobre vuestras vacaciones. Marisol, ¿adónde vas normalmente de vacaciones?**
- Soy muy deportista. Normalmente voy a la montaña en Alemania. Hago esquí y alpinismo. Pero el año pasado fui a la playa. ***Marisol***
- **¿Y tú, Isabel? ¿Adónde fuiste el año pasado?**
- Soy menos deportista que Marisol. Fui a República Dominicana. Nadé en el mar y también hice deportes acuáticos. Hice buceo y vi muchas tortugas marinas. ¡Fue guay! ***Isabel***
- **¿Y tú, Emilia?**
- Yo fui de excursión al campo, aquí en España. También fui al cine y vi muchas películas románticas y de aventura. ¡Fue bastante aburrido! Normalmente prefiero las vacaciones muy activas. Hago senderismo en las montañas o en el campo. ***Emilia***
- **¿Y Marta?**
- Normalmente voy a la ciudad de un país europeo y visito monumentos. El verano pasado fue muy diferente. Fui a África e hice un safari. ¡Fue fenomenal! Vi animales salvajes en libertad: elefantes, leones, jirafas… ***Marta***

2 *By using the context to help you, can you work out what these words mean?*

1 alpinismo .... 2 senderismo .... 3 el buceo ....

3 **Contesta a las preguntas en español.**

1 ¿Quién es más deportista, Isabel o Marisol? ....
2 ¿Lo pasó bien Emilia? ....
3 ¿Quién pasó sus vacaciones en el mar? ....
4 ¿Quién vio animales salvajes en libertad? ....
5 ¿Quién fue a la playa y no a la montaña como siempre? ....
6 ¿Normalmente quién prefiere las vacaciones culturales? ....

4 **Eres un miembro de tu grupo preferido. ¿Qué haces normalmente en vacaciones? ¿Y el año pasado?**

27

1 (AT3.5)

2 (AT3.5)

1 mountain climbing **2** trekking/walking **3** diving

3 (AT3.5)

1 Marisol **2** No, fue aburrido. **3** Isabel
4 Marta **5** Marisol **6** Marta

4 (AT3.5)

Cuaderno B, page 28

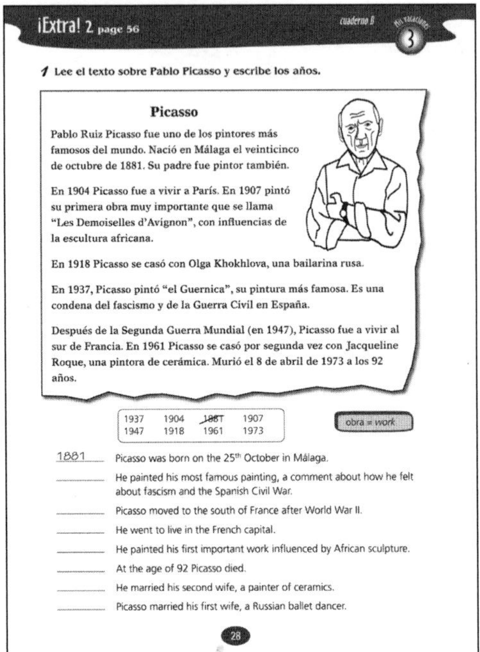

¡Extra! 2 page 56 — cuaderno B — Mis vacaciones 3

1 **Lee el texto sobre Pablo Picasso y escribe los años.**

Picasso

Pablo Ruiz Picasso fue uno de los pintores más famosos del mundo. Nació en Málaga el veinticinco de octubre de 1881. Su padre fue pintor también.

En 1904 Picasso fue a vivir a París. En 1907 pintó su primera obra muy importante que se llama "Les Demoiselles d'Avignon", con influencias de la escultura africana.

En 1918 Picasso se casó con Olga Khokhlova, una bailarina rusa.

En 1937, Picasso pintó "el Guernica", su pintura más famosa. Es una condena del fascismo y de la Guerra Civil en España.

Después de la Segunda Guerra Mundial (en 1947), Picasso fue a vivir al sur de Francia. En 1961 Picasso se casó por segunda vez con Jacqueline Roque, una pintora de cerámica. Murió el 8 de abril de 1973 a los 92 años.

1937 1904 ~~1881~~ 1907
1947 1918 1961 1973

obra = work

1881 Picasso was born on the 25th October in Málaga.
.... He painted his most famous painting, a comment about how he felt about fascism and the Spanish Civil War.
.... Picasso moved to the south of France after World War II.
.... He went to live in the French capital.
.... He painted his first important work influenced by African sculpture.
.... At the age of 92 Picasso died.
.... He married his second wife, a painter of ceramics.
.... Picasso married his first wife, a Russian ballet dancer.

28

1 (AT3.5)

1881 Picasso was born on the 25th October in Málaga.
1937 He painted his most famous painting, a comment about how he felt about fascism and the Spanish Civil War.
1947 Picasso moved to the south of France after World War II.
1904 He went to live in the French capital.
1907 He painted his first important work influenced by African sculpture.
1973 At the age of 92 Picasso died.
1961 He married his second wife, a painter of ceramics.
1918 Picasso married his first wife, a Russian ballet dancer.

Te toca a ti (Pupil's Book pages 118–119)

- Self-access reading and writing at two levels

A Reinforcement

1 *Solve the anagrams. Write out the sentences and match each one to a picture.* (AT4.2, AT3.2) ▸▸5.4◂◂

Writing. Pupils work out the anagrammed words, write out the completed sentences and match each to the correct picture.

Answers

1. *Lo pasé **guay**. – c*
2. Lo pasé **bien**. – d
3. Lo pasé **fenomenal**. – b
4. Lo pasé **mal**. – e
5. Lo pasé **bomba**. – a

2 *Write out the questions and answers in pairs.* (AT4.2, AT3.3) ▸▸4.6a/Y8◂◂

Writing. Pupils match each question with the correct answer, writing out both forms.

Answers

1. *¿Adónde fuiste de vacaciones?*
   Fui a Italia.
2. ¿Con quién fuiste?
   Fui con mis amigos.
3. ¿Cómo fuiste?
   Fui en avión.
4. Qué hiciste?
   Fui de excursión y visité monumentos. Por la noche, fuimos a la discoteca.
5. ¿Cómo fue?
   Fue guay.

3 *Match up the holidays to the descriptions. (There is one description too many.)* (AT3.3) ▸▸5.4◂◂

Reading. Pupils look at the three pictures and find the correct text for each from the four given.

Answers

1 b **2** d **3** a

B Extension

1 *Put the words in the wordsnake into three groups.* (AT4.2, AT3.3) ▸▸5.2◂◂

Writing. Pupils split the wordsnake into words, which they group under the three headings given: transport, verbs and countries. Remind them as necessary that countries take a capital letter.

Answers

Transporte: *coche,* tren, avión, autocar, barco
Verbos: *mandé,* jugué, fui, bailé, descansé
Países: *España*, Grecia, Portugal, Argentina, Escocia

2 *Who is talking: Claudia or Norberto? Write C or N.* (AT3.5) ▸▸5.3 5.4◂◂

Reading. Pupils read the two emails, from Claudia and Norberto. They decide for each of the ten pictures whether it refers to Claudia's text (by writing C) or Norberto's (by writing N).

Answers

1 *N* **2** N **3** C **4** C **5** C **6** N **7** C **8** C
9 N **10** C

3 *Copy out the text with the correct verbs.* (AT4.3, AT3.4) ▸▸4.5a/Y8◂◂

Writing. Pupils copy out the text and complete it by choosing the correct verb from the two options given each time.

Answers

El año pasado fui a Grecia de vacaciones. ***(1) Visité*** monumentos y (**2**) **mandé** mensajes. (**3**) **Jugué** al fútbol y (**4**) **monté** en bicicleta también. (**5**) **Tomé** el sol en la playa. Lo pasé bomba. (**6**) **Fue** guay.

Module 4 La comida (Pupil's Book pages 60–77)

Unit	Framework	Levels and PoS	Key language	Grammar	Skills
1 ¿Qué desayunas? (pp. 60–61) Talking about mealtimes Understanding time expressions	**4.2/Y8** Language – increasing vocabulary	**2–4** **2.1a** identify patterns **2.1b** memorising **2.1d** previous knowledge **4b** communicate in pairs etc.	*¿Qué desayunas/comes/meriendas/cenas?* *Desayuno/Como/Meriendo/Ceno…* *carne con verduras/cereales/fruta/galletas/ magdalenas/pasta/patatas fritas/pescado con ensalada/pizza/pollo/ostadas/un bocadillo* *¿Qué bebes?* *Bebo…* *Cola Cao/té/zumo de naranja* *No meriendo.* *No desayuno nada.* *Nunca como.* *¿A qué hora desayunas/cenas?* *Desayuno a las ocho.* *Como a la una.* *a mediodía* *siempre, generalmente, normalmente, a veces, de vez en cuando, todo el tiempo*	Time expressions	Using reading strategies to work out new words Developing vocabulary learning skills Writing creatively in Spanish
2 En el mercado (pp. 62–63) Shopping for food Using high numbers	**1.3/Y8** Listening – (a) understanding language for specific functions **1.3/Y8** Speaking – (b) using language for specific functions	**2–4** **2.1a** identify patterns **2.2e** ask and answer questions **2.2j** adapt previously learned language **3b** sounds and writing **3f** compare experiences **4b** communicate in pairs etc. **4f** language for interest/ enjoyment	*cien* *ciento diez* *doscientos, trescientos, cuatrocientos, quinientos, seiscientos, setecientos, ochocientos, novecientos, mil* *¿Qué quieres?* *un kilo de…* *dos kilos de…* *quinientos gramos de…* *medio kilo de…* *chorizo/jamón/manzanas/peras/queso/tomates/ uvas/zanahorias* *una barra de pan* *una lechuga* *un cartón de leche* *una botella de agua* *¿Algo más?* *Sí, quiero…* *por favor* *Nada más, gracias.* *¿Cuánto cuesta?* *Un euro.* *Dos euros y veinte.* *Cuatro euros y veinticinco.*	The preterite tense (revision of *-ar* verbs)	Predicting pronunciation Applying recognised patterns to new language

Module 4 La comida (Pupil's Book pages 60–77)

Unit	Framework	Levels and PoS	Key language	Grammar	Skills
3 En el restaurante (pp. 64–65) Eating at a restaurant Understanding the difference between *tú* and *usted*	**3.2/Y8** Culture – (b) customs, traditions **5.2** Strategies – memorising	**2–4** **2.1b** memorising **2.2a** listen for gist **2.2e** ask and answer questions **2.2f** initiate/sustain conversations **3e** different countries/ cultures **4b** communicate in pairs etc. **4e** use a range of resources	*¿Qué vas/va a tomar?* *De primer plato…* *De segundo plato…* *De postre…* *quiero…* *ensalada* *flan* *fruta* *gambas* *helado (de chocolate)* *paella* *pescado* *pollo* *sopa de mariscos* *¿Para beber?* *(Quiero)… , por favor.* *agua* *Coca-Cola* *limonada* *Tengo hambre.* *No tengo hambre.* *Tengo sed.* *La cuenta, por favor.*	*tú/usted*	Participating in an unscripted dialogue Developing vocabulary learning skills Developing independence as a learner Reviewing progress/ checking work using the Mini-test
4 Una cena especial (pp. 66–67) Talking about a past meal Using the preterite of *-er* and *-ir* verbs	**1.4/Y8** Speaking – (b) unscripted conversations **5.1** Strategies – patterns	**4–5** **2.1a** identify patterns **2.1b** memorising **2.1d** previous knowledge **2.1e** use reference materials **2.2g** write clearly and coherently **2.2h** redraft to improve writing **3c** apply grammar **4e** use a range of resources **4f** language for interest/ enjoyment	*El fin de semana pasado…* *salí con…* *fui a…* *un restaurante español* *un restaurante muy caro* *Comí ensalada.* *Mi compañero/a comió gambas.* *Compartimos una paella.* *Bebimos agua.* *Hablamos de fútbol/música.* *¡Fue genial!*	The preterite tense (*-er*/*-ir* verbs)	Using reading strategies to work out tense usage Developing grammar learning skills Recognising and using techniques to improve writing Writing an extended text in Spanish

continued

Module 4 La comida (Pupil's Book pages 60–77)

Unit	Framework	Levels and PoS	Key language	Grammar	Skills
5 ¿Qué te gusta comer? (pp. 68–69) Talking about likes and dislikes Using past, present and future together	**4.6/Y8** Language – (b) range of negatives **5.8** Strategies – evaluating and improving	**3–6** **2.1e** use reference materials **2.2e** ask and answer questions **2.2f** initiate/sustain conversations **2.2g** write clearly and coherently **2.2i** reuse language they have met **3c** apply grammar **4b** communicate in pairs etc. **4c** use more complex language	*¿Qué te gusta comer?* *Me gusta (mucho) comer…* *No me gusta nada comer…* *A veces como…* *Nunca como…* *Me gusta beber…* *Nunca bebo…* *Normalmente como…* *El fin de semana pasado comí…* *Mañana voy a comer…*	Using a range of tenses: preterite, present and near future	Using different tenses appropriately Using reference resources Participating in an unscripted dialogue Working on sounding authentic by copying Spanish models Recognising and using techniques to improve writing Communicating with native speakers
Resumen/ Prepárate (pp. 70–71) Pupils' checklist and practice test		**3–6**			Reviewing progress/ checking work
¡Extra! 1 (pp. 72–73) Practising using three tenses together Giving a spoken presentation	**1.5/Y8** Speaking – (a) unscripted talks **2.2/Y8** Reading – (b) personal response to text **5.7** Strategies – planning & preparing	**2–6** **3c** apply grammar **3d** use a range of vocab/ structures **4b** communicate in pairs etc. **4c** use more complex language **4g** language for a range of purposes	Revision of language from Module 4	Using a range of tenses: preterite, present and future	Using different tenses appropriately Understanding a longer/authentic text in Spanish (email) Participating in an unscripted dialogue Delivering a presentation

continued

Module 4 La comida (Pupil's Book pages 60–77)

Unit	Framework	Levels and PoS	Key language	Grammar	Skills
¡Extra! 2 (pp. 74–75) Reading extended texts Learning about authentic Spanish specialities	**2.2/Y8** Reading – (a) longer, more complex texts **5.5** Strategies – reference materials	3–5 **2.1d** previous knowledge **2.1e** use reference materials **2.2b** skim and scan **2.2d** pronunciation and intonation **3e** different countries/ cultures **4e** use a range of resources **4f** language for interest/ enjoyment	Revision of language from Module 4		Understanding a longer text in Spanish (ongoing photo story; website adverts) Identifying key information by skim-reading a text Using reference resources Using reading strategies to work out new words
Te toca a ti (pp. 120–121)	Self-access reading and writing at two levels				

1 ¿Qué desayunas? (Pupil's Book pages 60–61)

Launching objectives
- Talking about mealtimes
- Understanding time expressions

Framework objectives
4.2/Y8 Language – increasing vocabulary

Grammar
- Time expressions

Key language
¿Qué desayunas/comes/meriendas/cenas?
Desayuno...
Como...
Meriendo...
Ceno...
carne con verduras
cereales
fruta
galletas
magdalenas
pasta
patatas fritas
pescado con ensalada
pizza
pollo
tostadas
un bocadillo
¿Qué bebes?
Bebo...
Cola Cao/té/zumo de naranja
No meriendo.
No desayuno nada.
Nunca como.
¿A qué hora desayunas/cenas?
Desayuno a las ocho.
Como a la una.
a mediodía
siempre
generalmente
normalmente
a veces
de vez en cuando
todo el tiempo

High-frequency words
el, la, las
un
a
de
en
con
no
todo
¿qué?
beber (bebes)
comer (como, comes)
nada, nunca

Resources
CD2, tracks 22–24
Cuadernos A & B, p. 32
Flashcards 37–52

Teacher Presentations
Screen 1 – Module 4 overview
Screen 2 – Vocabulary: Flashcards
Screen 3 – p. 60 ex. 1
Screen 4 – p. 60 ex. 3
Screen 5 – Game

Starter 1 4.2/Y8 5.4

Aim

To use reading strategies to work out new language.

Write up:

¿Qué desayunas?
Desayuno cereales y zumo de naranja.
¿Qué comes?
Como pizza.
¿Qué meriendas?
Meriendo fruta. No bebo nada.
¿Qué cenas?
Ceno pasta con ensalada.

Give pupils three minutes working in pairs to translate the text into English.

If your pupils need extra support, you could draw a small clock for each section of text, showing 8 o'clock, 1 o'clock, 4 o'clock and 6 o'clock respectively.

Check answers, getting pupils to tell you how they worked out the new verbs. A good class should also be able to give you the infinitive forms of the verbs (*desayunar, comer, merendar, beber, cenar*): ask how they worked these out. Tell pupils that one of the verbs is a stem-changing verb and ask them to spot which one it is (*merendar – meriendo*).

Suggestion

Use Flashcards 37–52 to introduce items of food and drink. Do this meal by meal, encouraging pupils to spot words they already know and cognates, and to think of ways that will help them memorise this vocabulary.

1 Escucha y escribe la letra o las letras correctas. (1–13) (AT1.2)

4.2/Y8

Listening. Pupils listen to 13 short conversations about what people eat and drink for various meals and note the letter(s) of the food/drink item(s) mentioned, using the pictures *a–p*.

Audioscript Track 22

1 – *¿Qué desayunas?*
– *Desayuno tostadas.*
2 – *¿Qué desayunas?*
– *Desayuno magdalenas y cereales.*
3 – *¿Qué desayunas?*
– *No desayuno nada.*
4 – *¿Qué comes?*
– *Como carne con verduras.*
5 – *¿Qué cenas?*
– *Ceno pasta y pollo.*
6 – *¿Qué meriendas?*
– *Meriendo un bocadillo.*
7 – *¿Qué bebes?*
– *Bebo zumo de naranja.*
8 – *¿Qué bebes?*

– *No bebo nada.*
9 – *¿Qué meriendas?*
– *Meriendo fruta y galletas.*
10 – *¿Qué comes?*
– *Como pizza y patatas fritas.*
11 – *¿Qué bebes?*
– *Bebo Cola Cao.*
12 – *¿Qué cenas?*
– *Ceno pescado con ensalada.*
13 – *¿Qué bebes?*
– *Bebo té.*

Answers
1 b **2** c, a **3** p **4** d **5** k, l **6** i **7** o **8** p
9 h, g **10** e, f **11** m **12** j **13** n

Use the tip box to summarise the different Spanish verbs for talking about different meals: *desayunar, comer, merendar, cenar*.

2 Pregunta y contesta. Di la letra correcta del ejercicio 1. (AT2.2)

▸▸1.4a/Y8 4.6a/Y8◂◂

Speaking. In pairs: pupils take it in turn to ask and answer questions using the key language in exercise 1. A sample exchange is given.

+ Pupils take it in turn to prompt with a food (e.g. *pollo*) and to respond with the correct verb (e.g. *Ceno pollo*).

3 Escucha a Sergio y contesta a las preguntas. Escribe las letras del ejercicio 1 o una hora. (AT1.4)

▸▸1.1/Y8 4.6a/Y8◂◂

Listening. Pupils listen to Sergio talking about what he usually eats and drinks and answer the eight questions on what he says, using pictures *a–p* in exercise 1 and supplying the appropriate times.

Before you play the recording, read through the tip box contrasting the question forms *¿A qué hora... ?* and *¿Qué... ?*.

Audioscript Track 23

– *¿Qué desayunas, Sergio?*
– ***Normalmente** desayuno cereales.*
– *¿Y qué bebes?*
– *A ver... **siempre** bebo zumo de naranja.*
– *¿A qué hora desayunas?*
– ***Normalmente** a las siete y media.*
– *¿Qué comes generalmente?*
– *Pues depende, patatas fritas o **a veces** como carne con verduras.*
– *¿A qué hora comes, Sergio?*
– *Como **siempre** a la una.*
– *¿Qué meriendas?*
– ***Nunca** meriendo un bocadillo; **siempre** meriendo galletas.*
– *¿A qué hora cenas?*
– *Ceno a las ocho. **De vez en cuando** a las ocho y media.*
– *¿Qué cenas?*
– *Tomo pescado con ensalada.*

Answers
1 a **2** o **3** 7.30 **4** f, d **5** 1.00 (13.00) **6** g
7 8.00/8.30 (20.00/20.30) **8** j

Starter 2 ▸▸4.2/Y8 5.3◂◂

Aim
To review time expressions. To use reading strategies to work out new vocabulary.

Write up the following, jumbling the order of the column of English translations.

1	*por las mañanas*	in the mornings
2	*de vez en cuando*	from time to time
3	*siempre*	always
4	*normalmente*	normally
5	*a veces*	sometimes
6	*a mediodía*	at midday
7	*nunca*	never
8	*todo el tiempo*	all the time

Give pupils three minutes working in pairs to match the Spanish expressions with the correct English versions.

Check answers, asking what strategies they used to work out the new language. Can they work out how you would say 'in the afternoons'?

4 Escucha otra vez. ¿Qué palabras del cuadro entiendes? ¿Qué significan? (AT1.4) ▸▸4.2/Y8 4.4/Y8◂◂

Listening. Pupils listen to the recording in exercise 3 again, noting each instance of the expressions listed in the box. They then translate the expressions they note.

Audioscript Track 24

As for exercise 3.

Answers
See **bold** in audioscript for all instances of the words.
normalmente = normally
siempre = always
a veces = sometimes
nunca = never
de vez en cuando = from time to time

R Pupils working in pairs take it in turn to say what they eat at a particular meal or when they eat, using one of the expressions listed in the box (e.g. *De vez en cuando desayuno a las diez* or *Siempre meriendo galletas*). Each pupil should come up with a sentence for each time expression.

5 Empareja las bandejas con los animales. (Sobra una bandeja.) (AT3.4) ▸▸4.2/Y8 5.4◂◂

Reading. Pupils read the three animals' speech bubbles and select the appropriate tray for each animal from the four pictured. (There is one tray too many.) Some vocabulary is glossed for support.

Point out the non-literal use of *tener* in *tengo (mucha) hambre*. How is *tener* usually translated? How would pupils translate it here? Remind pupils that certain expressions in Spanish can't be translated word for word: an expression like this has to be memorised as a new vocabulary item.

Answers

1 Roberto el Ratón – c **2** Serafina la Serpiente – a
3 Pepe el Perro – d

+ Pupils invent an animal who would eat the things on the fourth tray and write a speech bubble for it.

6 Contesta al sondeo. Cambia los datos subrayados y completa las frases. (AT4.3–4) ▸▸4.4/Y8◂◂

Writing. Pupils do the survey, completing the sentences and replacing the underlined text with their own details. Ask pupils to identify the time expressions used in the model. Can they think of another one they could include? (*siempre*)

Plenary ▸▸5.2◂◂

Ask pupils which Spanish time expressions they have come across in this unit, getting them to translate each one into English.

Then write up *siempre, normalmente*, a *veces, nunca*.

Go round the class prompting with an item of food or drink in Spanish (e.g. *cereales*). Pupils in turn respond with a time expression that is appropriate for them (e.g. *a veces*).

Cuaderno A, page 32

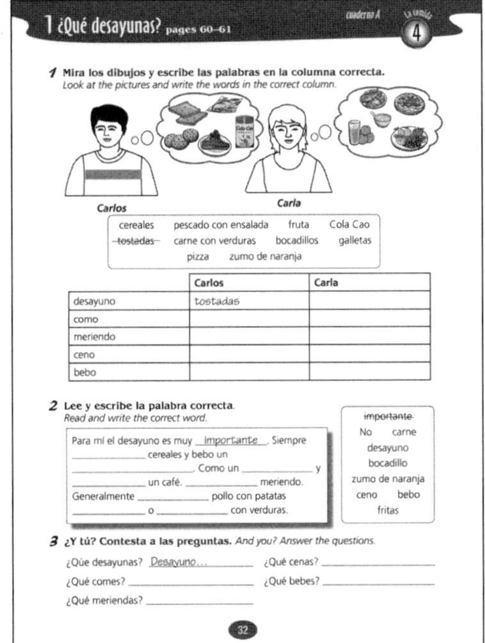

1 ¿Qué desayunas? pages 60–61 · cuaderno A · La comida 4

1 **Mira los dibujos y escribe las palabras en la columna correcta.**
Look at the pictures and write the words in the correct column.

Carlos · *Carla*

cereales · pescado con ensalada · fruta · Cola Cao
~~tostadas~~ · carne con verduras · bocadillos · galletas
pizza · zumo de naranja

	Carlos	Carla
desayuno	tostadas	
como		
meriendo		
ceno		
bebo		

2 **Lee y escribe la palabra correcta.**
Read and write the correct word.

Para mí el desayuno es muy __importante__. Siempre ______ cereales y bebo un ______. Como un ______ y ______ un café. ______ meriendo. Generalmente ______ pollo con patatas ______ o ______ con verduras.

~~importante~~ · No · carne · desayuno · bocadillo · zumo de naranja · ceno · bebo · fritas

3 **¿Y tú? Contesta a las preguntas.** *And you? Answer the questions.*

¿Qúe desayunas? Desayuno... ¿Qué cenas? ______
¿Qué comes? ______ ¿Qué bebes? ______
¿Qué meriendas? ______

32

1 (AT4.1)

	Carlos	Carla
desayuno	*tostadas*	cereales
como	bocadillos	pizza
meriendo	galletas	fruta
ceno	carne con verduras	pescado con ensalada
bebo	Cola Cao	zumo de naranja

2 (AT3.3, AT4.1)

Para mí el desayuno es muy *importante*. Siempre desayuno cereales y bebo un zumo de naranja. Como un bocadillo y bebo un café. No meriendo. Generalmente ceno pollo con patatas fritas o carne con verduras.

3 (AT4.3)

Cuaderno B, page 32

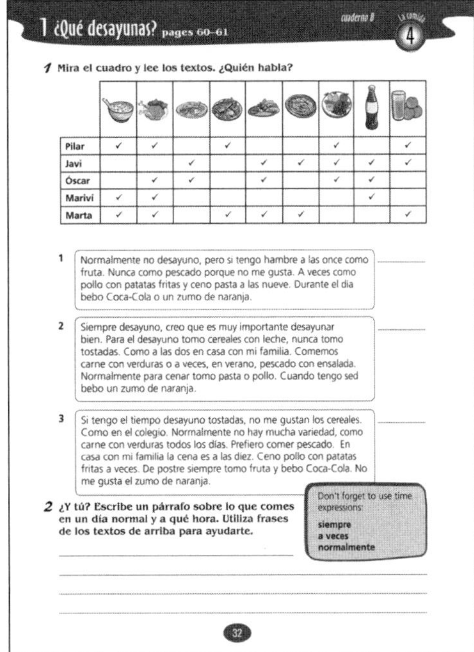

1 ¿Qué desayunas? pages 60–61 · cuaderno B · La comida 4

1 **Mira el cuadro y lee los textos. ¿Quién habla?**

Pilar	✓	✓		✓			✓		✓
Javi			✓		✓	✓	✓	✓	✓
Óscar		✓	✓		✓		✓	✓	
Mariví	✓	✓						✓	
Marta	✓	✓		✓	✓	✓			✓

1 Normalmente no desayuno, pero si tengo hambre a las once como fruta. Nunca como pescado porque no me gusta. A veces como pollo con patatas fritas y ceno pasta a las nueve. Durante el día bebo Coca-Cola o un zumo de naranja. ______

2 Siempre desayuno, creo que es muy importante desayunar bien. Para el desayuno tomo cereales con leche, nunca tomo tostadas. Como a las dos en casa con mi familia. Comemos carne con verduras o a veces, en verano, pescado con ensalada. Normalmente para cenar tomo pasta o pollo. Cuando tengo sed bebo un zumo de naranja. ______

3 Si tengo el tiempo desayuno tostadas, no me gustan los cereales. Como en el colegio. Normalmente no hay mucha variedad, como carne con verduras todos los días. Prefiero comer pescado. En casa con mi familia la cena es a las diez. Ceno pollo con patatas fritas a veces. De postre siempre tomo fruta y bebo Coca-Cola. No me gusta el zumo de naranja. ______

2 **¿Y tú? Escribe un párrafo sobre lo que comes en un día normal y a qué hora. Utiliza frases de los textos de arriba para ayudarte.**

Don't forget to use time expressions:
siempre
a veces
normalmente

32

1 (AT3.4)

1 Javi **2** Marta **3** Óscar

2 (AT4.4)

2 En el mercado (Pupil's Book pages 62–63)

Launching objectives

- Shopping for food
- Using high numbers

Grammar

- The preterite tense (revision of *-ar* verbs)

Framework objectives

- **1.3/Y8** Listening – (a) understanding language for specific functions
- **1.3/Y8** Speaking – (b) using language for specific functions

Key language

cien
ciento diez
doscientos, trescientos, cuatrocientos, quinientos, seiscientos, setecientos, ochocientos, novecientos
mil
¿Qué quieres?
un kilo de...
dos kilos de...
quinientos gramos de...
medio kilo de...
chorizo
jamón
manzanas
peras
queso
tomates
uvas
zanahorias
una barra de pan
una lechuga
un cartón de leche
una botella de agua
¿Algo más?
Sí, quiero...
por favor
Nada más, gracias.
¿Cuánto cuesta?
Un euro.
Dos euros y veinte.
Cuatro euros y veinticinco.

High-frequency words

un, una
de
y
sí
¿cuánto?
¿qué?
querer (quiero, quieres)
algo
nada
más

Resources

CD2, tracks 25–28
Cuadernos A & B, p. 33
R & A Pack, Gramática p. 17
Flashcards 53–64

Teacher Presentations

Screen 1 – Module 4 overview
Screen 2 – p. 62 ex. 1
Screen 3 – Vocabulary: Flashcards
Screen 4 – p. 62 ex. 3
Screen 5 – p. 63 ex. 4
Screen 6 – p. 63 ex. 6
Screen 7 – Game

Starter 1 ▸▸5.1◂◂

Aim

To introduce higher numbers (100, 200, etc.).
To predict the form of new language using recognised patterns.

Put a grid on the board with numbers between 100 and 1000. Ask pupils to complete the numbers in written form, using their knowledge of patterns. Make sure you include the words *quinientos*, *setecientos*, *novecientos* and *mil* as they will not be able to work these out.

cien	100
ciento diez	110
doscientos	200
doscientos diez	210
	300

1 Escucha y repite. (AT1.2) ▸▸4.2/Y8◂◂

Listening. Pupils listen to the recording of high numbers and follow the text at the same time. There is a pause after each item on the recording so they can repeat the word.

Audioscript Track 25

cien...
ciento diez...
doscientos...
trescientos...
cuatrocientos...
quinientos...
seiscientos...
setecientos...
ochocientos...
novecientos...
mil...

2 Juega con dos compañeros. Una persona dice un número del ejercicio 1. Hay que escribir el número correcto. (AT2.2) ▸▸1.4a/Y8◂◂

Speaking. In groups of three pupils take it in turn to prompt with one of the numbers from exercise 1 and to write down the number in numerals. A sample exchange is given.

R Give the class some simple mental arithmetic to do in Spanish. Remind them first of the meaning of *más* and *menos* in this context.

1 *doscientos más trescientos son...* *(quinientos)*
2 *cien más setecientos son...* *(ochocientos)*
3 *cuatrocientos más seiscientos son...* *(mil)*
4 *quinientos menos cien son...* *(cuatrocientos)*
5 *mil menos cien son...* *(novecientos)*
6 *setecientos diez menos cuatrocientos son...* *(trescientos diez)*

Suggestion

Write up:

- *¿Qué quieres?*
- *Un kilo de tomates.*

Ask pupils to translate it. Where would you hear a dialogue like this? Explain that the next section of the unit focuses on buying food in a shop.

Use Flashcards 53–64 to introduce items that you might buy in a food shop. You might find it useful to concentrate first on the food/drinks and then on the quantities.

3 Escucha y escribe la letra correcta. (1–12) (AT1.2) ⏩1.3a/Y8 4.2/Y8⏪

Listening. Pupils listen to 12 conversations in food shops and note the letter of the food item mentioned in each (from *a–l*).

Audioscript Track 26

1 – *¿Qué quieres?*
– *Una lechuga, por favor.*
2 – *¿Qué quieres?*
– *Un kilo de peras, por favor.*
3 – *Buenos días. ¿Qué quieres?*
– *Doscientos gramos de queso, por favor.*
4 – *¿Qué quieres?*
– *Una barra de pan, por favor.*
5 – *¿Qué quieres?*
– *Cien gramos de jamón, por favor.*
6 – *¿Qué quieres?*
– *Medio kilo de tomates, por favor.*
7 – *¿Qué quieres?*
– *Un cartón de leche, por favor.*
8 – *¿Qué quieres?*
– *Una botella de agua, por favor.*
9 – *¿Qué quieres?*
– *Quiero quinientos gramos de uvas, por favor.*
10 – *¿Qué quieres?*
– *Un chorizo, por favor.*
11 – *¿Qué quieres?*
– *Un kilo de zanahorias, por favor.*
12 – *Buenos días. ¿Qué quieres?*
– *Eh, dos kilos de manzanas, por favor.*

Answers

1 i **2** a **3** f **4** j **5** e **6** b **7** l **8** k **9** g
10 h **11** d **12** c

R Use Flashcards 53–64 as prompts to practise the key vocabulary. You could do this in teams to make it more motivating. Award one point for a correctly identified food/drink, two points if the person answering gets the quantity right too.

Starter 2 ⏩5.2⏪

Aim
To review the numbers (10, 20, etc.).

Ask pupils to stand. Starting at *cero*, each person gives the next number in the sequence 10, 20, etc., up to 100. If a pupil can't answer or makes a mistake, he/she sits down. The last person standing is the winner.

You can make this more challenging by including the fives (10, 15, 20, 25, etc.) or by starting at *cien* and going backwards.

Suggestion

Say *Quiero un kilo de tomates. ¿Cuánto cuesta?* and write up *1,00€.* Ask pupils to translate *¿Cuánto cuesta?* Explain that in this lesson they are going to learn more useful language for shopping in Spain.

Use the tip box to talk about Spanish currency. Give pupils a model for the pronunciation of *euro* and *céntimos* in Spanish. You could also ask pupils to find out the current value of a euro in pounds. Where will they research this?

4 Escucha y escribe el precio correcto. (a–j) (AT1.2) ⏩1.3a/Y8⏪

Listening. Pupils listen to ten conversations featuring prices in euros and note the price mentioned in each. The prices are all supplied for reference.

Audioscript Track 27

a – *¿Cuánto cuesta?*
– *Un euro.*
b – *¿Cuánto cuesta?*
– *Dos euros y veinte céntimos.*
c – *¿Cuánto cuesta, por favor?*
– *Cuatro euros y veinticinco céntimos.*
d – *¿Cuánto cuesta, por favor?*
– *Tres euros y cincuenta céntimos.*
e – *¿Cuánto cuesta?*
– *Un euro y cincuenta céntimos, por favor.*
f – *¿Cuánto cuesta?*
– *Tres euros y setenta y cinco céntimos.*
g – *¿Cuánto cuesta?*
– *Un euro y treinta céntimos.*
h – *¿Cuánto cuesta?*
– *Dos euros y veinticinco céntimos.*
i – *¿Qué quieres?*
– *Quiero dos kilos de manzanas, por favor. ¿Cuánto cuesta?*
– *Dos euros y cincuenta céntimos.*
– *Aquí tiene.*
– *¿Algo más?*
– *Nada más, gracias.*

j – *¿Qué quieres?*
– *Una lechuga, por favor. ¿Cuánto cuesta?*
– *Ochenta céntimos. ¿Algo más?*
– *Nada más, gracias.*

Answers

a *1,00€* **b** 2,20€ **c** 4,25€ **d** 3,50€ **e** 1,50€ **f** 3,75€
g 1,30€ **h** 2,25€ **i** 2,50€ **j** 0,80€

5 Con tu compañero/a, haz diálogos cambiando los datos subrayados. (AT2.3) ▸▸1.3b/Y8 1.4b/Y8◂◂

Speaking. In pairs: using the picture prompts supplied, pupils make up dialogues set in a food shop. A sample exchange is also given: pupils should replace the underlined text with their own choice of item and its price and also add other items where there is a gap in the sample. New vocabulary is glossed for support.

Use the tip box to revise the preterite form of *-ar* verbs using *comprar*. Pupils should be familiar with the 1st person form from Module 3, so focus on the other persons here. There is practice on this on page 132 of the Pupil's Book.

R Prompt in Spanish (e.g. *compraron*) for a pupil to respond in English (e.g. 'they bought'). That pupil then prompts the next pupil, and so on. You could set a time limit for pupils to beat, or do the activity twice, with pupils trying to beat their own timing.

6 Escucha y canta. (AT1.4) ▸▸5.2◂◂

Listening. Pupils listen to the song, following the words at the same time in their books. Play the recording again, this time getting pupils to sing along.

Audioscript Track 28

Para mis amigos

Fui al mercado y compré…
Medio kilo de tomates para Pilates.

Fui al mercado y compré…
Una barra de pan para Sebastián
y medio kilo de tomates para Pilates.

Fui al mercado y compré…
Cien gramos de jamón para Ramón,
Una barra de pan para Sebastián
y medio kilo de tomates para Pilates.

Fui al mercado y compré…
Un pepino para Severino,
Cien gramos de jamón para Ramón,
Una barra de pan para Sebastián
y medio kilo de tomates para Pilates.

Fui al mercado y compré…
Una lechuga para mi tortuga,
Un pepino para Severino,
Cien gramos de jamón para Ramón,
Una barra de pan para Sebastián
y medio kilo de tomates para Pilates.

Fui al mercado y compré…
Dos kilos de manzanas para mis hermanas,
Una lechuga para mi tortuga,
Un pepino para Severino,
Cien gramos de jamón para Ramón,
Una barra de pan para Sebastián
y medio kilo de tomates para Pilates.

Plenary ▸▸1.4a/Y8 5.2◂◂

Play a chain game round the class to practise shopping vocabulary and quantities. Start it off: *Fui al mercado y compré un kilo de tomates,…* Pupils in turn repeat the chain to date and add another item. If a pupil makes a mistake or forgets an item, he/she is out and the chain starts again from the beginning.

Cuaderno A, page 33

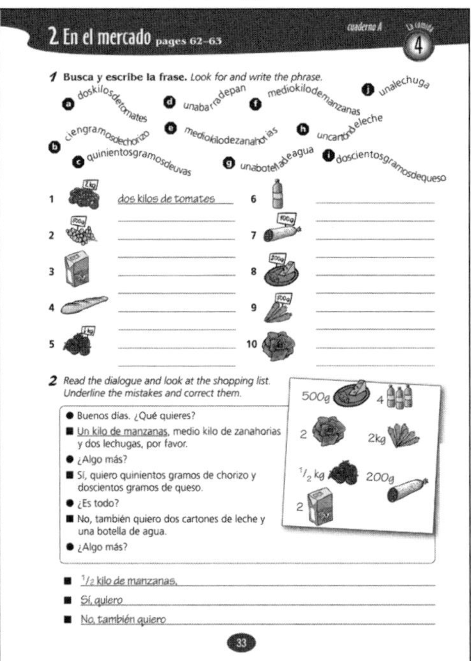
2 En el mercado pages 62–63 cuaderno A La comida 4

1 **Busca y escribe la frase.** *Look for and write the phrase.*

a doskilosdetomates
b ciengramosdechorizo
c quinientosgramosdeuvas
d unabarradepan
e mediokilodezanahorias
f mediokilodemanzanas
g unabotelladeagua
h uncartóndeleche
i doscientosgramosdequeso
j unalechuga

1 dos kilos de tomates
2
3
4
5
6
7
8
9
10

2 *Read the dialogue and look at the shopping list. Underline the mistakes and correct them.*

● Buenos días. ¿Qué quieres?
■ Un kilo de manzanas, medio kilo de zanahorias y dos lechugas, por favor.
● ¿Algo más?
■ Sí, quiero quinientos gramos de chorizo y doscientos gramos de queso.
● ¿Es todo?
■ No, también quiero dos cartones de leche y una botella de agua.
● ¿Algo más?

■ 1/2 kilo de manzanas,
■ Sí, quiero
■ No, también quiero

33

1 (AT4.2)

1 *dos kilos de tomates*
2 quinientos gramos de uvas
3 un cartón de leche
4 una barra de pan
5 medio kilo de manzanas
6 una botella de agua
7 cien gramos de chorizo
8 doscientos gramos de queso
9 medio kilo de zanahorias
10 una lechuga

2 (AT3.3, AT4.2)

Un kilo de manzanas, medio kilo de zanahorias, quinientos gramos de chorizo, doscientos gramos de queso, una botella de agua

Medio kilo de manzanas, Dos kilos de zanahorias, Doscientos gramos de chorizo, Quinientos gramos de queso, Cuatro botellas de agua

Cuaderno B, page 33

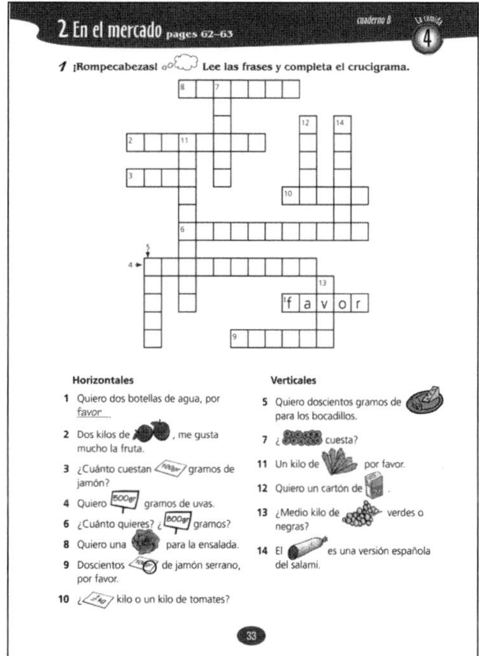

2 En el mercado pages 62–63 — cuaderno B — La comida 4

1 ¡Rompecabezas! Lee las frases y completa el crucigrama.

Horizontales

1 Quiero dos botellas de agua, por favor.
2 Dos kilos de , me gusta mucho la fruta.
3 ¿Cuánto cuestan gramos de jamón?
4 Quiero gramos de uvas.
6 ¿Cuánto quieres? ¿ gramos?
8 Quiero una para la ensalada.
9 Doscientos de jamón serrano, por favor.
10 ¿ kilo o un kilo de tomates?

Verticales

5 Quiero doscientos gramos de para los bocadillos.
7 ¿ cuesta?
11 Un kilo de por favor.
12 Quiero un cartón de .
13 ¿Medio kilo de verdes o negras?
14 El es una versión española del salami.

33

1 (AT3.3, AT4.2)

1 *favor* **2** manzanas **3** cien **4** quinientos **5** queso **6** ochocientos **7** cuánto **8** lechuga **9** gramos **10** medio **11** zanahorias **12** leche **13** uvas **14** chorizo

R & A Pack, Gramática page 17

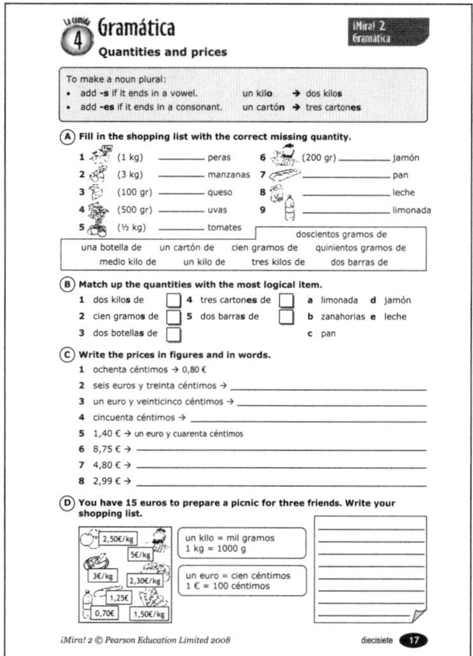

La comida 4 **Gramática** — ¡Mira! 2 Gramática

Quantities and prices

To make a noun plural:
- add **-s** if it ends in a vowel. un kilo → dos kilo**s**
- add **-es** if it ends in a consonant. un cartón → tres carton**es**

A Fill in the shopping list with the correct missing quantity.

1 (1 kg) ______ peras
2 (3 kg) ______ manzanas
3 (100 gr) ______ queso
4 (500 gr) ______ uvas
5 (½ kg) ______ tomates
6 (200 gr) ______ jamón
7 ______ pan
8 ______ leche
9 ______ limonada

doscientos gramos de / una botella de / un cartón de / cien gramos de / quinientos gramos de / medio kilo de / un kilo de / tres kilos de / dos barras de

B Match up the quantities with the most logical item.

1 dos kilos de ☐ 4 tres cartones de ☐ a limonada d jamón
2 cien gramos de ☐ 5 dos barras de ☐ b zanahorias e leche
3 dos botellas de ☐ c pan

C Write the prices in figures and in words.

1 ochenta céntimos → 0,80 €
2 seis euros y treinta céntimos → ______
3 un euro y veinticinco céntimos → ______
4 cincuenta céntimos → ______
5 1,40 € → un euro y cuarenta céntimos
6 8,75 € → ______
7 4,80 € → ______
8 2,99 € → ______

D You have 15 euros to prepare a picnic for three friends. Write your shopping list.

un kilo = mil gramos
1 kg = 1000 g

un euro = cien céntimos
1 € = 100 céntimos

¡Mira! 2 © Pearson Education Limited 2008 diecisiete 17

(A) **1** un kilo de **2** tres kilos de **3** cien gramos de **4** quinientos gramos de **5** medio kilo de **6** doscientos gramos de **7** dos barras de **8** un cartón de **9** una botella de

(B) **1** b **2** d **3** a **4** e **5** c

(C) **2** 6,30€ **3** 1,25€ **4** 0,50€ **6** ocho euros y setenta y cinco céntimos **7** cuatro euros y ochenta céntimos **8** dos euros y noventa y nueve céntimos

3 En el restaurante (Pupil's Book pages 64–65)

Launching objectives
- Eating at a restaurant
- Understanding the difference between *tú* and *usted*

Framework objectives
- **3.2/Y8** Culture – (b) customs, traditions
- **5.2** Strategies – memorising

Grammar
- *tú/usted*

Key language
¿Qué vas/va a tomar?
De primer plato...
De segundo plato...
De postre...
quiero...
ensalada
flan
fruta
gambas
helado (de chocolate)
paella
pescado
pollo
sopa de mariscos

¿Para beber?
(Quiero)... , por favor.
agua
Coca-Cola
limonada
Tengo hambre.
No tengo hambre.
Tengo sed.
La cuenta, por favor.

High-frequency words
la
a
de
para
no
¿qué?
beber
ir (vas, va)
querer (quiero)
tener (tengo)
tomar

Cross-curricular
Citizenship: Information about other cultures
English: Register (informal/ formal)
ICT: Internet research

Resources
CD2, tracks 29–32
Cuadernos A & B, p. 34
R & A Pack, Gramática p. 18

Teacher Presentations
Screen 1 – Module 4 overview
Screen 2 – p. 64 ex. 1
Screen 3 – p. 65 ex. 3
Screen 4 – p. 65 ex. 4
Screen 5 – p. 65 ex. 7

Starter 1 ▸▸ 4.6a/Y8 ◂◂

Aim
To revise the preterite tense (*-ar* verbs). To revise food vocabulary.

Write up:

En el mercado compré una barra de pan.
compré compró compramos

Get pupils working in pairs to write their own version of the sentence three times, each using a different form of *comprar* in the preterite ('I', 'we' and 'he/she') and changing the item purchased. They should also translate their sentences into English.

1 Escucha y escribe el plato y la letra correcta. (1–12) (AT1.2) ▸▸ 1.3a/Y8 ◂◂

Listening. Pupils listen to twelve conversations in which people order food or something to drink in a restaurant. They note in Spanish what each person is ordering (*primer plato,* etc.) and the specific item mentioned (from *a–l* in the menu).

Audioscript Track 29

1 – *¿Qué va a tomar?*
– *De primer plato quiero unas gambas.*
2 – *¿Qué vas a tomar?*
– *De segundo plato quiero pollo.*
3 – *¿Qué va a tomar?*
– *De postre quiero un helado.*
4 – *¿Qué vas a tomar?*
– *Para beber quiero una limonada.*
5 – *¿Qué vas a tomar?*
– *De primer plato quiero una sopa.*
6 – *¿Qué va a tomar?*
– *De segundo plato quiero una paella de mariscos.*
7 – *¿Qué vas a tomar?*
– *De postre quiero fruta.*
8 – *¿Para beber?*
– *Para beber quiero agua.*
9 – *¿Qué vas a tomar?*
– *De primer plato quiero una ensalada.*
10 – *¿Qué vas a tomar?*
– *De segundo plato quiero pescado.*
11 – *¿Qué va a tomar?*
– *De postre quiero un flan.*
12 – *Para beber quiero una Coca-Cola.*

Answers
1 *primer plato – b* **2** segundo plato – e
3 postre – h **4** beber – l **5** primer plato – a
6 segundo plato – f **7** postre – i **8** beber – j
9 primer plato – c **10** segundo plato – d
11 postre – g **12** beber – k

Suggestion

Ask pupils if they noticed anything about the verbs used in the questions of the recording (two verb forms were used: *vas* and *va*). Read through the tip box on *tú* and *usted*, explaining that the difference is one of register (*tú* is informal – used with children, young people, family and other adults you know well; *usted* is formal – used with adults you don't know). Make sure pupils are clear that *usted*, although it means 'you', takes the 'he/she' form of the verb.

R Play the recording again and ask pupils to note the verb used in each question: *vas* or *va*? Is the person in each case being addressed informally or formally?

2 Con tu compañero/a, haz diálogos. (AT2.3) ▸▸1.4a/Y8◂◂

Speaking. In pairs pupils make up dialogues set in a restaurant, taking it in turn to play the part of the waiter and the customer. They use the picture prompts and dialogue framework supplied.

Once they feel confident, pupils could close their books and attempt the dialogue without the prompts in front of them.

Starter 2 ▸▸5.2◂◂

Aim

 To revise vocabulary for restaurant food.

Write up the following words: tell pupils these are in code and they need to decipher them. Say that they are all things you might order in a restaurant. (Answers are in brackets for reference.)

1 fzlazr (*gambas*)
2 ekzm (*flan*)
3 odrbzcn (*pescado*)
4 ozdkkz (*paella*)
5 eqtsz (*fruta*)

You could give the answer to the first one if the class needs support.

Suggestion ▸▸1.5b/Y8◂◂

Ask pupils if they can remember what *Tengo hambre* means. Using this information, can they work out *Tengo sed*? Use mimes if they are struggling.

Use the tip box to cover expressions like this which don't translate word for word. Can pupils remember any other expressions like this? (e.g. *¡Lo pasé guay!*, *tengo que*, etc.)

3 Escucha y lee. (AT1.4) ▸▸1.3a/Y8◂◂

Listening. Pupils listen to a conversation which takes place in a restaurant, reading the text at the same time. Some vocabulary is glossed for support.

Audioscript Track 30

– *Tengo hambre. Quiero un helado de chocolate. ¿Qué vas a tomar?*
– *No tengo hambre pero tengo sed. Quiero una limonada.*
– *¿Qué va a tomar?*
– *Un helado de chocolate, por favor.*
– *¿Y usted? ¿Qué va a tomar?*
– *Una limonada, por favor.*
– *¿Algo más?*
– *Nada más. La cuenta, por favor.*

4 Escucha y escribe las letras correctas del ejercicio 1. (1–3) (AT1.4) ▸▸1.3a/Y8◂◂

Listening. Pupils listen to three conversations and note the food/drink items ordered, using the pictures in exercise 1 (*a–l*).

Audioscript Track 31

1 – *Tengo hambre. Quiero un flan. ¿Tú, qué vas a tomar?*
– *Quiero una Coca-Cola. No tengo hambre pero tengo sed.*
– *¿Qué va a tomar?*
– *Un flan, por favor.*
– *¿Y usted? ¿Qué va a tomar?*
– *Una Coca-Cola, por favor.*
– *¿Algo más?*
– *Nada más. La cuenta, por favor.*

2 – *Tengo hambre. Quiero una sopa. ¿Qué vas a tomar?*
– *Hmm… Voy a tomar una ensalada.*
– *¿Qué van a tomar?*
– *Una sopa y una ensalada, por favor.*
– *¿Algo de postre?*
– *No, gracias.*
– *¿Y para beber?*
– *Sí, eh… agua, por favor.*

3 – *Tengo hambre. De primer plato quiero unas gambas y una ensalada. ¿Qué vas a tomar?*
– *Una ensalada también. ¿Qué quieres de segundo plato?*
– *Quiero pollo. Es muy bueno.*
– *Y yo quiero una paella de mariscos. Voy a beber una limonada. ¿Y tú?*
– *Para mí, agua.*
– *¿Qué va a tomar?*
– *De primer plato, unas gambas y una ensalada, por favor. De segundo plato quiero pollo, y quiero beber agua.*
– *¿Y usted?*
– *También una ensalada y de segundo plato quiero una paella de mariscos. Para beber, quiero una limonada.*
– *¿Algo más?*
– *Nada más. La cuenta, por favor.*

Answers

1 *g, k* **2** a, c, j **3** b, c, e, f, j, l

Suggestion ▸▸5.2◂◂

Ask pupils to discuss in pairs ways in which they might note down and memorise this vocabulary. Pool suggestions:

Noting vocabulary
– organise by topic (here, by course – *primer plato: una sopa*, etc.)

- organise by gender
- organise alphabetically

Memorising
- writing out vocabulary in all the different ways above
- writing out vocabulary in two columns (Spanish and English), then covering up first the Spanish, then the English to test your ability to translate from one to the other
- working with a friend, with each of you taking it in turn to prompt in Spanish, then English

Encourage pupils to develop their independence as learners by trying these and other techniques to find out which way(s) work(s) best for them and using it/them regularly to memorise vocabulary.

5 Con otras dos personas, haz diálogos, cambiando los datos subrayados del ejercicio 3. (AT2.3) ▸▸1.3b/Y8 1.4a/Y8◂◂

Speaking. In groups of three: pupils make up dialogues in a restaurant, taking it in turn to play the waiter/the customers. They should use the picture prompts supplied to change the underlined details in exercise 3.

Once they are feeling confident, get the pupils to try this exchange without looking at the model dialogue: they can use their own choice of food items. Ask a few good groups to perform in front of the class, with the rest of the class giving constructive feedback.

6 Escribe un diálogo del ejercicio 5. (AT4.4) ▸▸4.4/Y8◂◂

Writing. Pupils write out one of the dialogues they made up in exercise 5, using exercise 3 as a model. Bright pupils could try doing it without looking at the model.

7 Escucha y lee el texto 'El tapeo'. Escribe las letras de los dibujos mencionados. (AT3.4) ▸▸3.2b/Y8◂◂

ZONA CULTURA *Listening.* Pupils read and listen to the Zona Cultura text on tapas and note the letters of the food items mentioned (from pictures *a–h*).

Ask pupils if they have ever eaten tapas, either in Spain or in a Spanish restaurant in this country. What did they eat? What did they think of them?

Audioscript Track 32

Zona Cultura – El tapeo
El tapeo es una costumbre muy famosa en España. El tapeo consiste en ir de bar en bar tomando tapas de jamón serrano, queso, tortilla o gambas, con vino o cerveza.

Answers
c, b, f, d, g, e

Pupils do further research on tapas using the internet. You could structure their research by challenging them to find the following in English:

- the meaning of the word *tapa*
- the possible origins of *tapas* in history
- three kinds of tapas not listed here

Plenary ▸▸5.8◂◂

Ask the class to read through the Mini-test section and take a vote on which of the points listed they have found the hardest. Identify the most popular response and ask them for suggestions on how it could be reviewed to help them. Make sure you cover ideas for learning vocabulary and using resources, such as the Gramática boxes in the text and the Gramática section at the back of the book. Suggest doing the written exercises in the modules again at home, to help consolidate language. Emphasise the usefulness of working in pairs and testing each other.

If it is a vocabulary-based topic, move on to a quickfire translation activity from English into Spanish, to help consolidate the words.

If it is a grammar-based topic, ask a confident pupil to review the rules and then give prompts in English to practise these.

Cuaderno A, page 34

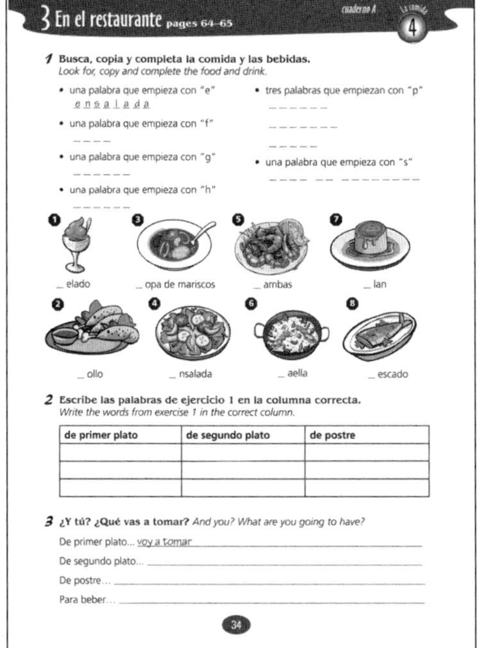
3 En el restaurante pages 64–65 cuaderno A La comida 4

1 **Busca, copia y completa la comida y las bebidas.**
Look for, copy and complete the food and drink.

- una palabra que empieza con "e" e n s a l a d a
- una palabra que empieza con "f" _ _ _ _
- una palabra que empieza con "g" _ _ _ _ _ _
- una palabra que empieza con "h" _ _ _ _ _ _
- tres palabras que empiezan con "p" _ _ _ _ _ _ / _ _ _ _ _ _ _ / _ _ _ _ _
- una palabra que empieza con "s" _ _ _ _ _ _ _ _ _ _ _ _ _ _

1 _ elado 3 _ opa de mariscos 5 _ ambas 7 _ lan
2 _ ollo 4 _ nsalada 6 _ aella 8 _ escado

2 **Escribe las palabras de ejercicio 1 en la columna correcta.**
Write the words from exercise 1 in the correct column.

de primer plato	de segundo plato	de postre

3 **¿Y tú? ¿Qué vas a tomar?** *And you? What are you going to have?*

De primer plato... voy a tomar

De segundo plato...

De postre…

Para beber…

34

1 (AT4.1)

ensalada; flan; gambas; helado; paella, pescado, pollo; sopa de mariscos

2 (AT4.1)

de primer plato	de segundo plato	de postre
sopa de mariscos	pollo	flan
gambas	paella	helado
ensalada	pescado	

3 (AT4.3)

Cuaderno B, page 34

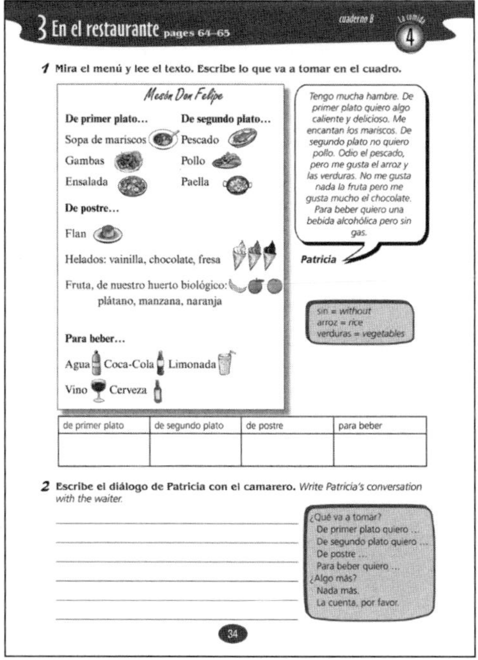
3 En el restaurante pages 64–65 cuaderno B La comida 4

1 **Mira el menú y lee el texto. Escribe lo que va a tomar en el cuadro.**

Mesón Don Felipe

De primer plato…
Sopa de mariscos
Gambas
Ensalada

De segundo plato…
Pescado
Pollo
Paella

De postre…
Flan
Helados: vainilla, chocolate, fresa
Fruta, de nuestro huerto biológico: plátano, manzana, naranja

Para beber…
Agua Coca-Cola Limonada
Vino Cerveza

Tengo mucha hambre. De primer plato quiero algo caliente y delicioso. Me encantan los mariscos. De segundo plato no quiero pollo. Odio el pescado, pero me gusta el arroz y las verduras. No me gusta nada la fruta pero me gusta mucho el chocolate. Para beber quiero una bebida alcohólica pero sin gas.

Patricia

sin = *without*
arroz = *rice*
verduras = *vegetables*

de primer plato	de segundo plato	de postre	para beber

2 **Escribe el diálogo de Patricia con el camarero.** *Write Patricia's conversation with the waiter.*

¿Qué va a tomar?
De primer plato quiero ...
De segundo plato quiero ...
De postre ...
Para beber quiero ...
¿Algo más?
Nada más.
La cuenta, por favor.

34

1 (AT3.3)

Answers

	de primer plato	de segundo plato	de postre	para beber
Patricia	sopa de mariscos	paella	helado de chocolate	vino

2 (AT4.4)

R & A Pack, Gramática page 18

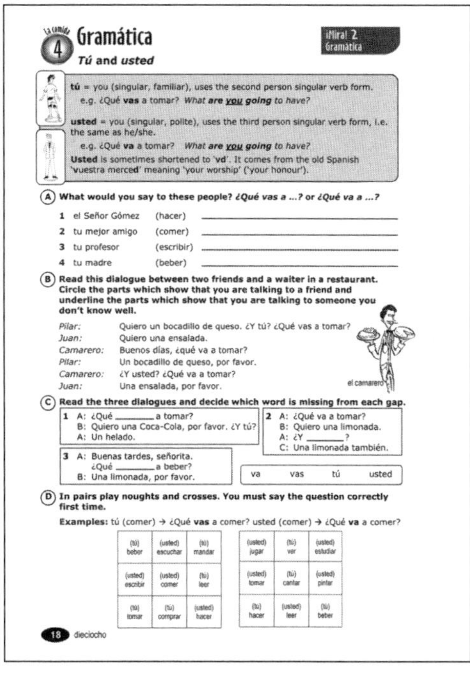
La comida 4 **Gramática** ¡Mira! 2 Gramática

Tú* and *usted

tú = you (singular, familiar), uses the second person singular verb form.
e.g. ¿Qué **vas** a tomar? *What **are** you **going** to have?*

usted = you (singular, polite), uses the third person singular verb form, i.e. the same as he/she.
e.g. ¿Qué **va** a tomar? *What **are** you **going** to have?*

Usted is sometimes shortened to '**vd**'. It comes from the old Spanish '**v**uestra merce**d**' meaning 'your worship' ('your honour').

(A) **What would you say to these people? *¿Qué vas a ...?* or *¿Qué va a ...?***

1 el Señor Gómez (hacer)
2 tu mejor amigo (comer)
3 tu profesor (escribir)
4 tu madre (beber)

(B) **Read this dialogue between two friends and a waiter in a restaurant. Circle the parts which show that you are talking to a friend and underline the parts which show that you are talking to someone you don't know well.**

Pilar: Quiero un bocadillo de queso. ¿Y tú? ¿Qué vas a tomar?
Juan: Quiero una ensalada.
Camarero: Buenos días, ¿qué va a tomar?
Pilar: Un bocadillo de queso, por favor.
Camarero: ¿Y usted? ¿Qué va a tomar?
Juan: Una ensalada, por favor.

el camarero

(C) **Read the three dialogues and decide which word is missing from each gap.**

1 A: ¿Qué ______ a tomar?
B: Quiero una Coca-Cola, por favor. ¿Y tú?
A: Un helado.

2 A: ¿Qué va a tomar?
B: Quiero una limonada.
A: ¿Y ______?
C: Una limonada también.

3 A: Buenas tardes, señorita.
¿Qué ______ a beber?
B: Una limonada, por favor.

va vas tú usted

(D) **In pairs play noughts and crosses. You must say the question correctly first time.**

Examples: tú (comer) → ¿Qué **vas** a comer? usted (comer) → ¿Qué **va** a comer?

(tú) beber	(usted) escuchar	(tú) mandar
(usted) escribir	(usted) comer	(tú) leer
(tú) tomar	(tú) comprar	(usted) hacer

(usted) jugar	(tú) ver	(usted) estudiar
(usted) tomar	(tú) cantar	(usted) pintar
(tú) hacer	(usted) leer	(tú) beber

18 dieciocho

(A) **1** ¿Qué va a hacer? **2** ¿Qué vas a comer? **3** ¿Qué va a escribir? **4** ¿Qué vas a beber?

(B) (circled) tú, vas; (underlined) va, usted, va

(C) **1** vas **2** usted **3** va

4 Una cena especial (Pupil's Book pages 66–67)

Launching objectives

- Talking about a past meal
- Using the preterite of *-er* and *-ir* verbs

Framework objectives

1.4/Y8 Speaking – (b) unscripted conversations
5.1 Strategies – patterns

Grammar

- The preterite tense (*-er/-ir* verbs)

Key language

El fin de semana pasado...
salí con...
Fui a...
un restaurante español
un restaurante muy caro
Comí ensalada.
Mi compañero/a comió gambas.
Compartimos una paella.
Bebimos agua.
Hablamos de fútbol/música.
¡Fue genial!

High-frequency words

el
un, una
mi
a
de
con
muy
comer (comí, comió)
beber (bebimos)
hablar (hablamos)
ir (fui)
ser (fue)

Cross-curricular

ICT: Internet research

Resources

CD2, tracks 33–34
Cuadernos A & B, p. 35
R & A Pack, Gramática p. 19

Teacher Presentations

Screen 1 – Module 4 overview
Screen 2 – p. 66 ex. 1
Screen 3 – p. 67 ex. 4
Screen 4 – Game

Suggestion ▸▸5.1◂◂

Make sure, as pupils work through this unit, that they understand that learning patterns for verb conjugations will save them time!

Starter 1 ▸▸5.1◂◂

Aim
To revise the preterite forms of *-ar* verbs. To practise distinguishing between present and preterite tense forms.

Write up the following:

Normalmente...		*El fin de semana pasado...*	
bailo	I dance	*bailé*	I danced

Give pupils 3 minutes working in pairs to sort the following verbs into the correct column and to translate each one.

bailaste	*bailo*	*bailaron*	*bailamos*
bailáis	*bailasteis*	*bailé*	*bailó*
bailan	*baila*	*bailas*	*bailamos*

(Answers – in any order)
1st column: *bailo, bailas, baila, bailamos, bailáis, bailan*

2nd column: *bailé, bailaste, bailó, bailamos, bailasteis, bailaron*

(Answers – in any order)
1st column: *bailo, bailas, baila, bailamos, bailáis, bailan*
2nd column: *bailé, bailaste, bailó, bailamos, bailasteis, bailaron*

For extra support, supply more forms in the table and/or suggest they use the verb tables in the Gramática section at the back of the Pupil's Book.

Check answers, asking pupils to identify the tense used in each column.

Suggestion

Write up: *El fin de semana pasado salí con David Beckham.*

Ask pupils to identify the verb and to tell you what tense it is. How did they work it out? (time expression *el fin de semana pasado*) Can they work out which verb it is from and translate the sentence? Explain that this unit introduces the preterite forms of *-er* and *-ir* verbs.

1 Escucha y lee. (AT1.5)

▸▸2.3/Y8 4.5a/Y8◂◂

Listening. Pupils listen to Alex's report on his dinner with David Beckham, following the text in the book at the same time. Some vocabulary is glossed for support.

Audioscript Track 33

El fin de semana pasado salí con David Beckham. Fui a Madrid en avión y fui a un restaurante muy caro con David. ¡Fue guay! El restaurante se llama El Mesón madrileño.
De primer plato comí una ensalada y David, gambas. De segundo plato compartimos una paella.
De postre comí un helado de chocolate – ¡delicioso! David no comió nada. Bebimos agua.
Durante la cena, David recibió unos mensajes de Victoria. Hablamos del Real Madrid y de fútbol.

Suggestion

Pick out the forms *compartimos (una paella)* and *hablamos (del Real Madrid)*. If these phrases had been used to describe something that Alex normally does and so were in the present tense, what would the verb forms have been? Give pupils a minute to look this up in the verb tables at the back of the Pupil's Book if necessary. Confirm that the 'we' form is the same in the present and preterite tenses and ask pupils how then they are to know which tense is meant. (use of context, recognition of time expressions)

Gramática: the preterite of *-er* and *-ir* verbs

Use the Gramática box to introduce the full preterite forms of *-er* and *-ir* verbs, using *comer* and *salir*. Ask pupils what they notice about the two verb types in the preterite. (They have the same endings as each other.) There is practice on this on page 132 of the Pupil's Book.

R Pupils use *comer* and *salir* as models to write out all the preterite forms of *beber* and *escribir*.

+ Pupils in pairs test each other on the different parts of *comer* and *salir* by taking it in turn to prompt in English and respond in Spanish. They then write out all the preterite forms of *beber* and *escribir* without looking at their books.

Suggestion

Pupils might find it useful to compare *-ar* preterite endings with *-ir*/*-er* endings. Can they identify similarities and differences that might help them remember the endings for all three groups?

2 Lee el texto y contesta a las preguntas en inglés. (AT3.5) ▸▸5.4◂◂

Reading. Pupils reread the text in exercise 1 and answer the six questions on it in English.

Answers

1. *In Madrid.*
2. Last weekend.
3. Salad, paella and chocolate ice cream.
4. Prawns and paella.
5. Water.
6. Real Madrid and football.

Starter 2 ▸▸5.1◂◂

Aim

To practise recognising verbs in the preterite tense.

Tell the class you are going to write up/reveal a mixture of verbs in the present and preterite tenses, one at a time. (Use the verbs *comprar*, *comer* and *salir*.) They need to stand up if the verb is in the preterite tense and sit down if it is in the present tense. Ask a pupil to translate each verb form before showing the next one.

3 Lee el texto otra vez. Copia y rellena la tabla con los verbos (en verde) del texto. (AT3.5) ▸▸4.5a/Y8 5.1◂◂

Reading. Pupils copy out the table. They reread the text in exercise 1 and then complete the table with the required verb details: as given in the headings below.

Answers

Preterite	English	Infinitive	English
salí	*I went out*	*salir*	*to go out*
fui (x 2)	I went	ir	to go
fue (x 3)	it was	ser	to be
comí (x 2)	I ate	comer	to eat
compartimos	we shared	compartir	to share
comió	he ate	comer	to eat
bebimos	we drank	beber	to drink
recibió	he received	recibir	to receive
hablamos	we talked	hablar	to talk

4 Escucha a Rosa y escribe la letra correcta. (AT1.4) ▸▸1.1/Y8◂◂

Listening. Pupils listen to Rosa describing her dinner with a famous person. They complete the ten sentences by choosing the correct ending for each, *a* or *b*.

Audioscript Track 34

El fin de semana pasado salí con Jennifer Lopez. Fui a Los Ángeles en avión.
Fui a un restaurante español con Jennifer. De primer plato comí una ensalada y Jennifer también. De segundo plato comimos pollo – mmm, ¡delicioso!
De postre comí un helado de chocolate. Jennifer comió fruta. Bebimos Coca-Cola.
¡Jennifer es muy, muy simpática y ahora es mi amiga! Hablamos de música y de películas. ¡Fue genial!

Answers

1 a **2** b **3** a **4** a **5** b **6** a **7** a **8** a **9** b **10** a

5 Con tu compañero/a, pregunta y contesta sobre una cena. (AT2.5) ▸▸1.4b/Y8 4.6a/Y8◂◂

Speaking. In pairs pupils make up a dialogue discussing a dinner in the past, possibly with a famous person, taking it in turn to ask and answer questions. A framework is supplied for support.

6 Describe una cena con una persona famosa. (AT4.5) ▸▸2.1/Y8 2.4a/Y8 4.4/Y8◂◂

Writing. Using Alex's text in exercise 1 as a model, pupils write a description of a dinner they had with a famous person. A structure is supplied for support.

Remind them to make their sentences as varied and interesting as possible, by including connectives and negatives and by introducing opinions and reasons. They can use a dictionary to extend their vocabulary range: suggest they read through the Estrategia feature in the Palabras section in the Pupil's Book (page 77), which contains advice on dictionary usage.

Get pupils to do a first draft and then swap with a partner to comment on each other's work. They should then do a second draft.

Pupils find some menus in Spanish on Spanish restaurant websites. They should note down five new dishes and look these up in a dictionary. They should aim to include at least two of these items in their work in unit 5.

Plenary ▸▸5.1◂◂

Put the class into three teams. Give them one minute to look at the verb paradigms on pages 63 (*comprar*) and 66 (*comer, salir*) of the Pupil's Book while you draw a grid as follows.

	Team 1 – *comprar*	Team 2 – *comer*	Team 3 – *salir*
I			
you (singular)			
he/she/it			
we			
you (plural)			
they			

Explain that this is a tag game: one person from each team comes to the front and writes in one verb form for their team's verb (it can be for any of the spaces still blank). He/She then runs back and tags the next player in the team, who fills in another verb. This continues until the grids are full. Award one point for a correct answer and give two bonus points to the team which finishes first.

You could make the game more challenging by using different regular verbs, e.g. *mandar, beber, escribir*.

Cuaderno A, page 35

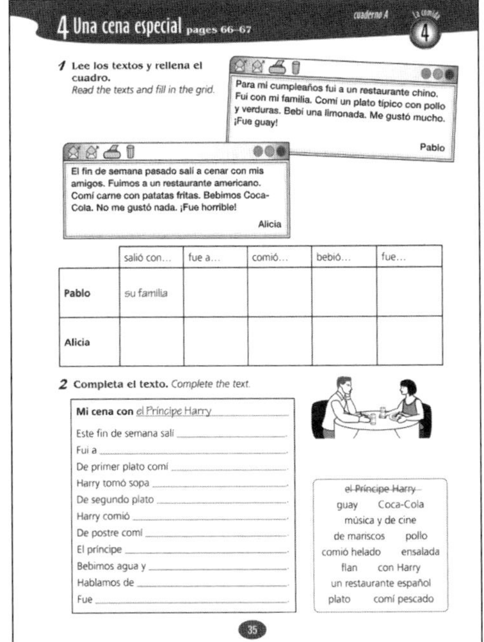

4 Una cena especial pages 66–67 cuaderno A La comida 4

1 **Lee los textos y rellena el cuadro.** *Read the texts and fill in the grid.*

Para mi cumpleaños fui a un restaurante chino. Fui con mi familia. Comí un plato típico con pollo y verduras. Bebí una limonada. Me gustó mucho. ¡Fue guay!

Pablo

El fin de semana pasado salí a cenar con mis amigos. Fuimos a un restaurante americano. Comí carne con patatas fritas. Bebimos Coca-Cola. No me gustó nada. ¡Fue horrible!

Alicia

	salió con…	fue a…	comió…	bebió…	fue…
Pablo	su familia				
Alicia					

2 **Completa el texto.** *Complete the text.*

Mi cena con el Príncipe Harry

Este fin de semana salí ________.
Fui a ________.
De primer plato comí ________.
Harry tomó sopa ________.
De segundo plato ________.
Harry comió ________.
De postre comí ________.
El príncipe ________.
Bebimos agua y ________.
Hablamos de ________.
Fue ________.

~~el Príncipe Harry~~ guay Coca-Cola música y de cine de mariscos pollo comió helado ensalada flan con Harry un restaurante español plato comí pescado

35

Cuaderno B, page 35

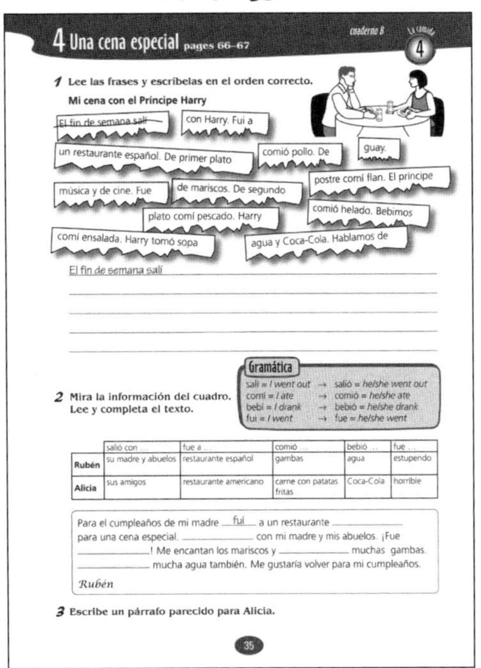

4 Una cena especial pages 66–67 cuaderno B La comida 4

1 **Lee las frases y escríbelas en el orden correcto.**

Mi cena con el Príncipe Harry

~~El fin de semana salí~~ | con Harry. Fui a | un restaurante español. De primer plato | comió pollo. De | guay. | música y de cine. Fue | de mariscos. De segundo | postre comí flan. El príncipe | plato comí pescado. Harry | comió helado. Bebimos | comí ensalada. Harry tomó sopa | agua y Coca-Cola. Hablamos de

El fin de semana salí

Gramática
salí = *I went out* → salió = *he/she went out*
comí = *I ate* → comió = *he/she ate*
bebí = *I drank* → bebió = *he/she drank*
fui = *I went* → fue = *he/she went*

2 **Mira la información del cuadro. Lee y completa el texto.**

	salió con …	fue a …	comió …	bebió …	fue …
Rubén	su madre y abuelos	restaurante español	gambas	agua	estupendo
Alicia	sus amigos	restaurante americano	carne con patatas fritas	Coca-Cola	horrible

Para el cumpleaños de mi madre fui a un restaurante ________ para una cena especial. ________ con mi madre y mis abuelos. ¡Fue ________! Me encantan los mariscos y ________ muchas gambas. ________ mucha agua también. Me gustaría volver para mi cumpleaños.

Rubén

3 **Escribe un párrafo parecido para Alicia.**

35

1 (AT3.3)

	salió con...	fue a...	comió...	bebió...	fue...
Pablo	*su familia*	un restaurante chino	(un plato típico con) pollo y verduras	una limonada	guay
Alicia	sus amigos	un restaurante americano	carne con patatas fritas	Coca-Cola	horrible

2 (AT3.2, AT4.2)

Mi cena con *el Príncipe Harry*
Este fin de semana salí **con Harry**.
Fui a **un restaurante español**.
De primer plato comí **ensalada**.
Harry tomó sopa **de mariscos**.
De segundo plato **comí pescado**.
Harry comió **pollo**.
De postre comí **flan**.
El príncipe **comió helado**.
Bebimos agua y **Coca-Cola**.
Hablamos de **música y de cine**.
Fue **guay**.

1 (AT3.4, AT4.3)

Mi cena con el Príncipe Harry
El fin de semana salí con Harry.
Fui a un restaurante español
De primer plato comí ensalada.
Harry tomó sopa de mariscos.
De segundo plato comí pescado.
Harry comió pollo.
De postre comí flan.
El príncipe comió helado.
Bebimos agua y Coca-Cola
Hablamos de música y de cine.
Fue guay.

2 (AT3.5, AT4.2)

Para el cumpleaños de mi madre *fui* a un restaurante español para una cena especial. Salí con mi madre y mis abuelos. ¡Fue estupendo! Me encantan los mariscos y comí muchas gambas. Bebí mucha agua también. Me gustaría volver para mi cumpleaños.

Rubén

3 (AT4.5)

R & A Pack, Gramática page 19

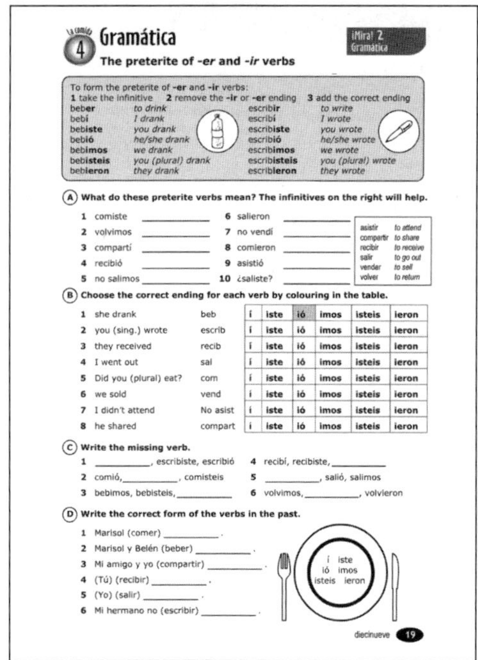

Gramática

iMira! 2 Gramática

The preterite of *-er* and *-ir* verbs

To form the preterite of **-er** and **-ir** verbs:
1 take the infinitive **2** remove the **-ir** or **-er** ending **3** add the correct ending

beb**er**	*to drink*	escrib**ir**	*to write*
bebí	*I drank*	escribí	*I wrote*
beb**iste**	*you drank*	escrib**iste**	*you wrote*
beb**ió**	*he/she drank*	escrib**ió**	*he/she wrote*
beb**imos**	*we drank*	escrib**imos**	*we wrote*
beb**isteis**	*you (plural) drank*	escrib**isteis**	*you (plural) wrote*
beb**ieron**	*they drank*	escrib**ieron**	*they wrote*

Ⓐ **What do these preterite verbs mean? The infinitives on the right will help.**

1 comiste ________ 6 salieron ________
2 volvimos ________ 7 no vendí ________
3 compartí ________ 8 comieron ________
4 recibió ________ 9 asistió ________
5 no salimos ________ 10 ¿saliste? ________

asistir	*to attend*
compartir	*to share*
recibir	*to receive*
salir	*to go out*
vender	*to sell*
volver	*to return*

Ⓑ **Choose the correct ending for each verb by colouring in the table.**

1 she drank	beb	í	iste	ió	imos	isteis	ieron
2 you (sing.) wrote	escrib	í	iste	ió	imos	isteis	ieron
3 they received	recib	í	iste	ió	imos	isteis	ieron
4 I went out	sal	í	iste	ió	imos	isteis	ieron
5 Did you (plural) eat?	com	í	iste	ió	imos	isteis	ieron
6 we sold	vend	í	iste	ió	imos	isteis	ieron
7 I didn't attend	No asist	í	iste	ió	imos	isteis	ieron
8 he shared	compart	í	iste	ió	imos	isteis	ieron

Ⓒ **Write the missing verb.**

1 ________, escribiste, escribió 4 recibí, recibiste, ________
2 comió, ________, comisteis 5 ________, salió, salimos
3 bebimos, bebisteis, ________ 6 volvimos, ________, volvieron

Ⓓ **Write the correct form of the verbs in the past.**

1 Marisol (comer) ________.
2 Marisol y Belén (beber) ________.
3 Mi amigo y yo (compartir) ________.
4 (Tú) (recibir) ________.
5 (Yo) (salir) ________.
6 Mi hermano no (escribir) ________.

í iste ió imos isteis ieron

diecinueve 19

Ⓐ **1** you (sing.) ate **2** we returned **3** I shared **4** he/she received **5** we didn't go out **6** they went out **7** I didn't sell **8** they ate **9** he/she attended **10** Did you (sing.) go out?

Ⓑ **1** beb**ió** **2** escrib**iste** **3** recib**ieron** **4** salí **5** ¿com**isteis**? **6** vend**imos** **7** no asistí **8** compart**ió**

Ⓒ **1** escribí **2** comimos **3** bebieron **4** recibió **5** saliste **6** volvisteis

Ⓓ **1** comió **2** bebieron **3** compartimos **4** recibiste **5** salí **6** escribió

5 ¿Qué te gusta comer? (Pupil's Book pages 68–69)

Launching objectives

- Talking about likes and dislikes
- Using past, present and future together

Framework objectives

4.6/Y8 Language – (b) range of negatives
5.8 Strategies – evaluating and improving

Grammar

- Using a range of tenses: preterite, present and future

Key language

¿Qué te gusta comer?
Me gusta (mucho) comer...
No me gusta nada comer...
A veces como...
Nunca como...
Me gusta beber...
Nunca bebo...
Normalmente como...
El fin de semana pasado comí...
Mañana voy a comer...

High-frequency words

el
me, te
a
de
mañana
mucho
no
¿qué?
beber
comer (como, comí)
ir (voy)
nada, nunca

Cross-curricular

English: Writing techniques

Resources

CD2, tracks 35–36
Cuadernos A & B, p. 36
R & A Pack, Gramática p. 20

Teacher Presentations

Screen 1 – Module 4 overview
Screen 2 – p. 68 ex. 1
Screen 3 – p. 69 exs 3 & 4
Screen 4 – Video

Starter 1 ▸▸5.2◂◂

Aim
To revise vocabulary for food.

Give pupils three minutes working in pairs to list as many items of food as they can. Each pair swaps with another pair to check answers, using the Palabras section of the Pupil's Book (pages 76–77). A correct food item wins a point, plus an extra point if the correct form of the article is given. The pair with the most points is the winner.

Suggestion

Use the key language grid to introduce the question forms *¿Qué te gusta comer/beber?* and the responses. Give English translations of this language as prompts for pupils to supply the Spanish.

Point out the tip box contrasting *Me gusta comer...* and *Como...* . Ask pupils what form of the verb *comer* is.

1 ¿Quién habla? Escucha y escribe el nombre correcto. (1–4) (AT1.3) ▸▸1.1/Y8 4.6b/Y8◂◂

Listening. Pupils listen to four people talking about what they like to eat and drink and identify each speaker using the pictures supplied.

Audioscript Track 35

1 *Me gusta comer pescado y pollo.*
Me gusta beber agua.
A veces como patatas fritas.
Nunca como gambas.
2 *Me gusta comer helado.*
También me gusta beber limonada.
A veces como fruta pero nunca como ensalada.
3 *A ver, me gusta comer magdalenas.*
Me gusta beber zumo de naranja.
A veces como tostadas pero nunca como cereales.
4 *– ¿Qué te gusta comer?*
– A ver, me gusta comer paella.
Me gusta beber agua.
A veces como pollo.
Nunca como pan.

Answers
1 *Juana* **2** Rico **3** Ramón **4** Elena

R Pupils working in pairs use the pictures in exercise 1 to practise the expressions in the key language grid. They pick a person each and describe what they eat/drink/don't eat using the openings provided (e.g. *A veces como...* or *Nunca como...*) with an appropriate item pictured (e.g. for Elena: *A veces como paella/pollo* or *Nunca como pan*).

2 Con tu compañero/a, haz un diálogo. (AT2.3) ▸▸1.4b/Y8◂◂

Speaking. In pairs: pupils take it in turn to ask and answer each other about what they like to eat and drink. A framework is supplied.

Once pupils are feeling more confident, they could try doing the dialogue without looking at the model. You could choose a few pairs to peform in front of the class and ask the rest of the class comprehension questions on what they hear.

Starter 2 ▸▸4.5a/Y8◂◂

Aim
To practise using the present, preterite and near future tenses appropriately.

Write up: *A veces...*
La semana pasada...
Mañana...

bebí, voy a comer, como, bebo, comí, voy a beber

Give pupils three minutes working in pairs to write three sentences, each using one of the time expressions given and two appropriate verbs, plus any additional language necessary.

Check answers, asking pupils to translate their sentences into English. Ask them which tense was used in each sentence.

Suggestion

Ask pupils to summarise time expressions associated with the present, preterite and near future tenses, translating them into English.

Then ask them to give you examples of verbs in these tenses.

Explain that this lesson is going to focus on using all three of the tenses together and that it will be very important for them to look out for time expressions and to remember verb forms to understand the written texts, and to use time expressions and verb forms appropriately in their own writing.

3 Escucha y lee. Copia y rellena la tabla. (AT1.6) ▸▸1.2/Y8 1.5b/Y8 4.6b/Y8 5.6◂◂

Listening. Pupils copy out the table. They listen to two people talking about what they ate and drank when they were in the jungle, reading the text in the book at the same time. The 'menu' glosses new vocabulary for support. They then complete the table with details of what each person likes and dislikes.

Audioscript Track 36

1 *Normalmente como mucha fruta y ensalada y bebo agua pero ayer comí arañas. ¡Qué horror! Y mañana voy a comer un bocadillo de moscas. ¡Ay! No puedo. Me gusta comer ensalada de lechuga y pepino... Quiero salir de aquí.*

2 *Normalmente como pasta. También me gusta comer nachos y hamburguesas. No quiero comer insectos. No me gustan nada. El fin de semana pasado bebí un cóctel de gusanos y mañana voy a comer cucarachas con mayonesa. ¡Buagh, qué asco!*

Answers

	Le gusta	No le gusta
Elisa	*fruta, ensalada,* agua	arañas, moscas
Alejandro	pasta, nachos, hamburguesas	insectos – gusanos, cucarachas

R Get pupils to read the texts aloud, encouraging them to put as much expression into their versions as possible.

+ Pupils re-read the texts and note down features which make them interesting. If necessary, prompt with the following so that pupils can locate the Spanish expressions: colloquialisms (*¡Ay!*, *¡Buagh!*); exclamations (*¡Qué horror!*, *¡Qué asco!*); humour (content – insects consumed; details like *con mayonesa* and *un cóctel de...*); the use of connectives to extend sentences; variety in sentence types.

Encourage pupils to keep this as a checklist of ideas for doing their own creative writing in Spanish.

4 Contesta a las preguntas en inglés por Elisa y Alejandro. (AT3.6)

▸▸1.2/Y8 4.5a&b/Y8◂◂

Reading. Pupils read the texts in exercise 3 again and answer the questions in English.

Answers

1 *Elisa normally eats salad and fruit.*
Alejandro normally eats pasta, nachos and hamburgers.
2 Elisa ate spiders.
Alejandro ate/drank maggots/a maggot cocktail.
3 Elisa is going to eat a fly sandwich.
Alejandro is going to eat cockroaches with mayonnaise.

+ Ask pupils to find expressions using the verbs *poder* and *querer* in the texts and to translate them: there are three. Then get them to rewrite the expressions featuring these verbs using the 'we' form, 'he/she' form and 'they' form, respectively, of the appropriate verb.

(*No puedo – No podemos, no podemos*
Quiero salir de aquí. – Quiere salir de aquí.
No quiero comer insectos. – No quieren comer insectos.)

5 Lee los textos otra vez. Escribe los verbos en la tabla. (AT3.6) ▸▸1.2/Y8 4.5a&b/Y8◂◂

Reading. Pupils copy out the table. They read the texts in exercise 3 again and note all the verbs used in the texts, sorting them by tense – present, preterite or future.

Read through the tip box as a class before pupils do the activity as a reminder that recognising time expressions can help them identify tenses. Ask pupils which tenses they would expect to find with *normalmente, ayer* and *mañana.*

Answers

Presente	Pretérito	Futuro
como	bebí	voy a comer
bebo		
(no) puedo		
me gusta(n)		
quiero		

Suggestion ▸▸3.2b/Y8 5.8◂◂

If you have a native Spanish-speaking assistant, you could use him/her to give pupils practice talking without prompts on the subject of eating habits. The assistant could also talk about his/her own eating preferences and about Spanish specialities.

Whenever an assistant works with the pupils, encourage him/her to give feedback in Spanish, using the expressions you use consistently to comment on pupils' work (and have perhaps already displayed in the classroom for pupils' reference).

6 ¿Qué te gusta comer? Copia y completa la ficha. Mira la sección Palabras (páginas 76 y 77). (AT4.3, AT3.5) ▸▸2.4a/Y8 4.2/Y8 4.4/Y8◂◂

Writing. Pupils copy out the grid and complete it with details of their own eating and drinking likes/dislikes, etc. They should use the Palabras section (pages 76–77) for a summary of useful food and drink vocabulary from the whole of the module.

Plenary ▸▸5.8◂◂

Ask pupils how they think they can get the most out of the Resumen section at the end of each module. Explain as necessary that it is a valuable tool for revising and can be used as follows:

- to test their progress so far
- as a prompt to review/look up other examples
- to identify and enable them to target weak areas
- for self-testing
- to test each other in pairs

Put the class into teams and tell pupils that you are going to use the Resumen section to test them. Each team chooses a unit: give them two minutes to review those pages in the Pupil's Book. They then close their books.

Ask the teams in turn to give a Spanish example for each point listed in the Resumen section. They can confer, but a different person must finally answer each time. A correct answer wins a point. The team with the most points wins.

Cuaderno A, page 36

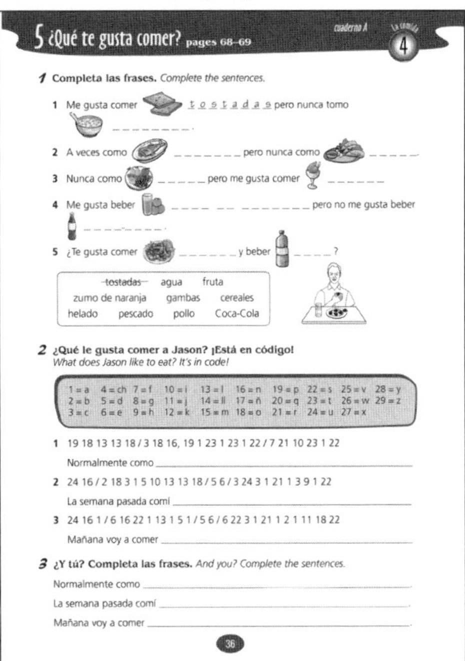

5 ¿Qué te gusta comer? pages 68–69 — cuaderno A — La comida 4

1 Completa las frases. *Complete the sentences.*

1 Me gusta comer t o s t a d a s pero nunca tomo ________.
2 A veces como ________ pero nunca como ________.
3 Nunca como ________ pero me gusta comer ________
4 Me gusta beber ________ pero no me gusta beber ________.
5 ¿Te gusta comer ________ y beber ________?

~~tostadas~~ agua fruta
zumo de naranja gambas cereales
helado pescado pollo Coca-Cola

2 ¿Qué le gusta comer a Jason? ¡Está en código!
What does Jason like to eat? It's in code!

1 = a 4 = ch 7 = f 10 = i 13 = l 16 = n 19 = p 22 = s 25 = v 28 = y
2 = b 5 = d 8 = g 11 = j 14 = ll 17 = ñ 20 = q 23 = t 26 = w 29 = z
3 = c 6 = e 9 = h 12 = k 15 = m 18 = o 21 = r 24 = u 27 = x

1 19 18 13 13 18 / 3 18 16, 19 1 23 1 23 1 22 / 7 21 10 23 1 22
Normalmente como ________
2 24 16 / 2 18 3 1 5 10 13 13 18 / 5 6 / 3 24 3 1 21 1 3 9 1 22
La semana pasada comí ________
3 24 16 1 / 6 16 22 1 13 1 5 1 / 5 6 / 6 22 3 1 21 1 2 1 11 18 22
Mañana voy a comer ________

3 ¿Y tú? Completa las frases. *And you? Complete the sentences.*
Normalmente como ________
La semana pasada comí ________.
Mañana voy a comer ________.

36

1 (AT4.1)

1 *tostadas,* cereales
2 pescado, pollo
3 fruta, helado
4 zumo de naranja, Coca-Cola
5 gambas, agua

2 (AT4.1)

1 pollo con patatas fritas
2 un bocadillo de cucarachas
3 una ensalada de escarabajos

3 (AT4.2)

Cuaderno B, page 36

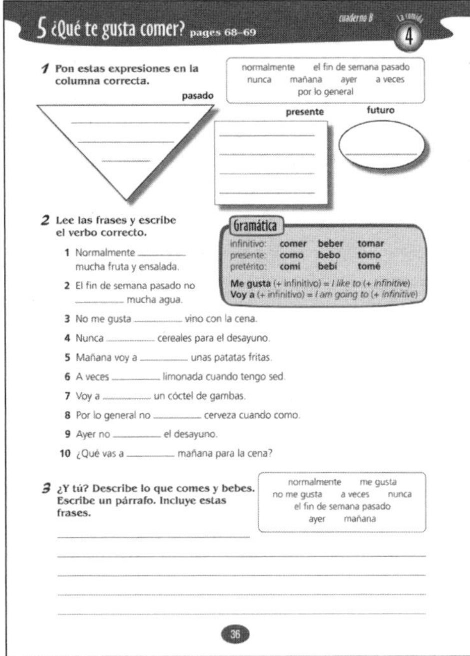
5 ¿Qué te gusta comer? pages 68–69 — cuaderno B — La comida 4

1 **Pon estas expresiones en la columna correcta.**

normalmente · el fin de semana pasado · nunca · mañana · ayer · a veces · por lo general

pasado · presente · futuro

2 **Lee las frases y escribe el verbo correcto.**

Gramática

infinitivo:	**comer**	**beber**	**tomar**
presente:	**como**	**bebo**	**tomo**
pretérito:	**comí**	**bebí**	**tomé**

Me gusta (+ infinitivo) = *I like to* (+ *infinitive*)
Voy a (+ infinitivo) = *I am going to* (+ *infinitive*)

1 Normalmente ______ mucha fruta y ensalada.
2 El fin de semana pasado no ______ mucha agua.
3 No me gusta ______ vino con la cena.
4 Nunca ______ cereales para el desayuno.
5 Mañana voy a ______ unas patatas fritas.
6 A veces ______ limonada cuando tengo sed.
7 Voy a ______ un cóctel de gambas.
8 Por lo general no ______ cerveza cuando como.
9 Ayer no ______ el desayuno.
10 ¿Qué vas a ______ mañana para la cena?

3 **¿Y tú? Describe lo que comes y bebes. Escribe un párrafo. Incluye estas frases.**

normalmente · me gusta · no me gusta · a veces · nunca · el fin de semana pasado · ayer · mañana

36

1 (AT4.1)

pasado: el fin de semana pasado, ayer
presente: normalmente, nunca, a veces, por lo general
futuro: mañana

2 (AT3.5, AT4.2)

1 como **2** bebí **3** beber **4** como **5** comer
6 bebo **7** comer **8** bebo **9** tomé **10** tomar/comer

3 (AT4.6)

R & A Pack, Gramática page 20

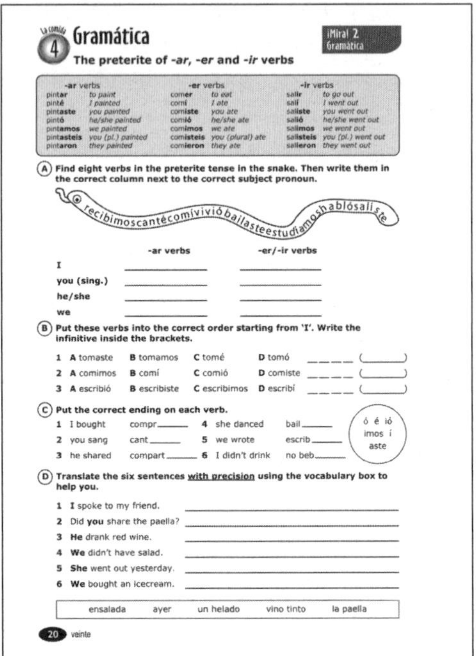
La comida 4 **Gramática** — ¡Mira! 2 Gramática

The preterite of *-ar*, *-er* and *-ir* verbs

-ar verbs		**-er** verbs		**-ir** verbs	
pint**ar**	*to paint*	com**er**	*to eat*	sal**ir**	*to go out*
pint**é**	*I painted*	com**í**	*I ate*	sal**í**	*I went out*
pint**aste**	*you painted*	com**iste**	*you ate*	sal**iste**	*you went out*
pint**ó**	*he/she painted*	com**ió**	*he/she ate*	sal**ió**	*he/she went out*
pint**amos**	*we painted*	com**imos**	*we ate*	sal**imos**	*we went out*
pint**asteis**	*you (pl.) painted*	com**isteis**	*you (plural) ate*	sal**isteis**	*you (pl.) went out*
pint**aron**	*they painted*	com**ieron**	*they ate*	sal**ieron**	*they went out*

(A) **Find eight verbs in the preterite tense in the snake. Then write them in the correct column next to the correct subject pronoun.**

recibimoscantécomívivióbailasteestudiamoshablósaliste

	-ar verbs	**-er/-ir verbs**
I	______	______
you (sing.)	______	______
he/she	______	______
we	______	______

(B) **Put these verbs into the correct order starting from 'I'. Write the infinitive inside the brackets.**

1 **A** tomaste **B** tomamos **C** tomé **D** tomó _ _ _ _ (______)
2 **A** comimos **B** comí **C** comió **D** comiste _ _ _ _ (______)
3 **A** escribió **B** escribiste **C** escribimos **D** escribí _ _ _ _ (______)

(C) **Put the correct ending on each verb.**

1 I bought compr______ 4 she danced bail______
2 you sang cant______ 5 we wrote escrib______
3 he shared compart______ 6 I didn't drink no beb______

ó é ió imos í aste

(D) **Translate the six sentences with precision using the vocabulary box to help you.**

1 **I** spoke to my friend.
2 Did **you** share the paella?
3 **He** drank red wine.
4 **We** didn't have salad.
5 **She** went out yesterday.
6 **We** bought an icecream.

ensalada · ayer · un helado · vino tinto · la paella

20 veinte

(A)

	-ar verbs	-er / -ir verbs
I	canté	comí
you (sing.)	bailaste	saliste
he/she	habló	vivió
we	estudiamos	recibimos

(B) **1** C A D B (tomar)
2 B D C A (comer)
3 D B A C (escribir)

(C) **1** compr**é** **2** cant**aste** **3** compart**ió** **4** bail**ó**
5 escrib**imos** **6** no beb**í**

(D) **1** Hablé con mi amigo.
2 ¿Compartiste la paella?
3 Bebió vino tinto.
4 No tomamos ensalada.
5 Salió ayer.
6 Compramos un helado.

4 Resumen y Prepárate (Pupil's Book pages 70–71)

Resumen

This is a checklist of language covered in Module 4. Pupils can work on this in pairs to check what they have learned and remembered. There is a Resumen page in the Resource and Assessment Pack. Encourage them to look back at the module and to use the grammar section to revise what they are unclear about. You can also use the Resumen as a useful plenary at the end of each unit.

Prepárate

These revision tests can be used for pupils to practise prior to the assessment tasks in the Resource and Assessment Pack.

Resources

CD2, track 37
R & A Pack, Module 4: Resumen, Prueba, I can...

1 Escucha. Copia y rellena la tabla. (AT1.4) ▸▸ 1.1/Y8 ◂◂

Listening. Pupils copy out the table. They listen to three people talking about what they normally eat and drink and complete the table with the details.

Audioscript Track 37

Gustavo
A ver… Normalmente desayuno cereales y bebo café. Como a las dos: como pollo o pescado con ensalada y de postre como fruta. Ceno a las nueve y tomo pizza o pasta.

Rosa
Desayuno tostadas o magdalenas y bebo Cola Cao. Como a la una. Normalmente tomo un bocadillo y bebo agua. Ceno tarde, a las nueve y media. De primer plato tomo sopa, de segundo carne y de postre fruta.

Enrique
– *¿Qué desayunas, Enrique?*
– *No desayuno nada.*
– *¿Qué comes generalmente?*
– *Pues depende, un bocadillo o una pizza.*
– *¿Y a qué hora cenas?*
– *Ceno a las ocho. Es mi comida principal. Tomo pescado con ensalada.*

Answers

	Desayuno	Comida	Cena
Gustavo	cereales, café	pollo/ pescado con ensalada, fruta	pizza/pasta
Rosa	tostadas/ magdalenas, Cola Cao	bocadillo, agua	sopa, carne, fruta
Enrique	nada	bocadillo/ pizza	pescado con ensalada

2 Con tu compañero/a, haz diálogos. (AT2.3) ▸▸ 1.4a/Y8 ◂◂

Speaking. In pairs: using the picture prompts supplied, pupils make up dialogues set in a food shop. They take it in turn to play the role of the shop owner and the customer. A sample exchange is supplied.

3 Lee y empareja las mitades de las frases. Escribe las frases completas en el orden correcto para hacer un diálogo. (AT3.3) ▸▸ 5.4 ◂◂

Reading. Pupils match the sentence halves, and then rewrite the completed sentences in order to make a dialogue.

Answers
5 d **2** a **3** b **4** c **1** f **6** e

4 Escribe un correo. Incluye los datos siguientes. (AT4.5–6) ▸▸ 2.4b/Y8 4.5a&b/Y8 ◂◂

Writing. Pupils write an email to a friend talking about their eating habits. The information they need to include is listed: what they usually eat/ drink for each meal; what they ate and drank yesterday; what they are going to have tomorrow; what they like to eat and drink; what they never eat. A framework is supplied for support.

4 ¡Extra! 1 (Pupil's Book pages 72–73)

Launching objectives
- Practising using three tenses together
- Giving a spoken presentation

Framework objectives
1.5/Y8 Speaking – (a) unscripted talks
2.2/Y8 Reading – (b) personal response to text
5.7 Strategies – planning & preparing

Grammar
- Using a range of tenses: preterite, present and future

Key language
Revision of language from Module 4

High-frequency words
Revision of language from Module 4

Resources
CD2, tracks 38–39

Starter ▸▸ 4.4/Y8 ◂◂

Aim

To revise the language and structures of the module.

Write up the following words and ask pupils to use them to write a short paragraph. There are two rules: they need to use *all* of the words and they need to give verbs and adjectives in the appropriate form.

pero el fin de semana pasado beber
comer no me gusta pollo agua
limonada y a veces paella de mariscos

Suggestion

Ask pupils to recap on which tense they would use when talking about:

- what they usually eat or drink
- what they're planning to eat or drink tomorrow
- what they ate and drank yesterday

Ask the class to give you the appropriate 'I' forms of the verbs *comer* and *beber* in all three tenses.

1 Escucha y elige el verbo correcto. Luego escribe las frases en inglés. (AT1.2, AT3.2) ▸▸ 4.6a/Y8 ◂◂

Listening. Pupils listen to the description of what Diego ate and drank yesterday. They complete the text version of the audioscript by choosing the correct verb from the two options given for each statement.

Audioscript Track 38

1 *Ayer Diego no* ***desayunó*** *nada…*
2 *… pero* ***tomó*** *chocolate con dos kilos de churros a las dos de la tarde.*
3 *Luego* ***vomitó****.*
4 ***Bebió*** *mucha agua…*
5 *… y más tarde* ***cenó*** *con su familia.*

Answers

See also ***bold*** *in audioscript.*

1 desayunó **2** tomó **3** vomitó **4** bebió **5** cenó

2 ¿Comes una dieta sana? ¡Compruébalo con este test! (AT2.6) ▸▸ 2.2b/Y8 ◂◂

Speaking. In pairs: pupils do the quiz to work out whether they have a healthy diet. They each choose an answer from the multiple choice options for each question, saying it aloud. They then tally their scores and read the appropriate comment.

3 Escucha a Lola. Completa las frases. (AT1.6) ▸▸ 4.3/Y8 4.4/Y8 ◂◂

Listening. Pupils listen to Lola. They note the key details of what she says by completing the six sentence openings, choosing from the options given.

Audioscript Track 39

Me gusta comer ensalada de lechuga, pepino y tomates porque es muy sana y también rica. No me gusta comer hamburguesas porque no son sanas, son grasientas. Todos los días como queso porque es delicioso. Algunas veces a la semana como pescado porque es muy sano. El fin de semana pasado comí pollo porque también es sano. Y mañana voy a comer helado de chocolate porque es mi cumpleaños.

Answers

1 *Me gusta comer* ensalada (con lechuga, pepino y tomates) porque es (muy) sana y (también) rica.
2 *No me gusta comer* hamburguesas porque no son sanas, son grasientas.
3 *Todos los días como* queso.
4 *Algunas veces a la semana como* pescado.
5 *El fin de semana pasado comí* pollo (porque es sano).
6 *Mañana voy a comer* helado de chocolate porque es mi cumpleaños.

4 Pon los dibujos en el orden del texto. (AT3.5) ▸▸4.2/Y8◂◂

Reading. Pupils read Lidia's email and put the pictures *a–m* in the order she mentions them.

Answers

b, a, f, h, c, e, g, d, k, j, i, l, m

R Pupils identify:

- two time expressions
- two 'I' form verbs in the preterite tense
- five 'we' form verbs in the preterite tense

+ Pupils rewrite the text in the 3rd person (so 'I' →'she' and 'we' → 'they').

5 Prepara una presentación. (AT2.6) ▸▸1.5a/Y8 4.4/Y8 5.7◂◂

Speaking. Pupils use the language of the module to structure a presentation on their eating habits. A list of all the points to cover (including cross-references to the relevant page of the module) is supplied. A tip box also summarises ways in which pupils can make their texts in Spanish more interesting (connectives, time expressions, negatives).

Encourage them to write out the text of what they want to say, but then to create a short list of notes to use as prompts when actually speaking. Using this technique is very useful preparation for coping with unscripted speech and for developing independence as a learner.

Give students the chance to practise their presentations in pairs, and to record themselves if possible. Hear a few presentations and give constructive feedback, both on the accuracy of the language and on the fluency of the Spanish.

Plenary ▸▸4.5a/Y8◂◂

Put the class into teams for a verb quiz. Team by team, give each pupil a verb: they have to tell you what tense it is in – present, preterite or near future. A correct answer wins two points. Pupils can ask you to write up the verb for support, but will only then win one point for a correct answer. The points for each team are totalled to get the overall winners.

4 ¡Extra! 2 (Pupil's Book pages 74–75)

Launching objectives

- Reading extended texts
- Learning about authentic Spanish specialities

Framework objectives

2.2/Y8 Reading – (a) longer, more complex texts
5.5 Strategies – reference materials

Key language

Revision of language from Module 4

High-frequency words

Revision of language from Module 4

Cross-Curricular

English: Recognising the features of different text types

Resources

CD2, track 40
Cuadernos A & B, pp. 37–38

Starter 5.4

Aim

To lead into episode 4 of the story, give pupils a minute to re-read episode 3 and then read out the following statements about it. Pupils need to put up their hand if the sentence is correct, put their hand on their heads if it's false or shrug their shoulders if that information is not given in episode 3.

Pupils could then correct the statements which are false (given in brackets for reference).

1 *El año pasado Diego fue a Cadaqués con su familia.* (*... con un amigo.*)
2 *A Patricia no le gustan las pinturas de Dalí.* (*Sí, a Patricia le gustan...*)
3 *Cadaqués está al norte de Barcelona.*
4 *El año pasado Patricia fue a México.* [information not given]
5 *En Cadaqués Diego jugó al voleibol en la playa.* (*... jugó al fútbol...*)
6 *A Diego le gusta el dibujo.*

1 Escucha y lee. (AT1.5)

2.2a/Y8 5.4

Listening. Pupils listen to the recording of the story and read along with the text. Some vocabulary is glossed for support.

Audioscript Track 40

1 – *Tengo hambre, Diego. ¿Vamos a comer algo?*
– *De acuerdo. ¿Qué te gusta comer?*

2 – *A ver... me gusta mucho la carne. Y me gusta mucho la fruta también, sobre todo las uvas, las peras y los plátanos. La fruta es rica y muy sana.*

3 – *Ayer fui a la Boquería, allí tienen mucha fruta.*
– *¿La Boquería? ¿Qué es?*
– *Es un mercado en las Ramblas de Barcelona.*

4 – *Pero... ¡tengo una idea! Te invito a ir de tapas y luego a comer paella.*

5 – *¿Qué van a tomar?*
– *Una ración de aceitunas, una ración de albóndigas y unas patatas bravas.*

6 – *¿Cuál es la comida típica de Barcelona?*
– *La escalibada y la paella negra o de marisco. La escalibada está hecha de pimiento, berenjena y cebolla.*

7 – *¿Te gusta la paella, Patricia?*
– *Hmm, está deliciosa... Gracias por invitarme.*
– *De nada, es un placer.*

2 Con tu compañero/a, lee en voz alta la historia de Patricia y Diego. (AT2.5) 5.6

Speaking. In pairs pupils read the story aloud, each taking the role of Diego or Patricia. Encourage them to focus on pronunciation and stress and to try and sound as fluent as possible, following the model of the recording.

3 Termina estas frases. (AT4.3)

4.4/Y8 5.4

Writing. Pupils summarise the key points of the photo story by writing endings for the six sentence openings listed.

Answers

1 *A Patricia le gusta comer* carne y fruta (sobre todo las uvas, las peras y los plátanos).
2 *Ayer Diego fue* a la Boquería.
3 *La Boquería es* un mercado (en las Ramblas de Barcelona).
4 *Diego y Patricia toman una ración de* aceitunas, una ración de albóndigas y unas patatas bravas.
5 *La comida típica de Barcelona es* la escalibada, la paella negra o de marisco.
6 *La escalibada está hecha de* pimiento, berenjena y cebolla.

4 Empareja las personas con los restaurantes. (AT3.4) ▸▸2.2a/Y8 5.3◂◂

Reading. Pupils read the four website adverts for different kinds of restaurants. They then read the four speech bubbles and identify an appropriate restaurant for each speaker. Some restaurants may be suitable for more than one speaker, but pupils need to match each person with a different restaurant.

Ask pupils to look for cognates and near-cognates and to explain how their knowledge of English helped them to complete the task.

Answers

1 d **2** b **3** a **4** c

+ Read through the adverts as a class and discuss the key features of this kind of text. What kind of information would pupils expect to get? (address, contact details) What kind of language would they expect to be used? (language which 'sells' the restaurant, i.e. makes you want to go there)

Can they pick out one example of this kind of language in each advert? Without a dictionary, they should be able to identify one of the following in each text:

- **a** *más de 10 clases... diferentes*
- **b** *especialidad, 150 tapas, las más famosas*
- **c** *deliciosa*
- **d** *típico, exquisitas, una gran variedad, todo tipo*

5 Choose two restaurants and write lists of what they offer. To help you, first look up the underlined words in the Vocabulario. (AT3.4) ▸▸5.4 5.5◂◂

Reading. Pupils choose two of the restaurants. They look up the underlined words in the Vocabulario section of the Pupil's Book, then make a list of the foods offered in each restaurant.

Answers

- **a** fish and seafood (octopus, fried vegetables), rice dishes
- **b** tapas (anchovy, ham, tuna, pork)
- **c** red meat (e.g. beef, lamb, pork) cooked on a hot stone, stuffed partridge, oxtail
- **d** pizzas, Italian dishes, pasta, salads, sandwiches

Encourage pupils to note down and learn some of the vocabulary here that they could use in their own speaking and writing. Remind them that when listing vocabulary, they should note the gender of nouns and the infinitive forms of verbs, and make sure they have the masculine singular form of adjectives. Check that they know how to work out these details using a dictionary as necessary.

+ Can pupils guess what the following expressions mean from the context?

- **a** *tampoco te los puedes perder* ('nor can you miss these')
- **b** *sin duda* ('without doubt')
- **c** *todo un lujo* ('always a luxury')
- **d** *platos para todos los gustos* ('dishes for all tastes')

Get them to look up vocabulary as necessary to check.

Plenary ▸▸5.8◂◂

Put the class in teams and ask each group to prepare three questions on what they have learned in Module 4. These can be questions on verb tenses, food vocabulary, high numbers, shopping transactions, etc. – encourage them to be inventive. Team 1 asks Team 2 a question. A correct answer wins Team 2 a point; an incorrect answer wins Team 1 a point. Team 2 then asks Team 3, and so on, until all questions have been asked. The winning team is the one with the most points.

Cuaderno A, page 37

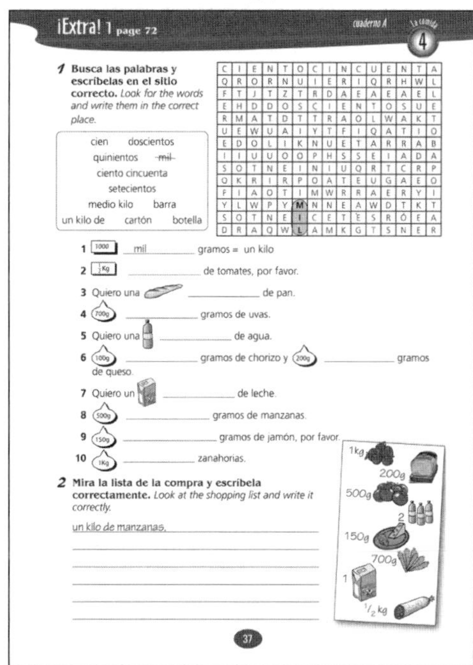

¡Extra! 1 page 72 cuaderno A La comida 4

1 Busca las palabras y escríbelas en el sitio correcto. *Look for the words and write them in the correct place.*

cien doscientos quinientos ~~mil~~ ciento cincuenta setecientos medio kilo barra un kilo de cartón botella

C	I	E	N	T	O	C	I	N	C	U	E	N	T	A
Q	R	O	R	N	U	I	E	R	I	Q	R	H	W	L
F	T	J	T	Z	T	R	D	A	E	A	E	A	E	L
E	H	D	D	O	S	C	I	E	N	T	O	S	U	E
R	M	A	T	D	T	T	R	A	O	L	W	A	K	T
U	E	W	U	A	I	Y	T	F	I	Q	A	T	I	O
E	D	O	L	I	K	N	U	E	T	A	R	R	A	B
I	I	U	U	O	O	P	H	S	S	E	I	A	D	A
S	O	T	N	E	I	N	I	U	Q	R	T	C	R	P
O	K	R	I	R	P	O	A	T	E	U	G	A	E	O
F	I	A	O	T	I	M	W	R	R	A	E	R	Y	I
Y	L	W	P	Y	M	N	N	E	A	W	D	T	K	T
S	O	T	N	E	I	C	E	T	È	S	R	Ó	E	A
D	R	A	Q	W	L	A	M	K	G	T	S	N	E	R

1 1000 mil gramos = un kilo
2 ½ Kg ______ de tomates, por favor.
3 Quiero una ______ de pan.
4 700g ______ gramos de uvas.
5 Quiero una ______ de agua.
6 100g ______ gramos de chorizo y 200g ______ gramos de queso.
7 Quiero un ______ de leche.
8 500g ______ gramos de manzanas.
9 150g ______ gramos de jamón, por favor.
10 1Kg ______ zanahorias.

2 Mira la lista de la compra y escríbela correctamente. *Look at the shopping list and write it correctly.*

un kilo de manzanas.

1kg 200g 500g 2 150g 700g 1 ½ kg

37

1 (AT4.1)

1 *mil* **2** medio kilo **3** barra **4** setecientos **5** botella **6** cien, doscientos **7** cartón **8** quinientos **9** ciento cincuenta **10** un kilo de

2 (AT4.2)

Un kilo de manzanas
Doscientos gramos de jamón
Quinientos gramos de tomates
Dos botellas de agua
Ciento cincuenta gramos de queso
Setecientos gramos de zanahorias
Un cartón de leche
Medio kilo de chorizo

Cuaderno A, page 38

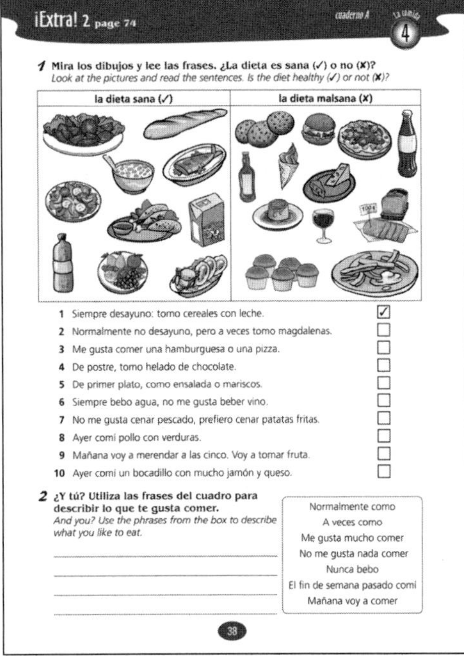

¡Extra! 2 page 74 — cuaderno A — La comida 4

1 Mira los dibujos y lee las frases. ¿La dieta es sana (✓) o no (✗)?
Look at the pictures and read the sentences. Is the diet healthy (✓) or not (✗)?

la dieta sana (✓)	la dieta malsana (✗)

1 Siempre desayuno: tomo cereales con leche. ☑
2 Normalmente no desayuno, pero a veces tomo magdalenas. ☐
3 Me gusta comer una hamburguesa o una pizza. ☐
4 De postre, tomo helado de chocolate. ☐
5 De primer plato, como ensalada o mariscos. ☐
6 Siempre bebo agua, no me gusta beber vino. ☐
7 No me gusta cenar pescado, prefiero cenar patatas fritas. ☐
8 Ayer comí pollo con verduras. ☐
9 Mañana voy a merendar a las cinco. Voy a tomar fruta. ☐
10 Ayer comí un bocadillo con mucho jamón y queso. ☐

2 ¿Y tú? Utiliza las frases del cuadro para describir lo que te gusta comer.
And you? Use the phrases from the box to describe what you like to eat.

Normalmente como
A veces como
Me gusta mucho comer
No me gusta nada comer
Nunca bebo
El fin de semana pasado comí
Mañana voy a comer

38

1 (AT3.2)

1 ✓ **2** ✗ **3** ✗ **4** ✗ **5** ✓ **6** ✓ **7** ✗ **8** ✓
9 ✓ **10** ✗

2 (AT4.3)

Cuaderno B, page 37

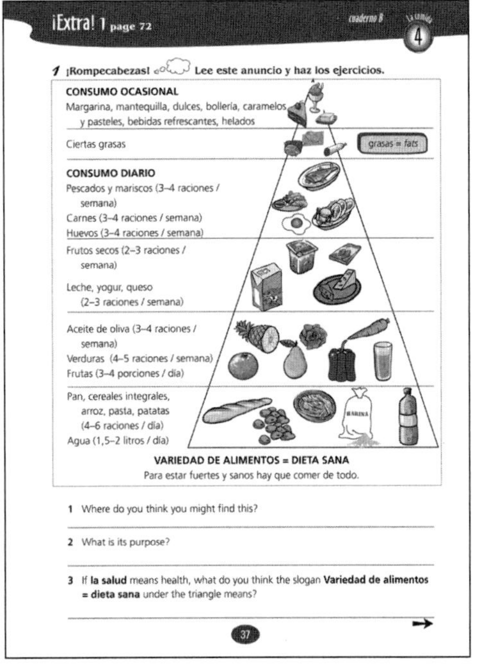

¡Extra! 1 page 72 — cuaderno B — La comida 4

1 ¡Rompecabezas! Lee este anuncio y haz los ejercicios.

CONSUMO OCASIONAL
Margarina, mantequilla, dulces, bollería, caramelos y pasteles, bebidas refrescantes, helados

Ciertas grasas — grasas = fats

CONSUMO DIARIO
Pescados y mariscos (3–4 raciones / semana)
Carnes (3–4 raciones / semana)
Huevos (3–4 raciones / semana)
Frutos secos (2–3 raciones / semana)
Leche, yogur, queso (2–3 raciones / semana)
Aceite de oliva (3–4 raciones / semana)
Verduras (4–5 raciones / semana)
Frutas (3–4 porciones / día)
Pan, cereales integrales, arroz, pasta, patatas (4–6 raciones / día)
Agua (1,5–2 litros / día)

VARIEDAD DE ALIMENTOS = DIETA SANA
Para estar fuertes y sanos hay que comer de todo.

1 Where do you think you might find this?
2 What is its purpose?
3 If **la salud** means health, what do you think the slogan **Variedad de alimentos = dieta sana** under the triangle means?

37

1 (AT4.6)

1 in a magazine or on a website
2 to inform the public about healthy eating
3 a variety of foods = a healthy diet

Cuaderno B, page 38

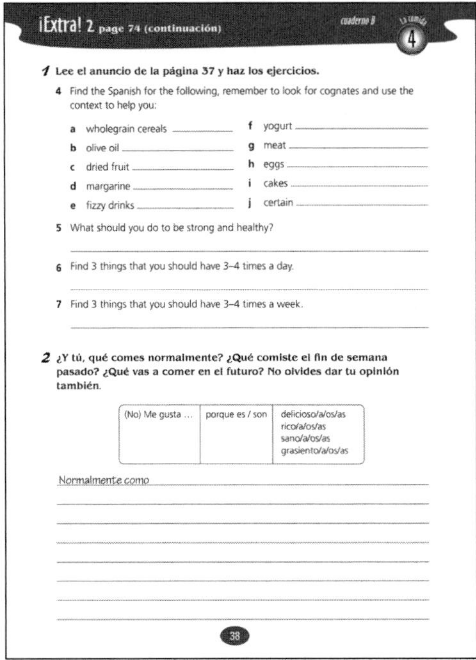

¡Extra! 2 page 74 (continuación) — cuaderno B — La comida 4

1 Lee el anuncio de la página 37 y haz los ejercicios.
4 Find the Spanish for the following, remember to look for cognates and use the context to help you:
a wholegrain cereals f yogurt
b olive oil g meat
c dried fruit h eggs
d margarine i cakes
e fizzy drinks j certain
5 What should you do to be strong and healthy?
6 Find 3 things that you should have 3–4 times a day.
7 Find 3 things that you should have 3–4 times a week.

2 ¿Y tú, qué comes normalmente? ¿Qué comiste el fin de semana pasado? ¿Qué vas a comer en el futuro? No olvides dar tu opinión también.

(No) Me gusta ...	porque es / son	delicioso/a/os/as rico/a/os/as sano/a/os/as grasiento/a/os/as

Normalmente como

38

4 **a** cereales integrales
b aceite de oliva
c frutos secos
d margarina
e bebidas refrescantes
f yogur
g carne
h huevos
i pasteles
j ciertas
5 eat a bit of everything
6 bread, wholegrain cereals, rice, pasta, potatoes
7 fish, seafood, meat, eggs, olive oil

2 (AT4.6)

Te toca a ti (Pupil's Book pages 120–121)

- Self-access reading and writing at two levels

A Reinforcement

1 *Match up the word halves and then write a sentence using each word.* (AT4.3) ▸▸4.5a/Y8 4.6b/Y8◂◂

Writing. Pupils match up the word halves to find the items of food/drink and then write a sentence using each word. Encourage them to include a range of time expressions and tenses in their sentences and to include some negatives.

Answers

The words featured:

cereales	tostadas	magdalenas	pescado
ensalada	lechuga	helado	pollo

2 *Put the pictures in the same order as the dialogue.* (AT3.3)

Reading. Pupils read the dialogue and note the pictures in the order they are mentioned.

Answers

d, c, a, b

3 *Match up the dinosaurs with the shopping bags. (There is one bag too many.)* (AT3.4) ▸▸5.4◂◂

Reading. Pupils read the speech bubbles from the three dinosaurs and select the appropriate shopping bag for each one from the pictures *a–d*.

Answers

1 *b* **2** c **3** a

B Extension

1 *Match up the sentence halves.* (AT3.3) ▸▸5.4◂◂

Reading. Pupils match each sentence opening to the correct ending.

Answers

1 c **2** b **3** d **4** a

2 *Copy out the text and fill in the gaps.* (AT4.3, AT3.4) ▸▸4.5a/Y8◂◂

Writing. Pupils copy and complete the text, choosing the correct verb from the two options given in each case. Some vocabulary is glossed for support.

Answers

Diego gana el premio de supervivientes
Para ganar el premio del día, el ganador Diego (**1**) **comió** gusanos, moscas, cucarachas y arañas. (**2**) **Ganó** una cesta de comida con pollo, pescado, ensalada y fruta. No (**3**) **compartió** su comida con sus amigos. (**4**) **Comió** todo en su tienda. No (**5**) **vomitó**.

3 *Translate these jokes into English.* (AT4.3, AT3.4) ▸▸5.4◂◂

Writing. Pupils translate the two jokes into English.

Answers

Do you want to have a Spanish omelette or a French omelette?
It doesn't matter. I'm not going to talk to it.

Aren't you going to eat the snails?
No. I prefer fast food.

Module 5 De moda (Pupil's Book pages 78–95)

Unit	Framework	Levels and PoS	Key language	Grammar	Skills
1 La ropa (pp. 78–79) Talking about clothes Making colours agree	**4.3/Y8** Language – gender and plurals	**2–3** **2.1a** identify patterns **2.1d** previous knowledge **2.1e** use reference materials **2.2h** redraft to improve writing **2.2k** deal with unfamiliar language **3f** compare experiences **4b** communicate in pairs etc. **4e** use a range of resources	*¿Qué llevas?* *Llevo...* *un jersey* *un vestido* *una camisa* *una camiseta* *una falda* *una gorra* *una sudadera* *unos pantalones* *unos vaqueros* *unos zapatos* *unas botas* *unas zapatillas de deporte* *nunca* *de vez en cuando* *a veces* *a menudo* *normalmente* *siempre* *amarillo/a* *blanco/a* *negro/a* *rojo/a* *azul* *gris* *marrón* *naranja* *rosa* *verde*	Indefinite article (*un/una/unos/unas*) Adjective endings: colours	Communicating with native speakers Applying recognised patterns to new language Using reference resources Using reading strategies to work out new words

continued

Module 5 De moda (Pupil's Book pages 78–95)

Unit	Framework	Levels and PoS	Key language	Grammar	Skills
2 El uniforme escolar (pp. 80–81) Talking about school uniform Using comparative adjectives (*más… que*)	**3.2/Y8** Culture – (b) customs, traditions	**2–4** **2.1e** use reference materials **3c** apply grammar **3f** compare experiences **4b** communicate in pairs etc. **4e** use a range of resources	*este jersey* *este vestido* *esta chaqueta* *esta corbata* *esta camiseta* *estos pantalones* *estos zapatos* *estas botas* *anticuado/a* *barato/a* *bonito/a* *caro/a* *cómodo/a* *feo/a* *guay* *incómodo/a* *Esta chaqueta es cómoda.* *Estos zapatos son incómodos.* *Tengo que llevar uniforme.* *Para ir al colegio, normalmente llevo…* *También llevo…* *(No) Me gusta llevar uniforme.* *Me gusta porque es práctico.* *No me gusta porque es incómodo.* *Es más elegante que llevar vaqueros.*	Comparatives Demonstrative adjectives (*este/esta/estos/estas*)	Carrying out a survey in the classroom Writing an extended text in Spanish

continued

Module 5 De moda (Pupil's Book pages 78–95)

Unit	Framework	Levels and PoS	Key language	Grammar	Skills
3 ¿Qué prefieres? (pp. 82–83) Choosing an item of clothing Using superlative adjectives		**3–4** **2.1b** memorising **2.1d** previous knowledge **2.2e** ask and answer questions **3c** apply grammar **4b** communicate in pairs etc. **4e** use a range of resources **4f** language for interest/ enjoyment	*¿Cuál prefieres?* *Este vestido / Esta camiseta es...* *el más bonito / la menos cómoda* *Estos zapatos / Estas botas son...* *los más baratos / las menos prácticas* *de rayas* *de lunares* *estampado/a* *de manga larga* *de manga corta* *de tirantes* *largo/a* *corto/a* *de cuadros* *de cuero* *de tacón*	Superlatives	Using reading strategies to work out new words Developing vocabulary learning skills Participating in an unscripted dialogue Reviewing progress/ checking work using the Mini-test
4 Vamos a visitar Argentina (pp. 84–85) Talking about a trip to Argentina Using the present and near future tenses	**4.6/Y8** Language – (a) range of questions	**3–5** **2.2a** listen for gist **3c** apply grammar **3d** use a range of vocab/ structures **4b** communicate in pairs etc. **4c** use more complex language	*Cuando estoy de vacaciones...* *Normalmente llevo...* *ropa de deporte* *una camiseta de fútbol* *Mañana voy a llevar...* *un bañador* *mis gafas de sol*	Using different tenses (present and near future)	Using different tenses appropriately

continued

Module 5 De moda (Pupil's Book pages 78–95)

Unit	Framework	Levels and PoS	Key language	Grammar	Skills
5 Un baile de disfraces (pp. 86–87) Saying what you wore to a fancy dress ball Using past, present and future tenses together	**4.1/Y8** Language – sounds/ spelling exceptions **5.5** Strategies – reference materials	**4–6** **2.1d** previous knowledge **2.1e** use reference materials **2.2a** listen for gist **2.2h** redraft to improve writing **2.2i** reuse language they have met **2.2j** adapt previously learned language **3c** apply grammar **3d** use a range of vocab/ structures **4c** use more complex language	*Ayer…* *salí con mis amigos* *fuimos a un baile de disfraces* *llevé…* *Bebí limonada.* *Bailé.* *Comí ensalada y tortilla.* *Llevé un vestido de princesa.* *Fui de vampiro.* *Mi amigo/a fue de vampiro.* *Fue muy divertido.* *Normalmente llevo…* *La próxima vez voy a llevar…*	Using different tenses (present, preterite and near future)	Using different tenses appropriately Developing grammar learning skills Using reference resources Developing independence as a learner
Resumen/ Prepárate (pp. 88–89) Pupils' checklist and practice test		**3–4**			Reviewing progress/ checking work

continued

Module 5 De moda (Pupil's Book pages 78–95)

Unit	Framework	Levels and PoS	Key language	Grammar	Skills
¡Extra! 1 (pp. 90–91) Using different tenses together Combining language from different topics	**1.2/Y8** Listening – new contexts **1.4/Y8** Speaking – (a) classroom exchanges (teacher-pupil)	**4–6** **2.2a** listen for gist **2.1e** use reference materials **2.2j** adapt previously learned language **3a** spoken and written language **3d** use a range of vocab/ structures	*Tengo el pelo…* *Tengo los ojos…* Revision of language from Module 5		Developing listening skills Using different tenses appropriately Understanding a longer/authentic text in Spanish (magazine quiz) Extending sentences, using connectives and negatives Writing an extended text in Spanish
¡Extra! 2 (pp. 92–93) Reading a story in Spanish Learning about cultural aspects of South America	**3.1/Y8** Culture – changes in everyday life	**3–5** **2.1d** previous knowledge **2.1e** use reference materials **3d** use a range of vocab/ structures **3e** different countries/ cultures **4e** use a range of resources **4f** language for interest/ enjoyment	Revision of language from Module 5		Understanding a longer text in Spanish (ongoing photo story; information on Latin American culture) Using reading strategies to work out new words Using reference resources Writing an extended text in Spanish
Te toca a ti (pp. 122–123)	Self-access reading and writing at two levels				

1 La ropa (Pupil's Book pages 78–79)

Learning objectives
- Talking about clothes
- Making colours agree

Framework objectives
4.3/Y8 Language – gender and plurals

Grammar
- Indefinite article (*un/una/unos/unas*)
- Adjective endings: colours

Key language
¿Qué llevas?
Llevo…
un jersey/vestido
una camisa/camiseta/falda/gorra/sudadera
unos pantalones/vaqueros/zapatos/botas/zapatillas de deporte
nunca
de vez en cuando
a veces
a menudo
normalmente
siempre
amarillo/a
blanco/a
negro/a
rojo/a
azul
gris
marrón
naranja
rosa
verde

High-frequency words
un, una
a
de
en
¿qué?
nunca

Cross-curricular
Citizenship: Information about other cultures
ICT: Email contact with a Spanish school

Resources
CD3, tracks 2–5
Cuadernos A & B, p. 42
R & A Pack, Gramática p. 21
Flashcards 65–76

Teacher Presentations
Screen 1 – Module 5 overview
Screen 2 – Vocabulary: Flashcards
Screen 3 – p. 78 ex. 1
Screen 4 – p. 78 exs 2 & 3
Screen 5 – p. 79 ex. 5
Screen 6 – Game

Starter 1 ▸▸ 4.3/Y8 ◂◂

Aim
To revise the indefinite article.

Write up: *un una unos unas*

Ask the class what these words mean and when they are used.

Give pupils working in pairs two minutes to list as many nouns to go with each of these words as possible (without using their Pupil's Books). When they have finished, each pair swaps with another and they check each other's answers. The pair with the most correct answers wins.

Suggestion

Use Flashcards 65–76 to introduce items of clothing. Make it clear that these are grouped according to the indefinite article (*un jersey… una falda*, etc.).

Introduce *¿Qué llevas?* and the response *Llevo…*, using items of clothing you are wearing.

1 Escucha y escribe las letras de la ropa mencionada. (1–6) (AT1.2)

▸▸ 4.2/Y8 ◂◂

Listening. Pupils listen to six people saying what clothes they are wearing and note the items of clothing mentioned using the pictures *a–l*.

Audioscript Track 2

1 – *¿Qué llevas?*
– *Normalmente llevo una camiseta y unos vaqueros.*
2 – *¿Qué llevas?*
– *Llevo un jersey y una falda.*
3 – *¿Qué llevas?*
– *Llevo una gorra y una sudadera.*
4 – *¿Qué llevas?*
– *Llevo un vestido y unas botas.*
5 – *¿Qué llevas?*
– *Llevo unas zapatillas de deporte. No llevo zapatos.*
6 – *¿Qué llevas?*
– *Llevo una camisa y unos pantalones.*

Answers
1 *f, h* **2** a, c **3** d, g **4** b, k **5** l, j **6** e, i

R Pupils working in pairs use their answers to exercise 1 to make statements about what they are wearing. So (e.g.) 1 f, h = *Llevo una camiseta y unos vaqueros.*

Gramática: the indefinite article *(un/una/unos/unas)*

Use this to revise the indefinite article.

+ Pupils working in pairs take it in turn to prompt with an item of clothing (e.g. *falda*). Partners (with Pupil's Books closed) respond using the indefinite article (e.g. *una falda*).

2 Escucha. ¿Qué llevan? Contesta en inglés. (1–5) (AT1.3) ▸▸1.1/Y8◂◂

Listening. Pupils listen to five people talking about what they wear and note the items of clothing mentioned in English.

Audioscript Track 3

1 *Normalmente llevo unos vaqueros y una sudadera. Siempre llevo una gorra.*
2 *A veces llevo un vestido y unas zapatillas de deporte. Me gusta mucho este estilo.*
3 *A ver, de vez en cuando llevo una falda y una camiseta con unas botas. Nunca llevo zapatillas de deporte.*
4 *– ¿Qué llevas normalmente?*
– A menudo llevo un vestido y unos zapatos, pero depende…
5 *Normalmente llevo unos vaqueros, una camiseta y unas zapatillas de deporte pero cuando salgo con amigos…*

Answers

1 *jeans, sweatshirt, baseball cap*
2 dress, trainers
3 skirt, t-shirt, boots; (doesn't wear) trainers
4 dress, shoes
5 jeans, t-shirt, trainers

3 Escucha otra vez. Escribe la expresión de frecuencia para cada artículo. (1–5) (AT1.3) ▸▸4.2/Y8◂◂

Listening. Pupils listen to the recording in exercise 2 again, this time noting details of how often each speaker wears the items mentioned, using the timeline of frequency expressions for reference.

Audioscript Track 4

As for exercise 2.

Answers

1 *jeans, sweatshirt – normalmente*
baseball cap – siempre
2 dress, trainers – a veces
3 skirt, t-shirt, boots – de vez en cuando; trainers – nunca
4 dress, shoes – a menudo
5 jeans, t-shirt, trainers – normalmente

Starter 2 ▸▸4.3/Y8◂◂

Aim

To revise endings for colour adjectives.

Write up:

	un vestido	*una camiseta*	*unos vaqueros*	*unas botas*
rojo	rojo		rojos	
negro		negra		negras
azul		azul		azules
gris	gris		grises	

Check pupils understand all the colours (*negro, azul, gris* have all come up already in the context of hair/eyes), pointing to appropriately coloured objects in the classroom to help them as necessary. Explain that colours are adjectives and change ending depending on the noun they are with.

Give pupils two minutes working in pairs to complete the grid, using the information supplied to work out the missing forms.

If pupils need more support, point out similarities in endings (e.g. noun ending in *-o*/ adjective ending in *-o* = same endings) and/or fill in a few of the blanks.

Suggestion

Read through the frequency expressions in the timeline in exercise 3 as a class. When pupils are familiar with them, get them to close their books. Prompt in Spanish (e.g. *a veces*) for them to respond in English (e.g. 'sometimes'). Move on to prompting in English for them to supply the correct Spanish version.

Explain that this lesson is going to focus on saying how often they wear certain items of clothing and describing what they wear.

4 Con tu compañero/a, haz diálogos. (AT2.3) ▸▸1.4b/Y8◂◂

Speaking. In pairs: pupils make up dialogues about what they wear, using the clothes from exercise 1 and the frequency expressions repeated in the box here. A sample exchange is given, showing the expressions that need to change and where details need to be added.

Gramática: agreement of colour adjectives

Use the Gramática box to revise the endings for colour adjectives before pupils do exercise 5. What other colours can pupils remember? Prompt as necessary with the masculine singular form and get pupils to come to the front of the class and write up the other forms (*amarillo*, *blanco*; *azul*, *gris*). Also cover the irregular colours *naranja* and *rosa*, which change only in the plural (*naranjas*, *rosas*).

Ask pupils why *marrón* loses its accent in the plural form. (Usual rules of stress mean that the stress falls on the *o* already, so no accent is required.)

Write up a few examples of expressions featuring an item of clothing and a colour e.g. *una camiseta roja*, *unos vaqueros azules*. Ask pupils how you would say in Spanish 'a black sweatshirt'. Can they come up with a rule for the position of colour adjectives?

+ Write up some prompts in English, consisting of a colour and an item of clothing for pupils to give the correct Spanish version.

With a less able class, you could supply prompts in Spanish.

5 Escucha y lee. Luego pon las personas en el grupo apropiado. (1–6) (AT1.3) ▸▸2.3/Y8 4.3/Y8◂◂

Listening. Pupils listen to the recording and follow the text in the six speech bubbles at the same time. They then study the pictures showing six different urban looks and identify which group each of the speakers belongs to.

Audioscript Track 5

- *Pepe, ¿qué llevas normalmente?*
- *Siempre llevo unos vaqueros negros y unas botas negras. Me encanta la música de los Sex Pistols y los piercings.*

- *Sergio, ¿qué llevas normalmente?*
- *Normalmente llevo una camiseta gris muy grande, unos vaqueros y una gorra azul. Me gustan las joyas preciosas.*

- *Marco, ¿qué llevas normalmente?*
- *Normalmente llevo una camiseta sin mangas, unos vaqueros y unas botas altas. Me encanta Kiss. Odio a los pijos.*

- *Ana, ¿qué llevas normalmente?*
- *A menudo llevo una camiseta blanca, un jersey rojo y unos vaqueros de marca. Me encanta el dinero. Odio a los heavies.*

- *Ricardo, ¿qué llevas normalmente?*
- *Siempre llevo una camisa blanca. Tengo el pelo largo y rizado. A veces llevo gafas de sol. Me gusta bailar. Me encanta el ritmo. ¡Olé!*

- *Lola, ¿qué llevas normalmente?*
- *Llevo una sudadera amarilla, unos vaqueros y unas zapatillas de deporte. De vez en cuando llevo una muñequera. Me gusta mucho ir al parque con mis amigos.*

Answers

Pepe – f Sergio – b Marco – d Ana – c
Ricardo – e Lola – a

R Pupils re-read the texts and identify all the colour adjectives used and give the gender/number for each.

6 ¿Qué significan las palabras en azul en los textos? Utiliza el contexto. (AT3.3) ▸▸5.2 5.3◂◂

Reading. Pupils re-read the texts in exercise 5 and work out what the words in blue mean, using the context and any other appropriate reading strategies. (Remind them as necessary to use the detail in the pictures.)

Pupils should swap with a partner and check each other's answers using the Vocabulario section or a dictionary. When checking answers, ask if they had problems with *de marca*. Where did they look it up? Explain that in expressions like this, small words/prepositions like *de* are generally disregarded and the expression is listed under the first letter of the main word (here *m* for *marca*).

Answers

las joyas preciosas – valuable jewellery
sin mangas – sleeveless
de marca – designer
gafas de sol – sunglasses
el ritmo – the rhythm
una muñequera – wristband

7 ¿En qué grupo estás tú? Contesta a la pregunta y describe tu estilo. (AT4.2–3) ▸▸2.2b/Y8 2.4a/Y8◂◂

Writing. Pupils decide which group in exercise 5 they fall into, or would like to be part of, and describe their style. Get them to check their adjectives carefully (using the Gramática section at the back of the Pupil's Book to confirm endings and position) before doing a second draft of their texts.

If you have contact with a Spanish school, pupils could swap details of what they wear in various situations (school, sport, at the weekend, parties, other special events, etc.). They could also exchange photos.

Plenary ▸▸ 4.3/Y8 ◂◂

Put the class into teams and get them to stand up. Prompt each team in turn with an item of clothing (e.g. *una sudadera*). A member of the team answers with an appropriate colour (e.g. *una sudadera roja*). If correct, he/she sits down. Play continues until the whole team is sitting. You can allow conferring if pupils need support. Each correct answer wins one point and the first team to finish gets three bonus points.

You can make the game more challenging by missing out the definite article in the prompt (so that the pupil has to supply it too) or by prompting in English (e.g. 'a red sweatshirt')

Cuaderno A, page 42

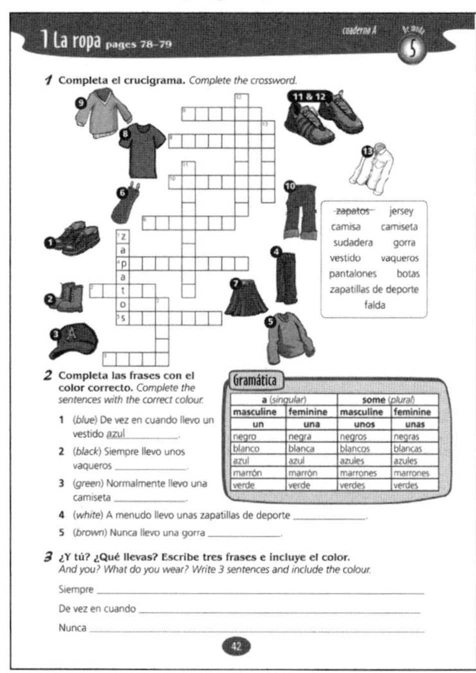

1 La ropa pages 78–79 — cuaderno A — De moda 5

1 **Completa el crucigrama.** *Complete the crossword.*

~~zapatos~~ jersey camisa camiseta sudadera gorra vestido vaqueros pantalones botas zapatillas de deporte falda

2 **Completa las frases con el color correcto.** *Complete the sentences with the correct colour.*

1 (*blue*) De vez en cuando llevo un vestido azul.
2 (*black*) Siempre llevo unos vaqueros ______.
3 (*green*) Normalmente llevo una camiseta ______.
4 (*white*) A menudo llevo unas zapatillas de deporte ______.
5 (*brown*) Nunca llevo una gorra ______.

Gramática

a (*singular*)		some (*plural*)	
masculine	**feminine**	**masculine**	**feminine**
un	**una**	**unos**	**unas**
negro	negra	negros	negras
blanco	blanca	blancos	blancas
azul	azul	azules	azules
marrón	marrón	marrones	marrones
verde	verde	verdes	verdes

3 **¿Y tú? ¿Qué llevas? Escribe tres frases e incluye el color.** *And you? What do you wear? Write 3 sentences and include the colour.*

Siempre ______
De vez en cuando ______
Nunca ______

42

1 (AT4.1)

1 zapatos **2** botas **3** gorra **4** pantalones **5** sudadera **6** vestido **7** falda **8** camiseta **9** jersey **10** vaqueros **11** zapatillas **12** de deporte **13** camisa

2 (AT4.1)

1 azul **2** negros **3** verde **4** blancas **5** marrón

3 (AT4.3)

Cuaderno B, page 42

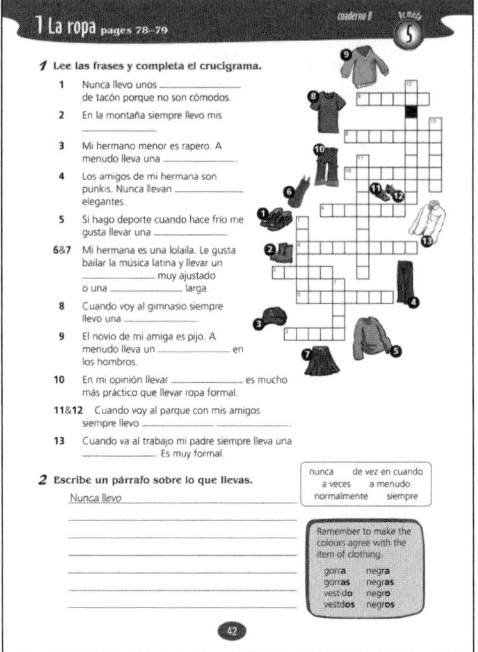

1 La ropa pages 78–79 — cuaderno B — De moda 5

1 **Lee las frases y completa el crucigrama.**

1 Nunca llevo unos ______ de tacón porque no son cómodos.
2 En la montaña siempre llevo mis ______.
3 Mi hermano menor es rapero. A menudo lleva una ______.
4 Los amigos de mi hermana son punkis. Nunca llevan ______ elegantes.
5 Si hago deporte cuando hace frío me gusta llevar una ______.
6&7 Mi hermana es una lolaila. Le gusta bailar la música latina y llevar un ______ muy ajustado o una ______ larga.
8 Cuando voy al gimnasio siempre llevo una ______.
9 El novio de mi amiga es pijo. A menudo lleva un ______ en los hombros.
10 En mi opinión llevar ______ es mucho más práctico que llevar ropa formal.
11&12 Cuando voy al parque con mis amigos siempre llevo ______ ______.
13 Cuando va al trabajo mi padre siempre lleva una ______. Es muy formal.

2 **Escribe un párrafo sobre lo que llevas.**

Nunca llevo ______

nunca de vez en cuando a veces a menudo normalmente siempre

Remember to make the colours agree with the item of clothing.

gorr**a** negr**a**
gorr**as** negr**as**
vestid**o** negr**o**
vestd**os** negr**os**

42

1 (AT3.2, AT4.2)

1 zapatos **2** botas **3** gorra **4** pantalones **5** sudadera **6** vestido **7** falda **8** camiseta **9** jersey **10** vaqueros **11** zapatillas **12** de deporte **13** camisa

2 (AT4.4)

R & A Pack, Gramática page 21

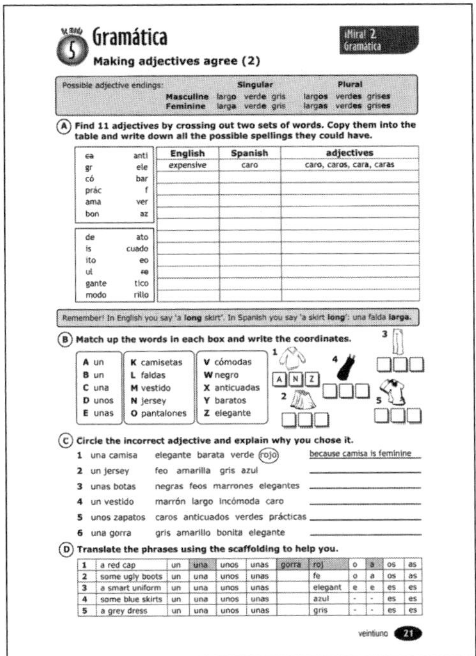

Gramática

¡Mira! 2 Gramática

Making adjectives agree (2)

Possible adjective endings:

	Singular			Plural		
Masculine	largo	verde	gris	largos	verdes	grises
Feminine	larga	verde	gris	largas	verdes	grises

(A) Find 11 adjectives by crossing out two sets of words. Copy them into the table and write down all the possible spellings they could have.

ca	anti
gr	ele
có	bar
prác	f
ama	ver
bon	az

de	ato
is	cuado
ito	eo
ul	ro
gante	tico
modo	rillo

English	Spanish	adjectives
expensive	caro	caro, caros, cara, caras

Remember! In English you say 'a **long** skirt'. In Spanish you say 'a skirt **long**': una falda **larga.**

(B) Match up the words in each box and write the coordinates.

A un	**K** camisetas	**V** cómodas
B un	**L** faldas	**W** negro
C una	**M** vestido	**X** anticuadas
D unos	**N** jersey	**Y** baratos
E unas	**O** pantalones	**Z** elegante

1 A N Z
2
3
4
5

(C) Circle the incorrect adjective and explain why you chose it.

1 una camisa elegante barata verde (rojo) because camisa is feminine
2 un jersey feo amarilla gris azul
3 unas botas negras feos marrones elegantes
4 un vestido marrón largo incómoda caro
5 unos zapatos caros anticuados verdes prácticas
6 una gorra gris amarillo bonita elegante

(D) Translate the phrases using the scaffolding to help you.

1	a red cap	un	una	unos	unas	gorra	roj	o	a	os	as
2	some ugly boots	un	una	unos	unas		fe	o	a	os	as
3	a smart uniform	un	una	unos	unas		elegant	e	e	es	es
4	some blue skirts	un	una	unos	unas		azul	-	-	es	es
5	a grey dress	un	una	unos	unas		gris	-	-	es	es

veintiuno 21

(A) old-fashioned, anticuado, **4**, anticuado, anticuada, anticuados, anticuadas
practical, práctico, **4**, práctico, práctica, prácticos, prácticas
ugly, feo, **4**, feo, fea, feos, feas
pretty, bonito, **4**, bonito, bonita, bonitos, bonitas
comfortable, cómodo, **4**, cómodo, cómoda, cómodos, cómodas
yellow, amarillo, **4**, amarillo, amarilla, amarillos, amarillas
cheap, barato, **4**, barato, barata, baratos, baratas
smart, elegante, **2**, elegante, elegantes
green, verde, **2**, verde, verdes
blue, azul, **2**, azul, azules
grey, gris, **2**, gris, grises

(B) **1** ANZ **2** ELX **3** DOY **4** BMW **5** EKV

(C) **2** amarilla (jersey is masculine singular)
3 feos (botas is feminine plural)
4 incómoda (vestido is masculine singular)
5 prácticas (zapatos is masculine plural)
6 amarillo (gorra is feminine singular)

(D) **2** unas botas feas **3** un uniforme elegante
4 unas faldas azules **5** un vestido gris

2 El uniforme escolar (Pupil's Book pages 80–81)

Learning objectives

- Talking about school uniform
- Using comparative adjectives (*más... que*)

Grammar

- Comparatives (revision)
- Demonstrative adjectives (*este/esta/estos/estas*)

Framework objectives

3.2/Y8 Culture – (b) customs, traditions

Key language

este jersey/vestido
esta chaqueta/corbata/camiseta
estos pantalones/zapatos
estas botas
anticuado/a
barato/a
bonito/a
caro/a
cómodo/a
feo/a
guay
incómodo/a
Esta chaqueta es cómoda.
Estos zapatos son incómodos.

Tengo que llevar uniforme.
Para ir al colegio, normalmente llevo...
También llevo...
(No) Me gusta llevar uniforme.
Me gusta porque es práctico.
No me gusta porque es incómodo.
Es más elegante que llevar vaqueros.

High-frequency words

a (al) · *me*
para · *también*
porque · *que*
ser (es, son) · *tener (tengo)*
no · *más*
este, esta, estos, estas

Cross-curricular

Citizenship: Information about other cultures
English: Comparatives
ICT: Producing charts

Resources

CD3, tracks 6–7
Cuadernos A & B, p. 43

Teacher Presentations

Screen 1 – Module 5 overview
Screen 2 – Vocabulary: Flashcards
Screen 3 – p. 80 ex. 1
Screen 4 – p. 81 ex. 4
Screen 5 – Game

Starter 1

Aim

 To revise vocabulary for items of clothing.

Write up the following (answers in brackets for reference only):

a 26, 1, 16, 1, 20, 15, 19 (*zapatos*)
b 22, 5, 19, 20, 9, 4, 15 (*vestido*)
c 2, 15, 20, 1, 19 (*botas*)
d 16, 1, 14, 20, 1, 12, 15, 14, 5, 19 (*pantalones*)
e 10, 5, 18, 19, 5, 25 (*jersey*)
f 3, 1, 13, 9, 19, 5, 20, 1 (*camiseta*)

Explain that these are Spanish items of clothing, presented in code. Give pupils three minutes working in pairs to work out what they are.

If pupils need support, do the first as an example.

To make the activity more challenging, ask pupils then to work out in code the form of the definite article that would go with each item.

Suggestion

Introduce *este* using two books, e.g. *Este libro es azul. Este libro es rojo.* Move on to introduce the other forms (*esta, estos, estas*) using items of clothing that you/the pupils are wearing, e.g. *esta falda, estos zapatos, estas zapatillas de deporte.* Ask pupils what other words they can think of that are like *este*, with four different forms and used before a noun (indefinite, definite articles). Ask pupils to look at the speech bubbles in exercise 1. How many instances of *este/esta/estos/estas* can they find?

Then get pupils to look specifically at the words with coloured letters at the end. What kind of words are these? Why are the endings highlighted? What does a blue/pink ending signify (adjectives/ to denote gender; blue = masculine, pink = feminine)? Explain that this unit is going to focus on describing clothes and will cover *este* (etc.) and adjective agreement.

Make sure pupils know the meaning of the new items of vocabulary (*esta chaqueta* and *esta corbata*) before you play the recording.

1 Escucha y escribe la letra correcta. (1–8) (AT1.2) ▸▸4.3/Y8◂◂

Listening. Pupils listen to the eight people describing the clothes they are wearing and note the correct picture for each (from *a–h*).

Audioscript Track 6

1 *Esta camiseta es guay.*
2 *Este jersey es feo.*
3 *Esta corbata es anticuada.*
4 *Estos pantalones son baratos.*
5 *Estos zapatos son incómodos.*
6 *Esta chaqueta es cómoda.*
7 *Estas botas son caras.*
8 *Este vestido es bonito.*

Answers

1 e **2** a **3** d **4** f **5** g **6** c **7** h **8** b

Gramática: this/these

This summarises the forms of *este*. There is practice on this on page 129 of the Pupil's Book.

R Pupils working in pairs prompt with an item of clothing, from this unit or Unit 1 (e.g. *una chaqueta*) and the other responds using the correct form of *este* (e.g. *esta chaqueta*).

+ Use Flashcards 65–76 as prompts to practise the forms of *este* with a broader range of items of clothing.

2 Empareja los antónimos. (AT3.2) ▸▸5.2◂◂

Reading. Pupils separate out the words on the coathanger and group them into opposites.

Answers

barato – caro
anticuado – guay
feo – bonito
incómodo – cómodo

3 Describe la ropa de tu profesor/profesora. (AT2.3) ▸▸1.4a/Y8 4.3/Y8◂◂

Speaking. In pairs: pupils describe the clothes their teacher is wearing, using the correct form of *este* and the adjectives in exercise 1.

Encourage pupils to use the Gramática box to check they are using the correct form of *este*.

+ Pupils could include colours in their descriptions (e.g. *Esta corbata roja es anticuada*).

Starter 2 ▸▸4.4/Y8◂◂

Aim
To revise the comparative.

Write up:

Una chaqueta es más incómoda que una sudadera.
Unas botas son más caras que una gorra.

Un jersey...
Unas zapatillas de deporte...
Unos vaqueros...

Give pupils three minutes working in pairs to translate the two sentences and to complete the three sentence openings, using any appropriate adjectives and items of clothing.

If pupils need more support, highlight the endings on the adjectives and the different verb forms used (*es/son*). You could also supply a range of adjectives for them to choose from.

Suggestion

Using some answers from Starter 2 as examples, ask the class to summarise how the comparative is formed.

4 Escucha y lee. Contesta a las preguntas para cada persona. (AT1.4) ▸▸3.2b/Y8◂◂

Listening. Pupils listen to three people giving an opinion of their school uniform and follow the texts at the same time. Pupils then say in Spanish whether each of the speakers wears a uniform and if so, whether he/she likes the uniform. Some vocabulary is glossed for support.

Read through the tip box on school uniform in Spain (generally not worn, except in private schools).

Audioscript Track 7

¿Te gusta el uniforme?

Alejandro
En mi colegio tengo que llevar uniforme. No me gusta nada porque es anticuado, feo y muy incómodo. También es caro. Prefiero la ropa de los fines de semana: vaqueros, una sudadera y zapatillas de deporte. Es más cómoda.

Belén
Yo no llevo uniforme. Normalmente para ir al colegio llevo una camiseta, unos vaqueros y zapatillas de deporte. Esta ropa es más cómoda que una corbata y una chaqueta.

Marisol
Tengo que llevar uniforme. Llevo una falda, un jersey, una camisa, una corbata y una chaqueta. Me gusta llevar uniforme. Es más práctico para ir al colegio. También es más elegante, pero a veces es menos cómodo.

Answers

Alejandro – Lleva uniforme. No le gusta nada.
Belén – No lleva uniforme. (No le gusta.)
Marisol – Lleva uniforme. Le gusta el uniforme.

+ Ask pupils to identify the three words/expressions used by the three speakers to introduce their opinions. (*No me gusta nada... Prefiero... Me gusta...*)

Use the tip box to revise how the comparative is formed and ask pupils to list the comparatives used in the texts in exercise 4. There is practice on the comparative on page 128 of the Pupil's Book.

5 Lee los textos otra vez. Corrige las frases. (AT3.4) ▸▸2.2/Y8◂◂

Reading. Pupils read the texts in exercise 4 again and rewrite the six statements, correcting the factual errors in them.

Answers

1. *A Alejandro **no** le gusta llevar uniforme.*
2. No le gusta nada el uniforme porque es **anticuado, feo y muy incómodo**.
3. Belén **no** lleva uniforme.
4. Para ir al colegio, lleva **una camiseta, unos vaqueros y zapatillas de deporte**.
5. Marisol lleva **una falda, un jersey, una camisa, una corbata y una chaqueta**.
6. A Marisol le gusta llevar uniforme.

6 Haz este sondeo en tu clase. (AT2.3) ▸▸2.2b/Y8 3.2b/Y8◂◂

Speaking. Pupils carry out a class survey, asking participants to say whether or not they agree with the five statements on uniform. Ask them about their findings: on balance, do pupils think that their class likes the British system of having a school uniform or would they prefer the Spanish system of choosing what you wear to school?

Pupils could present their results for the survey in exercise 6 on computer, as a bar or pie chart.

7 Escribe lo que llevas para ir al colegio. (AT4.4) ▸▸2.4a/Y8 4.3/Y8◂◂

Writing. Using the texts in exercise 4 as a model, pupils write a paragraph on what they normally wear to school and their opinion of it, giving reasons and making comparisons between what they wear to school and other clothes. A framework is given.

Encourage them to check agreement of adjectives using the Gramática section at the back of the Pupil's Book.

Plenary ▸▸5.8◂◂

Ask pupils to summarise what was covered in this unit, prompting them as necessary to give the different forms of *este* and how the comparative is structured, as well as the clothes vocabulary.

Then play a chain game round the class to practise these. Explain that you are going to construct a sentence together, with each person adding a single word at a time; once a sentence is complete, the next person starts a new sentence (e.g. Pupil 1 *Esta* – Pupil 2 *falda* – Pupil 3 *es* – Pupil 4 *menos* – Pupil 5 *cómoda*, etc.). The class is aiming to see how many sentences they can complete in an allotted time.

Cuaderno A, page 43

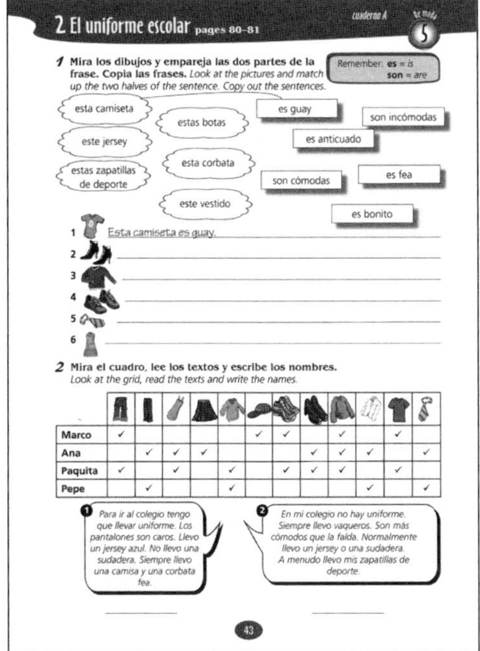
2 El uniforme escolar pages 80–81

cuaderno A De moda 5

1 Mira los dibujos y empareja las dos partes de la frase. Copia las frases. *Look at the pictures and match up the two halves of the sentence. Copy out the sentences.*

Remember: **es** = *is* **son** = *are*

esta camiseta | estas botas | este jersey | esta corbata | estas zapatillas de deporte | este vestido

es guay | son incómodas | es anticuado | son cómodas | es fea | es bonito

1 Esta camiseta es guay.
2
3
4
5
6

2 Mira el cuadro, lee los textos y escribe los nombres. *Look at the grid, read the texts and write the names.*

Marco	✓					✓	✓		✓		✓	
Ana		✓	✓	✓				✓	✓	✓		✓
Paquita	✓		✓		✓		✓	✓	✓		✓	
Pepe		✓			✓					✓		✓

1 *Para ir al colegio tengo que llevar uniforme. Los pantalones son caros. Llevo un jersey azul. No llevo una sudadera. Siempre llevo una camisa y una corbata fea.*

2 *En mi colegio no hay uniforme. Siempre llevo vaqueros. Son más cómodos que la falda. Normalmente llevo un jersey o una sudadera. A menudo llevo mis zapatillas de deporte.*

43

1 (AT4.2)

1 *Esta camiseta es guay.*
2 Estas botas son incómodas.
3 Este jersey es anticuado.
4 Estas zapatillas de deporte son cómodas.
5 Esta corbata es fea.
6 Este vestido es bonito.

2 (AT3.3)

1 Pepe 2 Paquita

Cuaderno B, page 43

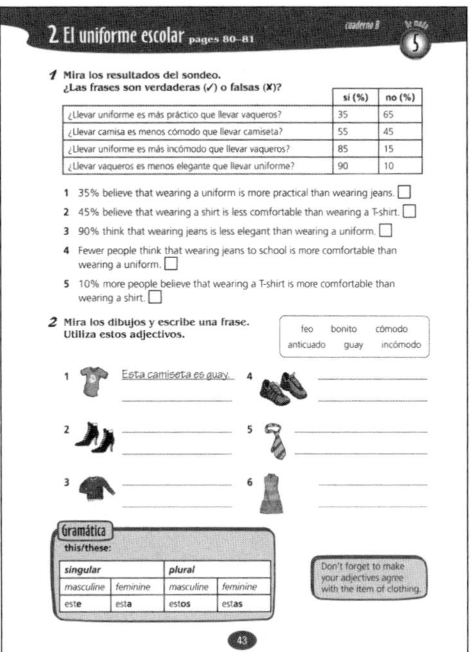
2 El uniforme escolar pages 80–81

cuaderno B De moda 5

1 Mira los resultados del sondeo. ¿Las frases son verdaderas (✓) o falsas (✗)?

	sí (%)	no (%)
¿Llevar uniforme es más práctico que llevar vaqueros?	35	65
¿Llevar camisa es menos cómodo que llevar camiseta?	55	45
¿Llevar uniforme es más incómodo que llevar vaqueros?	85	15
¿Llevar vaqueros es menos elegante que llevar uniforme?	90	10

1 35% believe that wearing a uniform is more practical than wearing jeans. ☐
2 45% believe that wearing a shirt is less comfortable than wearing a T-shirt. ☐
3 90% think that wearing jeans is less elegant than wearing a uniform. ☐
4 Fewer people think that wearing jeans to school is more comfortable than wearing a uniform. ☐
5 10% more people believe that wearing a T-shirt is more comfortable than wearing a shirt. ☐

2 Mira los dibujos y escribe una frase. Utiliza estos adjectivos.

feo bonito cómodo anticuado guay incómodo

1 Esta camiseta es guay.
2
3
4
5
6

Gramática
this/these:

singular		plural	
masculine	*feminine*	*masculine*	*feminine*
este	esta	estos	estas

Don't forget to make your adjectives agree with the item of clothing.

43

1 (AT3.3)

1 ✓ 2 ✗ 3 ✓ 4 ✗ 5 ✓

2 (AT4.3)

1 *Esta camiseta es guay.*
2 Estas botas son incómodas.
3 Este jersey es anticuado.
4 Estas zapatillas de deporte son cómodas.
5 Esta corbata es fea.
6 Este vestido es bonito.

Accept alternatives as long as grammatically correct.

3 ¿Qué prefieres? (Pupil's Book pages 82–83)

Learning objectives

- Choosing an item of clothing
- Using superlative adjectives

Grammar

- Superlatives

Key language

¿Cuál prefieres?
Este vestido / Esta camiseta es...
el más bonito / la menos cómoda
Estos zapatos / Estas botas son...
los más baratos / las menos prácticas
de rayas
de lunares
estampado/a
de manga larga/corta
de tirantes
largo/a
corto/a
de cuadros
de cuero
de tacón

High-frequency words

el, la, los, las
de
¿cuál?
ser (es, son)
este, esta, estos, estas

Cross-curricular

English: Superlatives

ICT: Using Paint/Powerpoint

Resources

CD3, tracks 8–11
Cuadernos A & B, p. 44
R & A Pack, Gramática p. 22

Teacher Presentations

Screen 1 – Module 5 overview
Screen 2 – p. 82 ex. 1
Screen 3 – p. 83 ex. 4
Screen 4 – p. 83 ex. 5
Screen 5 – p. 83 ex. 6

Starter 1 ▸▸ 4.3/Y8 ◂◂

Aim
To revise the superlative.

Write up the following, jumbling the order of the second column.

1 *Este vestido rojo es*	*el más práctico.*
2 *Esta camiseta azul*	*es la menos cómoda.*
3 *Estos pantalones negros*	*son los más baratos.*
4 *Estas botas marrones*	*son las menos bonitas.*
5 *Esta chaqueta blanca es*	*la más barata.*

Give pupils three minutes working in pairs to match the sentence halves and work out a translation for each sentence.

Suggestion

Use the sentences in Starter 1 to summarise how the superlative is formed. Ask pupils to translate the question openings in the speech bubbles in exercise 1 into English, and then to give you a Spanish adjective in the appropriate form to complete each question.

1 Escucha las preguntas y escribe la letra correcta. (1–8) (AT1.3) ▸▸ 2.2b/Y8 4.3/Y8 ◂◂

Listening. Pupils look at the catalogue and listen to the eight sets of questions and respond (for *1–4*) by identifying the correct item of clothing and (for *5–8*) with their own opinion.

Audioscript Track 8

1. *¿Qué vestido es el más caro? ¿El vestido negro de rayas, el vestido de lunares o el vestido estampado?*
2. *¿Qué camiseta es la más barata? ¿La camiseta de manga larga, la camiseta de manga corta o la camiseta sin mangas?*
3. *¿Qué pantalones son los más caros? ¿Los pantalones largos, los pantalones cortos o los pantalones de cuadros?*
4. *¿Qué botas son las más baratas? ¿Las botas marrones de cuero, las botas de tacón o las botas de rayas?*
5. *¿Qué vestido es el más bonito? ¿El vestido negro de rayas, el vestido de lunares o el vestido estampado?*
6. *¿Qué camiseta es la menos guay? ¿La camiseta gris y azul de manga larga, la camiseta verde de manga corta o la camiseta negra sin mangas?*
7. *¿Qué pantalones son los menos cómodos? ¿Los pantalones largos, los pantalones cortos o los pantalones de cuadros?*
8. *¿Qué botas son las menos prácticas? ¿Las botas marrones de cuero, las botas de tacón o las botas de rayas?*

Answers
1 c **2** f **3** h **4** k **5–8** *pupil's own opinion*

R To reinforce the superlative structure and further test pupils' comprehension, adapt the questions on the recording and use as new prompts, e.g. *¿Qué vestido es el menos caro?*

+ Write up the following prompts:

- cheapest dress
- most expensive t-shirt
- cheapest trousers
- most expensive boots

Ask pupils to write the appropriate question for each prompt, with their books closed. You could model the first one if necessary for support. (*¿Qué vestido es el más barato?*)

Gramática: superlatives

Use the Gramática box to summarise the superlative construction and to remind pupils of the different forms of *este*. Point out the use of pink and blue: suggest pupils use a similar system in their own vocabulary notebooks to help reinforce gender.

2 Con tu compañero/a, pregunta y contesta sobre cada sección del catálogo. (AT2.3) ▸▸1.4a/Y8 2.2a/Y8◂◂

Speaking. In pairs pupils take it in turn to ask and answer questions using the information in the catalogue in exercise 1. The questions are supplied.

Starter 2 ▸▸5.2◂◂

Aim
To revise vocabulary for describing clothes.

Pupils working in pairs do four simple drawings of items of clothing featured in exercise 1 on page 82 (e.g. short-sleeved t-shirt, striped boots, etc.). They swap drawings with another pair and then (with Pupil's Books closed) write out captions for each drawing (e.g. *camiseta de manga corta, botas de rayas*). They swap and check each other's answers against the Pupil's Book.

3 Escribe seis preguntas y respuestas sobre los artículos del catálogo. (AT4.3) ▸▸2.2b/Y8 4.6a/Y8◂◂

Writing. Pupils write six questions and appropriate responses on the items in the catalogue in exercise 1. An example is given.

➕ Pupils put together their own ideas for a fashion catalogue in Spanish, drawing and labelling items of clothing adapting the language in exercise 1. They could then work with a friend, discussing the clothes each other has designed using the superlative.

Pupils could go further with the topic, using Paint/Powerpoint to put together a fashion presentation/fashion show for the class.

4 Escucha y lee. (AT1.3) ▸▸4.4/Y8 4.6a/Y8◂◂

Listening. Pupils listen to the dialogue in a clothes shop and read the text at the same time. Point out the tip box on *¿Cuál?* and *¿Cuáles?* before playing the recording.

Check comprehension of the dialogue by asking a few simple questions in Spanish. Ask pupils how they would adapt the dialogue to talk about two pairs of boots, black and brown.

Then get pupils in pairs to practise reading the dialogue. With an able class, suggest they adapt the dialogue to feature different items and colours.

Audioscript Track 9

- *Quiero comprar una chaqueta. ¿Cuál prefieres? ¿La naranja o la roja?*
- *Me gusta esta chaqueta naranja con botones negros. Es la más barata.*
- *Sí, voy a comprar la chaqueta naranja.*

5 Escucha. Copia y rellena la tabla en inglés. (1–5) (AT1.4) ▸▸1.3a/Y8 4.6a/Y8◂◂

Listening. Pupils listen to conversations in which people are comparing different items of clothing and complete the table with the details in English.

After they have done the activity, write up the following expressions from the recording: *estas blancas* and *estas grises*. Ask pupils how to translate them. ('these white ones', 'these grey ones')

Audioscript Track 10

1 – *Quiero comprar un vestido. ¿Cuál prefieres? ¿El azul o el rojo?*
– *Hmm, no me gustan nada estos vestidos.*
– *Es verdad, prefiero este vestido verde. Es el más elegante. Sí... voy a comprar este vestido verde.*

2 – *Quiero comprar unos vaqueros. A ver... me gustan mucho estos negros.*
– *¿Cuáles prefieres tú, Ricardo?*
– *Prefiero estos blancos.*
– *No, no... creo que los negros son los más bonitos. Voy a comprar los vaqueros negros.*

3 – *Quiero comprar unas zapatillas de deporte. ¿Cuáles prefieres?*
– *Prefiero estas blancas pero son muy caras.*
– *Hmm, me gustan estas grises. Son bonitas y son las más baratas. Voy a comprar estas zapatillas grises.*

4 – *Quiero comprar unos pantalones. ¿Cuáles prefieres? ¿Los negros o los marrones?*
– *Prefiero los negros porque son los más baratos.*
– *A ver... pero no, no, no, son incómodos.*
– *¿Y estos pantalones blancos?*

– *No. Voy a comprar los pantalones marrones. Son los más elegantes.*

5 – *Quiero comprar una chaqueta. ¿Cuál prefieres? ¿La blanca, la roja o la violeta?*
– *Prefiero la blanca pero es la menos cómoda.*
– *Hmm, me gusta la roja… y es la más barata. Voy a comprar la chaqueta roja.*

Answers

	Article bought	Reason bought
1	*green dress*	*most elegant*
2	black jeans	nicest
3	grey trainers	nice, cheapest
4	brown trousers	most elegant
5	red jacket	cheapest

6 Escucha y completa el texto de la canción. (1–8) (AT1.4) ▸▸1.5b/Y8 4.3/Y8◂◂

Listening. Pupils listen to the song and complete the gap-fill version by finding the missing words. Some vocabulary is glossed for support.

Audioscript Track 11

Ir de compras

*¿Te gusta **este** jersey violeta?*
*No me gusta nada, prefiero esta **camiseta**.*
*Estos vaqueros son **los más caros**,*
pero me gustan porque son estampados.
Ir de compras, ir de compras, siempre un placer.

¿Te gusta este vestido de flores?
Pues no, prefiero la falda de muchos colores.
*¿Te gustan **estos** zapatos de cuero?*
*Prefiero **estas** botas, valen menos dinero.*
Ir de compras, ir de compras, siempre un placer.

***Esta** corbata negra es muy **elegante**.*
Yo prefiero la de lunares. Me gusta bastante.
*¿Cuál prefieres? ¿La camisa **de rayas** o la camiseta?*
Voy a comprar las dos, y también la sudadera.
Ir de compras, ir de compras, siempre un placer…
Ir de compras, ir de compras, siempre un placer…
Ir de compras, ir de compras, siempre un placer…

Answers
*Also in **bold** in the audioscript*
1 *este* **2** camiseta **3** los más caros **4** estos
5 estas **6** esta **7** elegante **8** de rayas

Plenary ▸▸5.8◂◂

Put pupils into teams and give them two minutes to prepare for a Mini-test challenge. Each team has to come up with a sample sentence in Spanish for each of the points listed. You will select pupils at random in the team to answer, so they all have to be ready on all of the points. A correct answer wins two points (or one if the same sentence has already been given by another pupil).

Cuaderno A, page 44

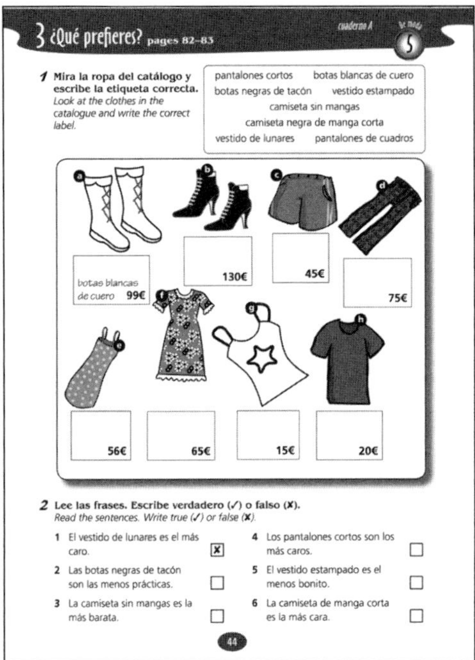

1 (AT4.2)

a *botas blancas de cuero*
b botas negras de tacón
c pantalones cortos
d pantalones de cuadros
e vestido de lunares
f vestido estampado
g camiseta sin mangas
h camiseta negra de manga corta

2 (AT3.2)

1 ✗ **2** ✓ **3** ✓ **4** ✗ **5** ✓ **6** ✓

Cuaderno B, page 44

1 (AT4.3)

2 (AT3.4)

1 d **2** c **3** b **4** e **5** a

R & A Pack, Gramática page 22

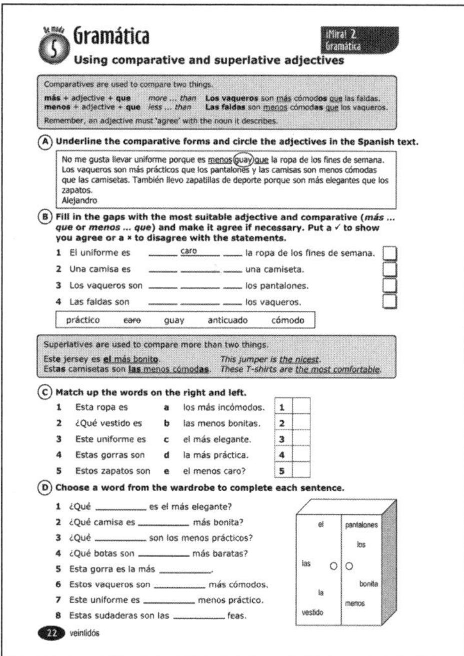

Ⓐ No me gusta llevar uniforme porque es <u>menos</u> guay <u>que</u> la ropa de los fines de semana. Los vaqueros son <u>más</u> prácticos <u>que</u> los pantalones y las camisas son <u>menos</u> cómodas <u>que</u> las camisetas. También llevo zapatillas de deporte porque son <u>más</u> elegantes <u>que</u> los zapatos. Alejandro

Ⓒ **1** d **2** e **3** c **4** b **5** a

Ⓓ **1** vestido **2** la **3** pantalones **4** las **5** bonita **6** los **7** el **8** menos

4 Vamos a visitar Argentina (Pupil's Book pages 84–85)

Learning objectives

- Talking about a trip to Argentina
- Using the present and near future tenses

Framework objectives

4.6/Y8 Language – (a) range of questions

Grammar

- Using different tenses (present and near future)

Key language

Cuando estoy de vacaciones...
Normalmente llevo...
ropa de deporte
una camiseta de fútbol
Mañana voy a llevar...
un bañador
mis gafas de sol

High-frequency words

un, una
mis
de
cuando
mañana
estar (estoy)

Cross-curricular

English: Verb tenses

Resources

CD3, tracks 12–13
Cuadernos A & B, p. 45
R & A Pack, Writing Skills p. 23 & Gramática p. 24

Teacher Presentations

Screen 1 – Module 5 overview
Screen 2 – pp. 84–85 exs 1, 2 & 3
Screen 3 – p. 85 ex. 4

Starter 1 ▸▸ 4.5a/Y8 ◂◂

Aim

To revise the near future tense.

Write up: *Mañana...*

I am going to...	We are going to...
go to the beach	play football
sunbathe	go for a bike ride
wear jeans	read

Give pupils in pairs three minutes to write two sentences starting *Mañana...* , using the English prompts to give details in Spanish of what they are going to do, using the 1st and 3rd persons of the near future tense, as appropriate.

If pupils need support, model the first ones as examples (*Mañana voy a ir a la playa, Mañana vamos a jugar al fútbol*).

Were pupils able to work out *voy a llevar* from the question form *¿Qué llevas?*

Suggestion

Explain that this unit will feature two tenses, the present and the near future. Ask pupils the 'I', 'he/she', 'we' and 'they' forms of *llevar* in both tenses.

1 Escucha y lee. Elige la frase apropiada para terminar cada texto. Escribe la letra correcta. (1–3) (AT1.4) ▸▸ 2.2/Y8 4.5a/Y8 ◂◂

Listening. Pupils listen to three people talking about their holidays in Argentina, and read the texts at the same time. They then choose the appropriate sentence (from *a–d*) to complete what each says. Some vocabulary is glossed for support.

Audioscript Track 12

1 *¿Qué tal? Me llamo Miguel. Soy estadounidense. Estoy de vacaciones en Chapelco con mi hermano. Me encanta Argentina, es un país muy bonito. El fútbol es mi deporte favorito. Me encanta ver partidos de fútbol. Normalmente llevo ropa de deporte. Llevo una camiseta, vaqueros y zapatillas de deporte. A veces llevo una gorra. ¡Mañana voy a hacer esquí, entonces voy a llevar algo diferente!*

2 *¡Buen día! ¿Qué tal? Me llamo Alba. Soy mexicana. Estoy de vacaciones en Mar del Plata. La gente argentina es muy simpática. En mi tiempo libre me encanta jugar a los videojuegos y chatear por internet. Aquí en Argentina no tengo ordenador. Normalmente llevo una falda con una camiseta y zapatillas de deporte. Pero mañana por la mañana voy a tomar el sol en la playa.*

3 *¡Hola! ¿Cómo estás? Me llamo Rodrigo. Soy chileno. Estoy de vacaciones en El Calafate. Me encanta leer cómics. Tengo una colección de cómics de Astérix. Normalmente llevo un jersey y unos vaqueros. Es ropa cómoda y práctica. No me interesa la moda. Mañana voy a ir al Perito Moreno en barco. Es un glaciar. No puedo llevar mi ropa habitual.*

Answers

1 c **2** d **3** b

R Pupils choose one of the texts and identify all the verbs in it as either present tense, near future tense or infinitive. Ask pupils when the present tense, the near future tense and the infinitive are used. Review time expressions associated with the present/near future tenses as necessary.

+ Translate the texts as a class, with each pupil doing a sentence.

2 Lee los textos. ¿Verdadero (V), falso (F) o no se sabe (NS)? (AT3.5) ▸▸ 2.2a/Y8 5.4 ◂◂

Reading. Pupils read the texts and decide whether the six statements are true (**V**) or false (**F**) or can't be identified as either as the information is not given in the texts (**NS**).

Answers

1 NS **2** V **3** F **4** NS **5** V **6** F

+ Pupils rewrite the F and NS sentences to make true statements.

3 Lee otra vez. Copia y rellena la tabla en español. (AT3.5) ▸▸ 4.5a/Y8 ◂◂

Reading. Pupils copy out the grid. They re-read the texts and complete the grid with details of what the three people normally wear and what they're going to do and wear tomorrow.

Answers

	Normalmente lleva...	Mañana va a...	Va a llevar...
Miguel	*una camiseta*, vaqueros, zapatillas de deporte y (a veces) una gorra	hacer esquí	unas botas, unos pantalones, unas gafas, una chaqueta y los esquís
Alba	una falda, una camiseta, zapatillas de deporte	tomar el sol en la playa	un bañador y unas gafas de sol
Rodrigo	un jersey y unos vaqueros	ir al Perito Moreno en barco	mucha ropa: botas, pantalones, chaqueta y gafas

Starter 2 ▸▸ 4.5a/Y8 5.2 ◂◂

Aim

To revise using the present and near future tenses. To revise vocabulary for clothes.

Write up:

1 play football – usually
2 go to the beach – tomorrow
3 go to a cybercafé – tomorrow
4 go out with friends – sometimes

Give pupils working in pairs three minutes to come up with a sentence for each of the four sets of English prompts, giving the Spanish for what they wear/are going to wear (as appropriate) for the occasions.

If pupils need more support, you could supply the activities and/or the frequency expressions in Spanish. You could also model the first answer.

4 Escucha y contesta a las preguntas en inglés para cada persona. (1–5) (AT1.5) ▸▸ 1.2/Y8 ◂◂

Listening. Pupils listen to five people talking about their holidays in Argentina and answer for each of the speakers the five comprehension questions in English.

Audioscript Track 13

1 *¡Hola! Me llamo Ana. Tengo diecisiete años. Soy estadounidense. Voy a ir de vacaciones a Argentina. Voy a escuchar música en la playa, voy a chatear por internet y también voy a mandar mensajes a mis amigas. Normalmente llevo una sudadera y una falda pero en las vacaciones voy a llevar falda y sudadera y también bañador.*

2 *¡Hola! Me llamo Mariela. Tengo quince años. Soy colombiana. Voy a ir de vacaciones a Buenos Aires, en Argentina. Voy a escuchar música y voy a bailar. Normalmente llevo una sudadera y vaqueros pero en las vacaciones voy a bailar tango, por eso voy a llevar un vestido rojo y zapatos negros.*

3 *¡Hola! Me llamo Antonio. Tengo dieciséis años. Soy mexicano. Voy a ir de vacaciones a Edimburgo, en Escocia. ¡Escocia me encanta! Voy a hacer deporte y también voy a bailar Ceilidh. Normalmente llevo una camiseta, unos vaqueros y unas zapatillas de deporte. En Escocia voy a llevar una falda escocesa para bailar Ceilidh.*

4 *¡Hola! Me llamo Arturo. Tengo quince años. Soy español. Voy a ir de vacaciones a Nueva York, en Estados Unidos. Voy a ir al teatro y al museo. Normalmente llevo una camiseta, pantalones y un jersey. Pero en Nueva York voy a llevar una chaqueta y una corbata.*

5 *¡Hola! Me llamo Teresa. Tengo diecisiete años. Soy portuguesa. Voy a ir de vacaciones a Irlanda. Voy a montar en bicicleta y voy a pasear a mi perro. Normalmente llevo el uniforme del colegio, pero en las vacaciones voy a llevar ropa de deporte.*

Answers

Ana
1 the United States
2 Argentina
3 listen to music (on the beach), chat online, send messages to her friends
4 a sweatshirt and a skirt
5 a skirt, a sweatshirt and a swimsuit

Mariela
1 Colombia
2 Argentina/Buenos Aires
3 listen to music, dance
4 a sweatshirt and jeans
5 a (red) dress and black shoes

Antonio
1 Mexico
2 Edinburgh/Scotland
3 do sports, dance
4 a t-shirt, jeans and trainers
5 a kilt

Arturo
1 Spain
2 the United States/New York
3 go to the theatre and a museum
4 a t-shirt, trousers and a jumper
5 a jacket and a tie

Teresa
1 Portugal
2 Ireland
3 go for bike rides, walk her dog
4 school uniform
5 sports clothes

5 Pon las palabras en el orden correcto. Traduce las preguntas al inglés. (AT4.3, AT3.3)

▸▸ **4.4/Y8 4.6a/Y8** ◂◂

Writing. Pupils put the words in each group in the correct order, to make eight complete questions, and translate each question into English.

Answers

1 *¿Cómo te llamas? – What are you called?*
2 ¿Cuántos años tienes? – How old are you?
3 ¿Cuál es tu nacionalidad? – What is your nationality?
4 ¿Qué te gusta? – What do you like?
5 ¿Qué haces en tu tiempo libre? – What do you do in your free time?
6 ¿Qué llevas normalmente? – What do you normally wear?
7 ¿Qué vas a hacer mañana? – What are you going to do tomorrow?
8 ¿Qué vas a llevar? – What are you going to wear?

6 Con tu compañero/a, pregunta y contesta por Javier. Utiliza las preguntas del ejercicio 5. (AT2.5)

▸▸ **1.4a&b/Y8** ◂◂

Speaking. In pairs using the prompts supplied, pupils put together a dialogue. They take it in turn to ask the questions and to play the part of Javier.

✚ Using the texts in exercise 1 as a model and the prompts in exercise 6, pupils write out a description of Javier's holiday.

Encourage more able students not to use the exercise 6 prompts, but to invent the details of what Javier does/likes/wears and is going to do/wear.

Plenary ▸▸ 4.5a/Y8 ◂◂

Ask the class to summarise when the present and near future tenses are used. Can they tell you any time expressions that are often used with these tenses? Then ask them how the future tense is formed, getting them to give examples using different verbs. You can either confine this to the 'I' form, or cover other forms, depending on the level of the class.

Put the class into teams. Teams take it in turn to challenge each other, prompting with an event in English (e.g. go to a party). You toss a coin each time: heads = present tense, tails = near future tense. The team being challenged has to come up with a statement about what they usually wear or what they are going to wear tomorrow (including the appropriate tense and a relevant time expression). A correct answer wins two points; an answer with a single error wins one point. The team with the most points wins.

Cuaderno A, page 45

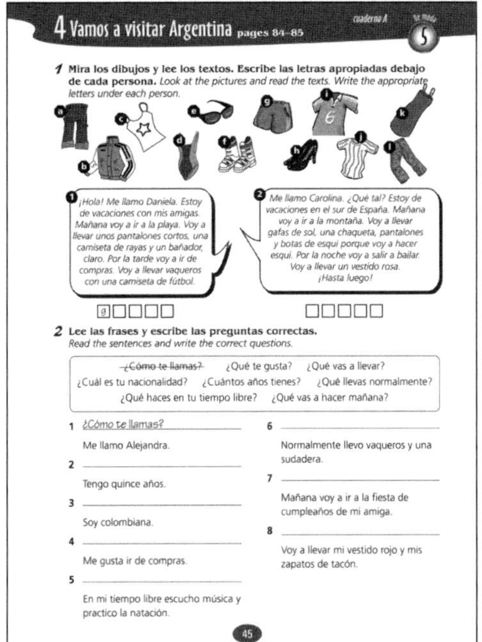

4 Vamos a visitar Argentina pages 84–85

cuaderno A

De moda 5

1 **Mira los dibujos y lee los textos. Escribe las letras apropiadas debajo de cada persona.** *Look at the pictures and read the texts. Write the appropriate letters under each person.*

a b c d e f g h i j k l

1 *¡Hola! Me llamo Daniela. Estoy de vacaciones con mis amigas. Mañana voy a ir a la playa. Voy a llevar unos pantalones cortos, una camiseta de rayas y un bañador, claro. Por la tarde voy a ir de compras. Voy a llevar vaqueros con una camiseta de fútbol.*

2 *Me llamo Carolina. ¿Qué tal? Estoy de vacaciones en el sur de España. Mañana voy a ir a la montaña. Voy a llevar gafas de sol, una chaqueta, pantalones y botas de esquí porque voy a hacer esquí. Por la noche voy a salir a bailar. Voy a llevar un vestido rosa. ¡Hasta luego!*

g ☐☐☐☐ ☐☐☐☐☐

2 **Lee las frases y escribe las preguntas correctas.** *Read the sentences and write the correct questions.*

~~¿Cómo te llamas?~~ ¿Qué te gusta? ¿Qué vas a llevar?
¿Cuál es tu nacionalidad? ¿Cuántos años tienes? ¿Qué llevas normalmente?
¿Qué haces en tu tiempo libre? ¿Qué vas a hacer mañana?

1 *¿Cómo te llamas?*
Me llamo Alejandra.

2 ______
Tengo quince años.

3 ______
Soy colombiana.

4 ______
Me gusta ir de compras.

5 ______
En mi tiempo libre escucho música y practico la natación.

6 ______
Normalmente llevo vaqueros y una sudadera.

7 ______
Mañana voy a ir a la fiesta de cumpleaños de mi amiga.

8 ______
Voy a llevar mi vestido rojo y mis zapatos de tacón.

45

1 (AT3.3)

1 *g* j d a i **2** e b l f k

2 (AT3.2, AT4.2)

1 *¿Cómo te llamas?*
2 ¿Cuántos años tienes?
3 ¿Cuál es tu nacionalidad?
4 ¿Qué te gusta?
5 ¿Qué haces en tu tiempo libre?
6 ¿Qué llevas normalmente?
7 ¿Qué vas a hacer mañana?
8 ¿Qué vas a llevar?

Cuaderno B, page 45

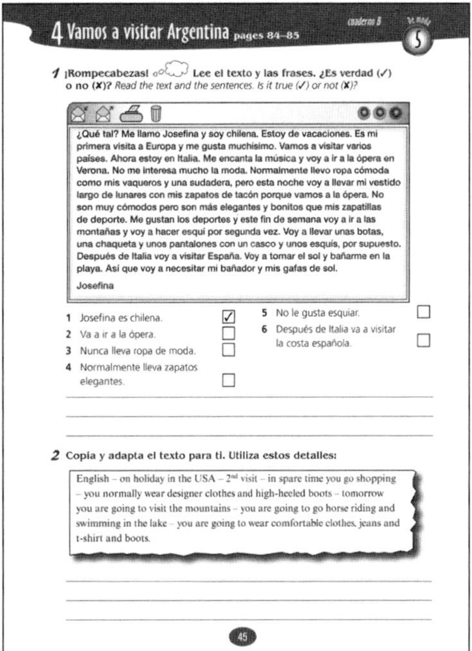

4 Vamos a visitar Argentina pages 84–85

cuaderno B

De moda 5

1 **¡Rompecabezas! Lee el texto y las frases. ¿Es verdad (✓) o no (✗)?** *Read the text and the sentences. Is it true (✓) or not (✗)?*

¿Qué tal? Me llamo Josefina y soy chilena. Estoy de vacaciones. Es mi primera visita a Europa y me gusta muchísimo. Vamos a visitar varios países. Ahora estoy en Italia. Me encanta la música y voy a ir a la ópera en Verona. No me interesa mucho la moda. Normalmente llevo ropa cómoda como mis vaqueros y una sudadera, pero esta noche voy a llevar mi vestido largo de lunares con mis zapatos de tacón porque vamos a la ópera. No son muy cómodos pero son más elegantes y bonitos que mis zapatillas de deporte. Me gustan los deportes y este fin de semana voy a ir a las montañas y voy a hacer esquí por segunda vez. Voy a llevar unas botas, una chaqueta y unos pantalones con un casco y unos esquís, por supuesto. Después de Italia voy a visitar España. Voy a tomar el sol y bañarme en la playa. Así que voy a necesitar mi bañador y mis gafas de sol.

Josefina

1 Josefina es chilena. ✓
2 Va a ir a la ópera. ☐
3 Nunca lleva ropa de moda. ☐
4 Normalmente lleva zapatos elegantes. ☐
5 No le gusta esquiar. ☐
6 Después de Italia va a visitar la costa española. ☐

2 **Copia y adapta el texto para ti. Utiliza estos detalles:**

English – on holiday in the USA – 2nd visit – in spare time you go shopping – you normally wear designer clothes and high-heeled boots – tomorrow you are going to visit the mountains – you are going to go horse riding and swimming in the lake – you are going to wear comfortable clothes, jeans and t-shirt and boots.

45

1 (AT3.5)

1 ✓ **2** ✓ **3** ✓ **4** ✗ **5** ✗ **6** ✓

2 (AT4.5)

R & A Pack, Writing Skills page 23

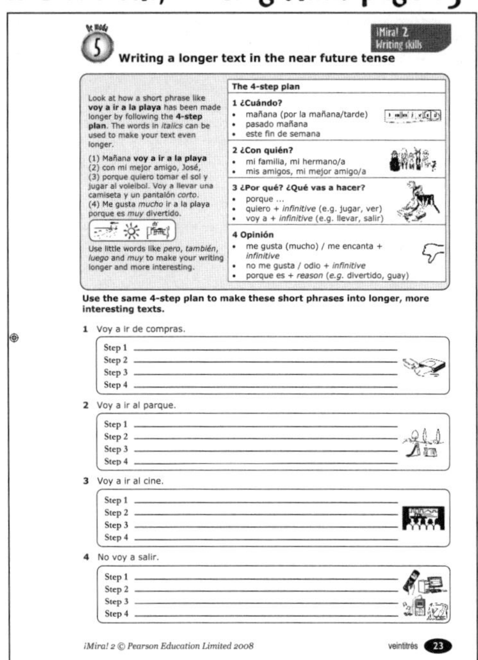

De moda 5

¡Mira! 2
Writing skills

Writing a longer text in the near future tense

Look at how a short phrase like **voy a ir a la playa** has been made longer by following the **4-step plan**. The words in *italics* can be used to make your text even longer.

(1) Mañana **voy a ir a la playa**
(2) con mi mejor amigo, José,
(3) porque quiero tomar el sol y jugar al voleibol. Voy a llevar una camiseta y un pantalón *corto*.
(4) Me gusta *mucho* ir a la playa porque es *muy* divertido.

Use little words like *pero*, *también*, *luego* and *muy* to make your writing longer and more interesting.

The 4-step plan

1 ¿Cuándo?
- mañana (por la mañana/tarde)
- pasado mañana
- este fin de semana

2 ¿Con quién?
- mi familia, mi hermano/a
- mis amigos, mi mejor amigo/a

3 ¿Por qué? ¿Qué vas a hacer?
- porque ...
- quiero + *infinitive* (e.g. jugar, ver)
- voy a + *infinitive* (e.g. llevar, salir)

4 Opinión
- me gusta (mucho) / me encanta + *infinitive*
- no me gusta / odio + *infinitive*
- porque es + *reason* (e.g. divertido, guay)

Use the same 4-step plan to make these short phrases into longer, more interesting texts.

1 Voy a ir de compras.
Step 1 ______
Step 2 ______
Step 3 ______
Step 4 ______

2 Voy a ir al parque.
Step 1 ______
Step 2 ______
Step 3 ______
Step 4 ______

3 Voy a ir al cine.
Step 1 ______
Step 2 ______
Step 3 ______
Step 4 ______

4 No voy a salir.
Step 1 ______
Step 2 ______
Step 3 ______
Step 4 ______

¡Mira! 2 © Pearson Education Limited 2008 veintitrés 23

R & A Pack, Gramática page 24

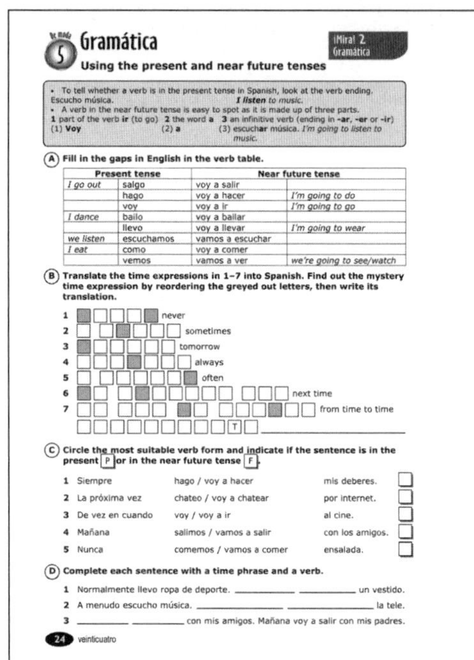

De moda 5

Gramática

¡Mira! 2
Gramática

Using the present and near future tenses

- To tell whether a verb is in the present tense in Spanish, look at the verb ending.
Escucho música. ***I listen** to music.*
- A verb in the near future tense is easy to spot as it is made up of three parts.
1 part of the verb **ir** (to go) **2** the word **a** **3** an infinitive verb (ending in **-ar**, **-er** or **-ir**)
(1) **Voy** (2) **a** (3) escuch**ar** música. *I'm going to listen to music.*

Ⓐ **Fill in the gaps in English in the verb table.**

Present tense		Near future tense	
I go out	salgo	voy a salir	
	hago	voy a hacer	*I'm going to do*
	voy	voy a ir	*I'm going to go*
I dance	bailo	voy a bailar	
	llevo	voy a llevar	*I'm going to wear*
we listen	escuchamos	vamos a escuchar	
I eat	como	voy a comer	
	vemos	vamos a ver	*we're going to see/watch*

Ⓑ **Translate the time expressions in 1–7 into Spanish. Find out the mystery time expression by reordering the greyed out letters, then write its translation.**

1 never
2 sometimes
3 tomorrow
4 always
5 often
6 next time
7 from time to time
T ______

Ⓒ **Circle the most suitable verb form and indicate if the sentence is in the present P or in the near future tense F.**

1 Siempre hago / voy a hacer mis deberes.
2 La próxima vez chateo / voy a chatear por internet.
3 De vez en cuando voy / voy a ir al cine.
4 Mañana salimos / vamos a salir con los amigos.
5 Nunca comemos / vamos a comer ensalada.

Ⓓ **Complete each sentence with a time phrase and a verb.**

1 Normalmente llevo ropa de deporte. ______ ______ un vestido.
2 A menudo escucho música. ______ ______ la tele.
3 ______ ______ con mis amigos. Mañana voy a salir con mis padres.

24 veinticuatro

Ⓐ I'm going to go out; I do; I go; I'm going to dance; I wear; we're going to listen; I'm going to eat; we see/watch

Ⓑ **1** nunca **2** a veces **3** mañana **4** siempre **5** a menudo **6** la próxima vez **7** de vez en cuando; normalmente – normally, usually

Ⓒ **1** hago, P, I always do my homework **2** voy a chatear, F, Next time I'm going to chat on the internet **3** voy, P, From time to time I go to the cinema **4** vamos a salir, F, Tomorrow we're going to go out with friends **5** comemos, P, We never eat salad

5 Un baile de disfraces (Pupil's Book pages 86–87)

Learning objectives

- Saying what you wore to a fancy dress ball
- Using past, present and future tenses together

Framework objectives

4.1/Y8 Language – sounds/ spelling exceptions
5.5 Strategies – reference materials

Grammar

- Using different tenses (present, preterite and near future)

Key language

Ayer…
salí con mis amigos
fuimos a un baile de disfraces
llevé…
Bebí limonada.
Bailé.
Comí ensalada y tortilla.
Llevé un vestido de princesa.
Fui de vampiro.
Mi amigo/a fue de vampiro.
Fue muy divertido.

Normalmente llevo…
La próxima vez voy a llevar…

High-frequency words

la
un
a
de
mi, mis
con
y
ayer
muy
beber (bebí)
comer (comí)
ir (voy, fui, fuimos)
salir (salí)
ser (fue)

Resources

CD3, tracks 14–15
Cuadernos A & B, p. 46

Teacher Presentations

Screen 1 – Module 5 overview
Screen 2 – p. 86 exs 1 & 2
Screen 3 – p. 86 ex. 4
Screen 4 – Game
Screen 5 – Video

Starter 1 ▸▸ 4.5a/Y8 ◂◂

Aim
To revise the preterite tense.

Write up the following, highlighting the options in bold (e.g. by using a different colour). The answers are underlined here for reference.

El fin de semana pasado ***<u>jugué</u>*** */* ***juego*** *al fútbol.* ***Llevo*** */* ***<u>Llevé</u>*** *pantalones cortos y zapatillas de deporte.* ***Fui*** */* ***<u>Fue</u>*** *muy divertido. Ayer* ***salgo*** */* ***<u>salí</u>*** *con mi amiga Paz.* ***Fue*** */* ***<u>Fuimos</u>*** *a la piscina y luego* ***comemos*** */* ***<u>comimos</u>*** *una pizza.*

Give pupils three minutes working in pairs to select the correct verbs and to translate the text into English.

Suggestion

Prompt with the following time expressions at random and ask pupils what tense they would expect to be used after each of them: *normalmente, generalmente, todos los días* (present); *ayer, el fin de semana pasado, el verano pasado* (preterite); *mañana, este fin de semana* (near future). Explain that this unit focuses on using these three tenses together.

1 Escucha y lee el texto de Dolores. (AT1.6) ▸▸ 1.2/Y8 4.5a/Y8 ◂◂

Listening. Pupils listen to someone describing a fancy dress party and read the text at the same time.

Can pupils work out the meaning of *la próxima vez* from the context and the fact that the near future tense is used?

Point out the use of different colours for the tenses in the Pupil's Book. Remind pupils that they might find a system like this useful for their own grammar revision.

Audioscript Track 14

Ayer salí con mis amigos y fuimos a un baile de disfraces. Yo llevé un vestido de princesa y fue muy divertido porque normalmente llevo vaqueros y una camiseta de fútbol todo el tiempo. Me encanta el fútbol, juego mucho, soy muy buena. En el baile comí ensalada y tortilla. Bebí limonada. Lo pasé guay. Fue muy, muy divertido.
La próxima vez voy a llevar unas botas, una camisa blanca muy larga y un sombrero rojo: voy a ser pirata del Caribe.

Use the tip box to summarise the preterite, present and near future tenses. Ask pupils if they can remember typical time expressions used with each tense.

2 Busca estos verbos en el texto. (AT3.6) ▸▸4.1/Y8 4.5a/Y8◂◂

Reading. Pupils find in the text the Spanish versions of the ten English verbs listed.

Answers

1 llevo **2** comí **3** salí **4** fue **5** fuimos
6 voy a ser **7** bebí **8** llevé **9** voy a llevar
10 me encanta

3 Con tu compañero/a, traduce las frases al español. (AT2.6) ▸▸4.4/Y8 4.5a/Y8◂◂

Speaking. In pairs: pupils work together to translate the seven sentences into Spanish.

Draw pupils' attention to the tip box, which recommends they identify related expressions in the text in exercise 1 and adapt these. Point out to pupils that using this technique whenever they can will make them more independent as learners and will help them make their Spanish more fluent.

Answers

1. *Ayer salí con mis padres.*
2. Fuimos a un restaurante.
3. ¡Lo pasé guay! / ¡Fue genial!
4. Comí ensalada, pollo y helado.
5. La próxima vez voy a comer paella.
6. Llevé vaqueros y una camiseta.
7. Normalmente llevo pantalones y una sudadera todo el tiempo.

4 Escucha y contesta a las preguntas por Eva y César (1–2). (AT1.5) ▸▸4.5a/Y8◂◂

Listening. Pupils listen to Eva and César talking about the fancy dress party they went to and answer the three questions for each speaker.

Audioscript Track 15

1a – *¿Fuiste al baile de disfraces, Eva?*
– *Sí, fui con mi hermano.*
– *¿Qué llevaste?*
– *Llevé unos pantalones azules y una camiseta azul de manga larga. También llevé una capa roja. Fui de Superman.*

b – *¿Qué llevas normalmente?*
– *Siempre llevo ropa de color negro porque soy gótica.*

c – *¿Qué vas a llevar al próximo baile?*
– *Al próximo baile voy a llevar unos pantalones blancos y una camiseta blanca de manga larga. Me voy a pintar la cara de blanco. Voy a ser una momia. ¡Uuuuuuh!*

2a – *Y tú, César, ¿fuiste al baile de disfraces?*
– *Sí, fui con mis amigos.*
– *¿Qué llevaste?*
– *Llevé unos pantalones negros, una chaqueta negra muy elegante, zapatos y una corbata. Fui de Bond, James Bond.*

b – *Normalmente tú no llevas ropa elegante, ¿verdad?*
– *¡Nunca! Siempre llevo ropa de deporte: zapatillas, sudaderas…*

c – *¿Qué vas a llevar al próximo baile?*
– *La próxima vez voy a llevar un vestido corto, zapatos de tacón y el pelo largo. Voy a ser una chica Bond.*

Answers

Eva

- **a** Llevé unos pantalones azules y una camiseta azul de manga larga. También llevé una capa roja.
- **b** Normalmente llevo ropa de color negro porque soy gótica.
- **c** Voy a llevar unos pantalones blancos y una camiseta blanca de manga larga.

César

- **a** Llevé unos pantalones negros, una chaqueta negra muy elegante, zapatos y una corbata.
- **b** Normalmente llevo ropa de deporte: zapatillas, sudaderas…
- **c** Voy a llevar un vestido corto, zapatos de tacón y el pelo largo.

Starter 2 ▸▸4.5a/Y8◂◂

Aim

To revise using different tenses.

Write up:

Normalmente…
Ayer fui a una fiesta (party) *y…*
La próxima vez…

Give pupils three minutes working in pairs to complete the sentences using *llevar* in an appropriate tense and items of clothing/details of a costume.

If pupils need more support, supply the 'I' forms of the three tenses in random order.

You could make it more challenging for able pupils by asking them to give colours with each item of clothing.

Suggestion

Write up *Fuimos a un baile de disfraces. Fui de vampiro y mi amiga Luisa fue de policía.* Ask pupils to translate the sentence, and to give you the Spanish for 'I went' and 'she went'. Then write up *Llevé unos pantalones negros y Luisa… un uniforme.* Ask pupils to work out the form of the missing verb. What tense is it? What is the infinitive form? If they cannot remember the ending, how will they find it?

Say that this lesson focuses on the 'he/she' form of the preterite.

5 Lee los textos. Empareja los dibujos con las personas. (AT3.4) ▸▸5.2 5.3◂◂

Reading. Pupils read the five texts, each describing a different person's fancy dress costume, and give the correct name for each of pictures *1–5*.

> **Answers**
> **1** *Juanita* **2** Rosa **3** Ángel **4** Carlos **5** Luisa

6 Elige el verbo correcto. (AT3.5) ▸▸4.1/Y8 4.5a/Y8◂◂

Reading. Pupils read the five sentences about the people who went to the fancy dress party in exercise 5. They complete the sentences by choosing the correct verb form from the two options given in each.

> **Answers**
> 1 ¡Qué miedo! Rosa **llevó** ropa negra, un vestido, un sombrero y bigote.
> 2 Mañana Ángel también **va a llevar** unos dientes blancos largos, una capa negra, unos pantalones negros y una camisa blanca.
> 3 Luisa llevó un uniforme, ella **fue** de policía.
> 4 Carlos **llevó** vaqueros, un sombrero y una camisa.
> 5 A Juanita **le gusta** Caperucita.

7 Copia las preguntas de la página web y completa las respuestas. (AT4.5) ▸▸4.5a/Y8 4.6a/Y8 5.5◂◂

Writing. Pupils copy out the questions from the web page and complete the answer for each, giving details about the fancy dress party and what they wore/usually wear/are going to wear next time, using the appropriate tense.

Encourage pupils to use the Gramática section at the back of the Pupil's Book to check verb forms and adjective endings and to use a dictionary to look up any new vocabulary they want to use.

Plenary ▸▸5.8◂◂

Put the class into teams and tell pupils that you are going to use the Resumen section to test them. Each team chooses a unit: give them two minutes to review that unit and its summary in the Resumen section. They then close their books.

Ask the teams in turn to give a Spanish example for each point listed in the Resumen section. They can confer, but a different person must finally answer each time. A correct answer wins a point. If a pupil can answer correctly without conferring, this wins two points. The team with the most points wins.

Cuaderno A, page 46

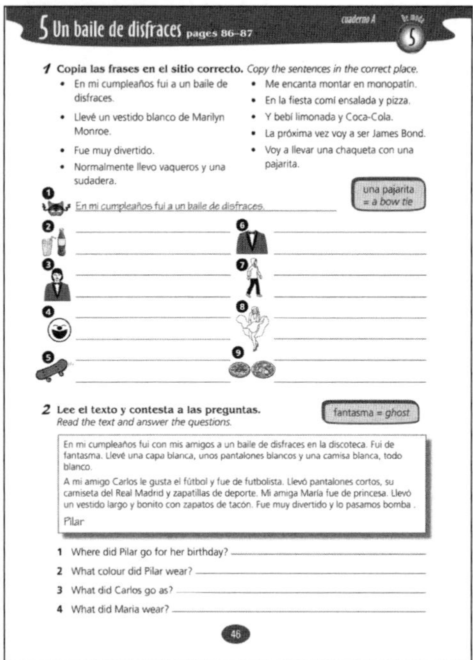

5 Un baile de disfraces pages 86–87 · cuaderno A · De moda 5

1 **Copia las frases en el sitio correcto.** *Copy the sentences in the correct place.*

- En mi cumpleaños fui a un baile de disfraces.
- Llevé un vestido blanco de Marilyn Monroe.
- Fue muy divertido.
- Normalmente llevo vaqueros y una sudadera.
- Me encanta montar en monopatín.
- En la fiesta comí ensalada y pizza.
- Y bebí limonada y Coca-Cola.
- La próxima vez voy a ser James Bond.
- Voy a llevar una chaqueta con una pajarita.

una pajarita = *a bow tie*

1 En mi cumpleaños fui a un baile de disfraces.
2
3
4
5
6
7
8
9

2 **Lee el texto y contesta a las preguntas.** *Read the text and answer the questions.*

fantasma = *ghost*

En mi cumpleaños fui con mis amigos a un baile de disfraces en la discoteca. Fui de fantasma. Llevé una capa blanca, unos pantalones blancos y una camisa blanca, todo blanco.

A mi amigo Carlos le gusta el fútbol y fue de futbolista. Llevó pantalones cortos, su camiseta del Real Madrid y zapatillas de deporte. Mi amiga María fue de princesa. Llevó un vestido largo y bonito con zapatos de tacón. Fue muy divertido y lo pasamos bomba .

Pilar

1 Where did Pilar go for her birthday?
2 What colour did Pilar wear?
3 What did Carlos go as?
4 What did Maria wear?

46

1 (AT3.2, AT4.2)

1 *Para mi cumpleaños fui a un baile de disfraces.*
2 Y bebí limonada y Coca-Cola.
3 La próxima vez voy a ser James Bond.
4 Fue muy divertido.
5 Me encanta montar en monopatín.
6 Voy a llevar una chaqueta con una pajarita.
7 Normalmente llevo vaqueros y una sudadera.
8 Llevé un vestido blanco de Marilyn Monroe.
9 En la fiesta comí ensalada y pizza.

2 (AT3.3)

1 She went to a fancy dress dance at the disco.
2 white
3 footballer
4 a long, pretty dress with high-heeled shoes

Cuaderno B, page 46

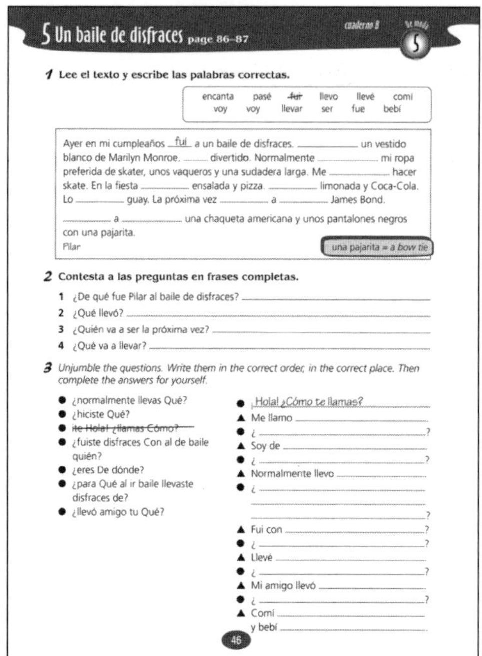

5 Un baile de disfraces page 86–87 · cuaderno B · De moda 5

1 **Lee el texto y escribe las palabras correctas.**

encanta pasé ~~fui~~ llevo llevé comí voy voy llevar ser fue bebí

Ayer en mi cumpleaños *fui* a un baile de disfraces. ______ un vestido blanco de Marilyn Monroe. ______ divertido. Normalmente ______ mi ropa preferida de skater, unos vaqueros y una sudadera larga. Me ______ hacer skate. En la fiesta ______ ensalada y pizza. ______ limonada y Coca-Cola. Lo ______ guay. La próxima vez ______ a ______ James Bond. ______ a ______ una chaqueta americana y unos pantalones negros con una pajarita.

Pilar

una pajarita = *a bow tie*

2 **Contesta a las preguntas en frases completas.**

1 ¿De qué fue Pilar al baile de disfraces?
2 ¿Qué llevó?
3 ¿Quién va a ser la próxima vez?
4 ¿Qué va a llevar?

3 *Unjumble the questions. Write them in the correct order, in the correct place. Then complete the answers for yourself.*

- ¿normalmente llevas Qué?
- ¿hiciste Qué?
- ~~ite Hola! ¿llamas Cómo?~~
- ¿fuiste disfraces Con al de baile quién?
- ¿eres De dónde?
- ¿para Qué al ir baile llevaste disfraces de?
- ¿llevó amigo tu Qué?

● ¡Hola! ¿Cómo te llamas?
▲ Me llamo ______
● ¿ ______ ?
▲ Soy de ______
● ¿ ______ ?
▲ Normalmente llevo ______
● ¿ ______ ?
▲ Fui con ______
● ¿ ______ ?
▲ Llevé ______
● ¿ ______ ?
▲ Mi amigo llevó ______
● ¿ ______ ?
▲ Comí ______ y bebí ______

46

1 (AT3.6)

Ayer en mi cumpleaños *fui* a un baile de disfraces. Llevé un vestido blanco de Marilyn Monroe. Fue divertido. Normalmente llevo mi ropa preferida de skater, unos vaqueros y una sudadera largos. Me encanta hacer skate. En la fiesta comí ensalada y pizza. Bebí limonada y Coca-Cola. Lo pasé guay. La próxima vez voy a ser James Bond. Voy a llevar una chaqueta americana y unos pantalones negros con una pajarita.

Pilar

2 (AT4.6)

1 Pilar fue al baile de disfraces de Marilyn Monroe.
2 Llevó un vestido blanco.
3 La próxima vez va a ser James Bond.
4 Va a llevar una chaqueta americana y unos pantalones negros con una pajarita.

3 (AT3.6, AT4.3)

¡Hola! ¿Cómo te llamas? Me llamo …
¿De dónde eres? Soy de …
¿Qué llevas normalmente? Normalmente llevo …
¿Con quién fuiste al baile de disfraces? Fui con …
¿Qué llevaste para ir al baile de disfraces? Llevé …
¿Qué llevó tu amigo? Mi amigo llevó …
¿Qué hiciste? Comí … y bebí …

Resumen y Prepárate (Pupil's Book pages 88–89)

Resumen

This is a checklist of language covered in Module 5. Pupils can work on this in pairs to check what they have learned and remembered. There is a Resumen page in the Resource and Assessment Pack. Encourage them to look back at the module and to use the grammar section to revise what they are unclear about. You can also use the Resumen as a useful plenary at the end of each unit.

Prepárate

These revision tests can be used for pupils to practise prior to the assessment tasks in the Resource and Assessment Pack.

Resources

CD3, track 16
R & A Pack, Module 5: Resumen, Prueba, I can...

1 Escucha y elige las dos cosas que menciona cada persona. (1–5) (AT1.3) ▸▸1.1/Y8◂◂

Listening. Pupils listen to five people saying what they usually wear and note the two items of clothing mentioned by each person.

Audioscript Track 16

1. *Normalmente llevo unos vaqueros azules y una sudadera blanca.*
2. *Normalmente llevo un vestido rosa o una falda rosa. Mi color favorito es el rosa, por supuesto.*
3. *A ver, normalmente llevo un vestido naranja y unos zapatos rojos de tacón.*
4. *– ¿Qué llevas normalmente?*
   – Normalmente llevo una falda negra y una camiseta azul.
5. *Normalmente llevo unos pantalones cortos naranjas y unas zapatillas de deporte.*

Answers

1 *a, g* **2** f, d **3** i, c **4** j, b **5** l, e

R Pupils write a caption for each of the pictures (e.g. *unos vaqueros azules*).

2 Con tu compañero/a, haz frases sobre José, Juan y Xavier. (AT2.3) ▸▸1.4a/Y8◂◂

Speaking. In pairs: pupils compare what the three boys pictured are wearing, using the comparative and superlative. Sentence openings are supplied.

3 Escribe las letras de la ropa que menciona Raúl. (AT3.3) ▸▸2.3/Y8◂◂

Reading. Pupils read Raúl's email and note the clothes in the order mentioned (using pictures *a–i*).

Answers

d, h, i, b, c, a, f

R Pupils identify all the adjectives used in the text, grouping them by number and gender.

4 Escribe un texto sobre tu uniforme. Utiliza el texto del ejercicio 3 como modelo. (AT4.3–4) ▸▸2.4a/Y8 4.5b/Y8◂◂

Writing. Using the text in exercise 3 as a model, pupils write a text describing their own uniform.

¡Extra! 1 (Pupil's Book pages 90–91)

Learning objectives
- Using different tenses together
- Combining language from different topics

Framework objectives
1.2/Y8 Listening – new contexts
1.4/Y8 Speaking – (a) classroom exchanges (teacher-pupil)

Key language
Tengo el pelo...
Tengo los ojos...

Revision of language from Module 5

High-frequency words
Revision of language from Module 5

Resources
CD3, tracks 17–18
Cuadernos A & B, pp. 47–48

Starter 4.3/Y8

Aim
To revise the vocabulary for colours.

Write up the following colours in anagram form (answers in brackets for reference):

joors	*(rojos)*	*dreev*	*(verde)*
ssaro	*(rosas)*	*gerans*	*(negras)*
nórrma	*(marrón)*	*luzeas*	*(azules)*
jaaanrn	*(naranja)*	*baclan*	*(blanca)*
sgir	*(gris)*	*lomalari*	*(amarillo)*

Say these are colours and they are given in a range of forms (masculine singular, feminine plural, etc.). Give pupils three minutes to work them out and to write each adjective with an appropriate noun (agreeing in number and gender with the form of the adjective given), e.g. *pantalones rojos*.

Check answers, getting pupils to give all four forms of each adjective.

1 Escucha. ¿Quién habla? (1–5) (AT1.4) 1.2/Y8

Listening. Pupils listen to five people describing themselves and identify the speaker each time using the labelled pictures.

Audioscript Track 17

1 *Tengo el pelo largo, rubio y ondulado. Tengo los ojos verdes. El rojo me queda bien pero el amarillo me queda mal. Soy inteligente y bastante divertida. No llevo gafas y me encantan las faldas.*

2 *Soy bastante alta. Creo que soy generosa y divertida. Me gusta mucho la ropa cómoda. Tengo el pelo largo, castaño y los ojos marrones. Mi color favorito es el azul y me encantan los pantalones cortos.*

3 *Tengo los ojos marrones y el pelo corto, negro y rizado. El verde me queda bien. Es mi color favorito. Soy hablador e inteligente y muy generoso.*

4 *Tengo el pelo corto y pelirrojo y los ojos azules. Llevo gafas. El naranja me queda mal – es horrible. Mi color favorito es el marrón. De carácter no soy perezoso. Soy trabajador y también simpático. Me gusta la ropa elegante.*

5 *Soy bastante inteligente. Tengo el pelo rubio, largo y liso. Tengo los ojos grises. Mi color favorito es el amarillo. Me gusta la ropa práctica. Me gustan los pantalones cortos y las camisetas de color amarillo.*

Answers
1 Juanita **2** Elena **3** David **4** Paco **5** Eduardo

+ Using the labelled pictures, pupils write a description of each person's hair and eyes.

Suggestion

Ask pupils what vocabulary they need to listen out for to do exercise 2.

Before playing the recording, read through the key language in the box on page 90. Go round the class getting pupils to give a statement about a colour which suits/doesn't suit them or their favourite colour.

2 Escucha otra vez. Elige la ropa apropiada para cada persona. (1–5) (AT1.4) 1.3a/Y8

Listening. Pupils listen to the recording again and choose the appropriate item of clothing (from pictures *a–e*) for each speaker.

Audioscript Track 18

As for exercise 1.

Answers

a Paco **b** Eduardo **c** Juanita **d** Elena **e** David

Play the recording again, asking pupils to note down the additional details each person gives about him/herself.

3 Con tu compañero/a, haz este test sobre la moda. (AT2.6) ▸▸2.2b/Y8 5.4◂◂

Speaking. In pairs: pupils do the test on their personal approach to fashion, working out their total scores and reading the findings.

They should use reading strategies to work out new vocabulary, and then check in the Vocabulario section or a dictionary to see if they are correct.

4 Copia y rellena este pasaporte de moda. (AT4.5) ▸▸2.2b/Y8 4.4/Y8◂◂

Writing. Pupils copy out the 'fashion passport' framework and complete it with a description of themselves and their own fashion preferences and choices.

5 Lee el pasaporte de moda de tu compañero/a y diseña algo para él/ella. (AT4.5–6) ▸▸2.2a/Y8 4.4/Y8◂◂

Writing. Pupils swap their answers to exercise 4 with a partner and, using the details supplied, draw and describe an appropriate outfit for each other.

Encourage pupils to make their texts as interesting as possible by writing complex sentences including connectives and negatives. They should use the Gramática section at the back of the Pupil's Book to check agreements before doing a second draft.

Plenary ▸▸1.4a/Y8◂◂

Prompt with a series of places or events in English or Spanish (e.g. a party, watching a football match, a school disco, going to the cinema) for pupils to say what they would wear. They should include colours.

Hold a conversation with the class about different clothes for different events.

Cuaderno A, page 47

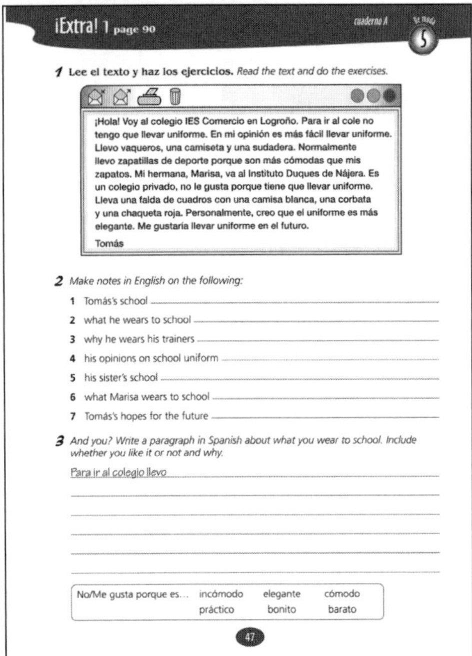
¡Extra! 1 page 90 cuaderno A De moda 5

1 **Lee el texto y haz los ejercicios.** *Read the text and do the exercises.*

¡Hola! Voy al colegio IES Comercio en Logroño. Para ir al cole no tengo que llevar uniforme. En mi opinión es más fácil llevar uniforme. Llevo vaqueros, una camiseta y una sudadera. Normalmente llevo zapatillas de deporte porque son más cómodas que mis zapatos. Mi hermana, Marisa, va al Instituto Duques de Nájera. Es un colegio privado, no le gusta porque tiene que llevar uniforme. Lleva una falda de cuadros con una camisa blanca, una corbata y una chaqueta roja. Personalmente, creo que el uniforme es más elegante. Me gustaría llevar uniforme en el futuro.

Tomás

2 *Make notes in English on the following:*

1 Tomás's school ______
2 what he wears to school ______
3 why he wears his trainers ______
4 his opinions on school uniform ______
5 his sister's school ______
6 what Marisa wears to school ______
7 Tomás's hopes for the future ______

3 *And you? Write a paragraph in Spanish about what you wear to school. Include whether you like it or not and why.*

Para ir al colegio llevo ______

No/Me gusta porque es... incómodo elegante cómodo práctico bonito barato

47

2 (AT3.4)

1 It is called IES Comercio in Logroño.
2 He wears jeans, T shirt, sweat shirt and trainers.
3 They are more comfortable than his shoes.
4 Uniform is easier.
5 It is called IES Duques de Nájera and is private.
6 She wears a checked skirt, a white shirt and tie and a red jacket.
7 He would like to wear uniform.

3 (AT4.4)

Cuaderno A, page 48

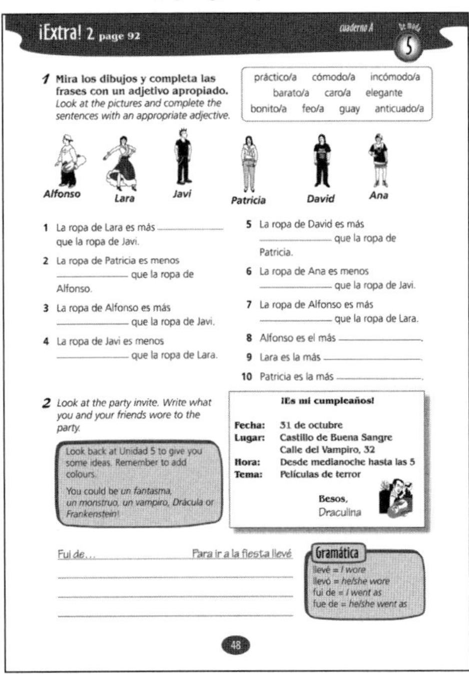
¡Extra! 2 page 92 cuaderno A De moda 5

1 **Mira los dibujos y completa las frases con un adjetivo apropiado.** *Look at the pictures and complete the sentences with an appropriate adjective.*

práctico/a cómodo/a incómodo/a barato/a caro/a elegante bonito/a feo/a guay anticuado/a

1 La ropa de Lara es más ______ que la ropa de Javi.
2 La ropa de Patricia es menos ______ que la ropa de Alfonso.
3 La ropa de Alfonso es más ______ que la ropa de Javi.
4 La ropa de Javi es menos ______ que la ropa de Lara.
5 La ropa de David es más ______ que la ropa de Patricia.
6 La ropa de Ana es menos ______ que la ropa de Javi.
7 La ropa de Alfonso es más ______ que la ropa de Lara.
8 Alfonso es el más ______.
9 Lara es la más ______.
10 Patricia es la más ______.

2 *Look at the party invite. Write what you and your friends wore to the party.*

Look back at Unidad 5 to give you some ideas. Remember to add colours.

You could be *un fantasma, un monstruo, un vampiro, Drácula* or *Frankenstein*!

¡Es mi cumpleaños!

Fecha: 31 de octubre
Lugar: Castillo de Buena Sangre, Calle del Vampiro, 32
Hora: Desde medianoche hasta las 5
Tema: Películas de terror

Besos,
Draculina

Fui de... Para ir a la fiesta llevé ______

Gramática
llevé = *I wore*
llevó = *he/she wore*
fui de = *I went as*
fue de = *he/she went as*

48

1 (AT3.3, AT4.1)

2 (AT4.3)

Cuaderno B, page 47

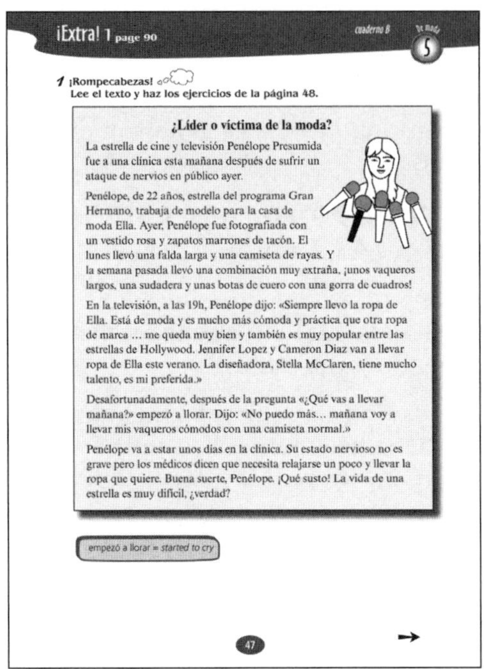
¡Extra! 1 page 90 cuaderno B De moda 5

1 **¡Rompecabezas! Lee el texto y haz los ejercicios de la página 48.**

¿Líder o víctima de la moda?

La estrella de cine y televisión Penélope Presumida fue a una clínica esta mañana después de sufrir un ataque de nervios en público ayer.

Penélope, de 22 años, estrella del programa Gran Hermano, trabaja de modelo para la casa de moda Ella. Ayer, Penélope fue fotografiada con un vestido rosa y zapatos marrones de tacón. El lunes llevó una falda larga y una camiseta de rayas. Y la semana pasada llevó una combinación muy extraña, ¡unos vaqueros largos, una sudadera y unas botas de cuero con una gorra de cuadros!

En la televisión, a las 19h, Penélope dijo: «Siempre llevo la ropa de Ella. Está de moda y es mucho más cómoda y práctica que otra ropa de marca ... me queda muy bien y también es muy popular entre las estrellas de Hollywood. Jennifer Lopez y Cameron Diaz van a llevar ropa de Ella este verano. La diseñadora, Stella McClaren, tiene mucho talento, es mi preferida.»

Desafortunadamente, después de la pregunta «¿Qué vas a llevar mañana?» empezó a llorar. Dijo: «No puedo más… mañana voy a llevar mis vaqueros cómodos con una camiseta normal.»

Penélope va a estar unos días en la clínica. Su estado nervioso no es grave pero los médicos dicen que necesita relajarse un poco y llevar la ropa que quiere. Buena suerte, Penélope. ¡Qué susto! La vida de una estrella es muy difícil, ¿verdad?

empezó a llorar = *started to cry*

47

1 (AT3.6)

Cuaderno B, page 48

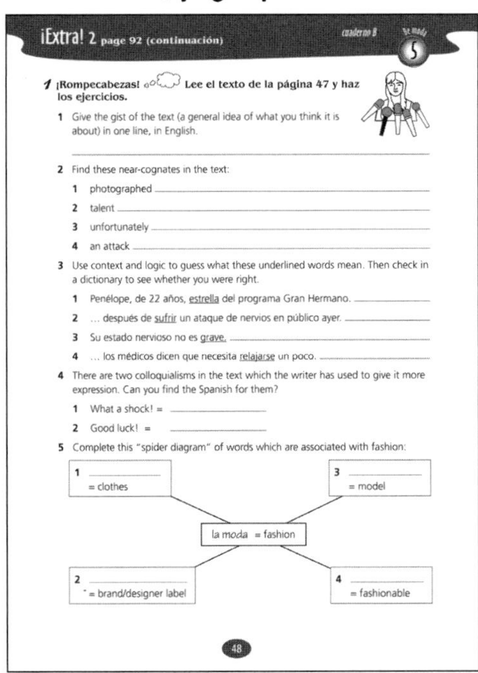
¡Extra! 2 page 92 (continuación) cuaderno B De moda 5

1 **¡Rompecabezas! Lee el texto de la página 47 y haz los ejercicios.**

1 Give the gist of the text (a general idea of what you think it is about) in one line, in English.

2 Find these near-cognates in the text:
1 photographed ______
2 talent ______
3 unfortunately ______
4 an attack ______

3 Use context and logic to guess what these underlined words mean. Then check in a dictionary to see whether you were right.
1 Penélope, de 22 años, estrella del programa Gran Hermano. ______
2 ... después de sufrir un ataque de nervios en público ayer. ______
3 Su estado nervioso no es grave. ______
4 ... los médicos dicen que necesita relajarse un poco. ______

4 There are two colloquialisms in the text which the writer has used to give it more expression. Can you find the Spanish for them?
1 What a shock! = ______
2 Good luck! = ______

5 Complete this "spider diagram" of words which are associated with fashion:

48

1 It is about a celebrity who has a break down because of the demands of fashion.
2 1 fotografiada
  2 talento
  3 desafortunadamente
  4 un ataque
3 1 star 2 suffering 3 serious 4 relax
4 1 ¡Qué susto! 2 ¡Buena suerte!
5 1 la ropa 2 de marca 3 modelo 4 de moda

¡Extra! 2 (Pupil's Book pages 92–93)

Learning objectives
- Reading a story in Spanish
- Learning about cultural aspects of South America

Framework objectives
3.1/Y8 Culture – changes in everyday life

Key language
Revision of language from Module 5

High-frequency words
Revision of language from Module 5

Cross-curricular
Citizenship: Information about other cultures
ICT: Internet research

Resources
CD3, tracks 19–20

Starter

Aim
To lead into episode 5 of the story.

Put the class into teams and tell them they have three minutes to come up with as many facts about either Diego or Patricia in Spanish as they can in that time. You will award a point for each correct statement and two points if none of the other teams has come up with that fact too.

1 Escucha y lee. (AT1.4) ▸▸2.2a/Y8 5.4◂◂

Listening. Pupils listen to the recording of the story and read along with the text. Some vocabulary is glossed for support.

Audioscript Track 19

1 – Te gusta mucho el dibujo, Patricia, ¿verdad?
– Sí, me encanta, me encanta. También me gusta ir de compras. Soy 'fashionista'. ¿Cuál es tu marca favorita, Diego?
2 – A ver, me gusta la ropa de Tommy Hilfiger y de Nike. ¿Quién es tu diseñador favorito?
3 – Bueno… me gusta mucho Stella McCartney. Es genial. Pero yo misma diseño unas cosas de vez en cuando. ¡Mira! ¡Tengo unas ideas para tu guardarropa!
4 – ¡Es chulo! Me gusta muchísimo.
– ¿Vamos a mirar escaparates un poco?
5 – ¡Qué guay! Me encantan estas zapatillas azules y amarillas. No son caras y son superchulas.
6 – Tenemos mucho en común, Patricia, ¿verdad?
– Sí, Diego, tenemos mucho en común…

2 Con tu compañero/a, lee en voz alta la historia de Patricia y Diego. (AT2.4) ▸▸5.6◂◂

Speaking. In pairs pupils read the story aloud, each taking the role of Diego or Patricia. Encourage them to focus on pronunciation and stress and to try and sound as fluent as possible, following the model of the recording.

3 Copia y completa las frases. (AT4.3, AT3.4) ▸▸4.4/Y8◂◂

Writing. Pupils copy out and complete the six sentences summarising episode 5 of the story.

Answers

1 A Patricia le gusta el dibujo e **ir de compras**.
2 Las marcas favoritas de Diego son **Tommy Hilfiger y Nike**.
3 La diseñadora favorita de Patricia es **Stella McCartney**.
4 Ella misma diseña **unas cosas (de vez en cuando)**.
5 Van a mirar **escaparates (un poco)**.
6 Tienen mucho **en común**.

4 Copia y completa el texto. (AT4.3) ▸▸5.4◂◂

Writing. Pupils copy and complete the gap-fill text, using the words supplied.

Answers

Me encanta ir de compras. ¡Jean Paul Gaultier es mi (**1**) **diseñador** favorito! Ayer compré dos (**2**) **vaqueros** negros y unas botas (**3**) **negras**. Por la noche (**4**) **fui** al concierto de Pink. Mañana (**5**) **voy a comprar** una camiseta de manga (**6**) **corta** y un jersey (**7**) **de lunares**. Normalmente llevo el pelo de color (**8**) **verde**.
Pepe

5 Pon las frases en el orden correcto. Luego escucha y comprueba tus respuestas. (AT3.5) ▸▸3.1/Y8 5.3 5.4 5.5◂◂

Reading. Pupils read the five sentences and put them in logical order. They should use reading strategies to work out new vocabulary as a first resort, and then use the Vocabulario section at the back of the Pupil's Book. They then listen and check their answers.

Audioscript Track 20

Un poncho consiste en un trozo de lana rectangular con abertura central.
Es un tipo de abrigo.
Hay muchos diseños y colores diferentes.
De origen andino, el poncho era parte de la vestimenta habitual de los nativos amerindios de la región.
Fue esencial para los gauchos que habitaron las llanuras argentinas.

Answers

c, b, e, d, a

6 Haz una lista de 12 palabras cognadas (cognates) en el texto del ejercicio 5. (AT3.5) ▸▸5.3◂◂

Reading. Pupils re-read the text in exercise 5 and make a list of 12 cognates.

Answers

Any 12 from:
esencial, argentinas, tipo, poncho, consiste, rectangular, central, origen, andino, parte, habitual, nativos, amerindios, región, muchos, diseños, colores, diferentes

7 Traduce el texto del ejercicio 5 al inglés. (AT3.5) ▸▸2.1/Y8 2.2a/Y8◂◂

Reading. Pupils translate the reordered text in exercise 5 into English.

Answers

A poncho consists of a piece of rectangular woollen cloth with an opening in the centre.
It is a type of coat.
There are many designs and different colours.
Of Andean origin/From the Andes in origin, the poncho is part of the typical clothing of the native Amerindians/American Indians of the region.
It was essential for the gauchos/cowboys who lived on the Argentinian plains.

Suggestion ▸▸3.1/Y8◂◂

Discuss the difference between the original use of the garments (utility, tradition) and their current use (tourism). Encourage the pupils to explain in Spanish using past and present tenses.

Pupils could choose and research an item of traditional Latin American clothing on the internet. They could then write a description, using the text in exercise 5 as a model.

Plenary ▸▸5.8◂◂

Put the class into teams for a verb quiz, revising the verbs and structures of the module. Team by team, give each pupil a verb form: they have to tell you what tense it is in – present, preterite or near future. A correct answer wins two points. Pupils can ask you to write up the verb for support, but will then only win one point for a correct answer. The points for each team are totalled to give the overall winners.

Te toca a ti (Pupil's Book pages 122–123)

- Self-access reading and writing at two levels

A Reinforcement

1 *Unjumble these items of clothing and then match them to the pictures.* (AT3.2) ▸▸5.2◂◂

Reading. Pupils unscramble the anagrams to find the items of clothing and match each one to the appropriate picture.

Answers

1 *unas botas – j*	**7** una gorra – d
2 una camiseta – f	**8** una sudadera – i
3 un jersey – a	**9** una falda – c
4 unos vaqueros – g	**10** unas zapatillas de deporte – e
5 un vestido – b	**11** una chaqueta – k
6 unos zapatos – h	**12** unos pantalones – l

2 *Write eight sentences saying whether or not you like these items of clothing.* (AT4.3) ▸▸4.3/Y8 4.6b/Y8◂◂

Writing. Using the picture + symbol prompts, pupils say whether or not they like the items of clothing. A tip box summarises the structures for expressing likes/dislikes.

Answers

1. *Me gusta este jersey.*
2. Me gustan estas botas.
3. No me gusta esta sudadera.
4. No me gustan estos vaqueros.
5. Me gustan estas zapatillas de deporte.
6. Me gusta esta falda.
7. No me gusta este vestido.
8. No me gusta esta camiseta.

3 *Copy out the text and fill the gaps with phrases from the box. (There is one phrase too many.)* (AT4.3, AT3.5) ▸▸4.5a/Y8◂◂

Writing. Pupils copy and complete the gap-fill text, replacing each picture prompt with the appropriate phrase from the list supplied. (There is one phrase too many.)

Answers

¡Hola! Me llamo Cintia. Soy chilena. Me gustan (**1**) **los videojuegos**. Me encanta (**2**) **leer** y (**3**) **escuchar música** también.
Normalmente llevo (**4**) **una falda** y (**5**) **una camiseta** pero mañana voy a ir de excursión.
Primero voy a montar en bicicleta y luego voy a montar a caballo. Voy a llevar (**6**) **unos vaqueros**, (**7**) **unas botas** y (**8**) **una sudadera**.

B Extension

1 *Which item is the most expensive? List the items in order, from least expensive to most expensive.* (AT3.3) ▸▸5.4◂◂

Reading. Pupils read the five statements about the items of clothing and use the information to work out how expensive the items are compared to one another. They list the items from cheapest to most expensive.

Answers

la gorra, la camiseta, la falda, las botas, las zapatillas de deporte, los zapatos

2 *Write the opposites of these adjectives.* (AT4.2, AT3.2) ▸▸4.2/Y8◂◂

Writing. Pupils write the opposites of the four adjectives listed.

Answers

1 bonito **2** cómodo **3** barato **4** guay

3 *Copy out the conversation and fill the gaps with words from the box. (There is one word too many.)* (AT4.3, AT3.3) ▸▸2.2a/Y8◂◂

Writing. Pupils copy out and complete the gap-fill text, using the words supplied. (There is one word too many.)

Answers

- Me gusta mucho (**1**) **esta** camiseta. ¿(**2**) **Cuál** prefieres, Anita?
- (**3**) **Prefiero** esta porque es (**4**) **menos** cara.
- No, no, esta es mucho (**5**) **más** bonita y además es (**6**) **cómoda**.

4 *Translate these sentences into Spanish.* (AT4.4) ▸▸4.4/Y8 5.3◂◂

Writing. Pupils translate the six sentences into Spanish.

Answers

1. *Este jersey es el más cómodo.*
2. Esta camiseta es la más barata.
3. Este vestido es el menos caro.
4. Esta sudadera es la menos cómoda.
5. Estos vaqueros son los más bonitos.
6. Estas botas son las más prácticas.

Module 6 Barcelona (Pupil's Book pages 96–113)

Unit	Framework	Levels and PoS	Key language	Grammar	Skills
1 La ciudad (pp. 96–97) Saying what there is to see and do in Barcelona Justifying your opinions of a place	**2.3/Y8** Reading – text features: emotive **2.5/Y8** Writing – using researched language	**2–4** **2.1d** previous knowledge **2.2g** write clearly and coherently **3c** apply grammar **3d** use a range of vocab/ structures **3e** different countries/ cultures **4e** use a range of resources **4f** language for interest/ enjoyment	*¿Qué hay en Barcelona?* *En Barcelona hay el acuario.* *¿Adónde vas?* *Voy...* *al acuario* *al Camp Nou* *al cine IMAX* *al monumento a Colón* *al museo Picasso* *al Tibidabo* *a la playa de la Barceloneta y el mar* *a la plaza de Cataluña* *a la Sagrada Familia* *a la torre Agbar* *a la Villa Olímpica* *a las Ramblas* *Me/Le gusta Barcelona porque...* *Me/Le encanta...* *Me/Le gusta mucho...* *ir de compras* *montar en las atracciones del parque* *sacar fotos* *tomar el sol* *ver esculturas* *ver partidos de fútbol* *ver películas* *ver tiburones*	Comparatives and superlatives (revision) *me gusta/me encanta* + verb/noun	Using reading strategies to work out new words Recognising and using techniques to improve writing

continued

Module 6 Barcelona (Pupil's Book pages 96–113)

Unit	Framework	Levels and PoS	Key language	Grammar	Skills
2 De compras en Barcelona (pp. 98–99) Talking about different types of shop Using *se puede* to say what can be bought there	**5.4** Strategies – working out meaning	**3–6** **2.1a** identify patterns **2.1b** memorising **2.1c** knowledge of language **2.1d** previous knowledge **2.1e** use reference materials	*¿Dónde se* ***puede*** *comprar… ?* *carne* *comida* *pan* *ropa* *un café* *un regalo* *¿Dónde se* ***pueden*** *comprar… ?* *pasteles* *joyas* *zapatos* *libros* *CDs* *Se puede(n) comprar… en…* *un supermercado* *una cafetería* *una carnicería* *una joyería* *una librería* *una panadería* *una pastelería* *una tienda de música* *una tienda de ropa* *una zapatería*	*se puede/se pueden* + infinitive	Using reading strategies to work out new words Developing vocabulary learning skills Developing independence as a learner Using reference resources

continued

Module 6 Barcelona (Pupil's Book pages 96–113)

Unit	Framework	Levels and PoS	Key language	Grammar	Skills
3 ¿Dónde está? (pp. 100–101) Asking for and giving directions Using *estar* to describe where something is		2–4 **2.1b** memorising **2.2c** respond appropriately **2.2e** ask and answer questions **2.2f** initiate/sustain conversations **3c** apply grammar **4b** communicate in pairs etc. **4e** use a range of resources **4f** language for interest/ enjoyment	*Perdón…* *¿Dónde está el museo Picasso?* *¿Dónde están las Ramblas?* *A ver…* *Bueno…* *Pues…* *luego* *Sigue todo recto.* *Dobla a la derecha.* *Dobla a la izquierda.* *Cruza la plaza.* *Toma la primera calle a la derecha.* *Toma la segunda calle a la izquierda.* *(Está) al final de la calle.* *Está a la derecha.* *Está a la izquierda.* *Está aquí.*	*estar* (present tense) Contrasting *ser* and *estar*	Developing vocabulary learning skills Using reference resources Participating in an unscripted dialogue Working on sounding authentic Reviewing progress/ checking work using the Mini-test
4 Soy turista en Barcelona (pp. 102–103) Describing a holiday in Barcelona Combining past, present and future tenses		5–6 **2.2g** write clearly and coherently **2.2j** adapt previously learned language **2.2k** deal with unfamiliar language **3c** apply grammar **3e** different countries/ cultures **3f** compare experiences **4b** communicate in pairs etc.	*Hoy…* *Estoy en Barcelona.* *Es genial.* *Anteayer…* *Ayer por la tarde…* *fui a la playa* *comí paella y bebí limonada* *descansé un poco* *Lo pasé fenomenal.* *Me gustó.* *No me gustó.* *Mañana…* *Pasado mañana…* *voy a ir al Tibidabo* *voy a ir de compras* *voy a comprar unas camisetas*	Using a range of tenses: preterite, present and near future	Using different tenses appropriately Communicating with native speakers Participating in an unscripted dialogue Writing an extended text in Spanish

continued

Module 6 Barcelona (Pupil's Book pages 96–113)

Unit	Framework	Levels and PoS	Key language	Grammar	Skills
5 Barcelona en tus sueños (pp. 104–105) Reading a story set in Barcelona Writing creatively	**2.4/Y8** Writing – (a) using text as stimulus	**2–6** **2.2b** skim and scan **2.2h** redraft to improve writing **2.2i** reuse language they have met **3a** spoken and written language **3d** use a range of vocab/ structures **4c** use more complex language **4e** use a range of resources **4f** language for interest/ enjoyment	Revision of language from Module 6		Identifying key information by skim-reading a text Working on sounding authentic by copying Spanish models Understanding a longer text in Spanish (comic strip) Using different tenses appropriately Writing creatively in Spanish
Resumen/ Prepárate (pp. 106–107) Pupils' checklist and practice test		**3–6**			Reviewing progress/ checking work
¡Extra! 1 (pp. 108–109) Learning about famous people Practising Spanish pronunciation	**3.1/Y8** Culture – changes in everyday life	**3–5** **2.1d** previous knowledge **2.2d** pronunciation and intonation **4f** language for interest/ enjoyment **4g** language for a range of purposes	Revision of language from Module 6		Working on sounding authentic Understanding a longer/authentic text in Spanish (historical information) Using reading strategies to work out new words

continued

Module 6 Barcelona (Pupil's Book pages 96–113)

Unit	Framework	Levels and PoS	Key language	Grammar	Skills
¡Extra! 2 (pp. 110–111) Looking for cognates within a text Learning cultural facts about Barcelona		2–4 **2.1d** previous knowledge **2.2d** pronunciation and intonation **2.2g** write clearly and coherently **3d** use a range of vocab/ structures **4e** use a range of resources **4f** language for interest/ enjoyment	Revision of language from Module 6		Using reading strategies to work out new words Understanding a longer text in Spanish (ongoing photo story)
Te toca a ti (pp. 124–125)	Self-access reading and writing at two levels				

1 La ciudad (Pupil's Book pages 96–97)

Learning objectives

- Saying what there is to see and do in Barcelona
- Justifying your opinions of a place

Framework objectives

2.3/Y8 Reading – text features: emotive
2.5/Y8 Writing – using researched language

Grammar

- Comparatives and superlatives (revision)
- *me gusta/me encanta* + verb/ noun

Key language

¿Qué hay en Barcelona?
En Barcelona hay el acuario.

¿Adónde vas?
Voy...
al acuario/Camp Nou/cine IMAX/monumento a Colón/ museo Picasso/Tibidabo
a la playa de la Barceloneta y el mar/plaza de Cataluña/Sagrada Familia/torre Agbar/Villa Olímpica
a las Ramblas
Me/Le gusta Barcelona porque...
Me/Le encanta...
Me/Le gusta mucho...
ir de compras
montar en las atracciones del parque
sacar fotos
tomar el sol
ver esculturas
ver partidos de fútbol
ver películas
ver tiburones

High-frequency words

el, la, las
me, le
a (al)
de (del)
en
mucho
porque
y
¿qué?
ir (voy, vas)
tomar
ver
hay

Cross-curricular

English: Comparatives and superlatives
ICT: Internet research

Resources

CD3, tracks 21–23
Cuadernos A & B, p. 52

Teacher Presentations

Screen 1 – Module 6 overview
Screen 2 – Vocabulary: Flashcards
Screen 3 – p. 96 ex. 2
Screen 4 – p. 97 ex. 4

Starter 1

Aim
To revise language for expressing an opinion.

Draw six groups of symbols:

☺, ☺☺, ☺☺☺; ☹, ☹☹, ☹☹☹

Give pupils working in pairs three minutes to come up with a suitable expression in Spanish for each of the symbols. If they need support, give them *me gusta mucho* as the expression for ☺☺ or give all the expressions in random order (*me gusta/me gusta mucho/me encanta; no me gusta/no me gusta nada/odio*).

Suggestion

Write up *¿Qué hay en* [+ the name of your town]? *Hay...*

Give a few examples of shops in your town (by name rather than type, so, e.g., Waterstones, M&S, etc.). Ask the class the question and get them to come up with some answers of their own.

Ask the class what *¿Qué hay en Barcelona?* means and how they would begin an answer. Ask if anyone has ever been to Barcelona. Can they complete the answer with places to visit there?

1 Escucha y repite. (AT1.2) ▸▸4.2/Y8◂◂

Listening. Pupils listen to someone listing all the things there are to see in Barcelona and repeat each of the 12 places mentioned.

Point out that although *las Ramblas* is plural the verb form remains the same: *hay*.

Audioscript Track 21

– ¿Qué hay en Barcelona?
– En Barcelona hay muchas cosas.
a *El monumento a Colón.*
b *El Camp Nou.*
c *El museo Picasso.*
d *El acuario.*
e *El Tibidabo.*
f *El cine IMAX.*
g *La torre Agbar.*
h *La Villa Olímpica.*
i *La Sagrada Familia.*
j *La plaza de Cataluña.*
k *La playa de la Barceloneta y el mar.*
l *Las Ramblas.*

Pupils working in pairs choose three of the Barcelona sights shown and research them in English on the internet. Set them the challenge of coming up with three facts on each.

This could form the basis of a project on Barcelona that pupils could work on throughout the time the class is doing Module 6. Suggestions have been made for research topics throughout the module.

You might prefer to put pupils in groups and allocate the groups specific areas of research, with each group working towards doing a short presentation to the class at the end of the module.

Suggestion

As a class, read through the key language box before playing the recording. Ask pupils to translate all the expressions into English. Can they work out what *ver tiburones* means using reading strategies? (specifically using the example and what they know to eliminate other options)

2 ¿Adónde van? Escucha y escribe la letra del ejercicio 1 y la razón en inglés. (1–8) (AT1.3) ▸▸1.2/Y8◂◂

Listening. Pupils listen to eight conversations and note where each person is going (using the pictures *a–l* in exercise 1) and his/her reason in English. Some vocabulary is glossed for support.

Audioscript Track 22

1 – *¿Adónde vas?*
– *Voy al acuario porque me gusta mucho ver tiburones.*
2 – *¿Y tú? ¿Adónde vas?*
– *Voy al museo Picasso. Me encanta mirar pinturas.*
3 – *¿Adónde vas?*
– *Voy al cine IMAX. Me gusta mucho ver películas.*
4 – *¡Hola! ¿Adónde vas?*
– *Ehh, bueno, me gusta ir de compras y voy al Corte Inglés en la plaza de Cataluña.*
5 – *¿Y tú? ¿Adónde vas?*
– *Voy a la torre Agbar. Me encanta sacar fotos.*
6 – *Buenos días. ¿Adónde vas?*
– *Voy al Camp Nou. Me encanta el fútbol y me gusta mucho ver partidos de fútbol.*
7 – *¿Adónde vas?*
– *Voy al Tibidabo. Me encanta montar en las atracciones del parque.*
8 – *¿Y tú? ¿Adónde vas?*
– *Voy a la playa de la Barceloneta a tomar el sol. Me gusta tomar el sol.*

Answers

1 *d – likes watching sharks*
2 c – loves looking at pictures
3 f – likes watching films a lot
4 j – likes shopping and is going to El Corte Inglés at the Plaza Cataluña
5 g – loves taking photos
6 b – loves football and likes watching football matches a lot
7 e – loves going on the rides at the theme park
8 k – likes sunbathing

Starter 2 ▸▸4.3/Y8◂◂

Aim

To revise *a* with the definite article.

Write up *a* + *el* = and ask pupils to supply the missing form. Ask them what happens when *a* is followed by *la/los/las*.

Give the places in exercise 1 as prompts, randomly organised (e.g. *el Tibidabo*). Pupils respond with *Voy* + the correct form of *a* + the place (e.g. *Voy al Tibidabo*).

3 Con tu compañero/a, pregunta y contesta. (AT2.3) ▸▸1.4a/Y8 4.4/Y8◂◂

Speaking. In pairs: pupils take it in turn to ask *¿Adónde vas?* and to respond with a place and reason, using the picture prompts supplied. A sample exchange is given.

➕ Pupils continue the activity using the other locations in Barcelona from exercise 1 and giving an appropriate reason.

4 Escucha y elige la frase correcta. (1–5) (AT1.3–4) ▸▸1.1/Y8◂◂

Listening. Pupils listen to five conversations in which people say whether they like living in Barcelona or not and why. They identify the sentence used in each conversation from the list supplied (*a–e*).

Audioscript Track 23

1 – *¡Hola! ¿Te gusta vivir en Barcelona?*
– *Por supuesto, es una ciudad histórica. Es muy interesante.*
2 – *¿Te gusta vivir en Barcelona?*
– *Sí, me gusta mucho. Es la ciudad más bonita de España. Es guay.*
3 – *¿Te gusta vivir en Barcelona?*
– *Ah, sí… me gusta vivir en Barcelona. Es grande, pero menos grande que Madrid.*
4 – *¿Te gusta vivir en Barcelona?*
– *No, no me gusta porque es muy turística. Es menos turística que Benidorm, por ejemplo, pero todavía hay muchos turistas.*
5 – *¿Te gusta vivir en Barcelona?*
– *Claro, me gusta mucho vivir en Barcelona porque es una ciudad importante. Es una ciudad industrial, pero también es antigua.*

Answers

1 *c* 2 e 3 a 4 d 5 b

Suggestion

Read through the tip box summarising the use of *me/le gusta(n)* and *me/le encanta(n)*.

5 Lee los textos y contesta a las preguntas para cada persona. (AT3.4) ▸▸2.3/Y8 4.6a/Y8◂◂

Reading. Pupils read the website texts and for each of the people answer the three questions. Some vocabulary is glossed for support.

Remind pupils as necessary that they should use the language of the questions to help them structure their responses.

Answers

Juanita

1 Sí, le gusta mucho Barcelona.
2 Hay mucha variedad. Hay barrios históricos y barrios modernos y más tranquilos.
3 Le gusta andar en monopatín y sacar fotos de la gente.

Hugo

1 No, no le gusta nada Barcelona.
2 Es muy turística. En el Camp Nou, las entradas son muy caras. Prefiere vivir en una ciudad menos turística y menos importante.
3 Le gusta ver partidos de fútbol.

Ask pupils to re-read the texts and to identify all the examples they can of the following:

- connectives
- negatives
- language for expressing ideas/attitudes/opinions
- the comparative
- the superlative
- any other features that emphasise how the writer feels (*superguay*, the emoticons)

6 Describe tu ciudad. (AT4.3–4) ▸▸2.1/Y8 2.4a/Y8 2.5/Y8◂◂

Writing. Using the texts in exercise 5 as models, pupils write a short text describing their own town. Sample paragraph openings are supplied.

Encourage pupils to include in their texts as many of the features listed in the Extension activity for exercise 5 as possible.

You could supply local information brochures or ask pupils to bring these in. Alternatively they could look on websites about local areas for ideas.

Plenary ▸▸5.8◂◂

Ask pupils how to ask what there is in a city and how to begin an answer. Then get them to tell you what expressions were used to give an opinion in this unit: *me gusta/me gusta mucho*, etc.

Put the class into teams. Give them three minutes to write down as many expressions as they can using one of the opinion expressions they have just summarised + a place in Barcelona or an activity from the unit (with Pupil's Books closed). Pupils then swap lists and check each other's answers, awarding two points for a completely correct item and one point if there is an error.

Cuaderno A, page 52

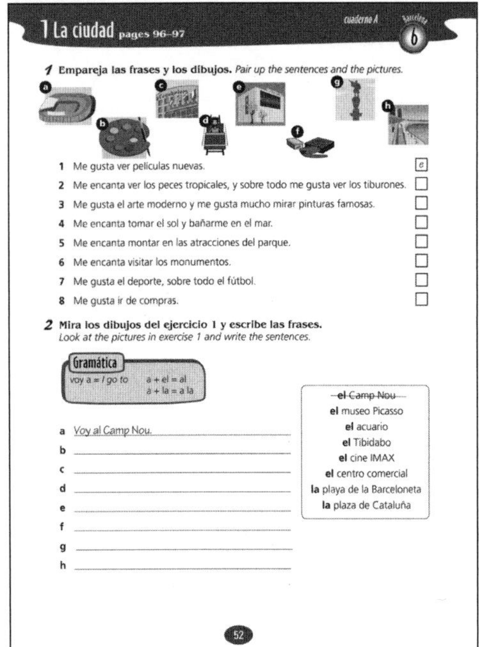

1 La ciudad pages 96–97 · cuaderno A · Barcelona 6

1 **Empareja las frases y los dibujos.** *Pair up the sentences and the pictures.*

1 Me gusta ver películas nuevas. [e]
2 Me encanta ver los peces tropicales, y sobre todo me gusta ver los tiburones. [ ]
3 Me gusta el arte moderno y me gusta mucho mirar pinturas famosas. [ ]
4 Me encanta tomar el sol y bañarme en el mar. [ ]
5 Me encanta montar en las atracciones del parque. [ ]
6 Me encanta visitar los monumentos. [ ]
7 Me gusta el deporte, sobre todo el fútbol. [ ]
8 Me gusta ir de compras. [ ]

2 **Mira los dibujos del ejercicio 1 y escribe las frases.**
Look at the pictures in exercise 1 and write the sentences.

Gramática
voy a = *I go to* a + el = al
a + la = a la

~~el Camp Nou~~
el museo Picasso
el acuario
el Tibidabo
el cine IMAX
el centro comercial
la playa de la Barceloneta
la plaza de Cataluña

a *Voy al Camp Nou.*
b ______
c ______
d ______
e ______
f ______
g ______
h ______

52

1 (AT3.2)

1 *e* **2** c **3** b **4** h **5** d **6** g **7** a **8** f

2 (AT4.3)

a *Voy al Camp Nou.*
b Voy al museo Picasso.
c Voy al acuario.
d Voy al Tibidabo.
e Voy al cine IMAX.
f Voy al centro comercial.
g Voy a la plaza de Cataluña.
h Voy a la playa de la Barceloneta.

Cuaderno B, page 52

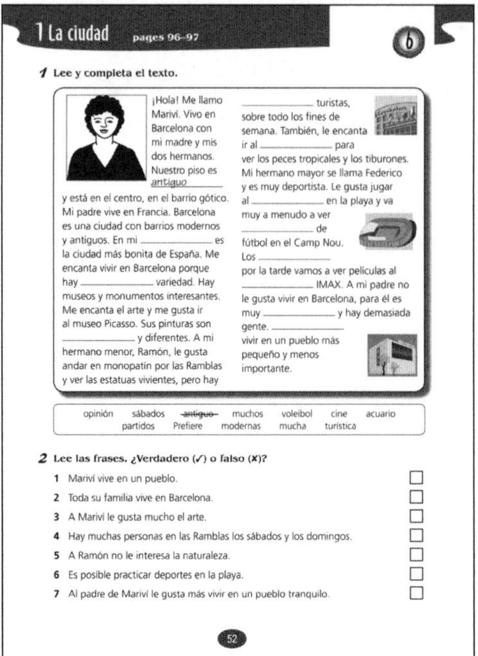

1 La ciudad pages 96–97 · 6

1 **Lee y completa el texto.**

¡Hola! Me llamo Mariví. Vivo en Barcelona con mi madre y mis dos hermanos. Nuestro piso es *antiguo* y está en el centro, en el barrio gótico. Mi padre vive en Francia. Barcelona es una ciudad con barrios modernos y antiguos. En mi ______ es la ciudad más bonita de España. Me encanta vivir en Barcelona porque hay ______ variedad. Hay museos y monumentos interesantes. Me encanta el arte y me gusta ir al museo Picasso. Sus pinturas son ______ y diferentes. A mi hermano menor, Ramón, le gusta andar en monopatín por las Ramblas y ver las estatuas vivientes, pero hay ______ turistas, sobre todo los fines de semana. También, le encanta ir al ______ para ver los peces tropicales y los tiburones. Mi hermano mayor se llama Federico y es muy deportista. Le gusta jugar al ______ en la playa y va muy a menudo a ver ______ de fútbol en el Camp Nou. Los ______ por la tarde vamos a ver películas al ______ IMAX. A mi padre no le gusta vivir en Barcelona, para él es muy ______ y hay demasiada gente. ______ vivir en un pueblo más pequeño y menos importante.

opinión sábados ~~antiguo~~ muchos voleibol cine acuario
partidos Prefiere modernas mucha turística

2 **Lee las frases. ¿Verdadero (✓) o falso (✗)?**

1 Mariví vive en un pueblo. [ ]
2 Toda su familia vive en Barcelona. [ ]
3 A Mariví le gusta mucho el arte. [ ]
4 Hay muchas personas en las Ramblas los sábados y los domingos. [ ]
5 A Ramón no le interesa la naturaleza. [ ]
6 Es posible practicar deportes en la playa. [ ]
7 Al padre de Mariví le gusta más vivir en un pueblo tranquilo. [ ]

52

1 (AT3.4, AT4.1)

¡Hola! Me llamo Mariví. Vivo en Barcelona con mi madre y mis dos hermanos. Nuestro piso es *antiguo* y está en el centro, en el barrio gótico. Mi padre vive en un pueblo pequeño en Francia. Barcelona es una ciudad con barrios modernos y antiguos. En mi opinión es la ciudad más bonita de España. Me encanta vivir en Barcelona porque hay mucha variedad. Hay museos y monumentos interesantes. Me encanta el arte y me gusta ir al museo Picasso. Sus pinturas son modernas y diferentes. A mi hermano menor, Ramón, le gusta andar en monopatín por las Ramblas y ver las estatuas vivientes, pero hay muchos turistas, sobre todo los fines de semana. También, le encanta ir al acuario para ver los peces tropicales y los tiburones. Mi hermano mayor se llama Federico y es muy deportista. Le gusta jugar al voleibol en la playa y va muy a menudo a ver partidos de fútbol en el Camp Nou. Los sábados por la tarde vamos a ver películas al cine IMAX. A mi padre no le gusta vivir en Barcelona, para él es muy turística y hay demasiada gente. Prefiere vivir en un pueblo más pequeño y menos importante.

2 (AT3.4)

1 ✗ **2** ✗ **3** ✓ **4** ✓ **5** ✗ **6** ✓ **7** ✓

2 De compras en Barcelona (Pupil's Book pages 98–99)

Learning objectives

- Talking about different types of shop
- Using *se puede* to say what can be bought there

Framework objectives

5.4 Strategies – working out meaning)

Grammar

- *se puede/se pueden* + infinitive

Key language

*¿Dónde **se puede** comprar... ?*
carne
comida
pan
ropa
un café
un regalo
*¿Dónde **se pueden** comprar... ?*
pasteles
joyas
zapatos
libros
CDs

Se puede(n) comprar... en...
un supermercado
una cafetería/carnicería/joyería/librería/panadería/pastelería/tienda de música/tienda de ropa/zapatería

High-frequency words

un, una
se
de
¿dónde?
comprar
poder (puede, pueden)

Resources

CD3, tracks 24–26
Cuadernos A & B, p. 53
Flashcards 77–86

Teacher Presentations

Screen 1 – Module 6 overview
Screen 2 – Vocabulary: Flashcards
Screen 3 – p. 98 ex. 1
Screen 4 – Vocabulary: Flashcards
Screen 5 – p. 98 ex. 2
Screen 6 – p. 99 ex. 5
Screen 7 – Game

Starter 1 ▸▸5.4◂◂

Aim

To use reading strategies to work out new vocabulary.

Write up the following, jumbling the order of the second column.

comida	*un supermercado*
un café	*una cafetería*
libros	*una librería*
zapatos	*una zapatería*
CDs	*una tienda de música*
pantalones	*una tienda de ropa*
carne	*una carnicería*
pan	*una panadería*

Give pupils two minutes working in pairs to match each item with the correct shop.

Check answers, getting pupils to translate all the items and shop names. (If they study French, prompt them with *pain* as a cognate for *pan.*)

Suggestion

Use Flashcards 77–86 to introduce the vocabulary for shops, prompting pupils to come up with the appropriate cognate(s), e.g. *zapatería – zapatos, zapatillas de deporte*, etc. (You will need to give them *joyas* and *pasteles* as these are new.)

Point out that spotting connections of this sort is a good way of becoming more independent as a learner. As well as improving their ability to cope when facing new vocabulary, making the link also helps with memorising vocabulary.

1 Escucha y escribe las letras en el orden correcto. (AT1.3) ▸▸4.2/Y8 5.4◂◂

Listening. Pupils note the shops in the order they are mentioned, using the pictures *a–j*.

Audioscript Track 24

En mi ciudad hay una tienda de música y una carnicería...
También hay una panadería y una librería... una joyería, un supermercado y una cafetería.
Hay una zapatería, una tienda de ropa y una pastelería.

Answers

h, c, a, g, e, j, b, f, i, d

R Pupils working in pairs take it in turn to prompt with an item in English (e.g. 'bracelet') and to respond in Spanish with the shop where you could buy it (e.g. *una joyería*).

Suggestion

Introduce *se puede* by asking and answering the question *¿Dónde se puede comprar un café?* Write up *se puede comprar*. Ask pupils to answer, prompting with *carne*, *ropa*, *comida* and *pan*.

Then ask and answer using the plural form *se pueden* (e.g. *¿Dónde se pueden comprar zapatos?*), writing up *se pueden comprar*. Ask pupils to answer, prompting with *libros*, *joyas*, *pasteles* and *CDs*.

Ask pupils to summarise when *se puede* and *se pueden* are used.

2 Escucha y escribe la letra correcta. Luego escucha y comprueba tus respuestas. (1–10) (AT1.3) ▸▸4.2/Y8 5.4◂◂

Listening. In each conversation the item to be purchased is beeped out. Pupils identify the item (from the pictures *a–j*), working it out from the shop that is mentioned.

Audioscript Track 25

(There are two recordings. In the first, the words in bold are beeped out.)

1 – *¿Dónde se puede comprar* ***carne****?*
– *Se puede comprar* ***carne*** *en la carnicería.*
2 – *¿Dónde se pueden comprar* ***libros****?*
– *Se pueden comprar* ***libros*** *en la librería.*
3 – *¿Dónde se pueden comprar* ***joyas****?*
– *Se pueden comprar* ***joyas*** *en la joyería.*
4 – *¿Dónde se puede comprar* ***ropa****?*
– *Se puede comprar* ***ropa*** *en la tienda de ropa.*
5 – *¿Dónde se pueden comprar* ***CDs****?*
– *Se pueden comprar* ***CDs*** *en la tienda de música.*
6 – *¿Dónde se puede comprar* ***un café****?*
– *Se puede comprar* ***un café*** *en la cafetería.*
7 – *¿Dónde se puede comprar* ***pan****?*
– *Se puede comprar* ***pan*** *en la panadería.*
8 – *¿Dónde se pueden comprar* ***zapatos****?*
– *Se pueden comprar* ***zapatos*** *en la zapatería.*
9 – *¿Dónde se puede comprar* ***comida****?*
– *Se puede comprar* ***comida*** *en el supermercado.*
10 – *¿Dónde se pueden comprar* ***pasteles****?*
– *Se pueden comprar* ***pasteles*** *en la pastelería.*

Answers

1 b **2** f **3** d **4** i **5** g **6** h **7** c **8** e **9** j **10** a

R Pupils working in pairs take it in turn to prompt with an item in Spanish (e.g. *libros*) and to respond with the correct form, *se puede* or *se pueden* + *comprar* (e.g. *se pueden comprar libros*).

Gramática: *se puede/se pueden* + infinitive

Use this to summarise how *se puede* and *se pueden* are used (with a singular/plural noun respectively). With a more able class, you could explain that this happens because the item being purchased is in fact the subject of the verb – *se pueden comprar libros* = 'books can be bought').

Ask pupils what the infinitive form of the verb forms *puede/pueden* is (*poder*). What kind of verb is it? Review stem-changing verbs briefly, directing pupils to the Gramática section at the back of the Pupil's Book for details of the various vowel changes.

What else can pupils tell you about *poder*, using *se puede comprar* as an example? (It is followed by the infinitive.)

There is practice on *se puede/se pueden* on page 134 of the Pupil's Book.

Starter 2 ▸▸1.5b/Y8 4.5b/Y8◂◂

Aim
To practise using *se puede/se pueden*.

Write up the following English prompts (answers in brackets for reference):

You can...

1	eat fruit	*(Se puede comer fruta.)*
2	send messages	*(Se pueden mandar mensajes.)*
3	drink tea	*(Se puede beber té.)*
4	watch television	*(Se puede ver la televisión.)*
5	read books	*(Se pueden leer libros.)*
6	buy a bottle of water	*(Se puede comprar una botella de agua.)*
7	take photos	*(Se pueden sacar fotos.)*
8	wear jeans	*(Se pueden llevar vaqueros.)*

Give pupils three minutes working in pairs to write a sentence for each of the English prompts, using the appropriate form: *se puede* or *se pueden*.

If pupils need support, you could supply the Spanish infinitives or all of the Spanish phrases in jumbled order.

Suggestion

Quickly review when *se puede* and *se pueden* are used. If pupils found Starter 2 difficult, consolidate the structures by giving further practice using the items in exercise 2 on page 98 as prompts.

3 Con tu compañero/a, pregunta y contesta sobre los artículos del ejercicio 2. (AT2.4) ▸▸1.4a/Y8◂◂

Speaking. In pairs pupils take it in turn to ask and answer questions about where the items in exercise 2 on page 98 can be bought. A sample exchange is given.

4 Lee los textos y elige los dibujos correctos. (AT3.6) ▸▸2.2a/Y8 5.4◂◂

Reading. Pupils read the two texts (by Elisa and Pepita) and use the details in them to choose the correct picture (from *a–c*) for each girl.

Answers

Elisa b **Pepita** a

R Translate the texts as a class, with each pupil translating a sentence in turn.

5 Escucha. Copia y rellena la tabla. (AT1.6) ▸▸1.2/Y8◂◂

Listening. Pupils copy out the table. They listen to five conversations about shopping in Barcelona and complete the table with details of what kind of shop each person goes to and what he/she buys there, plus the name or descriptionof the shop where the item(s) was/were purchased.

Audioscript Track 26

Isabel

– *¿Te gusta ir de compras en Barcelona?*
– *Sí, me gusta mucho. A mí, me encantan los zapatos. Hoy por la mañana fui a una zapatería. Se llama Camper. Compré unos zapatos muy bonitos.*

Javier

– *¿Te gusta ir de compras en Barcelona?*
– *Bueno, no mucho. Ayer fui al supermercado del Corte Inglés. Compré pan, pasteles, carne, pescado y lechuga.*

Natalia

– *Buenas tardes. ¿Te gusta ir de compras?*
– *Sí, me encanta. Ayer fui a la Casa del Libro. Es una librería enorme. Se pueden comprar libros de todo tipo. Compré un libro y dos cómics.*

Miguel

– *¡Hola! ¿Qué tal?*
– *Bien gracias, muy bien.*
– *¿Hay tiendas interesantes en Barcelona?*
– *Claro que sí. Hay muchas tiendas de ropa. Ayer fui de compras con una amiga y fuimos a Zara y Mango. En Zara y Mango se pueden comprar ropa y zapatos. Compré una chaqueta y unos pantalones.*

José

– *¿Te gusta Barcelona?*
– *Sí, me encanta Barcelona, sobre todo las tiendas. La semana pasada fui de compras y me lo pasé genial.*
– *¿Ah sí? ¿Qué compraste?*
– *Compré un CD de Shakira. Fui a una tienda de música muy pequeña que se llama Daily Records.*

Answers

Nombre	Tienda	Artículo(s)	Más información
Isabel	*zapatería*	*zapatos*	*Camper*
Javier	supermercado	pan, pasteles, carne, pescado, lechuga	(en) El Corte Inglés
Natalia	librería	un libro y dos cómics	La Casa del Libro
Miguel	tiendas de ropa	chaqueta y pantalones	Zara, Mango
José	una tienda de música	CD	muy pequeña

6 Copia y completa el texto con las palabras del cuadro. (AT4.3, AT3.4) ▸▸4.4/Y8 5.4◂◂

Writing. Pupils copy and complete the gap-fill text using the words supplied. Some vocabulary support is given.

Answers

Ayer (*1*) ***fui*** de compras por Barcelona con mi hermano. (**2**) **Primero** fui a la Boquería – el mercado en las Ramblas – donde (**3**) **compré** pan y carne para la cena. Luego fui a una joyería (**4**) **donde** compré un regalo muy bonito para mi novia.
Después, con mi hermano, (**5**) **fuimos** a una cafetería cerca de la Boquería donde (**6**) **bebimos** café y comimos (**7**) **pasteles** muy ricos. (**8**) **Me gusta** mucho ir de compras en Barcelona. Nunca es aburrido.

Plenary ▸▸1.5b/Y8 4.5b/Y8◂◂

Ask pupils to summarise when you use *se puede* and *se pueden*, giving examples from the unit.

Play a chain game to practise using *se puede* and *se pueden*, plus the vocabulary for shops/items in shops. Ask the class to stand. Each pupil adds a word in turn to form a sentence (e.g. P1 *Se* – P2 *puede* – P3 *comprar* – P4 *pan* – P5 *en* – P6 *una* – P7 *panadería*). When a sentence is finished, the next pupil begins another. If a pupil makes a mistake or can't think of a word, he/she sits down. The last pupil standing is the winner.

Cuaderno A, page 53

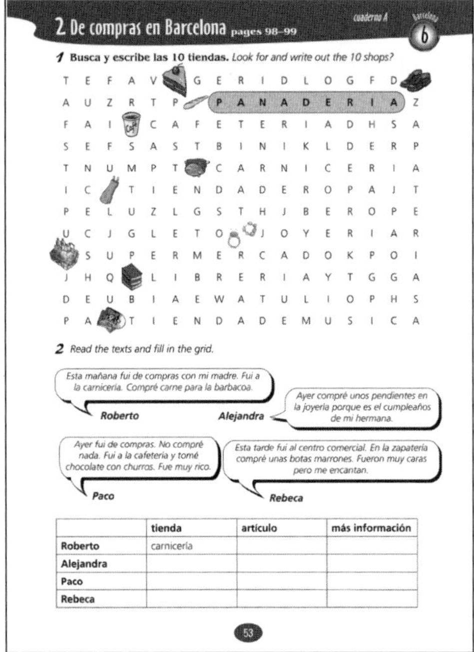
2 De compras en Barcelona pages 98–99 cuaderno A Barcelona 6

1 **Busca y escribe las 10 tiendas.** *Look for and write out the 10 shops?*

T E F A V G E R I D L O G F D
A U Z R T P P A N A D E R I A Z
F A I C A F E T E R I A D H S A
S E F S A S T B I N I K L D E R P
T N U M P T C A R N I C E R I A
I C T I E N D A D E R O P A J T
P E L U Z L G S T H J B E R O P E
U C J G L E T O J O Y E R I A R
S U P E R M E R C A D O K P O I
J H Q L I B R E R I A Y T G G A
D E U B I A E W A T U L I O P H S
P A T I E N D A D E M U S I C A

2 *Read the texts and fill in the grid.*

Esta mañana fui de compras con mi madre. Fui a la carnicería. Compré carne para la barbacoa. **Roberto**

Ayer compré unos pendientes en la joyería porque es el cumpleaños de mi hermana. **Alejandra**

Ayer fui de compras. No compré nada. Fui a la cafetería y tomé chocolate con churros. Fue muy rico. **Paco**

Esta tarde fui al centro comercial. En la zapatería compré unas botas marrones. Fueron muy caras pero me encantan. **Rebeca**

	tienda	artículo	más información
Roberto	carnicería		
Alejandra			
Paco			
Rebeca			

53

Cuaderno B, page 53

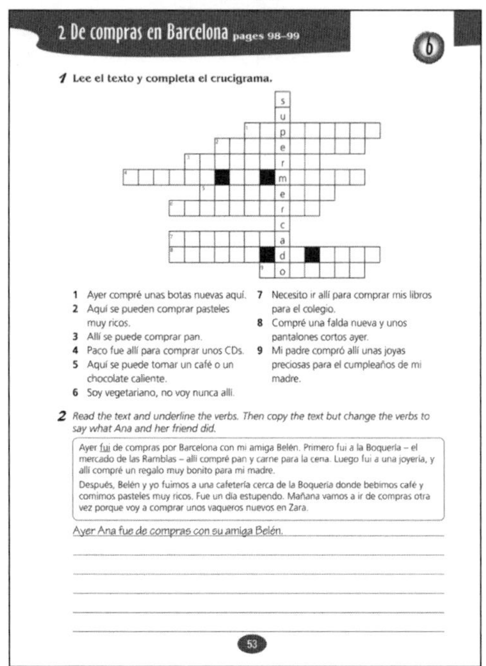
2 De compras en Barcelona pages 98–99 6

1 **Lee el texto y completa el crucigrama.**

s u p e r m e r c a d o

1 Ayer compré unas botas nuevas aquí.
2 Aquí se pueden comprar pasteles muy ricos.
3 Allí se puede comprar pan.
4 Paco fue allí para comprar unos CDs.
5 Aquí se puede tomar un café o un chocolate caliente.
6 Soy vegetariano, no voy nunca allí.
7 Necesito ir allí para comprar mis libros para el colegio.
8 Compré una falda nueva y unos pantalones cortos ayer.
9 Mi padre compró allí unas joyas preciosas para el cumpleaños de mi madre.

2 *Read the text and underline the verbs. Then copy the text but change the verbs to say what Ana and her friend did.*

Ayer fui de compras por Barcelona con mi amiga Belén. Primero fui a la Boquería – el mercado de las Ramblas – allí compré pan y carne para la cena. Luego fui a una joyería, y allí compré un regalo muy bonito para mi madre.

Después, Belén y yo fuimos a una cafetería cerca de la Boquería donde bebimos café y comimos pasteles muy ricos. Fue un día estupendo. Mañana vamos a ir de compras otra vez porque voy a comprar unos vaqueros nuevos en Zara.

Ayer Ana fue de compras con su amiga Belén.

53

1 (AT3.1)

panadería, cafetería, carnicería, tienda de ropa, joyería, supermercado, librería, tienda de música, pastelería, zapatería

2 (AT3.3, AT4.1)

	tienda	artículo	más información
Roberto	*carnicería*	carne	barbacoa
Alejandra	joyería	pendientes	cumpleaños de hermana
Paco	cafetería	chocolate con churros	muy rico
Rebeca	zapatería	botas marrones	caras pero le encantan

1 (AT3.2, AT4.2)

1 zapatería **2** pastelería **3** panadería
4 tienda de música **5** cafetería **6** carnicería
7 librería **8** tienda de ropa **9** joyería

2 (AT4.5)

Ayer *fui* de compras por Barcelona con mi amiga Belén. Primero fui a la Boquería – el mercado de las Ramblas – allí compré pan y carne para la cena. Luego fui a una joyería, y allí compré un regalo muy bonito para mi madre.

Después, Belén y yo fuimos a una cafetería cerca de la Boquería donde bebimos café y comimos pasteles muy ricos. Fue un día estupendo. Mañana vamos a ir de compras otra vez porque voy a comprar unos nuevos vaqueros en Zara.

Ayer Ana fue de compras por Barcelona con su amiga Belén. Primero fue a la Boquería – el mercado de Las Ramblas – allí compró pan y carne para la cena. Luego fue a una joyería, y allí compró un regalo muy bonito para su madre.

Después, Belén y Ana fueron a una cafetería cerca de la Boquería donde bebieron café y comieron pasteles muy ricos. Fue un día estupendo. Mañana van a ir de compras otra vez porque Ana va a comprar unos vaqueros nuevos en Zara.

3 ¿Dónde está? (Pupil's Book pages 100–101)

Learning objectives
- Asking for and giving directions
- Using *estar* to describe where something is

Grammar
- *estar* (present tense)
- Contrasting *ser* and *estar*

Key language
Perdón...
¿Dónde está el museo Picasso?
¿Dónde están las Ramblas?
A ver...
Bueno...
Pues...
luego

Sigue todo recto.
Dobla a la derecha.
Dobla a la izquierda.
Cruza la plaza.
Toma la primera calle a la derecha.
Toma la segunda calle a la izquierda.
(Está) al final de la calle.
Está a la derecha.
Está a la izquierda.
Está aquí.

High-frequency words
el, la, las
a (al)
aquí
todo
¿dónde?
estar (está, están)
tomar (toma)

Resources
CD3, tracks 27–30
Cuadernos A & B, p. 54
R & A Pack, Gramática pp. 25–26
Flashcards 87–96

Teacher Presentations
Screen 1 – Module 6 overview
Screen 2 – Vocabulary: Flashcards
Screen 3 – p. 100 ex. 1
Screen 4 – p. 100 ex. 2
Screen 5 – p. 101 ex. 3
Screen 6 – p. 101 ex. 6
Screen 7 – Game

Starter 1

Aim
To revise places in Barcelona.

Write up (missing words in brackets for reference):

1	** * Olímpica*	*(la Villa)*
2	** Ramblas*	*(las)*
3	** * a Colón*	*(el monumento)*
4	*el * IMAX*	*(cine)*
5	** Camp **	*(el, Nou)*
6	** torre Agbar*	*(la)*
7	** * * Cataluña*	*(la plaza de)*
8	** * Picasso*	*(el museo)*
9	** * de la Barceloneta*	*(la playa)*
10	*el **	*(acuario)*

Explain each star represents a missing word and give pupils three minutes to complete the names of these famous places in Barcelona.

1 Escucha y repite las direcciones. (AT1.2) ▸▸4.2/Y8◂◂

Listening. Pupils listen to ten directions, reading the text and looking at the picture given for each in the Pupil's Book at the same time. Pause the recording after each one for pupils to repeat the direction.

Point out to pupils the usefulness of making simple drawings like the ones in this exercise when noting and learning language like directions.

Audioscript Track 27

1 *Sigue todo recto.*
2 *Dobla a la derecha.*
3 *Dobla a la izquierda.*
4 *Cruza la plaza.*
5 *Toma la segunda calle a la derecha.*
6 *Toma la segunda calle a la izquierda.*
7 *Está al final de la calle.*
8 *Está a la derecha.*
9 *Está a la izquierda.*
10 *Está aquí.*

R Use Flashcards 87–96 to consolidate the language for directions.

Suggestion

Read the speech bubbles in exercise 2 together. Point out that when you are talking about something plural (e.g. *las Ramblas*), *está* changes to *están* – e.g.

– *¿Dónde están las Ramblas?*
– *Están aquí.*

2 Escucha y escribe el lugar y la dirección. (1–10) (AT1.3) ▸▸1.3b/Y8◂◂

Listening. Pupils listen to ten short recordings in which people are asking for directions. They identify the place mentioned (using pictures *a–j*) and note in English the direction given for each.

Audioscript Track 28

1 – *¿Dónde está el cine IMAX?*
– *A ver, sigue todo recto.*
2 – *¿Dónde están las Ramblas, por favor?*
– *¡¿Las Ramblas?! Están aquí.*
3 – *¿Dónde está la playa de la Barceloneta?*
– *Bueno, cruza la plaza y está al final de la calle.*

4 – *Perdón, ¿dónde está la plaza de Cataluña?*
– *Eh... toma la segunda calle a la izquierda.*
5 – *Por favor, ¿dónde está el monumento a Colón?*
– *A ver, sigue todo recto y está a la derecha.*
6 – *Dígame, ¿dónde está el Camp Nou?*
– *Mira, toma la segunda calle a la derecha y está al final de la calle.*
7 – *¿Dónde está la Villa Olímpica, por favor?*
– *A ver, sigue todo recto y está a la derecha.*
8 – *¿Dónde está el museo Picasso?*
– *El museo Picasso... a ver... dobla a la izquierda.*
9 – *Por favor, ¿por dónde se va al acuario?*
– *Bueno, a ver, toma la segunda calle a la derecha y luego sigue todo recto.*
10 – *Disculpe, ¿por dónde se va a la torre Agbar, por favor?*
– *Dobla a la derecha y está a la izquierda.*

Answers

1 *e – straight on*
2 j – here
3 i – cross the square; at the end of the street
4 h – the second street on the left
5 a – straight on; on the right
6 b – second street on the right; straight on
7 g – straight on; on the right
8 c – turn left
9 d – second street on the right; straight on
10 f – turn right; on the left

Gramática: *estar* (present tense)

Use this to cover the full present tense paradigm of *estar* and to point out when the two Spanish verbs meaning 'to be', *ser* and *estar*, are used:

estar = position/location and temporary states (e.g. to ask/say how someone feels)

ser = permanent states (e.g. to describe what someone looks like)

There is practice on using *ser/estar* appropriately on page 131 of the Pupil's Book.

R Ask pupils to look up the present tense of *ser* in the Gramática section at the back of the Pupil's Book. Get them working in pairs to test each other, prompting with the various forms of *estar* and *ser* in the present tense (e.g. *estamos*) for their partner to respond with the appropriate infinitive form (e.g. *estar*).

+ Pupils working in pairs prompt with *estar/ser* plus a pronoun in English (e.g. *ser* – she) for their partner to respond with the appropriate verb form in Spanish (e.g. *es*).

Starter 2 ▸▸ 4.5a/Y8 ◂◂

Aim

To practise using *ser/estar* as appropriate.

Write up the following, highlighting the options in each one (e.g. by using a different colour). (Answers underlined for reference.)

1 *Barcelona está/es bonita.*
2 *Estoy/Soy alto y delgado.*
3 *¿Dónde está/es tu casa?*
4 *Soy bajo y tengo el pelo negro. ¿Y tú? ¿Cómo estás/eres?*
5 *Estamos/Somos perezosos.*
6 *Mi casa está/es a la izquierda.*
7 *¡Hola! ¿Cómo estás/es?*

Give pupils three minutes working in pairs to choose the correct verb form in each sentence.

Check answers, getting pupils to translate the sentences into English and to give you the infinitive form of each correct verb.

3 Escucha los diálogos y mira el mapa de Barcelona. ¿Adónde van? Escribe la letra correcta. (1–6) (AT1.4) ▸▸ 1.3a/Y8 ◂◂

Listening. Pupils listen to six conversations in which people are asking for directions. The places the people want to go to are beeped out in the recording. Following the directions on the map in the Pupil's Book, pupils work out the place being discussed each time (from *a–i*).

Audioscript Track 29

1 – *Perdón, ¿dónde está [beep], por favor?*
– *A ver... es muy fácil, sigue todo recto, cruza la plaza y está al final de la calle.*
2 – *Perdón, ¿dónde está [beep]?*
– *Pues... sigue todo recto, toma la primera calle a la derecha y está al final de la calle.*
3 – *¿Dónde está [beep], por favor?*
– *Bueno... Sigue todo recto, dobla a la izquierda, luego toma la primera calle a la izquierda otra vez y sigue todo recto. Está al final de la calle.*
4 – *Perdón, señor, ¿dónde está [beep]?*
– *A ver... Sigue todo recto, dobla a la izquierda, luego toma la segunda calle a la derecha y está al final de la calle.*
5 – *Perdón, señor, ¿dónde está [beep]?*
– *Mira, sigue todo recto, toma la segunda calle a la derecha y luego toma la primera calle a la derecha. Está al final de la calle.*
6 – *Perdón, señor, ¿dónde está [beep]?*
– *Mira, sigue todo recto, toma la segunda calle a la derecha y luego toma la segunda calle a la izquierda. Está al final de la calle.*

Answers

1 g **2** b **3** j **4** h **5** c **6** e

4 Con tu compañero/a, pregunta y contesta. (AT2.4) ▸▸1.3b/Y8 1.4a/Y8◂◂

Speaking. In pairs using the map in exercise 3, pupils take it in turn to ask for directions to one of the places shown and to respond with appropriate directions. A sample exchange is given.

Point out the tip box on expressions that pupils can use to buy thinking time when speaking Spanish. Remind them too that when asking for important information in Spanish, such as directions, repeating what they hear will help them make sure they have heard and understood correctly.

5 Escribe cinco diálogos sobre el mapa. Utiliza el diálogo del ejercicio 4 como modelo. (AT4.3–4) ▸▸2.4a/Y8◂◂

Writing. Using the sample exchange in exercise 4 as a model and working out directions using the map in exercise 3, pupils write out five dialogues.

➕ Pupils could bring in and use a map of a different city to do the activity.

6 Escucha y completa la canción con palabras del cuadro. (1–6) (AT1.4) ▸▸4.4/Y8◂◂

Listening. Pupils listen to the song and complete the gap-fill version of the text with the words supplied.

Audioscript Track 30

Barcelona te quiero,
Todo aquí es bueno…
Barcelona te quiero,
Todo aquí es bueno…

¿Dónde está el museo Picasso?
***A ver**… sigue todo recto.*
*¿El cine IMAX, **por favor**?*
Al final de la calle, señor.

Barcelona te quiero,
Todo aquí es bueno…
Barcelona te quiero,
Todo aquí es bueno…

*¿Dónde **está** la Sagrada Familia?*
A la izquierda y cruza la plaza.
La playa de la Barceloneta – aquí está.
*Y **mira**, ¡hay una fiesta!*

Barcelona te quiero,
Todo aquí es bueno…
Barcelona te quiero,
Todo aquí es bueno…

¿Te gusta la Villa Olímpica?
*Es bonita pero **también** turística.*
¿El Camp Nou está por aquí?
*¿La casa del Barça? **Ah sí, sí, sí.***

Barcelona te quiero,
Todo aquí es bueno…
Barcelona te quiero,
Todo aquí es bueno…

Answers

*See also **bold** in audioscript.*

1 A ver **2** por favor **3** está **4** mira **5** también
6 Ah, sí, sí, sí

Plenary ▸▸5.8◂◂

In pairs: give pupils: time to read through the bullet points in the Mini-test and write a sentence for each, illustrating that they can do all the things listed. They should then swap texts with another pair and check the other pair's work. Ask for examples of mistakes made and take feedback from the class on where pupils should look for help in these areas (where summaries of adjective endings, verb endings, etc., are to be found).

Pupils could redraft their responses for homework.

Cuaderno A, page 54

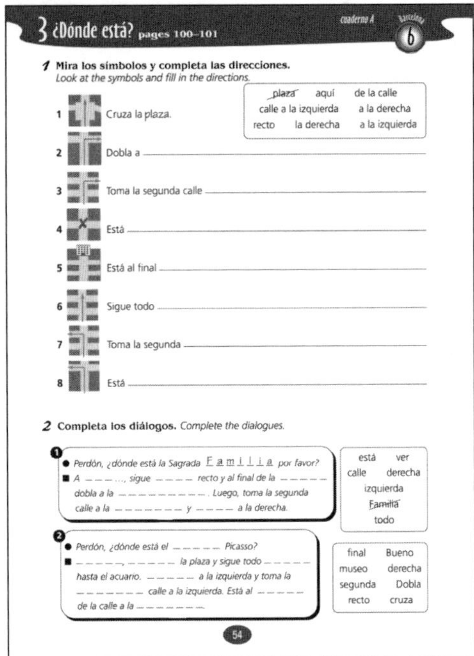

3 ¿Dónde está? pages 100–101 cuaderno A Barcelona 6

1 **Mira los símbolos y completa las direcciones.**
Look at the symbols and fill in the directions.

~~plaza~~	aquí	de la calle
calle a la izquierda		a la derecha
recto	la derecha	a la izquierda

1 Cruza la plaza.
2 Dobla a ______
3 Toma la segunda calle ______
4 Está ______
5 Está al final ______
6 Sigue todo ______
7 Toma la segunda ______
8 Está ______

2 **Completa los diálogos.** *Complete the dialogues.*

1
● *Perdón, ¿dónde está la Sagrada F a m i l i a por favor?*
■ *A ____..., sigue ____ recto y al final de la ____ dobla a la ________. Luego, toma la segunda calle a la ______ y ____ a la derecha.*

está ver calle derecha izquierda ~~Familia~~ todo

2
● *Perdón, ¿dónde está el ____ Picasso?*
■ *____, ____ la plaza y sigue todo ____ hasta el acuario. ____ a la izquierda y toma la ______ calle a la izquierda. Está al ____ de la calle a la ______.*

final Bueno museo derecha segunda Dobla recto cruza

54

Cuaderno B, page 54

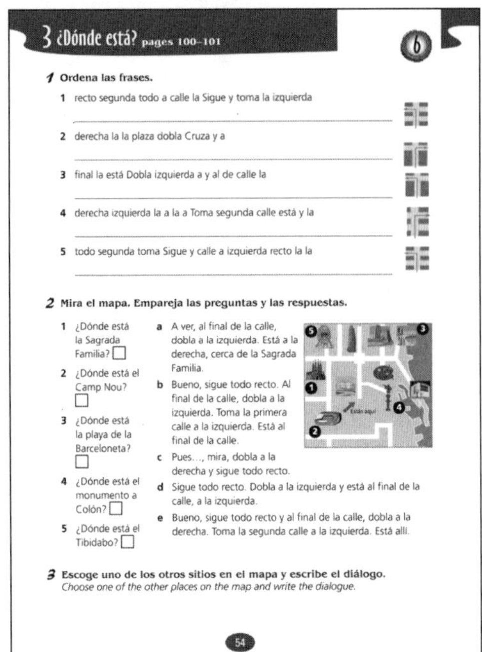

3 ¿Dónde está? pages 100–101 6

1 **Ordena las frases.**

1 recto segunda todo a calle la Sigue y toma la izquierda
______
2 derecha la la plaza dobla Cruza y a
______
3 final la está Dobla izquierda a y al de calle la
______
4 derecha izquierda la a la a Toma segunda calle está y la
______
5 todo segunda toma Sigue y calle a izquierda recto la la
______

2 **Mira el mapa. Empareja las preguntas y las respuestas.**

1 ¿Dónde está la Sagrada Familia? ☐
2 ¿Dónde está el Camp Nou? ☐
3 ¿Dónde está la playa de la Barceloneta? ☐
4 ¿Dónde está el monumento a Colón? ☐
5 ¿Dónde está el Tibidabo? ☐

a A ver, al final de la calle, dobla a la izquierda. Está a la derecha, cerca de la Sagrada Familia.
b Bueno, sigue todo recto. Al final de la calle, dobla a la izquierda. Toma la primera calle a la izquierda. Está al final de la calle.
c Pues..., mira, dobla a la derecha y sigue todo recto.
d Sigue todo recto. Dobla a la izquierda y está al final de la calle, a la izquierda.
e Bueno, sigue todo recto y al final de la calle, dobla a la derecha. Toma la segunda calle a la izquierda. Está allí.

3 **Escoge uno de los otros sitios en el mapa y escribe el diálogo.**
Choose one of the other places on the map and write the dialogue.

54

1 (AT4.1)

1 *Cruza la plaza*
2 Dobla a la derecha
3 Toma la segunda calle a la derecha
4 Está aquí
5 Está al final de la calle
6 Sigue todo recto
7 Toma la segunda calle a la izquierda
8 Está a la izquierda

2 (AT3.3, AT4.1)

1 Perdón, ¿dónde está la Sagrada *Familia*, por favor?

A ver..., sigue todo recto y al final de la calle dobla a la izquierda. Luego, toma la segunda calle a la derecha y está a la derecha.

2 Perdón, ¿dónde está el museo Picasso?

Bueno, cruza la plaza y sigue todo recto hasta el acuario. Dobla a la izquierda y toma la segunda calle a la izquierda. Está al final de la calle a la derecha.

1 (AT4.2)

1 Sigue todo recto y toma la segunda calle a la izquierda.
2 Cruza la plaza y dobla a la derecha.
3 Dobla a la izquierda y está al final de la calle.
4 Toma la segunda calle a la derecha y está a la izquierda.
5 Sigue todo recto, toma la segunda calle a la izquierda y aquí está.

2 (AT3.3)

1 d **2** b **3** e **4** c **5** a

3 (AT4.4)

R & A Pack, Gramática page 25

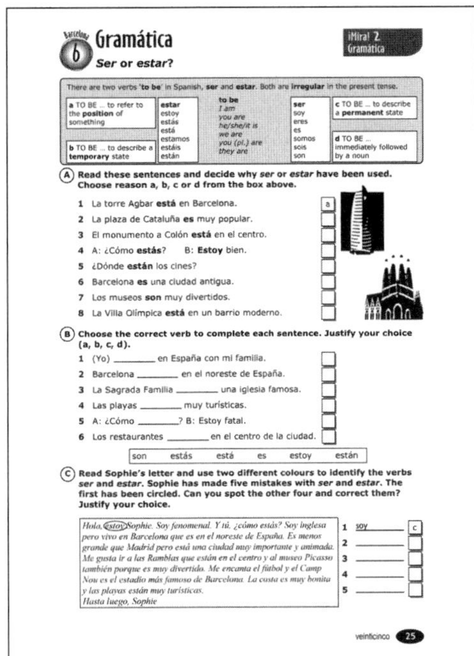

Barcelona 6 **Gramática**

¡Mira! 2 Gramática

***Ser* or *estar*?**

There are two verbs '**to be**' in Spanish, **ser** and **estar**. Both are **irregular** in the present tense.

	estar	to be	ser	
a TO BE ... to refer to the **position** of something	estoy	*I am*	soy	**c** TO BE ... to describe a **permanent** state
	estás	*you are*	eres	
	está	*he/she/it is*	es	
	estamos	*we are*	somos	**d** TO BE ... immediately followed by a noun
b TO BE ... to describe a **temporary** state	estáis	*you (pl.) are*	sois	
	están	*they are*	son	

A Read these sentences and decide why *ser* or *estar* have been used. Choose reason a, b, c or d from the box above.

1 La torre Agbar **está** en Barcelona. a
2 La plaza de Cataluña **es** muy popular.
3 El monumento a Colón **está** en el centro.
4 A: ¿Cómo **estás**? B: **Estoy** bien.
5 ¿Dónde **están** los cines?
6 Barcelona **es** una ciudad antigua.
7 Los museos **son** muy divertidos.
8 La Villa Olímpica **está** en un barrio moderno.

B Choose the correct verb to complete each sentence. Justify your choice (a, b, c, d).

1 (Yo) ________ en España con mi familia.
2 Barcelona ________ en el noreste de España.
3 La Sagrada Familia ________ una iglesia famosa.
4 Las playas ________ muy turísticas.
5 A: ¿Cómo ________? B: Estoy fatal.
6 Los restaurantes ________ en el centro de la ciudad.

son estás está es estoy están

C Read Sophie's letter and use two different colours to identify the verbs *ser* and *estar*. Sophie has made five mistakes with *ser* and *estar*. The first has been circled. Can you spot the other four and correct them? Justify your choice.

Hola, estoy Sophie. Soy fenomenal. Y tú, ¿cómo estás? Soy inglesa pero vivo en Barcelona que es en el noreste de España. Es menos grande que Madrid pero está una ciudad muy importante y animada. Me gusta ir a las Ramblas que están en el centro y al museo Picasso también porque es muy divertido. Me encanta el fútbol y el Camp Nou es el estadio más famoso de Barcelona. La costa es muy bonita y las playas están muy turísticas.
Hasta luego, Sophie

1 soy c
2 ________
3 ________
4 ________
5 ________

veinticinco 25

R & A Pack, Gramática page 26

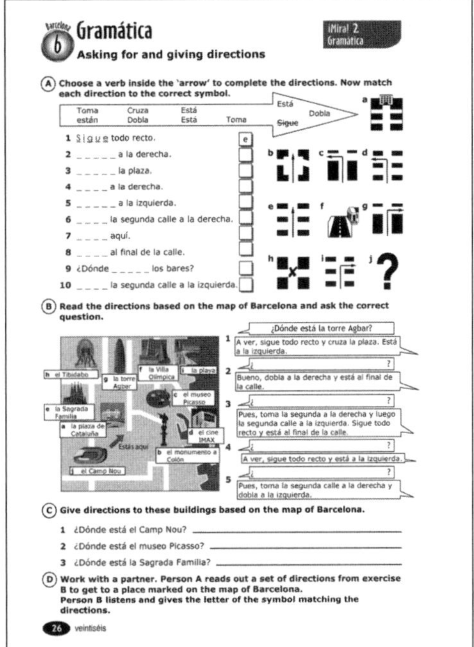

Barcelona 6 **Gramática**

¡Mira! 2 Gramática

Asking for and giving directions

A Choose a verb inside the 'arrow' to complete the directions. Now match each direction to the correct symbol.

Toma Cruza Está están Dobla Está Toma Está Dobla ~~Sigue~~

1 S i g u e todo recto. e
2 _ _ _ _ _ a la derecha.
3 _ _ _ _ _ la plaza.
4 _ _ _ _ a la derecha.
5 _ _ _ _ _ a la izquierda.
6 _ _ _ _ la segunda calle a la derecha.
7 _ _ _ _ aquí.
8 _ _ _ _ al final de la calle.
9 ¿Dónde _ _ _ _ _ los bares?
10 _ _ _ _ la segunda calle a la izquierda.

B Read the directions based on the map of Barcelona and ask the correct question.

1 ¿Dónde está la torre Agbar?
A ver, sigue todo recto y cruza la plaza. Está a la izquierda.
2 ¿ ?
Bueno, dobla a la derecha y está al final de la calle.
3 ¿ ?
Pues, toma la segunda a la derecha y luego la segunda calle a la izquierda. Sigue todo recto y está al final de la calle.
4 ¿ ?
A ver, sigue todo recto y está a la izquierda.
5 ¿ ?
Pues, toma la segunda calle a la derecha y dobla a la izquierda.

C Give directions to these buildings based on the map of Barcelona.

1 ¿Dónde está el Camp Nou? ________
2 ¿Dónde está el museo Picasso? ________
3 ¿Dónde está la Sagrada Familia? ________

D Work with a partner. Person A reads out a set of directions from exercise B to get to a place marked on the map of Barcelona. Person B listens and gives the letter of the symbol matching the directions.

26 veintiséis

A **2** c **3** a **4** b **5** a **6** d **7** c **8** a

B **1** estoy (a) **2** está (a) **3** es (d) **4** son (c) **5** estás (b) **6** están (a)

C The mistakes are: (2) soy fenomenal (estoy) (b); (3) es en el noreste de España (está) (a); (4) está una ciudad importante (es) (d); (5) las playas están muy turísticas (son) (c)

A **1** sigue (e) **2** dobla (g) **3** cruza (b) **4** está (f) **5** dobla (c) **6** toma (i) **7** está (h) **8** está (a) **9** están (j) **10** toma (d)

B **2** ¿Dónde está el monumento a Colón?
3 ¿Dónde está la playa?
4 ¿Dónde está la torre Agbar?
5 ¿Dónde está la Villa Olímpica?

C **1** Dobla a la izquierda, toma la primera a la izquierda y sigue todo recto.
2 Toma la segunda a la derecha y dobla a la derecha.
3 Dobla a la izquierda, toma la primera a la izquierda y está a la derecha.

4 Soy turista en Barcelona (Pupil's Book pages 102–103)

Learning objectives

- Describing a holiday in Barcelona
- Combining past, present and future tenses

Grammar

- Using a range of tenses: preterite, present and near future

Key language

Hoy...
Estoy en Barcelona.
Es genial.
Anteayer...
Ayer por la tarde...
fui a la playa
comí paella y bebí limonada
descansé un poco
Lo pasé fenomenal.
Me gustó.
No me gustó.
Mañana...
Pasado mañana...
voy a ir al Tibidabo
voy a ir de compras
voy a comprar unas camisetas

High-frequency words

el, la
un, unas
me
a (al)
de
por
y
hoy, mañana, ayer
no
beber (bebí)
comer (comí)
comprar
estar (estoy)
ir (voy, fui)
jugar (jugué)
ser (es)
tomar (tomé)

Cross-curricular

English: Verb tenses

Resources

CD3, tracks 31–32
Cuadernos A & B, p. 55
R & A Pack, Gramática p. 27

Teacher Presentations

Screen 1 – Module 6 overview
Screen 2 – p. 102 ex. 1
Screen 3 – p. 103 exs 4 & 5

Starter 1 ▸▸4.6a/Y8◂◂

Aim

To review the preterite, present and near future tenses.

Write up (answers in brackets for reference):

1 *restaurante ayer un fui a*
(Ayer fui a un restaurante.)
2 *ir al mañana voy Tibidabo a*
(Mañana voy a ir al Tibidabo.)
3 *tomé el voleibol al sol jugué y*
(Tomé el sol y jugué al voleibol./Jugué al voleibol y tomé el sol.)
4 *a vaqueros voy comprar unos*
(Voy a comprar unos vaqueros.)
5 *Barcelona genial en y es estoy*
(Estoy en Barcelona y es genial.)
6 *fenomenal lo pasé*
(Lo pasé fenomenal.)

Give pupils three minutes working in pairs to write out each sentence in the correct order.

Check answers, getting pupils to translate the sentences into English.

Suggestion

As a class read the tip box on recognising tenses.

1 Escucha y lee. Escribe las letras en la columna correcta de la tabla. (AT1.6) ▸▸1.2/Y8 4.5a/Y8◂◂

Listening. Pupils listen to the 10 statements about holidays and read the text at the same time. They then copy out and complete the table by identifying the tense used in each statement and putting the sentence label (from *a–j*) in the correct column.

Audioscript Track 31

a *Ayer por la tarde fui a un restaurante.*
b *Anteayer fui a la playa de la Barceloneta.*
c *Mañana por la tarde voy a ir al Tibidabo.*
d *Descansé un poco, tomé el sol y jugué al voleibol.*
e *Voy a comprar unas camisetas y unos vaqueros.*
f *Lo pasé fenomenal.*
g *Hoy voy al acuario y después al cine IMAX.*
h *Estoy en Barcelona y es genial.*
i *Pasado mañana voy a ir de compras.*
j *Comí paella y bebí limonada.*

Answers

Pasado	Presente	Futuro
a, b, d, f, j	g, h	c, e, i

+ Pupils continue their project work on Barcelona by researching and designing an itinerary for a holiday there. They then produce a postcard like the one in the Pupil's Book, detailing what they have done/are doing/are going to do.

2 Escribe las frases del ejercicio 1 en un orden lógico. (AT4.6) ▸▸2.4b/Y8◂◂

Writing. Pupils write out the sentences in exercise 1 in a logical order, using the time expressions to work out the structure.

Answers

Some variation possible, as long as the verb tenses are grouped together and time expressions are in the correct order.

h *Estoy en Barcelona y es genial.*
b Anteayer fui a la playa de la Barceloneta.
d Descansé un poco, tomé el sol y jugué al voleibol.
f Lo pasé fenomenal.
a Ayer por la tarde fui a un restaurante.
j Comí paella y bebí limonada.
g Hoy voy al acuario y después al cine IMAX.
c Mañana por la tarde voy a ir al Tibidabo.
i Pasado mañana voy a ir de compras.
e Voy a comprar unas camisetas y unos vaqueros.

Starter 2 ▸▸4.2/Y8◂◂

Aim

To revise time expressions.

Read out the following time expressions/tenses as prompts. Ask pupils to stand up if the time expression goes with the verb tense and to put their hands on their heads if it doesn't.

mañana – near future	(✓)
anteayer – near future	(✗)
hoy – preterite	(✗)
la semana pasada – preterite	(✓)
pasado mañana – near future	(✓)
ayer – present	(✗)
ayer por la tarde – preterite	(✓)
normalmente – present	(✓)
el verano pasado – present	(✗)
la próxima vez – near future tense	(✓)

3 Sigue las rayas y di las frases. (AT2.5) ▸▸1.4a/Y8◂◂

Speaking. In pairs: pupils take it in turn to follow the lines linking the time expressions to the pictures and to give a sentence using the appropriate tense.

Answers

Anteayer fui al restaurante.
Ayer fui de compras.
Hoy voy al Tibidabo.
Mañana voy a jugar al voleibol.
Pasado mañana voy a ir al cine.

+ Using the same time expressions and the appropriate tense, pupils make up statements about different activities.

Suggestion ▸▸3.2a/Y8◂◂

If you have a native Spanish-speaking assistant, you could use him/her to give pupils practice talking without a script about tourist activities they have done/are going to do, either in Spain or another country they have visited/are hoping to visit. The assistant could also talk about tourist activities he/she has done/is going to do in Britain while working as an assistant.

Whenever an assistant works with the pupils, encourage him/her to give feedback in Spanish, using the expressions you use consistently to comment on pupils' work (and have perhaps already displayed in the classroom for reference).

4 Escucha y lee. (AT1.6) ▸▸2.2a/Y8◂◂

Listening. Pupils listen to two people talking about Barcelona, and read the texts at the same time. Some vocabulary is glossed for support.

Audioscript Track 32

1 *¡Hola! ¿Qué tal? Me llamo Javier. Soy mexicano. Me encanta Barcelona. Es una ciudad guay. Ayer visité muchos monumentos: la Sagrada Familia, unas iglesias, las casas de Gaudí y el monumento a Colón. Saqué muchas fotos. Por la noche fui a la discoteca y lo pasé genial. Bailé y hablé con muchas personas interesantes.*

Hoy quiero ir al museo Picasso porque me gusta pintar y Picasso es mi pintor favorito. Mañana por la tarde voy a ver un partido de fútbol del Barça en el Camp Nou. Me gusta mucho el fútbol. Va a ser fenomenal. Creo que el Barça va a ganar.

2 *Me llamo Beverley. Lo siento, pero no me gusta Barcelona. Es una ciudad muy grande y para mí es demasiado turística. Vivo en un pueblo pequeño en Gales y prefiero la tranquilidad.*

Además estoy con mis padres y es muy, muy aburrido. Quiero hablar con mis amigos de mi pueblo. Ayer por la mañana les mandé muchos mensajes.

Ayer por la tarde fui al Tibidabo donde hay un parque de atracciones y me gustó bastante, pero hoy por la mañana fui a la Sagrada Familia y no me gustó nada. Ahora voy a la Villa Olímpica y mañana voy a ir al museo Picasso. Va a ser horrible.

5 ¿Es Javier o Beverley? Escribe J o B. (AT3.6) ▸▸2.2a/Y8 5.4◂◂

Reading. Pupils answer the six questions in English about the texts, by identifying who is being described in each one – Javier (by writing **J**) or Beverley (by writing **B**).

Answers

1 *B* **2** J **3** J **4** J **5** B **6** B

6 Con tu compañero/a, pregunta y contesta por Javier y Beverley. (AT2.6) ▸▸1.4a/Y8 4.6a/Y8◂◂

Speaking. In pairs: pupils take it in turn to ask questions and to respond in the role of Javier or Beverley. The questions are supplied.

More able pupils should re-read the appropriate text in exercise 4 to remind themselves of the details and do the dialogue without referring to it.

➕ Using Javier's or Beverley's text as a model, pupils write a text on their own town or a town they have visited.

Plenary ▸▸4.5a/Y8◂◂

Play a team game to review time expressions and tenses. Give each team an allocated time: you will prompt with a range of time expressions and the team responds with a verb in the appropriate tense for each one. How many correct verbs can they give in the time allowed?

With a less able class, you could make the game simpler by giving just one time expression to each team and getting them to give as many verbs as possible in the appropriate tense.

Cuaderno A, page 55

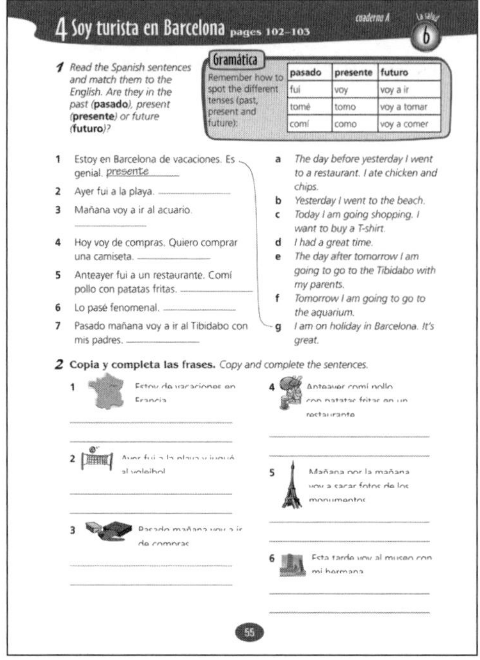
4 Soy turista en Barcelona pages 102–103 cuaderno A 6

1 *Read the Spanish sentences and match them to the English. Are they in the past (**pasado**), present (**presente**) or future (**futuro**)?*

Gramática
Remember how to spot the different tenses (past, present and future):

pasado	presente	futuro
fui	voy	voy a ir
tomé	tomo	voy a tomar
comí	como	voy a comer

1 Estoy en Barcelona de vacaciones. Es genial. presente
2 Ayer fui a la playa. ______
3 Mañana voy a ir al acuario. ______
4 Hoy voy de compras. Quiero comprar una camiseta. ______
5 Anteayer fui a un restaurante. Comí pollo con patatas fritas. ______
6 Lo pasé fenomenal. ______
7 Pasado mañana voy a ir al Tibidabo con mis padres. ______

a *The day before yesterday I went to a restaurant. I ate chicken and chips.*
b *Yesterday I went to the beach.*
c *Today I am going shopping. I want to buy a T-shirt.*
d *I had a great time.*
e *The day after tomorrow I am going to go to the Tibidabo with my parents.*
f *Tomorrow I am going to go to the aquarium.*
g *I am on holiday in Barcelona. It's great.*

2 **Copia y completa las frases.** *Copy and complete the sentences.*

1 Estoy de vacaciones en Francia
2 Ayer fui a la playa y jugué al voleibol
3 Pasado mañana voy a ir de compras
4 Anteayer comí pollo con patatas fritas en un restaurante
5 Mañana por la mañana voy a sacar fotos de los monumentos
6 Esta tarde voy al museo con mi hermana

55

1 (AT3.6)

1 *g presente* **2** b pasado **3** f futuro
4 c presente **5** a pasado **6** d pasado **7** e futuro

2 (AT4.2/3)

1. Estoy de vacaciones en Francia.
2. Ayer fui a la playa y jugué al voleibol.
3. Pasado mañana voy a ir de compras.
4. Anteayer comí pollo con patatas fritas en un restaurante.
5. Mañana por la mañana voy a sacar fotos de los monumentos.
6. Esta tarde voy al museo con mi hermana.

Cuaderno B, page 55

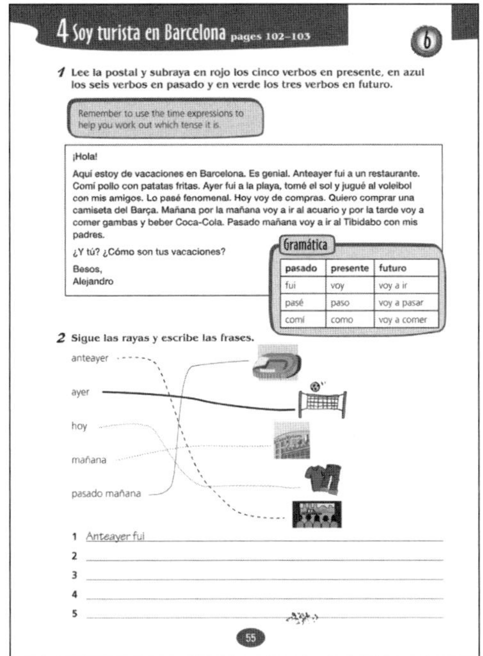
4 Soy turista en Barcelona pages 102–103

1 Lee la postal y subraya en rojo los cinco verbos en presente, en azul los seis verbos en pasado y en verde los tres verbos en futuro.

Remember to use the time expressions to help you work out which tense it is.

¡Hola!

Aquí estoy de vacaciones en Barcelona. Es genial. Anteayer fui a un restaurante. Comí pollo con patatas fritas. Ayer fui a la playa, tomé el sol y jugué al voleibol con mis amigos. Lo pasé fenomenal. Hoy voy de compras. Quiero comprar una camiseta del Barça. Mañana por la mañana voy a ir al acuario y por la tarde voy a comer gambas y beber Coca-Cola. Pasado mañana voy a ir al Tibidabo con mis padres.

¿Y tú? ¿Cómo son tus vacaciones?

Besos,
Alejandro

Gramática

pasado	presente	futuro
fui	voy	voy a ir
pasé	paso	voy a pasar
comí	como	voy a comer

2 Sigue las rayas y escribe las frases.

anteayer
ayer
hoy
mañana
pasado mañana

1 Anteayer fui
2
3
4
5

55

R & A Pack, Gramática page 27

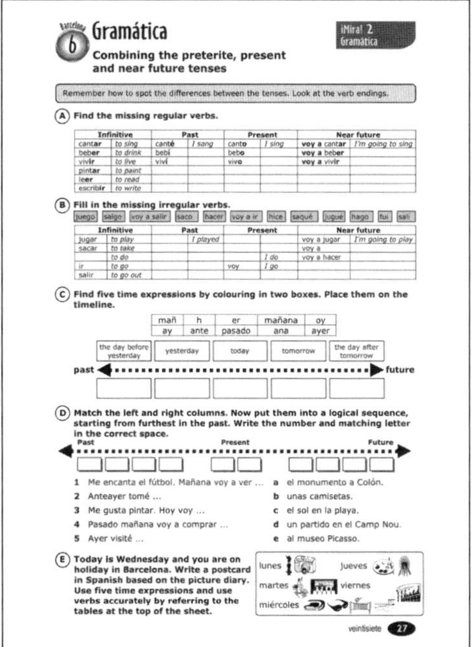
Gramática

¡Mira! 2 Gramática

Combining the preterite, present and near future tenses

Remember how to spot the differences between the tenses. Look at the verb endings.

(A) Find the missing regular verbs.

Infinitive		Past		Present		Near future	
cantar	*to sing*	canté	*I sang*	canto	*I sing*	voy a cantar	*I'm going to sing*
beber	*to drink*	bebí		bebo		voy a beber	
vivir	*to live*	viví		vivo		voy a vivir	
pintar	*to paint*						
leer	*to read*						
escribir	*to write*						

(B) Fill in the missing irregular verbs.

juego | salgo | voy a salir | saco | hacer | voy a ir | hice | saqué | jugué | hago | fui | salí

Infinitive		Past		Present		Near future	
jugar	*to play*		*I played*			voy a jugar	*I'm going to play*
sacar	*to take*					voy a	
	to do				*I do*	voy a hacer	
ir	*to go*			voy	*I go*		
salir	*to go out*						

(C) Find five time expressions by colouring in two boxes. Place them on the timeline.

mañ	h	er	mañana	oy
ay	ante	pasado	ana	ayer

the day before yesterday | yesterday | today | tomorrow | the day after tomorrow

past ◀ .... ▶ future

(D) Match the left and right columns. Now put them into a logical sequence, starting from furthest in the past. Write the number and matching letter in the correct space.

Past — Present — Future

1 Me encanta el fútbol. Mañana voy a ver …
2 Anteayer tomé …
3 Me gusta pintar. Hoy voy …
4 Pasado mañana voy a comprar …
5 Ayer visité …

a el monumento a Colón.
b unas camisetas.
c el sol en la playa.
d un partido en el Camp Nou.
e al museo Picasso.

(E) Today is Wednesday and you are on holiday in Barcelona. Write a postcard in Spanish based on the picture diary. Use five time expressions and use verbs accurately by referring to the tables at the top of the sheet.

lunes
jueves
martes
viernes
miércoles

veintisiete 27

1 (AT3.6)

red = estoy / es / voy / quiero / son
blue = fui / comí / fui / tomé / jugué / pasé
green = voy a ir / voy a comer … y beber / voy a ir

2 (AT4.6)

1 *Anteayer fui* al cine.
2 Ayer jugué al voleibol.
3 Hoy voy de compras.
4 Mañana voy a ir al acuario.
5 Pasado mañana voy a ir al Camp Nou.

(A) I drank, I drink, I'm going to drink
I lived, I live, I'm going to live
pinté, I painted, pinto, I paint, voy a pintar, I'm going to paint
leí, I read, leo, I read, voy a leer, I'm going to read
escribí, I wrote, escribo, I write, voy a escribir, I'm going to write

(B) jugué, juego, I play;
saqué, I took, saco, I take, sacar, I'm going to take;
hacer, hice, I did, hago, I'm going to do;
fui, I went, voy a ir, I'm going to go;
salí, I went out, salgo, I go out, voy a salir, I'm going to go out

(C) anteayer, ayer, hoy, mañana, pasado mañana

(D) **2** c **5** a **3** e **1** d **4** b

5 Barcelona en tus sueños (Pupil's Book pages 104–105)

Learning objectives
- Reading a story set in Barcelona
- Writing creatively

Framework objectives
2.4/Y8 Writing – (a) using text as stimulus

Key language
Revision of language from Module 6

High-frequency words
Revision of language from Module 6

Cross-curricular
English: Verb tenses
ICT: Word-processing

Resources
CD3, track 33
Cuadernos A & B, p. 56
R & A Pack, Writing Skills p. 28

Teacher Presentations
Screen 1 – Module 6 overview
Screen 2 – p. 104 ex. 1
Screen 3 – Game
Screen 4 – Video

Starter 1 4.4/Y8

Aim
To revise expressions used to give an opinion.

Write up:

Me gusta...	*No me gusta...*
Me gusta mucho...	*No me gusta nada...*
Me encanta...	*Odio...*
Prefiero...	

Ask pupils to write seven sentences, each using one of the phrases + an infinitive.

Suggestion

Give pupils a minute to skim-read the comic strip on page 104. Ask them to tell you what information they managed to glean in that time, prompting them as necessary to come up with answers to the following questions:

- Who is involved in the story? (Beverley and an angel)
- Where does Beverley go? (she flies over Barcelona)
- How does Beverley feel about Barcelona at the beginning of the story? What language conveys this? (negative: *no te gusta*)
- How does she respond to what the angel shows her? (she likes it: *me gusta mucho, me encanta*)
- How does she feel about Barcelona at the end? (positive: *la ciudad más bonita del mundo*, the list of different things she is going to do, *mágico*)

Ask pupils what they looked for when skim-reading the text. Stress how important it is to use any clues supplied – here the pictures give a lot of information that helps the reader to focus on the key points. Pupils should avoid being distracted by words they don't know, focusing instead on picking up information from language they recognise. One technique that could help in getting the gist of this text quickly is to read just the first few words in each speech bubble.

1 Escucha y lee. (AT1.6)

2.2a/Y8 5.4

Listening. Pupils listen to the recording of the comic strip, and read the text at the same time. Some vocabulary is glossed for support.

Encourage pupils to use intonation to help them understand. Copying models like this will also help pupils become more fluent in their spoken Spanish.

Audioscript Track 33

1 – *Érase una vez una niña llamada Beverley. Una noche vino un ángel...*
– *Beverley, no te gusta Barcelona, ¿verdad? Prefieres las montañas negras de Gales, pero Barcelona es bonita también.*

2 – *Vamos a volar. Uno, dos, tres... Primero vamos al acuario. A ver, todo recto, luego a la derecha, ahora a la izquierda... y aquí está.*

3 – *Mira, Beverley, los tiburones. Me encanta el acuario. ¿Te gusta, Beverley?*
– *Sí, Ángel, me gusta mucho... No hay tiburones en Gales.*

4 – *¿Te gusta nadar, Beverley?*
– *Ah sí, me encanta.*
– *Muy bien, vamos a la playa entonces. Todo recto, luego a la izquierda. Mira – el mar.*
– *¡Qué hermoso! ¡Qué bonito es!*

5 – *Y mañana vas al museo Picasso...*
– *¡Oh no! Va a ser horrible... ¡A-bu-rri-do!*
– *No, Beverley, el museo Picasso es fantástico. Es un museo mágico.*

6 – *Por favor, Beverley, Barcelona es una ciudad muy bonita. Disfruta.*
– *Ahora duerme, buenas noches...*

7 – *El día siguiente...*
– *Papi, mami, ayer por la noche soñé una cosa rarísima...*
– *¡Oh Beverley, por favor! No empieces, no seas negativa...*

8 – *¿Qué va a hacer hoy en Barcelona, señorita?*
– *Un montón de cosas. Barcelona es la ciudad más bonita del mundo. Primero voy al acuario y luego a la playa. Después voy al museo Picasso, es mágico...*
– *... Y colorín colorado este cuento se ha terminado.*

R Ask comprehension questions on the text in Spanish.

2 Lee el carné de identidad y contesta a las preguntas por Beverley. (AT1.5) ▸▸1.4a/Y8 4.6a/Y8◂◂

Reading. Pupil read Beverley's identity card and answer the four questions as though they were her.

Answers

1 Tengo 14 años.
2 Soy galesa.
3 Me gusta mandar mensajes, escuchar música, pasear al perro y salir con mis amigos.
4 No me gusta viajar.
No me estudiar español.

Starter 2 ▸▸4.5a&b/Y8◂◂

Aim

To revise *le gusta*, etc. To revise the preterite and near future tenses.

Write up the following, jumbling the order of the second column of Spanish:

1	*A Beverley no*	*le gusta Barcelona.*
2	*A Ángel*	*le encanta el acuario.*
3	*Ayer Beverley*	*soñó una cosa rarísima.*
4	*A Beverley le*	*gusta nadar.*
5	*Beverley va*	*a ir al museo Picasso.*
6	*Luego Beverley va a*	*ir a la playa.*

Give pupils three minutes working in pairs to match the sentence halves.

Check answers, getting pupils to translate the completed sentences into English.

3 Con tu compañero/a, lee en voz alta el cómic de Beverley (página 104). (AT2.6) ▸▸5.6◂◂

Speaking. In pairs: pupils read aloud the comic strip on page 104, taking it in turn to play the role of Beverley and the angel. Encourage them to focus on pronunciation and stress and to try and sound as fluent as possible, following the model of the recording.

4 Lee otra vez y busca estas frases en el cómic. (AT3.6) ▸▸5.3 5.4◂◂

Reading. Pupils re-read the comic strip and find the Spanish for the eight English phrases/sentences listed.

Answers

1 *Érase una vez…*
2 una noche
3 Vamos a volar.
4 A ver, todo recto, luego a la derecha, ahora a la izquierda…
5 Mira – el mar.
6 Ahora duerme.
7 ¿Qué vas a hacer hoy en Barcelona?
8 Es la ciudad más bonita del mundo.

5 Inventa la identidad de una persona que va a visitar una ciudad con Ángel. (AT4.2–3) ▸▸2.4a/Y8◂◂

Writing. Using Beverley's identity card as a model and the picture prompts supplied, pupils write a card for another person who is going to visit a city in the company of Ángel.

6 Escribe la historia de Ángel y tu personaje. (AT4.4–5) ▸▸2.4a/Y8◂◂

Writing. Pupils write their own story about Ángel and the person they have described in the identity card in exercise 5. They can locate the story in any city they want. Key expressions to include are supplied for support. Pupils should also look back at the comic strip on page 104 for guidance on the kind of detail to include.

An extended writing activity like this can be done on computer. It makes the process of correcting/redrafting much easier and more encouraging.

+ Pupils could work together to create a comic strip of their text, producing drawings as well as text.

Plenary ▸▸5.8◂◂

Put the class into teams and tell pupils that you are going to use the Resumen section to test them. Each team chooses a unit: give them two minutes to review that unit and its summary in the Resumen section. They then close their books.

Ask the teams in turn to give a Spanish example for each point listed in the Resumen section. They can confer, but a different person must finally answer each time. A correct answer wins a point. If a pupil can answer correctly without conferring, this wins two points. The team with the most points wins.

Cuaderno A, page 56

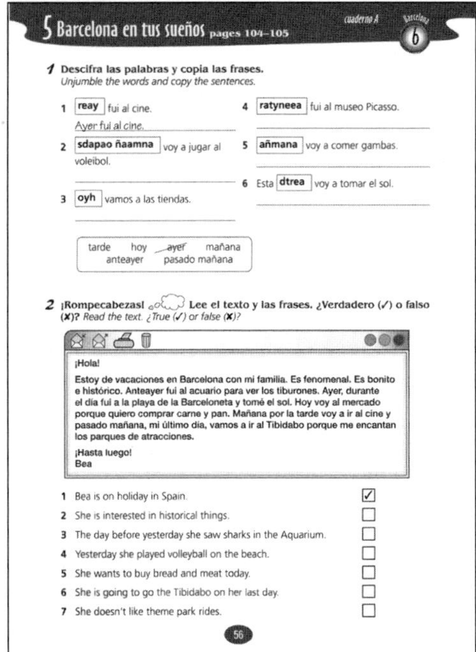
5 Barcelona en tus sueños pages 104–105

cuaderno A · Barcelona 6

1 Descifra las palabras y copia las frases.
Unjumble the words and copy the sentences.

1 **reay** fui al cine.
Ayer fui al cine.
2 **sdapao ñaamna** voy a jugar al voleibol.
3 **oyh** vamos a las tiendas.
4 **ratyneea** fui al museo Picasso.
5 **añmana** voy a comer gambas.
6 Esta **dtrea** voy a tomar el sol.

tarde hoy ~~ayer~~ mañana anteayer pasado mañana

2 ¡Rompecabezas! Lee el texto y las frases. ¿Verdadero (✓) o falso (✗)? *Read the text. ¿True (✓) or false (✗)?*

¡Hola!

Estoy de vacaciones en Barcelona con mi familia. Es fenomenal. Es bonito e histórico. Anteayer fui al acuario para ver los tiburones. Ayer, durante el día fui a la playa de la Barceloneta y tomé el sol. Hoy voy al mercado porque quiero comprar carne y pan. Mañana por la tarde voy a ir al cine y pasado mañana, mi último día, vamos a ir al Tibidabo porque me encantan los parques de atracciones.

¡Hasta luego!
Bea

1 Bea is on holiday in Spain. ☑
2 She is interested in historical things. ☐
3 The day before yesterday she saw sharks in the Aquarium. ☐
4 Yesterday she played volleyball on the beach. ☐
5 She wants to buy bread and meat today. ☐
6 She is going to go the Tibidabo on her last day. ☐
7 She doesn't like theme park rides. ☐

56

1 (AT3.3)

1 *Ayer* **2** pasado mañana **3** hoy **4** anteayer
5 mañana **6** tarde

2 (AT3.6)

1 ✓ **2** ✓ **3** ✓ **4** ✗ **5** ✓ **6** ✓ **7** ✗

Cuaderno B, page 56

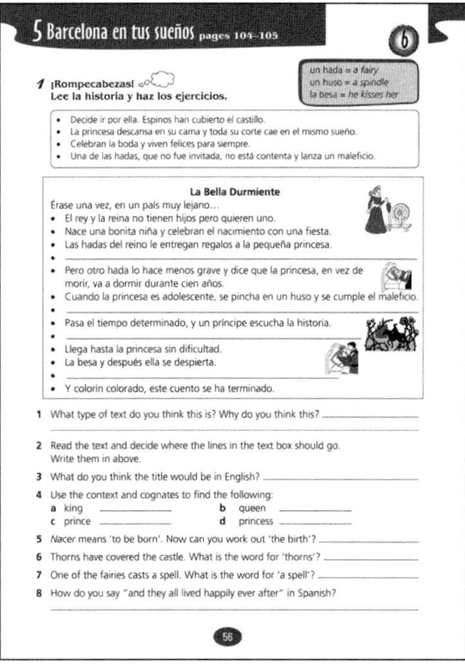
5 Barcelona en tus sueños pages 104–105

6

1 ¡Rompecabezas!
Lee la historia y haz los ejercicios.

un hada = *a fairy*
un huso = *a spindle*
la besa = *he kisses her*

- Decide ir por ella. Espinos han cubierto el castillo.
- La princesa descansa en su cama y toda su corte cae en el mismo sueño.
- Celebran la boda y viven felices para siempre.
- Una de las hadas, que no fue invitada, no está contenta y lanza un maleficio.

La Bella Durmiente

Érase una vez, en un país muy lejano…
- El rey y la reina no tienen hijos pero quieren uno.
- Nace una bonita niña y celebran el nacimiento con una fiesta.
- Las hadas del reino le entregan regalos a la pequeña princesa.
- ___
- Pero otro hada lo hace menos grave y dice que la princesa, en vez de morir, va a dormir durante cien años.
- Cuando la princesa es adolescente, se pincha en un huso y se cumple el maleficio.
- ___
- Pasa el tiempo determinado, y un príncipe escucha la historia.
- ___
- Llega hasta la princesa sin dificultad.
- La besa y después ella se despierta.
- ___
- Y colorín colorado, este cuento se ha terminado.

1 What type of text do you think this is? Why do you think this? ___
2 Read the text and decide where the lines in the text box should go. Write them in above.
3 What do you think the title would be in English? ___
4 Use the context and cognates to find the following:
a king ___ b queen ___
c prince ___ d princess ___
5 *Nacer* means 'to be born'. Now can you work out 'the birth'? ___
6 Thorns have covered the castle. What is the word for 'thorns'? ___
7 One of the fairies casts a spell. What is the word for 'a spell'? ___
8 How do you say "and they all lived happily ever after" in Spanish? ___

56

1 (AT3.6)

1 Fairy tale – talks about princesses etc. and starts with *Érase una vez* – once upon a time.

2
- El rey y la reina no tienen hijos pero quieren uno.
- Nace una bonita niña y celebran el nacimiento en una fiesta.
- Las hadas del reino le entregan regalos a la pequeña princesa.
- Una de las hadas, que no fue invitada, no está contenta y lanza un maleficio.
- Pero otro hada lo hace menos grave y dice que la princesa, en vez de morir, va a dormir durante cien años.
- Cuando la princesa es adolescente, se pincha en un huso y se cumple el maleficio.
- La princesa descansa en su cama y toda su corte cae en el mismo sueño.
- Pasa el tiempo determinado, y un príncipe escucha la historia.
- Decide ir por ella. Espinos han cubierto el castillo.
- Llega hasta la princesa sin dificultad.
- La besa y después ella se despierta.
- Celebran la boda y viven felices para siempre.
- Y colorín colorado este cuento se ha terminado.

3 Sleeping Beauty
4 **a** el rey **b** la reina **c** un príncipe **d** la princesa
5 el nacimiento
6 espinos
7 un maleficio
8 viven felices para siempre

R & A Pack, Gramática page 28

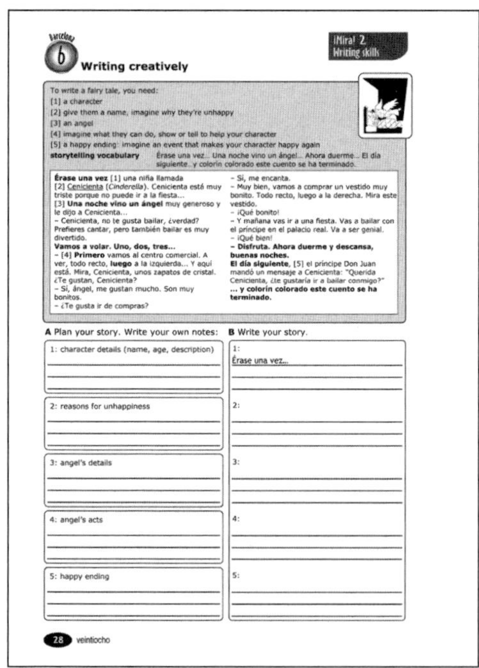
Barcelona 6 **Writing creatively**

¡Mira! 2 Writing skills

To write a fairy tale, you need:
[1] a character
[2] give them a name, imagine why they're unhappy
[3] an angel
[4] imagine what they can do, show or tell to help your character
[5] a happy ending: imagine an event that makes your character happy again

storytelling vocabulary Érase una vez… Una noche vino un ángel… Ahora duerme… El día siguiente… y colorín colorado este cuento se ha terminado.

Érase una vez [1] una niña llamada [2] Cenicienta (*Cinderella*). Cenicienta está muy triste porque no puede ir a la fiesta…
[3] **Una noche vino un ángel** muy generoso y le dijo a Cenicienta…
– Cenicienta, no te gusta bailar, ¿verdad? Prefieres cantar, pero también bailar es muy divertido.
Vamos a volar. Uno, dos, tres…
– [4] **Primero** vamos al centro comercial. A ver, todo recto, **luego** a la izquierda… Y aquí está. Mira, Cenicienta, unos zapatos de cristal. ¿Te gustan, Cenicienta?
– Sí, ángel, me gustan mucho. Son muy bonitos.
– ¿Te gusta ir de compras?
– Sí, me encanta.
– Muy bien, vamos a comprar un vestido muy bonito. Todo recto, luego a la derecha. Mira este vestido.
– ¡Qué bonito!
– Y mañana vas ir a una fiesta. Vas a bailar con el príncipe en el palacio real. Va a ser genial.
– ¡Qué bien!
– Disfruta. Ahora duerme y descansa, buenas noches.
El día siguiente, [5] el príncipe Don Juan mandó un mensaje a Cenicienta: "Querida Cenicienta, ¿te gustaría ir a bailar conmigo?"
… y colorín colorado este cuento se ha terminado.

A Plan your story. Write your own notes:
1: character details (name, age, description)
2: reasons for unhappiness
3: angel's details
4: angel's acts
5: happy ending

B Write your story.
1: Érase una vez…
2:
3:
4:
5:

28 veintiocho

Resumen y Prepárate (Pupil's Book pages 106–107)

Resumen

This is a checklist of language covered in Module 6. Pupils can work on this in pairs to check what they have learned and remembered. There is a Resumen page in the Resource and Assessment Pack. Encourage them to look back at the module and to use the grammar section to revise what they are unclear about. You can also use the Resumen as a useful plenary at the end of each unit.

Prepárate

These revision tests can be used for pupils to practise prior to the assessment tasks in the Resource and Assessment Pack.

Resources

CD3, track 34
R & A Pack, Module 6: Resumen, Prueba, I can...

1 Escucha a Paolo y a Mariana. Escribe las letras en la columna correcta de la tabla. (AT1.6) ▸▸4.5a/Y8◂◂

Listening. Pupils copy out the table. They listen to Paolo and Mariana saying what they think of Barcelona and note the activities mentioned (using pictures *a–j*) in the correct column of the table.

Audioscript Track 34

– *¡Hola! ¿Qué tal?*
Soy argentino. Me llamo Paolo.
Me encanta Barcelona. Es una ciudad genial. Ayer visité las Ramblas y saqué muchas fotos.
Por la noche fui a la Villa Olímpica y lo pasé genial.
Hoy quiero ir al Camp Nou porque me interesa mucho el fútbol.
Mañana por la tarde voy a ir al cine IMAX. Va a ser guay.
Me gustaría ir al casino pero no puedo porque no tengo 18 años.

– *¡Hola! Me llamo Mariana. Soy chilena.*
Me gusta Barcelona pero es muy grande. Ayer fui de excursión a la playa. Me gustó porque fue tranquilo. En la playa jugué al voleibol con un grupo de amigos.
Hoy quiero ir a la Villa Olímpica. Me interesa la arquitectura y quiero ver los rascacielos. Mañana por la tarde voy a ir al acuario con mis amigos.
También quiero ir al parque de atracciones.

Answers

	Ayer	**Hoy**	**Mañana**
Paolo	*i*, c, e	h	b, d
Mariana	a, f	e	g, j

2 Con tu compañero/a, haz cinco diálogos. (AT2.4) ▸▸1.4a/Y8◂◂

Speaking. In pairs using the picture prompts supplied, pupils make up five dialogues in which they ask for and give directions. A sample exchange is given.

3 Copia las frases con el verbo correcto. (AT3.3) ▸▸4.5a/Y8◂◂

Reading. Pupils copy out the sentences, selecting the correct verb from the two options given in each.

Answers

1 Ayer **fui** a la Sagrada Familia con mis padres.
2 Anteayer **fuimos** al museo Picasso. Fue genial.
3 Hoy **voy** al Camp Nou. Voy a ver un partido de fútbol.
4 Mañana **voy** a comer en un restaurante en las Ramblas.
5 Pasado mañana **voy** a tomar el sol en la playa de la Barceloneta.

4 Escribe frases por Paolo y Mariana del ejercicio 1. (AT4.5) ▸▸2.4a/Y8◂◂

Writing. Using their answers to exercise 1, pupils write out sentences as though they were Paolo/Mariana, saying what they did/are doing/are going to do. An example is given.

¡Extra! 1 (Pupil's Book pages 108–109)

Learning objectives

- Learning about famous people
- Practising Spanish pronunciation

Framework objectives

3.1/Y8 Culture – changes in everyday life)

Key language

Revision of language from Module 6

High-frequency words

Revision of language from Module 6

Resources

CD3, tracks 35–36

Starter 1 ▸▸5.3 5.4◂◂

Aim

To use reading strategies to work out new vocabulary.

Write up the following, jumbling the order of the second column.

su reinado	her reign
el emperador	the emperor
la reina	the queen
un imperio	an empire
nació	he was born
real	royal
la dictadura	the dictatorship
actual	current
el rey	the king

Give pupils two minutes working in pairs to match each Spanish expression with the correct English version.Check answers, getting pupils to explain how they worked each one out.

1 Escucha y lee. (AT1.5)
▸▸2.2a/Y8 3.1/Y8◂◂

Listening. Pupils listen to the descriptions of four famous people and read the texts at the same time.

Audioscript Track 35

Personajes importantes de la historia española

Trajano nació el 18 de septiembre de 53 y murió el 9 de agosto de 117. El emperador romano nació en la ciudad de Itálica en España. Hoy en día la ciudad se llama Santiponce. Está cerca de Sevilla.

Abderramán III nació el 7 de enero de 891 y murió en Córdoba en el año 961. Primero fue Emir de Córdoba y luego Califa. Abderramán III convirtió Córdoba en el centro de un nuevo imperio musulmán en Occidente y en la principal ciudad de Europa.

Isabel la Católica nació el 22 de abril de 1451 y murió el 26 de noviembre de 1504. Hija del rey Juan II de Castilla, Isabel fue reina de Castilla y León desde 1474 hasta 1504. Isabel hizo de la defensa de la fe católica un motivo principal de su reinado.

El Rey Don Juan Carlos I es el actual rey de España. Nació en Roma, Italia, el 5 de enero de 1938. Fue proclamado rey el 22 de noviembre de 1975. Restableció la democracia después de la dictadura de Francisco Franco. Vive en Madrid en la Casa Real con la Reina Doña Sofía, su mujer.

Suggestion ▸▸3.1/Y8◂◂

Discuss in English how the religious background of Spanish life has changed over the centuries: under the Romans, the Moors, the Catholics, and today a democracy that respects diverse religions. Compare this with their knowledge of the situation in the UK.

2 Lee el texto otra vez. Copia y rellena la tabla. (AT3.5)
▸▸2.2a/Y8 3.1/Y8◂◂

Reading. Pupils re-read the text. They copy the table and complete it with details from the texts: the names of the people described and the dates they were born/died.

Answers

Name	Birth	Death
Trajano	*18/9/53*	9/8/117
Abderramán III	7/1/891	961
Isabel la Católica	22/4/1451	26/11/1504
Juan Carlos I	5/1/1938	–

Read through the tip box on how to say years in Spanish.

R Pupils working in pairs take it in turn to say the years in the texts in exercise 1 (53, 117, etc.). They could make this more challenging by using their answers to exercise 2 as prompts and supplying the whole date.

3 Busca estas frases en español en el texto. (AT3.5) ▸▸5.3 5.4◂◂

Reading. Pupils read the text again and find the Spanish for the eight English phrases listed.

Answers

1 un nuevo imperio musulmán
2 hoy en día
3 reinado
4 el emperador romano
5 restableció la democracia
6 convirtió
7 fue proclamado rey
8 la defensa de la fe católica

4 Escucha estos trabalenguas y emparéjalos con los dibujos correctos. (1–5) (AT1.5) ▸▸4.1/Y8◂◂

Listening. Pupils listen to the five tongue-twisters and match them to the correct pictures.

Audioscript Track 36

1 *Pedro Pablo Pérez Pereira, pobre pintor portugués, pinta pinturas por poca plata, para pasar por París.*
2 *En tres tristes trastos de trigo,*
Tres tristes tigres comían trigo.
Comían trigo tres tristes tigres,
En tres tristes trastos de trigo.
3 *Pepe Pecas pica papas con un pico,*
Con un pico pica papas Pepe Pecas.
4 *Cuando cuentes cuentos, cuenta cuántos cuentos cuentas, cuando cuentos cuentes.*
5 *El perro de San Roque no tiene rabo porque Ramón Ramírez se lo ha robado.*

Answers

1 d **2** c **3** a **4** e **5** b

5 Con tu compañero/a, repite y traduce los trabalenguas al inglés. (AT2.3) ▸▸5.6◂◂

Speaking. In pairs: pupils read the tongue-twisters aloud, competing with each other to see how quickly they can say them without making mistakes. Encourage them to have fun doing this: they should exaggerate their pronunciation and try to sound as Spanish as possible. Pupils then translate the texts into English.

6 Empareja los proverbios españoles con el inglés. (AT3.4) ▸▸3.2a/Y8◂◂

Reading. Pupils read the four Spanish proverbs and match each with the correct English version. Encourage them to use reading strategies to identify and work out the meaning of key words.

Check answers, asking pupils how they worked out the pairings. Point out how recognising/working out just a few words was enough to make the connections. Translate/Work with them to translate the Spanish proverb literally.

Answers

1 d **2** a **3** b **4** c

Plenary ▸▸5.8◂◂

Play a team game to practise giving dates in Spanish. Write up 10 different years in digits and give the teams two minutes to prepare these. Each team then takes a turn to give the Spanish when you prompt with one of the dates at random. Award one point for a correct answer. The team with the most points wins.

You could make the game more challenging by not giving pupils preparation time.

¡Extra! 2 (Pupil's Book pages 110–111)

Learning objectives
- Looking for cognates within a text
- Learning cultural facts about Barcelona

Key language
Revision of language from Module 6

High-frequency words
Revision of language from Module 6

Cross-curricular
Citizenship: Information about other cultures
ICT: Internet research

Resources
CD3, track 37
Cuadernos A & B, p. 57
Hoja de Gramática, pp. 25–28

Starter 1 ▸▸2.2a/Y8 5.4◂◂

Aim
To revise key language of the module.

Write up the following, jumbling the phrases in the second column.

1	*Nunca fui*	*al museo Picasso.*
2	*¿Dónde está*	*el parque Güell?*
3	*¿No te gustan*	*las pinturas?*
4	*Está al*	*final de la calle.*
5	*Toma*	*la segunda calle a la izquierda.*
6	*Me encantan*	*estos colores.*

Give pupils two minutes to match the sentence halves.

Check answers, getting pupils to translate the completed sentences and to explain how they worked out which halves matched.

Suggestion

Ask the class to review in English what has happened in the story so far.

1 Escucha y lee. (AT1.4) ▸▸3.2a/Y8◂◂

Listening. Pupils listen to the recording of the story and read along with the text. Some vocabulary is glossed for support.

Audioscript Track 37

1 – *Me interesa mucho el arte y me encanta la arquitectura de Gaudí pero nunca fui al parque Güell. ¿Dónde está exactamente?*
2 – *A ver, ¿ves la montaña? Desde el metro vamos todo recto, luego a la izquierda y está al final de la calle.*
3 – *Mira, Diego, este dragón es precioso. Me encantan estos colores. Estamos en un mundo mágico…*
4 – *¿Sabes que la arquitectura de Gaudí es modernista? Él siempre utiliza curvas y formas contorneadas. Me encantan sus mosaicos de cerámica. ¡Todo es impresionante!*
5 – *¿Qué pasa, Diego? ¿No te gusta el parque Güell?*
– *Pues, no Patricia, no me gusta mucho. Creo que no es mi estilo, las esculturas son aburridas.*
6 – *Diego, no pasa nada. No estamos de acuerdo pero te quiero de todas maneras.*

2 Con tu compañero/a, lee en voz alta la historia de Patricia y Diego. (AT2.4) ▸▸5.6◂◂

Speaking. In pairs: pupils read the story aloud, each taking the role of Diego or Patricia. Encourage them to focus on pronunciation and stress and to try and sound as fluent as possible, following the model of the recording.

Suggestion ▸▸2.5/Y8 3.2b/Y8◂◂

Read through the Zona Cultura box on Gaudí.

Pupils could research more information on Gaudí as part of their Barcelona project. They could:

- find out about five things that Gaudí designed, giving three facts about each in Spanish or English
- look at pictures of Gaudí designs on the internet
- choose one picture and describe the style of Gaudí's design in Spanish or English.

3 Busca estas palabras en la historia de Patricia y Diego. (AT3.4) ▸▸5.3◂◂

Reading. Pupils reread the photo story and find the Spanish for the eight English expressions listed.

Answers

1	arte	**5**	modernista
2	mosaicos	**6**	esculturas
3	arquitectura	**7**	estilo
4	curvas	**8**	formas contorneadas

4 Empareja las frases que significan lo mismo. (AT4.2, AT3.2) ▸▸5.4◂◂

Reading. Pupils match the expressions that mean the same thing.

Answers

a *más bonito =* ***i*** *menos feo*
b más histórico = **g** menos moderno
c menos grande = **f** más pequeño
d más feo = **j** menos bonito
e menos aburrido = **h** más interesante

5 Haz una lista de las ciudades en España, desde la más grande hasta la más pequeña. (AT3.4) ▸▸5.4◂◂

Reading. Pupils read six statements about cities in Spain and use them to work out the relative sizes of the cities. They write a list of the cities, starting with the largest and ending with the smallest.

Check answers, asking pupils to explain how they worked out the list.

Answers

Madrid, Barcelona, Sevilla, Gijón, Benidorm

6 Escribe seis frases sobre el Reino Unido, utilizando las frases del ejercicio 5 como modelo. (AT4.4) ▸▸2.4a/Y8◂◂

Writing. Using exercise 5 as a model, pupils create their own puzzle using information about cities in the UK. First they write down (without showing it to anyone) the cities in order of size, from largest to smallest. They need to use their best judgment on the relative sizes of the cities rather than looking up information. They then write six sentences, each comparing one city with another, and giving in total enough information for a partner to work out the order.

When pupils have written their sentences, they swap texts with a partner and check each other's work. Have they given the correct information for the cities to be listed in the right order?

If pupils need support, they can work in pairs or small groups and swap with another pair/group.

Before moving on, confirm what the actual order of the cities is: *London, Glasgow, Manchester, Bristol, Cardiff, Belfast*. Did anyone get it right?

Plenary ▸▸5.8◂◂

Congratulate the pupils on completing the course! Ask them what the highlights have been and if there were any features they didn't like.

Finish by getting the class to imagine they are going on holiday to Barcelona. Each pupil has to say one thing he/she is going to do while there using *voy a...*

Cuaderno A, page 57

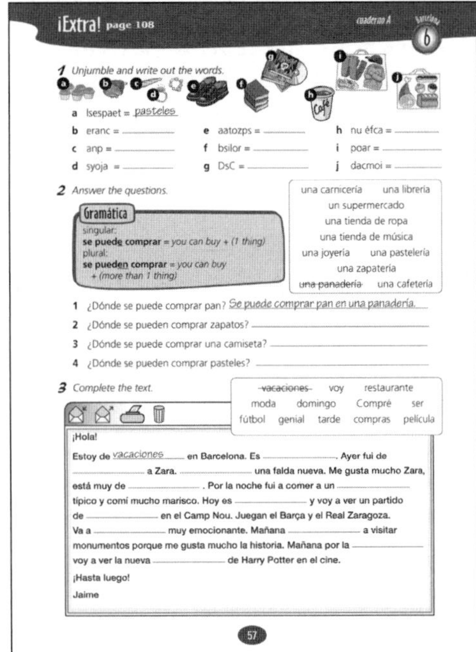

¡Extra! page 108 cuaderno A Barcelona 6

1 *Unjumble and write out the words.*

a lsespaet = pasteles
b eranc = ______ e aatozps = ______ h nu éfca = ______
c anp = ______ f bsilor = ______ i poar = ______
d syoja = ______ g DsC = ______ j dacmoi = ______

2 *Answer the questions.*

Gramática
singular:
se puede comprar = *you can buy + (1 thing)*
plural:
se pueden comprar = *you can buy + (more than 1 thing)*

una carnicería una librería un supermercado una tienda de ropa una tienda de música una joyería una pastelería una zapatería ~~una panadería~~ una cafetería

1 ¿Dónde se puede comprar pan? Se puede comprar pan en una panadería.
2 ¿Dónde se pueden comprar zapatos? ______
3 ¿Dónde se puede comprar una camiseta? ______
4 ¿Dónde se pueden comprar pasteles? ______

3 *Complete the text.*

~~vacaciones~~ voy restaurante moda domingo Compré ser fútbol genial tarde compras película

¡Hola!

Estoy de vacaciones en Barcelona. Es ______. Ayer fui de ______ a Zara. ______ una falda nueva. Me gusta mucho Zara, está muy de ______. Por la noche fui a comer a un ______ típico y comí mucho marisco. Hoy es ______ y voy a ver un partido de ______ en el Camp Nou. Juegan el Barça y el Real Zaragoza. Va a ______ muy emocionante. Mañana ______ a visitar monumentos porque me gusta mucho la historia. Mañana por la ______ voy a ver la nueva ______ de Harry Potter en el cine.

¡Hasta luego!

Jaime

57

1 (AT4.1)

a *pasteles* **b** carne **c** pan **d** joyas **e** zapatos
f libros **g** CDs **h** un café **i** ropa **j** comida

2 (AT4.2)

1 *Se puede comprar pan en una panadería.*
2 Se pueden comprar zapatos en una zapatería.
3 Se puede comprar una camiseta en una tienda de ropa.
4 Se pueden comprar pasteles en una pastelería.

3 (AT3.6, AT4.1)

¡Hola!

Estoy de *vacaciones* en Barcelona. Es genial. Ayer fui de compras. Compré una falda nueva. Me gusta mucho Zara, está muy de moda. Por la noche fui a comer a un restaurante típico y comí mucho marisco. Hoy es domingo y voy a ver un partido de fútbol en el Camp Nou. Juegan el Barça y el Real Zaragoza. Va a ser muy emocionante. Mañana voy a visitar monumentos porque me gusta mucho la historia. Mañana por la tarde voy a ver la nueva película de Harry Potter en el cine.

¡Hasta luego!

Jaime

Cuaderno B, page 57

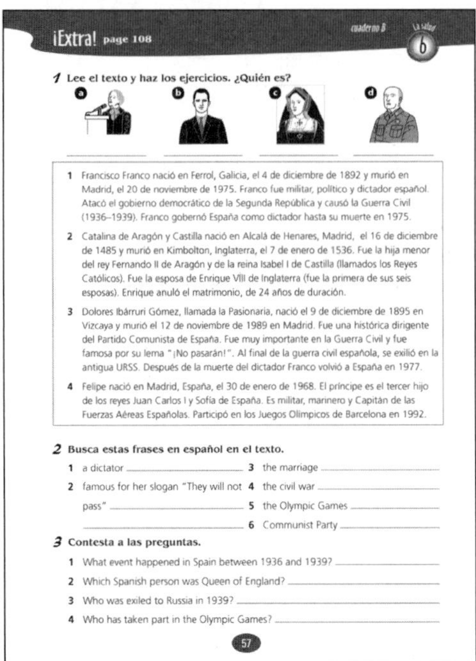

¡Extra! page 108 cuaderno B La salud 6

1 **Lee el texto y haz los ejercicios. ¿Quién es?**

a b c d

1 Francisco Franco nació en Ferrol, Galicia, el 4 de diciembre de 1892 y murió en Madrid, el 20 de noviembre de 1975. Franco fue militar, político y dictador español. Atacó el gobierno democrático de la Segunda República y causó la Guerra Civil (1936–1939). Franco gobernó España como dictador hasta su muerte en 1975.

2 Catalina de Aragón y Castilla nació en Alcalá de Henares, Madrid, el 16 de diciembre de 1485 y murió en Kimbolton, Inglaterra, el 7 de enero de 1536. Fue la hija menor del rey Fernando II de Aragón y de la reina Isabel I de Castilla (llamados los Reyes Católicos). Fue la esposa de Enrique VIII de Inglaterra (fue la primera de sus seis esposas). Enrique anuló el matrimonio, de 24 años de duración.

3 Dolores Ibárruri Gómez, llamada la Pasionaria, nació el 9 de diciembre de 1895 en Vizcaya y murió el 12 de noviembre de 1989 en Madrid. Fue una histórica dirigente del Partido Comunista de España. Fue muy importante en la Guerra Civil y fue famosa por su lema "¡No pasarán!". Al final de la guerra civil española, se exilió en la antigua URSS. Después de la muerte del dictador Franco volvió a España en 1977.

4 Felipe nació en Madrid, España, el 30 de enero de 1968. El príncipe es el tercer hijo de los reyes Juan Carlos I y Sofía de España. Es militar, marinero y Capitán de las Fuerzas Aéreas Españolas. Participó en los Juegos Olímpicos de Barcelona en 1992.

2 **Busca estas frases en español en el texto.**

1 a dictator ______
2 famous for her slogan "They will not pass" ______
3 the marriage ______
4 the civil war ______
5 the Olympic Games ______
6 Communist Party ______

3 **Contesta a las preguntas.**

1 What event happened in Spain between 1936 and 1939? ______
2 Which Spanish person was Queen of England? ______
3 Who was exiled to Russia in 1939? ______
4 Who has taken part in the Olympic Games? ______

57

1 (AT3.6)

1 d **2** c **3** a **4** b

2 (AT3.6)

1 dictador **2** famosa por su lema "No pasarán"
3 el matrimonio **4** la Guerra Civil
5 los Juegos Olímpicos **6** Partido Comunista

3 (AT3.6)

1 Spanish Civil War
2 Catalina de Aragón, wife of Henry VIII
3 Dolores Ibárruri
4 el Príncipe Felipe

Te toca a ti (Pupil's Book pages 124–125)

- Self-access reading and writing at two levels

A Reinforcement

1 *Fill in the missing letters in these time expressions. Then match up the Spanish and the English.* (AT4.2) ▸▸ 4.1/Y8 ◂◂

Writing. Pupils complete the time expressions by filling in the missing letters, then match each one to the correct English version.

Answers

ayer = yesterday, hoy = today, mañana = tomorrow, pasado mañana = the day after tomorrow, anteayer = the day before yesterday

2 *Write out the questions and answers.* (AT4.3) ▸▸ 4.6a/Y8 ◂◂

Writing. Pupils use the picture prompts to write four short dialogues asking for/giving directions.

Answers

1 ¿Dónde está el museo? Sigue todo recto y cruza la plaza. 2 ¿Dónde está la piscina? Toma la segunda calle a la izquierda, luego dobla a la derecha. 3 ¿Dónde está el hospital? Sigue todo recto y está a la izquierda. 4 ¿Dónde está la plaza de toros? Toma la segunda calle a la derecha, luego dobla a la izquierda.

3 *Write out the sentences correctly. Are they about the past, present or future?* (AT4.2) ▸▸ 4.5a/Y8 ◂◂

Writing. Pupils separate the wordsnakes and write out the sentences, identifying whether each one is talking about the past, present or future.

Answers

1 *Estoy en Barcelona y me encanta el acuario. – present*
2 Ayer fui a la playa por la mañana. – past
3 Luego fui a un restaurante con mis amigos. – past
4 Después fui a la discoteca y bailé mucho. – past
5 Hoy quiero ver la televisión en casa. – present
6 Mañana voy a hacer surf. – future
7 Después voy a comer tapas en un bar. – future

B Extension

1 *Which adjective in each group is the odd one out? Give a reason for your answer (there may be more than one answer!). Then write a sentence in Spanish using the adjective.* (AT3.2, AT4.3) ▸▸ 4.3/Y8 ◂◂

Reading. Pupils read the six groups of three words and identify the odd one out in each group, giving a reason for their answer. They then write a sentence in Spanish using the word.

Answers

1 *bonita – it's feminine – Vivo en una ciudad bonita.*
2 históricas – it's plural *or* histórico – it's masculine
3 grande – it's a different adjective/it has the same form for masculine and feminine *or* moderno – it's masculine *or* moderna – it's feminine
4 grandes – it's plural *or* industrial – it ends in a consonant in the singular and the others end in a vowel in the singular/it adds *-es* in the plural
5 bonito – it's masculine *or* pequeña – it can be used in a positive or negative sense; the others are used only in a positive sense
6 turístico – it's a form of a different adjective *or* fea – it's feminine

2 *Match up the sentence halves and write out the completed text.* (AT4.3) ▸▸ 4.4/Y8 ◂◂

Writing. Pupils match the sentence halves and write out the completed text.

Answers

Me encanta vivir en Manchester porque hay monumentos y museos.
También es una ciudad moderna e importante.
Es muy animada.
Sobre todo me gusta bailar en las discotecas.

3 *Read what Antonia says and correct the mistakes in the sentences.* (AT3.5) ▸▸ 4.3/Y8 ◂◂

Reading. Pupils read Antonia's email. They then read the eight sentences and use the details of the email to correct the errors in them.